Andrew Lang, William Young Sellar

The Roman Poets of the Augustan Age

Horace and the Elegiac Poets

Andrew Lang, William Young Sellar

The Roman Poets of the Augustan Age
Horace and the Elegiac Poets

ISBN/EAN: 9783744695770

Printed in Europe, USA, Canada, Australia, Japan

Cover: Foto ©Thomas Meinert / pixelio.de

More available books at **www.hansebooks.com**

THE ROMAN POETS OF THE AUGUSTAN AGE

HORACE AND THE ELEGIAC POETS

SELLAR

HENRY FROWDE, M.A.

PUBLISHER TO THE UNIVERSITY OF OXFORD

LONDON, EDINBURGH, AND NEW YORK

THE ROMAN POETS

OF THE

AUGUSTAN AGE

HORACE AND THE ELEGIAC POETS

BY

W. Y. SELLAR, M.A., LL.D.

LATE PROFESSOR OF HUMANITY IN THE UNIVERSITY OF EDINBURGH
AND FORMERLY FELLOW OF ORIEL COLLEGE, OXFORD

WITH A MEMOIR OF THE AUTHOR
BY ANDREW LANG, M.A.

SECOND EDITION

Oxford
AT THE CLARENDON PRESS
1899

Oxford
PRINTED AT THE CLARENDON PRESS
BY HORACE HART, M.A.
PRINTER TO THE UNIVERSITY

EDITOR'S PREFACE

THE manuscript of Mr. Sellar's book was entrusted to me at the end of last year, and the duty of seeing it through the press undertaken, in accordance with his wishes.

The chapters on *Horace*, and the four chapters on the *Elegiac Poets*, ending with the criticism of the poetry of Propertius, are complete. The chapter on the Odes of Horace (from the middle of Section II. p. 149, 'If Horace lived,' &c., to the end, p. 199) has had less of the author's revision than the others: the manuscript, however, is perfectly clear and continuous. The rest of the *Horace* and the four chapters of the *Elegiac Poets* were written out for the printers by Mr. Sellar.

The passage on the birthplace of Propertius was sent by the author to the *Classical Review*, and appeared in November 1890.

The chapter on *Ovid* (*Elegiac Poets*, chapter V) is not in the same condition as the rest of the book. It represents the notes made by Mr. Sellar for chapters on the same scale as the others. These notes leave some parts of the subject untouched—the biography of Ovid, for example, and his later poems. It might have been possible to supplement this chapter from the essay on *Ovid* contributed by Mr. Sellar to the *Encyclopaedia Britannica*, and the publishers of the *Encyclopaedia*, Messrs. Adam and Charles Black, generously gave permission to make use of it for the present volume. But it was thought better, in the end, to add nothing to the notes left by Mr. Sellar, except the merely formal modifications necessary in order to complete or to arrange some of the more fragmentary passages.

The proofs of Mr. Sellar's book have been read by Professor Butcher and Mr. J. W. Mackail. Of my private debt, for help and advice, this is not the place for me to speak.

W. P. KER.

LONDON,
 10 *October*, 1891.

CONTENTS

HORACE

CHAPTER I.

LIFE AND PERSONAL CHARACTERISTICS OF HORACE.

I.

	PAGE
Horace as representative of the Augustan age	1
The permanent charm of his writings	4
Biographical sources	6
The Sabellian race: Venusia	8
Horace's father	11
Education in Rome and Athens	13
Horace in the army of Brutus	15

II.

HORACE'S LITERARY LIFE.

[*First Period:* from 41 B.C. to 29 B.C.]

His return to Rome	19
Friendship with Virgil and Varius: introduction to Maecenas	20
Maecenas and his influence on Horace	22
Journey to Brundisium	26
Life in Rome: the Epodes and Satires	27

III.

[*Second Period:* from 29 B.C. to 19 B.C.]

Horace and the Monarchy	29
The Sabine farm	30
The Odes, Books i-iii	32
The Epistles, Book i	33
Death of Virgil	34

IV.

[Third Period: from 19 B.C. to 8 B.C.]

	PAGE
Carmen Seculare	34
The Odes, Book iv	35
The Epistles, Book ii, and Ars Poetica	34
Date of the Ars Poetica	36
Horace in closer relations with the court of Augustus	38
Death of Maecenas	39
Death of Horace	39

V.

PERSONAL CHARACTERISTICS.

Horace's sincerity	39
Irony	40
Independence of spirit	41
Horace's masters: Lucilius	42
Aristippus	42
Relations to society: the management of life	44
Influences in Horace's poetry	47
His tastes in art and literature	48

CHAPTER II.

THE SATIRES.

I.

The Satires and Epistles the expression of Horace's familiar moods	51
Horace's purpose in the Satires	52
Difference in character between the first and the second book	53

II.

THE SATIRES. BOOK I.

Horace's earlier manner in the Satires	53
Sat. i. 7 the earliest in date	53
Humours of the camp of Brutus	54
Tigellius and his allies (i. 2)	54
The journey to Brundisium (i. 5) (imitated from Lucilius)	55
Canidia (i. 8)	56
Horace's self-defence (i. 4, 6, and 10)	57

	PAGE
Apology for Satire (i. 4)	57
Horace on Lucilius (i. 10)	57
His answer to his detractors (i. 6)	59
Horace's dramatic manner: the encounter in the Via Sacra (i. 9)	60
Ethical discourses (Sermones) (i. 1 and 3)	60
Stoicism criticised	61
Discontent: the malady of the time and its remedy	61
The progress of Satire	62

III.

THE SATIRES. BOOK II.

Interval between the two books: change of view	63
Dramatic character of the second book: Horace's personages	64
Prologue to the second book	66
Satires on luxury of the table	66
The yeoman Ofellus, 'wise without the rules' (ii. 2)	67
Gastronomy as a fine art: Catius (ii. 4)	67
The banquet of Nasidienus (ii. 8)	69
Dialogue on baseness (ii. 5)	70
Town and Country (ii. 6)	71
Ethical discussions: Damasippus and Davus (ii. 3 and 7)	71

IV.

Place of the Satires in Augustan literature	74
Scope of satire in the Augustan age	75
Horace and Lucilius	76
Horace's distinction as a satirist: his moderation and truth to nature	79
Style of the Satires	81
The Horatian hexameter	82

CHAPTER III.

HORACE AS A MORALIST.

EPISTLES. BOOK I.

The Epistles included in the term *Sermones*	85
The Epistles distinguished from the Satires by more definite ethical purpose	86
The epistolary form in earlier poetry	87
Advantages of the form as used by Horace	88
The shorter Epistles	89

	PAGE
Resemblances between Epistles and Odes: letter to Tibullus	90
to Iccius, Aristius Fuscus, the 'villicus,' Bullatius: the wise enjoyment of life	91
to Julius Florus: public virtue	92
Maecenas in town	92
The didactic element in the longer Epistles	93
The Prologue to Maecenas: philosophic culture	94
Epistle to Lollius on the formation of character	95
'Nil admirari'	95
True and apparent happiness (i. 16)	96
Worldly wisdom (i. 17 and 18)	96
Horace on his critics and imitators (i. 19)	97
Epilogue: his estimate of himself	97
Ethical value of the Epistles	98
Relation between Horace and his readers	98
Poetical value of the Epistles	99
The Epistles an original addition to poetic forms	102

CHAPTER IV.

HORACE AS A LITERARY CRITIC.

EPISTLES. BOOK II. ARS POETICA.

The Epistle to Augustus	103
The Epistles to Julius Florus and to the Pisos	104
The Epistle to Augustus a defence of poetry	104
Criticism of the older Latin poets	105
Perfection to be learned from the Greeks	106
The literary temperament	107
The Epistle to Julius Florus: its date	108
Horace's account of his poetical and critical powers	110
The cultivation of style	110
Ethical teaching in this Epistle: Horace's final message to his generation	111
The Ars Poetica	111
Its sources and contents	112
The cultivation of Roman tragedy	113
Education of the Poet	114
The Ars Poetica not a systematic didactic poem	115
Its main object to protest against careless workmanship in literature: difference in value between Horace's rules for tragedy and his original advice to authors	116
Horace's literary ideals	117

CHAPTER V.

HORACE AS A LYRICAL POET.

THE EPODES.

	PAGE
Horace's imitations of Archilochus	119
'Iambi' of Catullus	120
Horace's iambic couplets	120
Date of the Epodes: their subjects	121
The enemies of society	122
Political Epodes: Epod. 16 a lament after the civil wars: its poetical character	123
Cleopatra: Epod. 9	124
The more gentle poems among the Epodes: Maecenas: the virtue of wine	126
Praise of a country life: Epod. 2: difficulty of the last four lines	127
The Epodes not fully representative of Horace's mind at the time when they were written	130
Catullus, Horace, and Martial	131

CHAPTER VI.

HORACE AS A LYRICAL POET.

THE ODES.

I.

Various aspects of the Odes	133
Graver and lighter moods	134
Horace and the Greek lyric poets: Alcaeus	135
Earlier and later Odes	136
The first book of Odes: imitations of Greek poets	137
Predominance of the lighter themes	138
The second book reflective and didactic	139
The third book: culmination of Horace's lyrical faculty	140
The fourth book and the Carmen Seculare	141
Books i–iii a complete series	141
Date of publication: difficulties in regard to certain Odes	142
Virgil (i. 3)	142
Eastern victories (ii. 9)	144
Marcellus	145
Murena (iii. 19, etc.)	145
Books i–iii probably published in 23 or 22 B.C.	147

II.

	PAGE
Horace a poet of culture: Greek element in the Odes	147
Horace's study of the older Greek poets and neglect of the Alexandrians	148
Intellectual and artistic movements in the Augustan age	149
National element in the Odes: the ideal of Rome	150
Three chief kinds of Ode to be considered: (1) the national, religious, and ethical Odes; (2) the lighter poems in the Greek manner, ἐρωτικά and συμποτικά; (3) the occasional poems of Horace's own life and experience	151

III.

The national, religious, philosophical, and ethical Odes	152
Earlier political poems: 'Caesaris ultor' (i. 2)	153
The Saviour of the State (i. 12); Cleopatra (i. 37); lament over civil wars (i. 35, ii. 1)	153
The great national Odes of Book iii (1–6)	154
Horace's lyrical art at its best in the best years of the Augustan age (27–23 B.C.)	154
The mission of Rome and Augustus	155
Political anxieties: warning and reproof (iii. 5 and 6)	156
The need for reformation (iii. 24)	157
Apotheosis of the Emperor (iii. 25)	157
Odes of the Fourth Book on the victories of Tiberius and Drusus: the glories of the rule of Augustus	157
Changes in the national feeling as expressed by Horace: three stages: the longing for peace after the civil wars; faith in the high destiny of Rome; glorification of the Emperor	159
The religious revival: Horace and the national religion	160
Association of religion with the political ideals of Horace	161
The deification of the Emperor	162
Rustic beliefs and holiday observances	163
Natural piety	164
Horace's graver philosophy	165
Horace and Lucretius	165
The highest good	168

IV.

The poems of love and wine	169
General character of Horace's lighter poems: his heroines	171
Praise of wine	174

V.

	PAGE
Horace's occasional poems	176
Their likeness to the Epistles: Horace's friends	176
His respect for rank; urbanity	177
Degrees of friendship	178
Horace's most intimate feelings expressed in the praise of his favourite places in Italy	180
Influence of Nature in the poetry of Horace	180
His artistic life	182

VI.

Horace's style	184
Progress of his art	185
Forms of verse	186
The Sapphic and Alcaic measures	187
Varieties of the Asclepiad	188
'Curiosa felicitas': characteristics of his phrases	194
Imaginative force of his diction	196
The reflective element in his lyrical poetry	197
Horace and Catullus	197
Law and impulse	199

THE ELEGIAC POETS

CHAPTER I.

ROMAN ELEGY.

Horace on elegiac poetry	203
'Querimonia': 'voti sententia compos'	204
The earliest Greek elegy allied to lyric poetry	204
Early Greek elegiac poets: Mimnermus	205
Antimachus of Colophon: the Alexandrian elegiac poets: Philetas	206
Callimachus	207
The earlier Roman elegy: Ennius and Lucilius	208
The elegies of Catullus	209
The elegiac poetry of the Augustan age related to Alexandrian elegy as the pastorals of Virgil to those of Theocritus: cultivation of amatory poetry	210

	PAGE
Quintilian's four elegiac poets of Rome—Gallus, Tibullus, Propertius, and Ovid	211
Common aims and methods of the elegiac poets	212
The poetry of pleasure: 'dulcedo otii'	212
The perfection of Roman elegy in Tibullus and Ovid	214
Change of literary taste: the circle of Maecenas and the circle of Messalla	215
Messalla and Tibullus	216
Exceptional character of Propertius and his poetry: Ovid the representative of his age	217
The 'bondage' of love as represented by these poets: decay of fortitude	218
Roman strength subdued by Italian 'mollitia'	219
Roman elegiac poetry the best product of the great age of Roman literature	220
Value of the elegiac poets: their rendering of personal feeling and experience	221
Their mastery of verse	221

CHAPTER II.

GALLUS, TIBULLUS, LYGDAMUS, SULPICIA.

I.

Cornelius Gallus and his fortunes: 'Lycoris'	223
Place of Gallus in Roman literature: his character: Gallus and Virgil	224
Gallus styled 'durior' by Quintilian, in comparison with Tibullus and Propertius	225

II.

Albius Tibullus	225
His life	226
Tibullus and Horace: identity of Horace's 'Albius' (Od. i. 33, Ep. i. 4) with Albius Tibullus the poet	227
His delineation of himself in the elegies	233
The first book: his home—'patrii lares'	235
Messalla's Aquitanian campaign, B.C. 30	235
Delia	235
Messalla's mission to the East: Tibullus detained by illness in Corcyra	236
Return to Rome: estrangement of Delia	237
Messalla's triumph (i. 7)	238

	PAGE
The second book: Nemesis	238
Materials and character of the poetry of Tibullus	239
Melancholy	240
The spirit of Italy: love of the country: resemblances to Virgil	241
Love of peace	242
Friendship for Messalla	242
Tibullus and the greatness of Rome: an exceptional passage (ii. 5)	243
Relation of Tibullus to other poets: affinities with Virgil	244
Elegy brought to perfection by Tibullus	245
Versification, style, and diction	246
Idyllic passages	248
Relation of Tibullus to his contemporaries and to the Empire	250
His rank among poets	251

III.

Lygdamus: the author of six elegies in the third book ascribed to Tibullus: a member of the circle of Messalla	252
Problems regarding Lygdamus	253
Lygdamus and Neaera	254
Character of the poems, and of the author	255

IV.

The Panegyric on Messalla, in hexameters: its value as an illustration of the taste of the time	256

V.

Sulpicia	258
Eleven poems relating to the fortunes of Sulpicia: six of these by Sulpicia herself	258
The story of Sulpicia and Cerinthus	259
Value of the poems	260

CHAPTER III.

PROPERTIUS: LIFE AND PERSONAL CHARACTERISTICS.

Varying estimates of Propertius	262
Fortunes of his poetry in different ages	263
His biography: founded chiefly on his own statements	264
Problems of his biography	265
Dates of his poems	267

	PAGE
The birthplace of Propertius	270
Interpretation of the passages in which his birthplace is referred to	270
His early life and recollections	278
The siege of Perusia	279
Propertius taken to Rome by his mother	280
Studies and friends: Tullus	281
Bassus, Lynceus, and Ponticus: Gallus: Paetus	282
Cynthia	283
The record of the first book—'Cynthia Monobiblos'	286
Publication of the first book: Propertius recognised by Maecenas	288
The second book: protestations and reproaches	288
The third book: disillusion	289
Cynthia in the fourth book	289
The fourth book probably left unfinished at the death of Propertius	290
Poetical ambition: relation of Propertius to other poets	291
The Roman Callimachus: Horace's estimate of Propertius	292
Character	293

CHAPTER IV.

THE ART AND GENIUS OF PROPERTIUS.

The poet's claim to be the first Latin representative of Alexandrian elegy	295
'Querimonia': 'lacrimae'	296
'Cynthia Monobiblos': artistic excellence of the first book	297
The second book—34 elegies: reasons for and against subdivision of the book	298
Themes of the second book: want of chronological or artistic sequence: Prologue to Maecenas: Epilogue—praise of Virgil	299
The third book more orderly and less passionate: new motives	300
The fourth book, containing two sets of poems: projected series on the antiquities of Rome	301
Elegies on various subjects: Cynthia's ghost	302
Arethusa: Cornelia	303
Defects of the antiquarian poems: variety and interest of the others	305
Manner of Propertius	305
Imagery and diction	306
Verse	308
The strength of Propertius: the temper of his poetry	312
The thought of death	313
Lament for Paetus	314
Paetus and Lycidas	315

	PAGE
Lament for Marcellus	316
Gloom and terror of the grave: 'sunt aliquid Manes'	316
Descriptive passages: the City	317
Nature in lonely places: the mountains	318
'Vesani murmura ponti'	319
The solitudes of Nature associated with the romance of Greek mythology	319
Milanion in Arcadia: Ariadne: Andromeda: Antiope	320
Hylas: imaginative value of mythology	321
National themes: Cleopatra	321
Roman myths and ritual	322
Estimate of the art and genius of Propertius	324

CHAPTER V.

OVID.

I.

AMORES.

Want of seriousness in Ovid's love poetry: the *Amores*	326
'Musa genialis': the elegy on Tibullus an exception among the lighter poems	327
Corinna	328
Subjects treated in the *Amores*	330
Spirit of the *Amores*	330

II.

HEROIDES.

Two sources of interest in Ovid's poetry—knowledge of Roman society, and exuberance of fancy	332
The *Heroides*: matter and form of Ovid's heroic epistles: their rhetorical and modern character	333
Spurious epistles	334
Ovid's heroines	335
Picturesque, romantic, and pathetic elements in the *Heroides*	336
Style	337

III.

ARS AMANDI.

Publication of the *Ars Amandi*	337
Roman society: the pursuit of pleasure	338

	PAGE
Ovid's didactic poem	339
His purpose in the *Ars Amandi*	340
Ovid's theory of life	341
Excellence of the poem as representative of the time, and of the author's genius: Ovid's wit, vivacity, and sane judgment	342
Picturesque and fanciful passages	343

IV.

METAMORPHOSES.

Ovid's recognition of his twofold power, as a poet of society, and an imaginative artist (Amores iii. 1): the Muses of Elegy and Tragedy	344
Ovid's essay in tragedy: the Medea	345
Failure of tragedy in Rome	345
Ovid's strength and weakness in dealing with mythological and heroic subjects: his imaginative revival of old stories	346
Mythology in the Greek poets	347
Greek mythology in Latin literature: spontaneity and freshness of Ovid's work	349
The Gods in Ovid's poetry: their loss of majesty: want of reverence in the *Metamorphoses*	351
The Fauns and Nymphs	351
Cultivation of epic poetry by Ovid's contemporaries	352
Ovid's own estimate of his poem: his renunciation of the strict epic form	352
Plan of the *Metamorphoses*	353
Ingenuity of the structure	354
Imperial sentiment employed to give unity to the poem	354
Motives of the stories: love and adventure: scenes of war: occasional exaggeration of repulsive details	355
The battle of the Centaurs	356
Predominance of rhetoric: unimaginative precision: absence of mystery and sublimity	357
Ovid's congenial ground: Arcadia: the loves of the Gods	359
The Palace of the Sun: Phaethon: power of description: command of poetical associations	360
Psychological insight	362
Romance and pathos: Cadmus and Harmonia: the sea-idyll of Ceyx and Alcyone: Baucis and Philemon: Ovid's homelier passages: humanity of the *Metamorphoses*	362

MEMOIR OF W. Y. SELLAR

ANDREW LANG

W. Y. S.

1890

WHERE nineteen summers' festal feet had gone,
The darkness gathers round thee, laid alone;
And there, unchanged, unshadowed, lie with thee
Kindness and Truth and Magnanimity.

J. W. M.

WILLIAM YOUNG SELLAR

To the last work of Mr. Sellar, it has been thought well to prefix a brief introductory memoir. As his nephew, his pupil, and one who found in his house another home, I attempt to tell, very briefly, the uneventful story of his life. By the aid of letters [1], and the reminiscences of friends, it would not be difficult to fill a volume with Mr. Sellar's biography. But it is improbable that he, who was absolutely devoid of literary self-consciousness and vanity, would have cared to be remembered, except in the affection of his friends and in the gratitude of his pupils. It must suffice, therefore, to give with brevity all that the readers of his books may find it desirable to know about the Author of the 'Roman Poets of the Republic.'

Mr. Sellar was born at Morvich in Sutherland on Feb. 22, 1825, being the son of Mr. Patrick Sellar and his wife, whose maiden name was Craig. The name of Sellar is very common in Oxfordshire, and it is not impossible that a progenitor of the family, which had long been settled in Elgin, came north with the Cromwellian forces. Mr. Sellar's father was an agent, or Factor, of the Sutherland family. In middle life he purchased the estates of Ardtornish and Acharn, on the Sound of Mull. His children were seven boys and two girls, Mr. William Young Sellar being his fourth child, and third son. Their childhood

[1] Mr. Sellar wrote full and interesting letters to many of his friends: in these it was his habit to express the thoughts that most interested him at the moment. Here they would be out of place; nor is it certain that he would have cared for their publication.

was passed at Morvich, a house of the Duke of Sutherland's, near the river Fleet, not far from Golspie. Morvich is pleasantly situated beneath high crags, and close to a burn flowing into the Fleet, wherein the children learned their first lessons in trout-fishing, being afterwards promoted to salmon and sea-trout in the river. The elder Mr. Sellar was a man of great energy, and expected great energy and industry from others. His wife was a lady who can never be mentioned without affection by any who were fortunate enough to know her, above all by any of her numerous descendants. With her, kindness was a passion: her generosity, hospitality, and sympathy were unbounded, and she had a great love of literature, which she retained into advanced old age.

In such a home, where there were plenty of brothers to play with, and where sport abounded to an extent now unknown, Mr. Sellar's childhood must have passed happily. But the home life of his childhood was extremely brief. At the early age of seven, he was sent with his brother, Mr. Patrick Plenderleith Sellar, his senior by little more than two years, to the junior class, or 'Gytes,' of the Edinburgh Academy. Among the children there he was probably the youngest, though he was to take, with ease, the foremost place in their studies.

The Edinburgh Academy, a large plain building standing in sufficient 'yards' on the north side of the slope of the new town, was founded in 1824. The first head master, or Rector, was the Rev. Dr. Williams, formerly Vicar of Lampeter, and a friend of Lockhart's. Sir Walter Scott, himself the chief glory of the High School, had taken a great part in founding the new Classical Academy. Through Lockhart he became acquainted with Dr. Williams, whom, though Scott was not fond of schoolmasters, he liked and respected. Williams gave him some of the materials for 'The Betrothed,' and it was he who read the service over the grave in Dryburgh. In opening the school, on October 1, 1824, Scott naturally deprecated any suspicions of prejudice against that ancient institution, the High School. He quoted Dr. Johnson's remark, that, of learning, 'every man in Scotland had a mouthful, but no man a bellyful.' The Directors were anxious to wipe off this reproach, to make the pupils begin Greek earlier, and 'prosecute it to a greater extent' than had been usual in Scotland. Sir Walter himself, as we know, began Greek late at school, was at a disadvantage in it when he went to the University, and did not 'prosecute it' at all.

The Edinburgh Academy is a day-school. At that time, and in the time of the present writer, the boys went up from class to class by seniority, getting a remove every year. Through their whole course they were under the same master with whom they started, and from the fifth class to the seventh they also studied with the Rector. This scheme has glaring disadvantages. A boy of parts who is indifferent to medals and prizes bound in calf, has no stimulus to ambition. He cannot, or then, at least, he could not, gain a remove by industry or ability. Moreover, the master who can keep in order, and teach the Latin Grammar to, a mob of disorderly 'gytes,' may be sadly to seek in more advanced studies. The school used to open at nine o'clock, and, with two breaks of a quarter of an hour, boys went from class-room to class-room till three in the afternoon. Preparation, if done at all, was done at home, under the superintendence of tutors often quite amusingly incompetent.

The young Sellars did not suffer, at least, from ignorant private instructors. They lived in the house of one of the masters, Mr. Andrew Carmichael, who has left a reputation for minute and anxious accuracy. At his establishment life was far from joyous; and the drudgery was extreme. Games were forbidden, especially cricket, a pastime which Mr. Sellar, in later life, was very fond of watching at Lord's, and at which he played a good deal when a Fellow of Oriel. But at school he was not permitted to relax his mind with amusements. His father considered it a positive duty that he should be head-boy, or *dux*, as it was called, of his class, and Mr. Carmichael assuredly refuted Dr. Johnson by giving him his bellyful of learning. Thus urged, Mr. Sellar, after conquering his chief competitor, his brother, won and retained the place of *dux*, and, at the early age of fourteen, gained the gold medal as head of the school, besides accumulating almost all the other prizes. His Greek Iambics appear to myself remarkable productions for a boy of his age, but, at the University, he discovered that extreme and original elegance in composition was not his *forte*. 'Don't you think, Sellar, you may have a genius for mathematics?' his tutor asked him (as he used to tell), after considering a very elaborate essay in Greek verse.

Of the Edinburgh Academy, in spite of his regard and esteem for Dr. Williams, Mr. Sellar did not retain a very happy memory. With a natural disposition to enjoy life, and with an appetite for work which would have been easily contented, with a keen enjoyment of literature, and a heart ardent in friendship, the boy was kept to a dull and plodding course of study. The strange thing is that his mind was not outworn in youth, that he did not become a pedant, or turn in distaste from scholarship. He sometimes attributed the frequent ill-health of his later life to the years of incessant strain at school. But then his holidays were always delightful, and he was saved from results which often follow too strenuous application by his native vigour and his sense of humour. Of the masters at the Edinburgh Academy he had some cheerful recollections. The teacher of Mathematics was Dr. Gloag, the Keate of the northern seminary. Dr. Gloag, who still survived and thrashed in my own time, was immensely appreciated by the boys as a practical humorist. Boys forgive, and even enjoy, a great deal that is not agreeable at the time, from an unaffected and energetic person of sterling honesty. 'Menzies was looking at the clock, was he? He thought to escape,' he would remark, when the hour was almost ended, and some terrible proposition was making havoc in the class—'Tak' it, Menzies.' Then the unlucky boy would come to grief, and would have the little, stumpy, broken pointer rattling on his shins, or would be sent 'behind the board,' to copy out the proposition at full length.

From the Edinburgh Academy, Mr. Sellar went, before he was fifteen, to Glasgow University. The College buildings were then an old, black, and malodorous pile in a crowded and squalid part of the town. Lectures used to begin at 7.30 in the morning, and, to an industrious and punctual student, Glasgow was a place of hard work, and of no pleasure. Fortunately, Mr. Sellar found, in the Greek Chair, Mr. Edmund Law Lushington, then a young professor of twenty-seven years. Probably the Scottish universities have never enjoyed a teacher in all respects so admirable, and so inspiring, as Mr. Lushington. To read under him was to gain a new conception of what scholarship might be, and, in him, was. The range of his knowledge lives in one's memory as almost miraculous; his accuracy was of the finest Cambridge pattern: it was as if some such Greek as Longinus had been reborn to teach his native tongue in Scotland. As Mr. Lushington is, fortunately, still with us, it would be unbecoming to dilate on the rare personal qualities and charms which endeared him to his pupils, and on the occasional touch of irony which shewed that dulness could annoy even his temper[1].

Under the Greek Professor, Mr. Sellar improved his scholarship, and, no doubt, acquired that sound and earnest taste for and love of the literature of Greece which distinguished him. He also enjoyed Mr. Lushington's personal friendship, which remained with him, as true and admiringly affectionate as ever, to the close of his life. From Professor Ramsay, also, he learned much in Latin literature and Latin antiquities, and the friendship between these two was continued, after Mr. Ramsay's death, with his nephew and successor, who at present holds the Chair of 'Humanity.'

The chief prizes at Glasgow are the Snell Exhibitions to Balliol, which were then worth about £120 a year. They were

---

[1] 'Mr. ——,' said Mr. Lushington, to a pupil who had first blundered through the Greek of a passage, and then, with new false quantities, had massacred the English,—'Mr. ——, you have made *more* mistakes than the words admit of'!

not awarded, like the prizes in the Lectures, by the votes of the students, a curious method which works with remarkable accuracy, but were given to distinguished students. Adam Smith, Lockhart, and Sir William Hamilton had all been Snell Exhibitioners. The foundation has been most serviceable to young Scots, and the biographer himself is 'more especially bound to pray' for John Snell, Esq. Mr. Sellar obtained this Exhibition at the early age of seventeen. After some months of study with his friend, the Rev. Mr. Dobson, Head Master of Cheltenham College, he won the Balliol Scholarship, which was then, and still is, a great object of ambition with schoolboys. He went up to Balliol after most of the men whom the late Principal Shairp commemorated in his poem. Northcote had gone, but Mr. Clough was still in Oxford, Mr. Matthew Arnold, in the glory of his youth, Mr. Morier (Sir Robert Morier), Mr. Shairp, Sir Alexander Grant, the Editor of 'Aristotle's Ethics,' Mr. T. C. Sandars, and others. Here Mr. Sellar was in society which liked him well. Though still industrious, he did not, as at school, waste his youth on books and nothing but books. He rode, he played cricket and whist, in which he excelled. Among others of his acquaintances was Mr. George Lawrence, author of 'Guy Livingstone.' But his chief friends at that time have already been mentioned. Others were Mr. Poste, Bishop Patteson, Mr. F. T. Palgrave, Mr. Theodore Walrond, Sir Francis Sandford, and Mr. Cumin. Mr. Sellar was a friend of singular loyalty and ardency. The biographer well remembers how, some time after the death of Bishop Patteson, martyred in the South Seas, Mr. Sellar, at the mention of his name, was unable to subdue his emotion, and left the room. Once a friend with him was always a friend, and it often seemed as if the doings and the successes of those he loved were of more moment to him, and dearer to him, than his own. He was happy in retaining the affection of many of these college friends through all his life. But he survived Mr. Matthew Arnold, Sir Alexander Grant (Principal in his own University of Edinburgh), Mr. Walrond, and Mr. H. H. Lancaster, a friend of later date. Of all these, perhaps, Principal Shairp was the man who was nearest to his affections, unlike as they were in many ways.

Among friends rather senior to Mr. Sellar at Oxford, doubtless Mr. Jowett, then a Tutor of Balliol, had most influence. Scotchmen are not, as a rule with many exceptions, favourable to sacerdotal ideas in religious matters. They are apt to think about such controversies as Newman was then engaged in, much what Charles Perrault thought of Pascal's discussions in the 'Lettres Provinciales,' that too much importance is assigned to them. The tendency among Mr. Jowett's pupils was rather in the direction of critical and philosophical thought. From Mr. Jowett, in particular, was expected some philosophical work, in place of which he has enriched the world by making Plato speak English. It is usual, at the Universities, for the pupils of some teacher to believe that 'he has the Secret,'—a sanguine expectation which has often been disappointed. Mr. Jowett's ideas, however, were of considerable influence with Mr. Sellar, though less momentous to him than Mr. Jowett's friendship. In later life, at least, and with his juniors certainly, he was not wont to discuss Theological topics. He might, perhaps, have said—

> Myself when young did eagerly frequent
> Doctor and saint, and heard great argument
>   About it, and about: but evermore
> Came out by the same door where in I went.

It is improbable that the Tractarian discussions and the Oxford movement interested him much more than they appear to have interested Mr. Matthew Arnold.

Mr. Sellar took a distinguished degree, a First Class in the Classical Final Schools (there were then no Moderations), which included scholarship, history, and philosophy. He next won the Oriel Fellowship, at that time the most distinguished of those prizes (1850). His terms at Oriel were probably among the happiest periods of his life, as he had achieved complete academic success, and could now afford to look round, and choose his opening in the profession of education. Many a tired young fellow in the beautiful college gardens may have inwardly blessed pious founders, and said to himself, *deus nobis haec otia fecit.*

Mr. Sellar was not cast for a college don, and did not linger late in the paradise of the academic Armida. For a short time he taught in the University of Durham, and thence went to assist his friend, Professor Ramsay, in the Latin Chair at Glasgow (1851–53). In the neighbourhood of Glasgow he met the lady whom he shortly afterwards married, Miss Eleanor Dennistoun, daughter of Mr. Dennistoun of Golf-hill. A happier marriage, and one which gave more happiness to a larger circle of people, was never made. It is impossible here to say more than that Mr. Sellar's home, wherever it might be, was henceforth a source of light, of mirth, of the friendliest hospitality to all old and to many new friends. The children who were born into the house did not lack the charm, the sympathetic kindness and the wit, which endeared their mother to all who made her acquaintance. But the best parts of a man's life, the best for himself, for his work, and for the world, are those which a biographer dares hardly touch upon.

The Greek Professor in the University of St. Andrews was at this time old, and suffering from the local malady of deafness. Mr. Sellar went from Glasgow to St. Andrews to act as his assistant in 1853–1859, and later succeeded him as Professor (1859–1863). St. Andrews has always been a small University, and the Colleges of St. Leonard's and St. Salvator probably did not contain more than two hundred students. The Greek Professor had to instruct his junior class in the rudiments of the language: in his second and senior class he was able to lead them to much higher things. Mr. Sellar, however, had leisure enough to write his two remarkable studies on Lucretius and Thucydides, in the volumes of Oxford Essays for 1855 and 1857.

In the way of relaxation from study, St. Andrews was then peculiarly fortunate. There was a small but lively and learned society in the place. Mr. Ferrier, the author of 'Institutes of Metaphysics,' was then Professor of Moral Philosophy. He was a man of noble character and of striking appearance, the ideal of what a philosopher should be. His wife and his family were remarkable for humour and social charm, and many famous people in literature visited the house of the daughter of Christopher North. Mr. Shairp was then Professor of Latin; Mr. Veitch, now of Glasgow, taught Logic; Principal Tulloch was at St. Mary's Hall, the Divinity College. They were very merry days at St. Andrews, and the Professors played Golf with more energy and enthusiasm, it must be admitted, than success. 'Ye may teach laddies Greek, Professor,' said a candid old caddie to Mr. Sellar, 'but gowf needs a heid.' At this time, Mr. Sellar's home, in the vacations, was at Harehead, a beautiful house situated where the battle of Philiphaugh ended, on a hill above the deep black pools of Yarrow, and within sight of Newark Castle. Here he had less opportunities of fishing and shooting, exercises very necessary to his health, than at Ardtornish, for that delightful place had been sold soon after the death of the elder Mr. Sellar. For many summers he had enjoyed the salmon and sea-trout fishing in the river and Loch Ari-Innes, at Ardtornish he had been visited by Mr. Tennyson, and other men of letters. But the new home all but made up for the loss of the older and still more beautiful one. It was here that the biographer first saw much of Mr. Sellar, or first remembers much of him, though he has a lively recollection of bungling in an attempt to land a sea-trout which he had hooked in the Aline. Mr. Sellar was at this time in the vigour of life; tall, powerfully made, and an excellent walker. In his company and that of Mr. Lancaster, Dr. John Brown made his pilgrimage to Minchmoor, and the Bush above Traquair, celebrated by Mr. Shairp in the most musical of his poems. Dr. Brown immortalised Harehead, and the children, in his prose idyll of 'Minchmoor.' It seems but yesterday that the children, in their scarlet cloaks, were running on the green beside the Yarrow, and now their own children are of the age that then they had, and Mr. Sellar, Dr. John Brown, Mr. Shairp and Mr. Lancaster are all gone from us. To us, as to Minstrel Burne, Yarrow is a sad place to revisit, and her dowie dens have more than 'a pastoral melancholy.' There are new faces at Hangingshaw, the storms have thinned Black Andro: we are all changed, all but the changeless hills, and Yarrow, that, as he rolls along, still 'bears burden to the minstrel's song.' These were probably Mr. Sellar's happiest years, nor was he idle, for he was engaged on his 'Roman Poets of the Republic.'

In 1861, the present biographer went to St. Leonard's Hall, at St. Andrews, and was a member of Mr. Sellar's Greek class. Thus he can add his testimony to the general voice in which Mr. Sellar's pupils praise his power, and one may say his charm, as a teacher. He had the great gifts of keeping perfect order and of thoroughly interesting those who studied under him. He taught them that Greek was no mere dead language, but the speech of a living and immortal literature. His lectures on Thucydides were perhaps especially interesting, but to all his work he brought a peculiar and indefinable power of stimulating and elevating the mind. Some of his pupils came from English public schools, others from such Scotch institutions as the Edinburgh Academy, others from country schools, where perhaps the elementary teaching had often been less copious and prolonged. It was extraordinary to see the advance which all who cared to work made under Mr. Sellar's instructions. His most distinguished pupil in these years (1861-62) was doubtless Mr. Wallace, now Professor of Moral Philosophy at Oxford, and Fellow of Merton College. Mr. Wallace was so easily our foremost scholar, that competition with him was hardly to be dreamed of. But the stimulus of competition was needless to all who were able to feel the inspiration of Mr. Sellar's educational influence. It is not easy for his biographer to refrain from saying that, having come to St. Andrews with no purpose of working, he left it in another mind, and that to Mr. Sellar he owes the impulse to busy himself with letters. But similar expressions of affection and of gratitude to Mr. Sellar might be made, and indeed have been made, by very many of his students, who were not fortunate enough to see so much of him in private life. No less important than his work as an author, important as that is, was his example as a scholar, and as a man; his loyal, honourable, simple, and generous life.

In 1863, to the great regret of St. Andrews, Mr. Sellar went to Edinburgh, to fill the Chair of Latin. While he was still a candidate for that post, appeared his first book, the fruit of some years of work,—'The Roman Poets of the Republic[1].'

This volume treats of Roman Poetry from the beginning of the literature to the death of Catullus. It is not, the biographer hopes, merely the partiality of a kinsman which makes him rank this work very highly. Perhaps there is not, in English, its companion, nor its equal, as an account of the national genius of Rome, of its debt to Greece, of its own original character and powers, of its expression in poetry, from the Saturnian *naïveté* to Catullus's success in modulating Latin to the Grecian melodies. The style is thoughtful, scholarly, and, in contrast with a great deal of modern criticism of the antique, is remarkably sober. It is probable that an author who was writing to-day on the very origins of Roman literature, would deal more in comparisons with the popular and oral poetry of other peoples. But this is comparatively a recent study, though Wolf expected much from it, and Mr. Sellar's tastes were not exactly antiquarian. Icelandic and Eskimo satiric songs, for example, might have been made to illustrate the Fescennine verse.

> Fescennina per hunc inventa licentia morem
> Versibus alternis opprobria rustica fudit.

The custom still survives in the extreme North, but Mr. Sellar did not look so far afield, and these comparative exercises were then hardly in vogue. He did not elucidate the retention in memory of historical ballad traditions by the hymns of the Maoris. Opinions may differ as to the value of such *rapprochements*, but there can be little doubt as to their interest. The

---

[1] Edmonston & Douglas, Edinburgh, 1863.

most excellent parts of the work, and the most popular, are doubtless the chapters on Lucretius and on Catullus. Lucretius has never found a more sympathetic and lucid interpreter: one more appreciative of what we may almost call his 'religious earnestness,' of his criticism of life, of his delight in nature, and in the spectacle of the world. 'No other writer,' says Mr. Sellar, 'makes us feel with more reality the quickening of the spirit which is caused by the sunrise or the early spring, by fine weather or fair and peaceful landscapes. The freshness of this feeling is one of the great charms of the poem, especially as a relief to the gloom and sadness of his thought on human life... No morbid or distempered fancies coloured the natural aspect which the world presented to his eyes and mind... His feeling is profoundly solemn, as well as infinitely tender. Above all the tumult of life, he hears incessantly the funeral dirge over some one departed, and the infant wail of a new-comer into the stormy sea of life—

> mixtos vagitibus aegris
> Ploratus mortis comites et funeris atri.'

Such was the favourite poet of Molière. Like a good, but not an affectedly patriotic Scotsman, Mr. Sellar shewed the unity of great poetry, by passages in which the thought and language of Burns strangely and happily coincided with the inspirations both of Lucretius and Catullus. Of Catullus he wrote with a sympathy which may be called even affectionate and which he communicates to his readers. The biographer recalls, however, that Mr. Sellar did not approve of his own boyish criticism, that Catullus was to Horace as Tennyson to Moore. 'As a lyrical poet,' says Mr. Sellar, 'Catullus cannot indeed be placed on the same level with Horace. He wants altogether the variety and range of interest, the subtlety and irony, the meditative spirit and the moral strength, of the great and genial Augustan poet.' To appreciate Horace is not given to boys; intelligence and love of him come with the maturer mind. And yet, one still has an instinct which tells one that, of the two lyrists, Catullus is a poet more poetical.

Mr. Sellar's book would, in France, have given him probably a claim to membership of the Academy. In our own country, and in Germany, it was well received, and it remains 'a standard book,' as the phrase goes. The blending of literary appreciation with sound scholarship and dignity of style is singular in this age, when, if we do praise the classics, we 'praise them too much like Barbarians.' There is nothing freakish in the book, and an element of freakishness is apparent enough amidst the many and delightful excellences of Mr. Matthew Arnold's 'Lectures on the Translation of Homer.' In England (including Scotland), a sane and thorough criticism of ancient literature leads to no particular honours. But these were the last things that Mr. Sellar had in his mind. He was never heard to complain of criticism, nor, indeed, did he concern himself about it in the slightest degree. When he was appreciated, either by a reviewer, or when, for example, Dublin gave him an honorary degree, and the Athenaeum Club elected him as a member, through the Committee, without ballot, he was pleased, of course, but he never thought of desiring recognition. He loved his studies entirely for their own sake: he dwelt with the great of old because he enjoyed their company. As he says about Catullus, 'though fastidious in his literary judgments, he was not only without a single touch of envy in his nature, but he felt a generous pride and pleasure in the fame and the accomplishments of his associates.' One of the last books which he read was a posthumous collection of Mr. Matthew Arnold's 'Essays,' including that on Tolstoi. 'There is nobody like him,' he said, as he laid them down.

At this point, something may be said of Mr. Sellar's tastes in modern literature. He did not keep up an acquaintance with recent verse. When Mr. Swinburne first appeared, in 1865, he naturally fascinated the young, among whom the biographer was then numbered. But Mr. Sellar did not seem to be allured by the author of 'Atalanta in Calydon,' and Mr. Rossetti did not appeal to him. *His* 'ply was taken long ago.' Among his contemporaries, not including seniors like the Laureate, he most appreciated Mr. 'Matthew Arnold, and he would not allow Mr. Clough to be depreciated. When his biographer began to rhyme, he looked at the performances dubiously. 'Do you think they are as good as ———'s, now?' he asked. The author replied with confidence that he did not think much of them, but that he *did* think they were as good as ———'s, of whom, to be sure, Mr. Sellar was not an admirer. To Lord Tennyson's poems he was much attached, and he must have been among Mr. Browning's earliest readers, though he did not keep up with all the later works. Perhaps Wordsworth was his favourite English poet, and Sir Walter and Mr. Thackeray his favourite novelists. In the leisure of his last vacation he was engaged in a steady perusal of Mr. Dickens. He had, like many men of active mind, a great power of devouring novels for which, perhaps, nobody would claim a high place in literature. M. Xavier de Montépin beguiled many of his hours; a favourite was *Le Médecin des Folles*. To one or two popular and admired novelists he had rather a rooted objection, which gave rise to animated discussions, but to no conversion on either side. Of modern novelists, he chiefly admired Mr. Norris. He thoroughly enjoyed *Richard Feverel*, on its first appearance, and twenty years before the world discovered Mr. Meredith. It is fair to add that he was defeated by *Diana of the Crossways*.

In French, German, and Italian he chiefly read works bearing on his own studies: the books of M. Gaston Boissier were often in his hands. Briefly, in literature he was a lover of what is sound, and has stood the test of time: he did not care to make new experiments, and was indifferent to a modern vogue. One literary taste of Mr. Sellar's was unusual in peaceful men of letters. He was extremely fond of reading military history, especially such books as Napier's 'Peninsular War.' His acquaintance with the details of battles and manœuvres used to astonish soldiers, when, after specially preparing a subject for examination, they found that Mr. Sellar's knowledge of it exceeded their own.

Mr. Sellar went to fill the Chair of Humanity at Edinburgh

in 1863; he was still Professor at his death in 1890. The course of his life in Edinburgh was happy but uneventful. He did his daily work at College; he walked, rode, and played whist. He was surrounded by many friends, among whom were Dr. John Brown, and Sir Alexander Grant, who became Principal of the University. Others were of a younger generation, with whom he was brought acquainted by a brother to whom he was deeply attached, Mr. Alexander Craig Sellar. One of these was Mr. Henry Hill Lancaster, whose remarkable geniality and humour were particularly acceptable to him. Mr. Lushington often came to Edinburgh from Glasgow, a welcome visitor, Mr. E. F. S. Piggott from London, and Professor Nichol of Glasgow was another companion. Dr. Harvey, at that time Rector of the Edinburgh Academy, Mr. Sellar's successor at St. Andrews, Professor Campbell, and Professor Jebb, were also among his more intimate associates. He was always fond of society, and enjoyed the friendly and kindly entertainments of the Northern town. His work with his classes he also enjoyed, and took particular pleasure in the successes of his pupils. The students were inclined to think him distant in his manner, which was merely the result of short-sightedness and its usual accompaniment, shyness. The short-sighted man is always addressing strangers by mistake, or failing to recognise acquaintances, and the memory of such adventures makes him reserved. It was only very late in Mr. Sellar's career that students began to invite professors to suppers. An occasion of this sort gave him much pleasure, and he regretted that the custom had not come sooner into vogue. There may be scholars who would feel thrown away and isolated in a city so little academic as Edinburgh, but this was never Mr. Sellar's case. He could usually find a few friends interested in his own studies, and he did not by any means limit his own interests, but was an excellent talker on most themes, and good company for most men. On the Continent, in his almost yearly visits to Italy and to Switzerland, he met Mr. Alfred Benn, author of a work on Greek Philosophy, and enjoyed his vivacious learning and originality. Mr. Sellar contradicted the saying that we make no new friends after forty. His heart was always open to new friendships, though his taste rather rebelled against new books. The chief pleasure of his later years was the arrival of Mr. Butcher as Professor of Greek in Edinburgh. Many another aging man might have felt an unconscious jealousy of so young a colleague; of one so rich in learning, in vigour, in every amiable and attractive quality. But Mr. Sellar's attachment to Mr. Butcher resembled the affections of youth.

In his Edinburgh vacations, when Harehead was given up, Mr. Sellar's family found, for a year, a beautiful home at Tullymet, some miles distant from Pitlochry, a house charmingly situated among woods, above an old-fashioned garden, with a wide and broken valley below. Here Mr. Jowett came, and many other guests; here the biographer gratefully remembers that he passed the happiest of all long vacations, reading Thucydides beneath the trees, while the squirrels chattered in the boughs, and the voices of the children, his friends of these days and of all days, called him to play from the distance.

Among the things that can be done in life, the best is to make others happy. Of such good deeds the record is difficult to write, and must only be treasured in remembrance. Yet, even in the briefest biography, there may be mention of what Mr. Sellar's hospitality and kindness and genial humour added to the well-being of his friends, and of his friends' friends; not in Scotland alone, but wherever he and his found themselves. To have lived thus is, indeed, to have lived to some purpose, for, if all else were nothing but vanity,—learning and taste, work and its rewards,—love is not given in vain.

After leaving Tullymet, Mr. Sellar passed a summer at Cray, near the Spital of Glenshee, in a country somewhat bleak, but where the air was supposed to be keen and freshening. He was obliged henceforth to take thought about climates and atmospheres, for, in 1868 and 1869, his health suffered severely, and with him bad health often meant an access of melancholy. No unmixed good is given to us: his life might have seemed as fortunate as mortal life could be, happy in abundant leisure, provided with congenial work, enlivened by friendship, enriched by every domestic felicity, and free from all anxiety. But in ill health he saw the world in dark colours. To some extent his illness may have arisen from, or it may have caused, lack of interest in many things that had interested him of old. His sight was not very quick or keen, and he ceased to care for shooting, while for modern fishing, and educated salmon and trout, he had been spoiled by the easier and more abundant sport of Morvern and Sutherland in old times. Nature gradually lost her old charm: buoyancy was no longer his, and he found it desirable to give up his work for a session, and to live abroad with his family, at Bonn, in Switzerland, and in the Black Forest. He was at St. Blasien in the Albthal with his family when the sudden rumours of war between France and Germany were first heard. The war broke out, a French invasion of Southern Germany was expected; the able-bodied men went to their regiments, the horses were 'requisitioned,' and a rather melancholy autumn was passed in Switzerland, on the heights above Zug, and at Engelberg. After Sedan Mr. Sellar came back to Edinburgh, and to his classes, which he did not again desert, except for part of a session when a return of indisposition induced him to seek the Riviera. His home in summer was now a cottage, gradually augmented with the additions which his hospitality required, on a hill above the brown waters of the Ken. Galloway is a country but little known to tourists, perhaps partly because its centre was untouched by Scott, partly because it is little crossed by railways. The landscape has all the charm and sentiment of the Border, with a Highland richness in colour and variety of outline. In the friendly Glen Kens, among the kindliest society of all ranks, Mr. Sellar wrote his *Virgil*, and the present volume, which completes his study of the Roman Poets of the Republic. Occasionally he visited the Continent, generally in spring, and especially interested himself in examining the birthplace of Propertius, and other scenes sacred to the Latin Muse. Of these twenty years, little is to be said, except that time brought its wonted griefs in the deaths of old friends, of Mr. Lancaster, Sir Alexander Grant, and Principal Shairp. All these caused him deep sorrow, and above all he suffered in the long illness and death of his youngest brother, Mr. Alexander Craig Sellar, the Member for Partick, in whose political career he took a sympathetic interest. He himself never mixed much in politics. He was a Liberal, and the biographer remembers his defining Liberalism as 'the desire that every one should as much as possible have his full share of all that is best.' On the matter of Home Rule for Ireland he did not go with Mr. Gladstone and the majority of the Party. On the other hand, he was an extremely staunch Unionist, and was much consulted by his brother Mr. Craig Sellar, one of the Scottish leaders of the party. On platforms of any kind Mr. Sellar never appeared, though he was present at a political dinner given in Edinburgh to Mr. A. J. Balfour. His interest in politics was as keen and eager as if he had been, what he never was, an active politician. He was not among the men of letters who would have come under that law of Solon's against those who, in civil disputes, took neither side. They are never likely to be so powerful as to bring in a law against partisans of all sides.

In 1877 Mr. Sellar published, with the Clarendon Press of Oxford, his most elaborate work, a volume on Virgil, as a first instalment of 'The Roman Poets of the Augustan Age.' He remarks that the characteristics of Virgil's art are not unlikely to be overlooked in an age which demanded from the literature of the imagination 'a rapid succession of varied and powerful impressions.' Such an age will perhaps find that Mr. Sellar's own essay on Virgil is less to its taste than a shorter study, rich in a rapid succession of brilliant and picturesque touches. If one's object were to inspire an English reader with a sudden desire to know more of Virgil, it is certain that the remarkable paper of Mr. F. W. H. Myers in his volume of 'Classical Essays' (Macmillan, 1883) would serve that particular purpose better. But if a student desires a full and exhaustive statement of all that is to be said about Virgil,—about his life, about the political, social, and literary condition of his age, about his relations to the Greek poets and to older Latin poetry,—then Mr. Sellar's volume is probably, or certainly, the most useful in our language. On reading it over again, one observes, perhaps, a certain languor in the style. The sentences are often too long, an effort is made to put too much into each period, and it cannot be said that 'bright speed' or striking effects are the characteristics of the volume. Deep study, profound reflexion, and unexaggerated truthfulness of statement, are its merits. 'The word *meditari*, applied by Virgil to his earlier art, expresses the process through which his mind passed,' says Mr. Sellar, 'in acquiring its mastery over words. In appreciating the charm of his style it is not of the spontaneous fertility of Nature that we think, but of the harvest yielded to assiduous labour by a soil at once naturally rich and obedient to cultivation—*justissima tellus*.' The same word *meditari* applies well to Mr. Sellar's own method in the treatment of Virgil's art. He writes about it rather as a conscientious critic than as a poet, or with the charm of a poet. He had not very much interest in a subject which Mr. Myers has handled so well—the posthumous fortunes of Virgil, as the Guide of Dante, as the magician of the Middle Ages, as the Prophet of the Gentiles. In one point the biographer finds himself differing from both these critics, namely, in appreciation of Virgil's master in the romantic treatment of Love, Apollonius Rhodius. Mr. Myers tells us that Apollonius Rhodius 'shrouded in long-drawn sweetness the inanity of his soul.' Mr. Sellar says that, in painting the passion of Dido, it was comparatively easy 'for Virgil to produce a more noble and vital impersonation than the Medea of Apollonius'; and elsewhere, probably with Euripides, not Apollonius, in his mind, remarks that Dido 'satisfies modern feeling more legitimately than the representation of the cruel and treacherous rancour of Medea.' To others it may well seem that, after Nausicaa, no woman in ancient literature appeals to modern sentiment so powerfully as the Medea of

Apollonius, with her passion, so sudden, so pure, so tender, and true, though, when thwarted, as destructive as a flame. Virgil's heroine was a widow, the hero of Apollonius was a maiden. Both portraits are masterpieces, but the Greek is the earlier, is the model, and is not the less great, as it is certainly the more original. But this apology for the neglected greatness of Apollonius Rhodius may be out of place.

Next to the extreme thoroughness of Mr. Sellar's Virgil, perhaps its chief merit is the clear discernment of what is Roman and native, in the poet's genius. 'It was the peculiarity of the Roman mind to be capable of receiving deep and lasting impressions from other natures with which it came in contact, without sacrifice of the strong individuality of its own character. What Columella says of the Italian soil—"curae mortalium obsequentissimam esse Italiam, quae paene totius orbis fruges, *adhibito studio colonorum*, ferre didicerit,"—might be said with equal truth of the Italian mind.' How this is exemplified in Virgil, how fruitfully the Greek seeds fell in the Italian soil of his genius, how Greek, yet with what an original colour and flavour, were the fruits and flowers that sprang from them, is the burden of the whole study. Virgil's is an art derived from the Alexandrian period of Greek literature, but enlarged, but enriched, but fortified by the consciousness of 'the greater freshness and vigour of the Roman genius, of the more vital force of their language, of their grander national life, of the privilege of being Romans, and the blessing of breathing Italian air.' The charming character of Virgil himself is treated with much sympathy. 'If any one ever succeeded in securing that which Tacitus says "should be to a man the one object of an insatiable ambition," to leave after him "a happy memory of himself," that may be truly said of Virgil.' Yet, after being 'the whole world's darling,' Virgil had sunk to a lower place in human esteem, partly through the revival of Greek studies, the discovery of his masters, of poets greater than himself, partly through the disparaging estimate of Niebuhr and other German scholars. Mr. Sellar's 'Virgil' is a substantial and successful effort to give the poet his own place as 'one of the great interpreters of the secret of Nature, and of the meaning of human life,' especially of 'the change which was then preparing for the human spirit and for the nations of the future.' No more loyal service has been done to the great Italian, who himself foresaw and felt what the world saw far later, his own inability to put on the armour of Homer, to bend the Bow of Eurytus, and make the string that sang in battle, ring clear as the swallow's song. Above all, the critic appreciated the magic of Virgil's language, his 'sayings that affect the mind with a strange potency, of which perhaps no account can be given except that they make us feel, as scarcely any other words do, the burden of the mystery of life, and by their marvellous beauty,—the reflexion, it may be, from some light dimly discerned or imagined beyond the gloom,—they make it seem more easy to be borne. *Aut videt aut vidisse putat.*' So faint, yet so charmed and so holy, is the light in the Arician thicket, from the

> 'Golden branch amid the shadows,
> kings and realms that pass to rise no more.'

Of Mr. Sellar's career, little remains to be told. In the summer of 1890 he had been in unusually good health, and was working very hard to complete this book, to which he gave all but the final touches. One evening in September he caught what seemed nothing more serious than a slight chill, but his constitution was unable to rally. The illness declared itself as jaundice, with other complications. After many days of weakness and distress, the end came.

He is buried in the churchyard of Dalry, on a grassy slope that takes the westering sun. The Ken flows by his grave, and by the tomb of the Covenanters who fell in the troublous times. 'It might make one in love with death to be buried in so sweet a place.' The scene is beautifully described by Mr. Sellar's pupil, Mr. Mackail:

> 'Here, where no lovelier ground
> Stands open to the mute perpetual sky;
> The eternal mountains watching all around,
> The pastoral river always rippling by.'

These are, shortly told, the chief incidents in the course of a scholar's life. Mr. Sellar was not well known to a very large circle. His shortness of sight made him somewhat shy and reserved. Though deeply interested in the welfare of his students, both while they were with him, and in after life, he was not one of the Professors who attempt to live much with them in friendly familiarity,—a task difficult to a man no longer young, and at no time demonstrative. His reserve might have been, and probably often was, mistaken for haughtiness, no failing of his. His likings were by no means confined to men of his own order of intellect, and as he waxed older he seemed to become more tolerant, even of bores. At the same time a certain lassitude grew upon him; fewer things appealed to his interest: but he never lost interest in his friends. Their arrival, or any occurrence which was of moment to them, never found him indifferent. Among friends of his later years, in addition to those already spoken of, may be mentioned Professor Knight, Professor Ramsay, Mr. Mackail, Mr. W. P. Ker, who has seen this volume through the Press, Mr. Strachan Davidson, Mr. William Arnold, Mr. Charles Maconochie, and the daughters of Dr. Norman Macleod, one of whom, Miss Agnes Macleod, was with him in his last days.

The most notable features in Mr. Sellar's character were simplicity, kindness, humour, frankness, loyalty, and a most delicate and lofty sense of honour. The charm of such a character, so free from thought of self, from vanity, pride, envy, display, it is difficult to express in words. All professions and pursuits have their besetting sins: a restless desire to be recognised, the attachment of undue importance to one's work, a tendency to jealousy and to petty criticism of others, are the besetting sins of the man of letters and of the scholar. From all these faults Mr. Sellar was so entirely free that it seemed as if, in his mind, they had no recognised existence. If he met a charlatan he smiled at him, but did not otherwise concern himself with pretenders and their performances. Among the best gifts of humour is, or should be, a clear sense of our own lack of importance ; a disposition not to be fretted by the unfriendly, nor elated by the sympathetic reception which the world may give to ourselves and to our work. This element of equanimity Mr. Sellar possessed in full measure. To know him well was to love him, but so great and so genuine was his modesty that, with a heart full of affection and of longing for affection, he never guessed how much nor by how many he was loved.

THE ROMAN POETS OF THE AUGUSTAN AGE

HORACE

CHAPTER I.

LIFE AND PERSONAL CHARACTERISTICS OF HORACE.

I.

THE spirit of the Augustan Age survives in the verse of the five poets whose works remain, out of many which were written and enjoyed their share of popularity during the half century in which Augustus was master of the Roman world. The great prose-writer of the age, the historian Livy, tells us little directly about his own time. It is from him and Virgil that we best understand how the past career and great destiny of Rome impressed the imagination during the time of transition from the Republic to the Empire. But of the actual life, and the spiritual and intellectual movement of the age, our best and almost our sole witnesses are the poets, Virgil, Horace, Tibullus, Propertius, and Ovid. These five poets are of very different value as representatives of their time. The three elegiac poets, although men of refined sensibility and culture, are, in comparison with Virgil and Horace, men of essentially lighter character, living for pleasure, making the life of pleasure the subject of their art, and showing little sympathy with the new ideas in the sphere of government, which were shaping the future of the world. The idea of Rome acting on their imagination was not that of the Rome of Ennius, of Virgil, and of Livy, but that of which one of their number writes,

<blockquote>Mater et Aeneae constat in urbe sui.</blockquote>

They came too late to feel deeply the change which was coming over the world. None of them lived in close intimacy with the great minister who bore so large a part in shaping the policy of the new Empire, and in reconciling the old governing class to the change. They had neither the profound feeling and serious imagination of Virgil, nor the many-sided versatility and strong reflective vein which made Horace the most complete representative and interpreter of his age.

It is to Virgil and Horace that the Augustan era owes its rank among the great eras of poetry. Virgil is the exponent of its highest hopes and ideas. In the spheres of government, of national and religious feeling, of all the finer influences of nature and human relationship, it was through him that the most searching, the most idealising, and the most enduring revelation was made. It was in him too that the national literature, after a century and a half of effort, attained its final perfection. But for our knowledge of the actual life of the time, of its manners and humours, of its gaiety on the surface, and of some of its deeper currents of serious feeling, we must go to another representative of the age. And it is in a poet born five years after Virgil, among the Sabellian people of the South of Italy, born like him of obscure parentage, but who, notwithstanding, enjoyed similar advantages of education, who though in early youth separated from him by difference of political sympathy as well as divided by difference of place, became in the first years of his manhood united to him by affection and devotion to kindred studies, that the complement of the genius of the gentle poet from the Cisalpine province is to be found. As Virgil is the most idealising exponent of what was of permanent and catholic significance in the time, Horace is the most complete exponent of its actual life and movement. He is at once the lyrical poet, with heart and imagination responsive to the deeper meaning and lighter amusements of life, and the satirist, the moralist, and the literary critic of the age.

The phases of public life and feeling during twenty eventful years, the reflexions suggested by the vicissitudes of national and individual fortune, the pleasures of youth in their refined and piquant aspects, the happiness and the pathetic regrets of the friendships and the social intercourse of maturer years, the idyllic delight of days passed among beautiful scenes endeared by the sense of possession and long familiarity, are so idealised in his lyrical poetry, as to preserve their life and meaning for all after times. The social follies and personal eccentricities, the pedantry and pretention, the avarice and meanness as well as the luxurious indulgence of the age are made to pass before us and to teach their lessons in his satire. The true wisdom of life for the individual under these new social and political conditions, the knowledge how to adapt oneself to the world, and the higher knowledge how to be independent of it, are taught in his Moral Epistles. The criticism which the age needed, and which, so far as criticism could, pointed the way to a more masculine type of poetry than that actually realised by the poets who came after him, was expounded in the poetical Epistles of his later years. On the whole, we find in his writings the completest picture and the justest criticism of his time, expressed with equal mastery in the language of idealising poetry and of common sense. In no Greek or Roman poet do we find so complete a representation of any time, as we find in Horace of those years of the Augustan age which most deserve to live in the memory of the world.

This is the first, and perhaps the chief ground of the prominent place assigned to him in the study of Roman literature. But he has another claim which makes him still less likely to be neglected. Among all ancient poets he suits the greatest variety of modern tastes. To a large number of those who receive a classical education he is the earliest, to some the only friend they make within its range. But whatever attraction the gaiety of his spirit and the music of his verse have for the young, it is only after mature experience of life that his full charm is felt, his full meaning understood. He has an attraction not merely of early association for educated men whose lives are cast in other spheres than that of literature: while to those who seek in the study of great poets to gain some temporary admission within the circle of some of the better thoughts, the finer fancies, the happier and more pathetic experiences of our race, he is able to afford this access. To each successive age or century, he seems to express its own familiar wisdom and experience. To Montaigne, to Addison and Johnson, as to our own times, he speaks with the voice of a contemporary. So true beyond his largest expectations was his prophecy:—

> Usque ego postera
> Crescam laude recens.

He is one of the few ancient writers who unite all the cultivated nations of modern times in a common admiration. They each seem to claim him as especially their own.

But the strongest hold which he has on every generation and every variety of cultivated reader, is that no other writer, ancient or modern, seems equally to speak to each individual as a familiar friend. Among the few happy expressions which meet us occasionally amid the strained phraseology of his imitator Persius, is that in which he characterises this peculiar gift:—

> Admissus circum praecordia ludit.

He enters into the mind and heart of every reader through the medium of a style of which, if he is not the inventor, he was at least one of the earliest masters; one which combines the grace of finished art with the familiar tones of natural conversation. But more than by the medium of his style he excites interest and conciliates affection by the frank trust in himself and in his reader, and the self-respect with which he admits the world into his confidence. He was not indeed the first to establish this relation between an author and his readers. For it was the sense of this relation, of the intimate knowledge of all the secrets of his life, imparted through his works, which was one of the chief attractions to Horace in Lucilius, and which may have attracted Lucilius himself to the Parian poet Archilochus. But no one before Horace had established this relation with such good humour, good taste, and perfect urbanity. There is, consequently, scarcely any figure in literature who seems to be so truly and familiarly known. He lives in his own writings as Dr. Johnson lives for us in the pages of Boswell. Perhaps the impression produced by the correspondence of Cicero may be deemed more trustworthy than that produced by the apparently artless, yet carefully meditated self-delineation in Horace's familiar writings. But we have many phases of Cicero's mobile nature rather than any distinct image of the man. Hence, though there is no man in antiquity about whom so many particulars are known, there is no one about whose personal character there has been, and still is, so much controversy. The self-delineation of Horace, on the other hand, is a work at once of 'Wahrheit' and of 'Dichtung,' natural and frank and yet a study of art and reflexion. He has not left out the faults or exaggerated the virtues of the original, but he has given to the whole picture of his life, though sketched at different times, unity and consistency and the stamp of reality. The personality of Horace may not have been more interesting than that of some of his predecessors among Roman poets, but he applied a keener criticism to himself, and had a more intimate knowledge of himself. His interest in national affairs, in literature, in art and nature, is intermittent; his interest in human life and character never flags; and he was especially interested in watching and retracing the current of that life which was best known to him. The mode of life deliberately adopted by him in Rome and in the country, though as far as possible from being unsocial and ascetic, threw him from time to time largely on his own mind for companionship. He studied himself, as he studied his books, with the enthusiasm of self-culture. In the maturity of his powers, he looks back on his past experience as a process of education; while he is ever striving to realise to his own mind how he stands in the present, and in what spirit he is prepared to meet the chances and the certainties of the future. We are thus able to accompany him better perhaps than any other writer of antiquity, not only in the record of his life, but in marking the trace left by each event and circumstance on the development of his character and intellect.

As a set-off to the fullness and frankness of his own self-portraiture, we have to place the scanty evidence we have of the impression which he made on his contemporaries. There is no mention of him in Tibullus and Propertius, and only one slight notice of him in Ovid; and that expressive not of any personal interest, but only of appreciation of the musical charm of his verse. The last two of these writers speak often of other contemporary poets with whom they lived in intimacy. Horace belonged to an older set of men of letters, which included Virgil and Varius, Pollio, Fundanius, Octavius, Aristius Fuscus, etc., with all or most of whom, in the earlier years of his literary career, he lived on terms of friendly intimacy; and in his later years he wished to guide and encourage younger men, in whom he recognised promise of literary distinction. But he seems to have felt that preference which Goethe and Scott, and other men of genius in modern times, have felt for the society of men of action and men of the world over that of men of letters. Though he lived in intimacy and made common cause with the writers of distinction, such as Virgil and Varius, and critics such as Quintilius, he disliked and was probably disliked by the grammarians and literary cliques, who swarmed amid the decay of political life, just as Pope disliked and was disliked by the critics and minor poets of his time. But it was by critics and grammarians that the personal memory of great writers was kept alive; and one reason why there was no such traditional admiration or affection attaching to the memory of Horace, as there was to the memory of Virgil after his death, was probably that in his lifetime there was no love lost between him and the writers by whom the impression made by a great writer on the world in which he lived was transmitted to after times. Thus the only contemporary evidence we have of the regard in which he was held is that of Maecenas and that of Augustus preserved by Suetonius, who quotes the beginning of an epigram in which Maecenas imitated the playful terms of affection applied by Catullus to Calvus—

> Ni te visceribus meis, Horati,
> Plus iam diligo—

and the statesman's dying commendation of his 'vatis amici' to the Emperor—'Horati Flacci ut mei esto memor.' The tone of the Emperor's letters quoted by the biographer implies an appreciation of the social charm of the poet, and respect for his independence of character.

The short life of Horace written by, or abridged from, Suetonius, is based almost entirely on the poet's own writings, and on these scanty memorials of the Emperor and Maecenas; though it adds one or two facts probably preserved by contemporary grammarians. The statements of Suetonius amount to this:—That he was born on the 8th of December in the year 65 B.C., and died on the 27th of November in the year 8 B.C., a few weeks after the death of Maecenas; that he was a native of Venusia, the son of a freedman, who was also 'auctionum coactor'—i.e. the collector of money paid at public auctions—and combined other avocations with this; that he served under Brutus with the rank of military tribune; that, availing himself of the amnesty granted to the defeated party, he procured the post of clerk in the office of the Quaestor; that he became intimate with Maecenas and Augustus, and secured a high place in the friendship of both. The biographer adds that the Emperor endeavoured to obtain his services as secretary, and showed no resentment when this favour was denied him. By his command, Horace composed the Carmen Seculare, the two Odes (iv. 4, iv. 14) celebrating the victories of his step-sons over the Rhaetians and Vindelici, and the Epistle (ii. 1) which begins

> Cum tot sustineas et tanta negotia solus.

From the same account we learn that he died somewhat suddenly, having only time to declare the Emperor his heir by word of mouth, and that he was buried on the Esquiline, close to the tomb of Maecenas. Suetonius tells us further that he was small in stature and fat, and that this circumstance exposed him to some unseemly jocularity on the part of the Emperor; also that he lived much in his country retreats, in the Sabine district and in the neighbourhood of Tibur, where his house was still shown in the time of Suetonius, near the grove of Tiburnus.

This bare outline of facts we are able to fill up from the autobiographical record—the 'Dichtung und Wahrheit'—contained in the lyrical poetry and the familiar writings of the poet. We are able, too, to follow his own guidance in noting the influence exercised by the facts and circumstances of his life on his heart, character, and imagination.

In more than one passage of his Odes and familiar writings (Odes iii. 21. 1, Epod. 13. 6, Ep. i. 20. 27) he mentions or indicates 65 B.C., the year of the consulship of L. Manlius Torquatus and L. Aurelius Cotta, as the year of his birth. Born in the same decennium as the other leaders in action and literature who played their part in the Augustan age, he was in the maturity of his powers in the happiest and brightest epoch of the new era. At the same time his character was formed to independence before the freedom of thought and action, enjoyed under the Republic, was lost. In the final crisis of the Republic he was old enough to be not only a spectator but an actor. Had he been born a few years earlier he might have been too far committed to the Republican cause ever to become reconciled to the new government. Had the date of his birth been somewhat later, he would probably have been as little interested in the national fortunes, as little braced to manliness in thought and feeling, as Tibullus and Propertius.

His birth-place was the old colony of Venusia on the borders of Apulia and Lucania, or, more probably, the farm in its neighbourhood which his father had bought with the proceeds

of his business. The district in which he was born was peopled
by men of the old Sabellian stock; and although, in consequence of his father's servile origin, we cannot be sure of the
race to which he belonged by birth, yet the strong grain of
Italian character and the Italian shrewdness of observation,
apparent in his familiar writings, suggest his affinity with that
branch of the race which retained longest its original stamp;
just as Virgil's more romantic imagination, and his greater
susceptibility of spiritual feeling, suggest his affinity with the
more impressible Celtic race of the Cisalpine district. In one
of his earliest poems (Epod. 2) Horace speaks, with sympathetic
pride, of the homely virtues of industry and chastity as being
the inheritance of the Sabellian stock; and in a later poem
(Od. iii. 6), the stern discipline of a Sabellian mother is spoken
of as the training of the breed of peasant soldiers who over-
threw Pyrrhus and Antiochus, and stained the seas with
Carthaginian blood. The 'Marsian and Apulian' (Od. iii. 5)
are mentioned together as representatives of the Italian soldiery.
One of the best types of the Italian yeoman is introduced to us
in the person of Ofellus (Sat. ii. 2), living a thrifty and genial
life on his small farm, and, after the confiscations which followed
the battle of Philippi, working as a hired labourer upon it and
applying the lessons of a philosophy not of the schools to his
changed circumstances. It is in his mouth that Horace puts
the most serious discourse in all his Satires, assigning to him
the same office as Lucilius assigned to Laelius in his satire.
A type of business-like sagacity is indicated in Servius Oppidius
of Canusium (Sat. ii. 3. 168), whose history would be known to
Horace from the vicinity of that town to Venusia. In Sat. i. 9.
29, he professes to recall the prophecy of a Sabellian crone, that
the fate which awaited him in after years was to be talked to
death by a bore. Such notices as these scattered through his
writings imply that Horace had lived as a child among the
peasantry of his native district, that he appreciated their homely
virtues and robust character, and that he bore through all his
life a happy recollection of the years passed among them.

From these early associations he was prepared to enjoy the conversation and ways of his country neighbours in the Sabine highlands as a welcome change from the society of statesmen and men of letters in the metropolis. His childhood and boyhood passed among the Apulian yeomen must have aided in developing those intellectual gifts and moral tendencies which fitted him to be the genial satirist of his age.

Another, and quite different gift, he seems first to have become conscious of in the early years passed near Venusia. He has, like the other great Italian poets, a genuine love of Nature. This susceptibility manifests itself in him in a way peculiar to himself and is discernible in the earliest impressions made by outward objects on his imagination. In Horace, the love of nature is shown in the vividness of impression produced by particular scenes[1], and by the hold which these scenes gained on his affections. The earliest trace of this definiteness of perception is seen in the familiar passage of the fourth Ode of the third book, in which, with more probably of fancy than of actual memory, he tells the story of the adventure which marked him out as 'a poetic child,'—

> Non sine dis animosus infans.

In such graphic touches as 'celsae nidum Acherontiae,' 'arvum pingue humilis Forenti,' we note the individual distinctness of the impressions made on his mind. The affection for particular places which he shows in later life, in his mention of Tibur, Lucretilis, the stream Digentia, and the fountain of Bandusia, seems to have been first awakened by the great natural objects by which his childhood was surrounded; such as the 'impetuous' and 'loud-sounding' Aufidus, whose name he more than once associates with his hope of immortality, the Monte Voltore and the 'Venusian woods' which clothed its sides, and the range of Apulian hills whose familiar outlines he

---

[1] Besides many vivid descriptive touches in the Odes, cf. such phrases as 'saxis late candentibus Anxur,' 'rugosus frigore pagus,' from the Satires and Epistles.

recognises in his journey to Brundisium. The name of the
fountain, whose sound charmed his ear in his poetical meridian,
and which he has made as famous as the names of the fountains
haunted by the Muses on Helicon and Parnassus, was probably
transferred by him from a fountain in the neighbourhood of his
early home to that which charmed his ear and fancy in later life.

The most important moral influence of his early years was
that exercised on his character by the worth, sagacity, and pious
devotion of his father. We hear of no other members of his
family; and the fact that his father was able to make him the
exclusive object of his care, to accompany him to Rome, and
to leave him means sufficient to support him in the station in
which he was educated, suggests the inference that he was an
only son and that he lost his mother in his early years. The
attachment between himself and his father is of the kind often
found subsisting between father and son when they are the sole
surviving members of their race. After Horace had enjoyed
the intimacy of the best men of his day, he looks back to his
father's influence as one of the happiest circumstances of his
life, and attributes to his precepts and example whatever claim
he had to moral worth and social attraction. To the same
influence he ascribes the intellectual habit of observing and
judging character. To his care also he owed the advantage
of the highest education which Rome could give, and the provision of the means which enabled him to complete his studies
at Athens. The original position of his father appears to have
been that of a public slave of the town of Venusia; and it is
supposed that he owed the ancient patrician name of Horatius
to the fact that Venusia was included in the Horatian tribe.
Horace was himself 'ingenuus'—i.e. born after his father had
obtained his emancipation. His father had first held the post
of 'coactor,' or collector of money at public auctions. From
the scanty emoluments of this post, combined with other
business, he saved enough to become the owner of the small
farm in the neighbourhood of Venusia where the poet probably
was born. Though careful and thrifty like the best type of the

Italian yeoman, he was free from the narrowness of self-made men, and while preparing his son for a career more suitable to the promise of his genius than likely to advance him in the race for wealth, he inculcated upon him the wisdom of being content with the provision he had himself made for him. To his training Horace attributes his exemption from the meanness and avarice of which he is so caustic an observer, as well as his immunity from the more ruinous vices of a corrupt society. Not satisfied with sending him to the school at Venusia where the sons of the provincial magnates were educated, he gave up his own occupation, took him to Rome, acted there as his attendant, enabled him to appear like the sons of men of old hereditary estate, and procured for him the best instruction which Rome could provide. He became the companion, guide, and friend of his son; and imparted to him the lessons on human life drawn from his own experience. There is scarcely any individual portrait in all ancient literature which leaves on the mind so real an impression of worth, affection, and good sense, as this picture of the poet's father. It reminds us of the peasant fathers of two men of genius in modern times, Burns and Carlyle; of the serious sense of duty in the one and his reverence for the 'traditus ab antiquis mos;' of the other's habit of shrewd and caustic observation on the lives and characters of his neighbours. The admiration which these men of genius had for the homely worth and sagacity of their fathers is exactly like that which Horace expresses for his peasant father. There are no passages in his writings, among those in which Horace speaks of and from himself, which afford surer evidence of the soundness of his heart and the true metal out of which his character was tempered, than those in which he recalls with candour and pride the debt which he owed his father. The vein of genius which made him one of the great poets of the world, is one of the incommunicable gifts—

θεῶν ἐρικυδέα δῶρα
ὅσσα κεν αὐτοὶ δῶσιν, ἑκὼν δ' οὐκ ἄν τις ἕλοιτο—

but the grain of character which saved him from becoming the slave of society or of the pleasures to which the mobility and geniality of his temperament exposed him, was clearly his by inheritance.

At Rome he received the ordinary literary education under the severe discipline of Orbilius, one of the line of famous grammarians and schoolmasters, dating from the time of Lucilius, to whose writings and teaching much of the definiteness and clearness of Latin style is to be attributed. A line from Domitius Marsus, preserved in a fragment of Suetonius,—

Si quos Orbilius ferula scuticaque cecidit—

justifies the epithet 'plagosus' applied by Horace to his old schoolmaster. In him, according to the account of Suetonius and Macrobius (ii. 6. 3), Horace had a living example of the caustic and censorious freedom of speech which he admired in Lucilius. Orbilius taught with 'more reputation than remuneration,' and wrote a book 'on the wrongs which schoolmasters suffered at the hands of parents.' If Horace received any literary impulse from him, it was probably towards satire rather than artistic poetry. The school-book which he mentions in connexion with the teaching he received at Rome is the 'poems of Livius Andronicus,' probably his Latin-translation of the Odyssey, the retention of which as a text-book in education in the Ciceronian age is a proof of Roman conservatism in educational as in other matters. But Horace received also, before he left Rome, some direct initiation into Greek literature and some knowledge of the Iliad. The object of the higher school-education during the last half-century of the Republic was to impart an intelligent mastery of Latin and Greek; to enable the pupil to become in after-life 'doctus sermones utriusque linguae.' Horace was familiar with, though he did not greatly value, most of the old Latin poets, and through all his life was a diligent student of the whole range of Greek poetry from Homer to Menander.

The crown of a liberal education in that age was to pass some years at Athens, which attracted the youth of Rome by the spell of its memories and the fame of its living teachers, and afforded them the combined advantages which a visit to the old seats of art and letters, and residence at a great University, afford to a modern Englishman. But these advantages were not accessible to every one; and it must have been quite an exceptional thing for a man of Horace's birth and means to share in the life led there by the younger members of the Roman aristocracy. The enthusiasm for intellectual culture, and the ambition to live with people of distinction, were through all his life powerful motives with Horace; and he was influenced by both motives in completing his education at Athens. The intellectual gains which he attributed to his stay there were an advance in literary accomplishment,

> Adiecere bonae paulo plus artis Athenae,

and his first introduction to the questions of ethical philosophy, which occupied much of his attention in his later years. It was probably at this time that he became an admirer of Archilochus and the old lyrical poets with whom his own earliest lyrical poems indicate long familiarity. He tells us that his earliest literary ambition was by the composition of Greek verses to be numbered among Greek poets, till warned from so preposterous a purpose by what he poetically calls a vision of Romulus, but what prosaically may be regarded as the suggestion of his own common sense and national feeling. Yet this early attempt to catch the melodies of the old Greek lyrical poets in their own language may have prepared him for that mastery over musical effect and poetical expression which he afterwards attained; just as their exercises in Latin or Italian verse trained the most classic of our English poets to their consummate mastery of metre and diction. One negative advantage he gained from the completion of his studies at Athens instead of under Greek teachers at Rome, that he escaped the influence of Alexandrinism, under which all the other contemporary poets were educated. But Athens was to him a school of life and social pleasure as well as of literary and philosophic culture. He writes of the time he spent there in the genial spirit in which men recall in after years their college life when it lives in their memory as a time in which they enjoyed their youth with congenial companions, as well as felt the first stirring of intellectual life. It is probable that the tie which bound him to some of the men of his own age and standing, whom he addresses in the language of old intimacy, was first formed in the 'pleasant time' of his Athenian residence.

The arrival of Brutus in Athens in the autumn after the assassination of Julius Caesar was the occasion of great enthusiasm among the Athenian people, who, living more in the memory of their past than in the interests of the present[1], saw in the act of the conspirators a parallel to the deeds of their own Harmodius and Aristogeiton. The devotion of Brutus to philosophy had been recently proclaimed in those works of Cicero which gave a new impulse to the study in Rome; and his appearance in the lecture-rooms of the philosophers attracted to his cause, by personal sympathy, the young Romans who were finishing their education at Athens. Horace followed the same impulse which moved his associates. Of the share which he took in the civil war he writes with reserve; but we have his own assertion that he took part in the battle of Philippi, and held the post of military tribune at the time. His appointment to that post in an army the officers of which were largely drawn from the oldest and noblest families excited considerable envy in ancient, and has given rise to some astonishment in modern times. It seems improbable that Brutus should have appointed a youth of obscure birth and of no military experience immediately to so high a rank. But the presence of Catullus and Cinna with Memmius in his provincial government, and, somewhat later, of Julius Florus, Titius and other young poets with Tiberius, suggests the inference that his

---

[1] Cf. Tacitus, Annals, ii. 53: 'Hinc ventum Athenas, foederique sociae et vetustae urbis datum ut uno lictore uteretur. Excepere Graeci quaesitissimis honoribus vetera suorum facta dictaque praeferentes, quo plus dignationis adulatio haberet.'

love of literature may have induced Brutus to attach him to his staff, and that the ardour which he showed in the cause, or the proof which he gave of capacity, may have led to his subsequent promotion. In the succinct statement of his claims to distinction which Horace makes in the last Epistle of the first book, he states emphatically the approval of the first men of his time in war and peace,

> Me primis urbis belli placuisse domique.

In what is probably the earliest of all his writings, the 7th Satire of Book i., he gives a graphic account of a scene enacted in presence of the staff when Brutus held his praetorial court at Clazomenae. The sole interest of the piece is the impression it produces of being drawn from actual experience, while the scene was still fresh in the memory of the writer and of those for whose entertainment it was written. The Epistle to Bullatius (i. 11) shows his familiarity not only with the more famous cities of Asia and the Greek isles, but with such deserted towns as Lebedos. Expressions in the Odes, such as the 'fesso maris ac viarum militiaeque' (ii. 6), a parallel to the 'odio maris atque viarum' of the Epistle referred to, and,

> O saepe mecum tempus in ultimum
> Deducte (ii. 7),

show that he had his share in the alarms and hardships of the campaign which preceded the final conflict with the arms of the Triumvirs. But lines in the Ode last quoted speak also of convivial pleasures often enjoyed with the comrade who had shared his dangers; and these reminiscences may be either of the pleasant times when they were students together at Athens, or of the relaxations from military duties which the luxurious cities of Asia afforded. Of his actual part in the battle, he tells us only that he shared in the general rout and that he left his shield ingloriously behind him. As one of the officers in command of a legion, he probably bore his part in the first action in which the wing under Brutus was successful; and though he escaped from the final battle unharmed, 'owing to the protection

of Mercury,' as he tells us, veiling, as he occasionally does, the
actual incidents of his life under mythological allusions, there
is no more reason to attribute cowardice to him than to any
other survivor of a defeat. To take seriously his ironical adaptation of words long before used of themselves by poets of a most
combative and martial spirit, Archilochus and Alcaeus, would
be to attribute to a man, who, with all his irony, maintained in
his life and writings a habitual self-respect, sentiments which
were a habitual source of ridicule in the slaves of Roman
comedy. The mode in which he makes his confession is in
accordance with his habitual candour and ironical self-depreciation. But perhaps his description of himself some ten years
later as 'imbellis et firmus parum' (Epod. 1) implies that the
experience of defeat had chilled the ardour with which, 'in his
hot youth, in the Consulship of Plancus,' he had fought for the
Republic. It cannot be thought discreditable to him that he
did not adhere to the cause after its leaders had shown their
despair of it by committing suicide. If there is any discredit
in such action, it is one which he shares with men of high
character and position, like Valerius Messalla, whose birth
would have made it more incumbent on him to adhere to the
Senatorian cause, if it had not been irretrievably lost. Yet,
without pressing his own admission against him, it may be
granted that in this crisis of his life Horace showed, as he
showed in all his later course and in his criticism of the world
of action and letters, a subordination of enthusiasm to a sober
estimate of things as they were. There is nothing of the spirit
of a renegade in his subsequent conversion and acceptance of
the new government. Along with the best among the survivors
of the defeated cause, he felt that the reconciliation of parties
was the first need of the age; and what was at first a cold
acquiescence in re-established order, became sympathetic advocacy, after a common danger and common triumph had united
the conquered and the conquerors. The immediate feelings with
which he regarded the overthrow of the Republican cause find
expression in some of the earliest of his lyrical compositions.

In the sixteenth Epode, written probably during the short war of Perusia, he calls on the better part of his countrymen to follow the example of the Phocaeans and to find a new home among the happy islands of the Western Ocean. In the fourteenth Ode of the first book, an allegory written in imitation of Alcaeus, he appears to remonstrate in tones of passionate earnestness with the remnants of the republican party. Both of these lyrical compositions may have exposed him to the charge of having too soon and too absolutely despaired of the Republic. Yet they are written in a spirit the very opposite of the gay and careless tone in which a few years later he expresses his indifference to the public topics of the day, and they betray no unworthy haste in welcoming the star of the new Empire.

The permanent effect of the defeat of his cause was to cure him of all illusions. It checked any personal ambition for public distinction. It brought home to him the lesson which he ever afterwards applied, not to expect too much from life, neither to trust the smiles nor to fear the frowns of fortune. He thus learned his philosophy 'vita magistra,' from the teaching of life, and his experience of the vicissitudes of fortune, common in an age of revolution, imparts a reality to maxims or reflexions, which otherwise might appear conventional. His opinions in the years immediately following the battle of Philippi, recorded in the first book of the Satires, imply his adherence to the speculative doctrines of Epicurus, inculcating political quietism. With the later revival of his sympathy with the national fortunes, we note a greater sympathy with the attitude of Stoicism, the teachers of which school are introduced merely as objects of ridicule in his early writings.

His life as a poet and man of letters, after the years of education and adventure were over, divides itself into three periods of about ten years each, and is reflected in the writings of these different periods. Of his habits, state of mind, ordinary avocations, in the years between 41 B.C. and 29 B.C., which were passed chiefly at Rome, we learn all that we can know from the two books of Satires, published about the years 35 B.C. and 29 B.C., and from the Epodes, published a little before the latter date. These different works show different aspects of his experience, life, and character. The Satires present him to us as the disinterested spectator of life, the Epodes as one sharing in its passions, animosities, and pleasures. The one work is the expression of his critical and observant faculty, the other of his more ardent feelings, and of that vein of poetry which had not yet found its truest and happiest outlet. The second period, 29 B.C. to 19 B.C., when he was between thirty-six and forty-six years of age, was the meridian of his genius; the time when he seems to have been happiest as a man, and was most truly inspired as a poet. The record of this period is contained in the larger number of the Odes of the three books published together during this decennium, and in the first book of the Epistles. During the last ten years of his life, his literary activity was much more intermittent, and of his personal position and relations at this time we learn only from the Odes of the fourth book, and from the second book of the Epistles: for the Ars Poetica, even if it belongs to this period, a point about which doubts have recently been raised, is unlike all his other works in this respect, that it tells us scarcely anything about himself.

II.

Horace's Literary Life.

[**First Period**: from 41 B.C. to 29 B.C.]

Horace returned to Rome probably in the year after the battle of Philippi, and found himself, in consequence of the confiscation of the territory attached to Venusia, stripped of his home and estate. He speaks in one of his Odes of a narrow escape from shipwreck in the Sicilian sea; and he often indicates a lively sense of the dangers and terrors of the sea. It is probable that this danger was incurred on his homeward voyage.

The comparison which he draws between himself and the soldier of Lucullus—

> vehemens lupus, et sibi et hosti
> Iratus pariter, ieiunis dentibus acer—

is a record of the angry and reckless mood in which he first entered on literature. The evidence of the Epodes leads to the conclusion that between his bright days at Athens and on the staff of Brutus, and the position which he soon afterwards enjoyed as a favoured member of the best circle in Rome, he passed through a short interval of struggle and discomfort, and was thrown into the society of men and women towards whom his feelings were uncongenial. He must have lost many of his old comrades by the fortune of war, and he had not yet made new friends among the partisans of Caesar. He not only had the critical faculty of a satirist, but was at this period of his life capable of feeling violent personal animosity; and he retained the resentment of a partisan against some of the prominent representatives of the victorious cause. His earliest writings were in the style of Archilochus, which afforded vent to his private animosities and opened up a field to him in which he might assert his originality, and in the more personal and aggressive vein of Lucilius, in adopting which he aspired to revive a form of the national literature which no one had successfully cultivated since the older satirist. Several of the Epodes and the second Satire of the first book show by the greater coarseness of their tone and their more aggressive personalities, that Horace, on his first return to Rome, was neither so happy in his immediate social relations, nor so fastidious in his pleasures, as he became in the time 'when the Odes and the Epistles were composed.

The happiest circumstance of his life in the early years after Philippi was the friendship which he formed with Virgil and Varius. The appreciation of their qualities expressed in the lines

> animae quales neque candidiores
> Terra tulit neque quis me sit devinctior alter,

and the appreciation which he received from them, must have done much to restore his natural kindliness and to place his relation to the world on a pleasanter footing. These older poets had made for themselves friends among the chiefs of the Caesarian party. They were thus able to exercise a determining influence not on the fortunes only, but on the whole life and art of Horace, by introducing him to Maecenas. The date of this introduction was probably in 39 B.C., but it was not till nearly a year afterwards that the relations between the poet and the statesman became intimate. From this time, till the death of the great Minister some thirty years later, his affection for Maecenas became the dominant feeling in the life of Horace. The relation between them was as nearly that of equal friendship as such a relation could be in a society based on aristocratic traditions, such as that of Rome was at all times. Although Horace does not conceal a natural sense of gratified vanity, especially in the earlier stages of their friendship, and though he owed to it the prosperity of his life, yet through all their intercourse he was resolute in maintaining his independence. It is from Horace chiefly that we learn to know and value the character of Maecenas, and to understand the kind of influence that he exercised. He bears strong testimony to the absence of all jealousy and intrigue from the circle of which Maecenas was the centre. When he himself became the most favoured guest in the mansion on the Esquiline, he owed this distinction more to his personal qualities than to his genius. Horace cultivated more carefully and valued more highly the qualities which fit men for life, than those which secure distinction in literature. The urbanity and tone of the world which appear natural to him and which in him were combined with perfect frankness and sincerity, the tact and reticence which he inculcates and which he seems to have carried into his conduct, must have recommended him to one whose especial function it was to understand and to manage men, and who, if his sympathetic nature required a confidant, wanted one on whose discretion and honour he could rely. His intercourse with

Maecenas tended to develope these qualities in Horace. There is a great difference in tone between the ignoble bitterness of the invectives against Canidia, or the coarse personality of the second Satire, and the geniality of those compositions which were written after Horace became the intimate friend of Maecenas. Coincidently with this change in tone and temper we find that he attaches himself in literature more to his own countryman the 'comis et urbanus' Lucilius, than to the angry Greek for whom 'rage forged the weapon of the iambus,' and that it is the urbanity and the frank communicativeness, not the aggressive personality of his master that he reproduces. The fastidiousness which characterized Horace in his literary and social judgments was also a quality which he shared with his patron. Not only the kindlier spirit of his writings, and the tone at once of the world and of distinction, which are a great ground of Horace's modern popularity, but also the more serious aims which he set before himself in his art may be ascribed to the influence of Maecenas. From the testimony, not of poets only, but of historians, we learn that under an appearance of indolence and an entire abnegation of personal ambition, Maecenas concealed great capacity and public spirit, and the most loyal devotion to Augustus. This devotion was not a mere personal sentiment, but was associated with his desire to promote a large, humane, and enlightened policy. It was while Augustus acted in accordance with his advice and that of Agrippa that his rule was most prosperous, and most beneficent. He encouraged the poets associated with him to great and serious undertakings, and to the use of their genius to enlist the national sentiment in favour of the great reformation in manners and character, which he had at heart. It was under this influence that Horace at a later period used his lyrical art to commend to the imagination of his countrymen the ideal of the new Empire[1]. The two Epodes apparently written

---

[1] The best commentary on many of the utterances of Horace on public policy, as in Od. iii. 2, iii. 24, is to be found in the long speech in which Dion (lii. 14–40) represents Maecenas as advising Augustus on the principles

immediately before and immediately after the battle of Actium, show that Horace's sympathy with the national cause was at first identified with his personal anxiety for Maecenas. But it is not only in the employment of his lyrical art for the celebration of national glory and the advancement of state policy that we recognise the more serious aims imparted to Horace by this relation. It was owing to his attachment to Maecenas and to the circle of eminent men with whom that relation brought him into contact, that he took the leading part in that consciously directed effort to produce a great national literature which so conspicuously distinguishes the Augustan age. Among those who took part in this effort were men who in the previous generation would have devoted themselves to a political career, but who, when that was denied to them, united with men of obscure or provincial origin in the creation of a literature, more comprehensive in its scope, more serious in its aim, more perfect in form and style, than had existed in any previous age. There was no rivalry among these competitors for fame. Each selected a province for himself, and did not interfere with any

in accordance with which he should govern. The necessity for severity of punishment insisted on in iii. 24. 25–36, 'O quisquis volet impias,' &c., gains new significance by being compared with such phrases as μεταρρύθμισον αὐτήν (i. e. τὴν πατρίδα) καὶ κατακόσμησον πρὸς τὸ σωφρονέστερον and κἄν γε καὶ ὡς νεωχμώσῃ τι, καὶ ἐλεγχθήτω καὶ κολασθήτω. The 'Nescit equo rudis Haerere ingenuus puer,' (iii. 24. 54), and the precepts of manliness for the training of the sons of Senators and Knights in iii. 2, 'Angustam amice,' are illustrated by lii. 26, ἵνα ἕως τε ἔτι παῖδές εἰσιν, ἐς τὰ διδασκαλεῖα συμφοιτῶσι, καὶ ἐπειδὰν ἐς μειράκια ἐκβάλωσιν, ἐπί τε τοὺς ἵππους καὶ ἐπὶ τὰ ὅπλα τρέπωνται. The stanzas about immortality being the reward of virtue and not of popular favour, 'Virtus repulsae nescia sordidae,' and the reference which they undoubtedly have to the 'Justum et tenacem propositi virum' of the following Ode, in which the deification of the Emperor is for the first time formally declared to be the result of his virtues, are best explained by the words (c. 35), ἀρετὴ μὲν γὰρ ἰσοθέους πολλοὺς ποιεῖ, χειροτονητὸς δ' οὐδεὶς πώποτε θεὸς ἐγένετο. And the importance of the revival of the forms and worship of the national religion as a bond of social and political order, insisted on by Horace, is in accordance with the whole tenour of chapter 36, καὶ προσέτι τὸ μὲν θεῖον πάντῃ πάντως αὐτός τε σέβου κατὰ τὰ πάτρια καὶ τοὺς ἄλλους τιμᾶν ἀνάγκαζε, &c. That the policy of bringing about a great moral and religious reformation, attributed by the historian to Maecenas, was really his, appears to be confirmed by the emphasis with which the Epicurean poet, as he is usually regarded, urges this policy during the years in which Maecenas had most influence in the counsels of Augustus.

other. Varius claimed that of epic poetry, Pollio of tragedy, Fundanius of comedy, Virgil of pastoral and rural poetry, Octavius of history, and Horace himself of satire. As their relative capabilities developed themselves, these parts were altered or interchanged. Varius resigns epic for tragic poetry: Pollio does not seem to have resumed 'the Cecropian buskin' after he applied himself to history. Those among this circle who were not poets contributed to the advancement of the national literature as critics, grammarians, and orators. There had been a similarly combined and consciously directed effort in the previous century, made by the members of that Scipionic circle by which Roman culture was first established on a firm basis. Maecenas, though himself a man of no literary or oratorical genius, was by his sympathetic appreciation of genius, as well as by the position which he filled in the early and best years of the new Empire, able to exercise over the most gifted members of this new circle an influence similar to that exercised by Scipio over his in the preceding century.

There is another side to the character of Maecenas which also formed a bond between Horace and himself. Historians and moralists attribute to him, not only the almost universal love of pleasure, but an effeminate weakness conspicuous in his dress, manner, and literary style. The tone in which Horace occasionally addresses Maecenas leaves no doubt that a common love of pleasure was one of the bonds of union between them, as it was in a friendship not unlike theirs, that of Goethe and the Duke of Weimar. The appearance of effeminacy was the unfavourable aspect of a sensibility and tenderness of feeling, which perhaps it is not fanciful to trace, combined with a careworn look, in the expression of the bust preserved, along with many of the same age of a harder and stronger type, in the Museum of the Vatican. His one irretrievable error, his betrayal to his wife Terentia of the danger to which her brother Murena was exposed, arose from an excess of tenderness. More than one of Horace's writings show how dependent Maecenas was on the sympathy and affection of his friend.

The relation of dependence and protection was thus not all on one side. The character of Horace was probably either naturally of a stronger metal, or better tempered by his philosophy and experience. The inequality between them was thus lessened, and the affection of Horace must have been strengthened by the knowledge that he was necessary to the happiness of his patron. Though Horace expresses a loyal feeling of regard for many friends and a deep affection for one or two, there was no man or woman who really shared his devotion to Maecenas.

He makes frequent acknowledgement that he owes his independent position to the liberality of his patron. On his first return to Rome he had procured as a means of livelihood a post in the order of *scribae*, attached to the great administrative offices. We find in the sixth Satire of the second book that that body availed themselves of his friendly offices and consulted him on matters concerning their interests: but the account he gives of his daily occupations some years previously leaves no room for the ordinary round of official duties. Within a year or two of the time when he is admitted to the intimacy of Maecenas, Horace writes of himself as having his time entirely at his own disposal, and as occupying himself with the ordinary amusements and exercises of a Roman gentleman, with that quiet observation of the peculiarities of Roman life apparent in his satire, with reading, and with writing down for his amusement the results of his observation and reflection. Thus the leisure and freedom from care which enabled him to devote himself to literature were the immediate results of his relation to Maecenas. A year or two later he received from him a gift which may without exaggeration be described as the condition which enabled him to become one of the great lyrical poets of the world—the gift of his Sabine farm. Though this gift was received and though Horace's enjoyment of it began in his first literary period, yet the great influence which it exercised on his life and his literary art belongs to the second period; and any further reference to it may be deferred till that is reached. The Satires and the Epodes reflect the habits, the pleasures, the society of the town: the inspiration of the Odes comes from the heart of the Sabine hills, and the cool stream of Digentia mingles its refreshment with the current of philosophic meditation in the Epistles.

Of the other incidents of this decennium, of his mode of life, and his growth in opinion and character, we learn something from both the Satires and the Epodes. The most notable incident of the earlier part of this time is his journey to Brundisium, in company with Virgil, Varius, Plotius, and the Greek rhetorician Heliodorus, in the train of Maecenas and Cocceius, who, as friends respectively of Caesar and Antony, had been sent to arrange some important matter between the rivals. The mission referred to, as has been shown by Mr. Palmer in his edition of the Satires, must have been that of Maecenas in the autumn of 38 B.C. to arrange with Antony for assistance against Sextus Pompeius. From the terms in which Maecenas is spoken of in this Satire, compared with all the later notices of him, we should infer that the poet's intimacy with him had not been fully established at this time. At a later time, before the battle of Actium, he professes his anxiety to accompany him to the scene of danger: and expressions in the song of triumph which utters the feelings of exultation and scorn called forth by the victory over Cleopatra, have been understood to imply that Horace was on board ship, and a witness of the scene of the battle of Actium. But even if the meaning of the words was perfectly unambiguous, it would be impossible to say in such a poem whether we were reading of a real experience, or of a situation imagined to give more force to the passion of the hour.

The Epodes and the Satires are the expression of the two different sides of Horace's nature. In later life these two sides became thoroughly harmonised in the union of self-command with the full enjoyment of life. He was, by his own account, naturally impressible and fond of pleasure, irascible and impatient, and at the same time, genial and sociable. This is the nature apparent in some of the Odes and in many of the Epodes.

In the Epodes the love of pleasure is less restrained and refined than in the Odes; there are indications of strong animosities, which in the Odes take the milder form of a contemptuous toleration. In later life he looks back to his youth and early manhood as a time of pleasure, but of a pleasure that left no painful sting behind it.

In some of the more Anacreontic Odes written about his eighth lustre, we have probably the reflex, softened by memory and glorified by fancy, of his life in Rome between the age of twenty-five and thirty-five. But the other side of Horace's nature asserted itself also during this time, and has found expression in both books of the Satires. In the sixth Satire of the first book we have a sketch of his ordinary daily life, which is far removed from the careless life of a man of pleasure —from that for instance of Catullus and his young associates, or from that of Propertius and Ovid at a later time. If he enjoyed the good things and the good conversation at the 'parasitica mensa' of Maecenas, he knew equally the pleasures of simple living both in town and country, of being alone, of reading, and of studying the life which passed before his eyes in the streets, and the strange characters who gathered in the Forum after the business of the day was over. He could tolerate the society of parasites like Milvius or Maenius, in the interest of that study of character which he carried on along with his self-examination. His liaisons with the Leuconoes and Neobules of his Odes, whether they are of the 'Dichtung' or of the 'Wahrheit' of his life, seem to be as much inspired by an interest in human nature as by any more ardent feeling. We hear little about them in the Satires, which record the reality of his life. He could extract the good from every variety of social life, from intercourse with Maecenas or Messalla, and with Milvius or Maenius, without being absorbed by it; and, without ever losing his hold on the world, he could retire from time to time into the solitude of his own thoughts and live the life of a meditative recluse.

His intimacy with Maecenas did not produce an immediate

change in his political sympathies. The tone of the earlier Epodes (the seventh and sixteenth) expresses merely a general horror of the continuance of civil war. In the two (the first and ninth) written immediately before and immediately after the battle of Actium, Caesar is identified with the national cause, but the earlier poem is called out by personal anxiety for Maecenas; and even the later poem (if we adopt Plüss's interpretation of lines 23-26) does not err on the side of flattery[1]. In the first book of Satires the name of Caesar occurs only once, and then in not too respectful connexion with the Sardinian Tigellius. But in the first Satire of Book ii, written after the capture of Alexandria, but before the title of Augustus was conferred on the Emperor, his tone is different. The epithet 'invictus' is there applied to him; and Horace already contemplates the duty of celebrating him in his verse. Though it was not till a later period, probably after the publication of the three books of Odes, that he began to enjoy the personal favour of the Emperor, there is no doubt that, with the close of the first period of his literary activity, he had become reconciled to the Monarchy, not only as a necessity, but as a form of government desirable and beneficent in itself; and this reconcilement was the necessary condition of the second and the maturer period in his literary career, that extending from 29 B.C. to 19 B.C.

III.

[Second Period: from 29 B.C. to 19 B.C.]

Two conditions mainly determined the current of his literary inspiration and activity during this second period. The first was the state of public affairs; the second the enjoyment which he derived from his Sabine farm. The enthusiasm awakened by the triumph of the national cause in the victory of Actium

[1] Cf. p. 124, 125, infra.

and the capture of Alexandria made Horace one of the great lyrical poets of the world. Although the earliest of his public Odes—the second and the twelfth of Book i—may have been composed to celebrate the successes over Sextus Pompeius, yet in those Odes of Book i, which appear to have been composed before the year 30 B.C., Horace is essentially the Anacreontic singer of the lighter joys of life, and the exponent of a philosophy suited to them. But his deeper nature was powerfully moved in sympathy with the general enthusiasm which hailed Octavianus as the saviour of the world, and also with the new ideas and the new policy which were introduced at the establishment of the Empire. His imagination was impressed by the spectacle of power and re-established order; and his higher nature responded to the revival of the moral and social ideals of the happier days of the Republic. The same influences acted on him, as had acted on Virgil in the composition of the Georgics and the conception of the Aeneid. His philosophy, in its two aspects of Epicurean renunciation and of Stoical devotion to duty, assumes a deeper and graver note. His satire, as in Od. iii. 24, becomes, for the first time, severe and earnest, allies itself with his poetical imagination, and is employed, not in the form of light ridicule of personal follies, nor as a weapon of personal animosity, but as the censorial condemnation of the corruption which was eating into the heart of the commonwealth. In the great revolution which had come over the world, in the new hopes which it awakened and the new ideals which it presented to the imagination, in the striking personality, in the prestige and fortune, in the actual career, of the remarkable man by whom this revolution was accomplished, there was a theme prepared for lyrical and for epic poetry. And it was the good fortune of the age to have, in the culminating crisis of the national destinies, two poets in the maturity of their powers and still in the freshness of their inspiration, who both by the susceptibility of their imagination and their intimate relation to the statesman at the centre of affairs, were enabled to perpetuate in lyrical song and in epic poetry the ideal aspirations and the romantic memories by which the heart of the world was then stirred.

Horace owed his knowledge of, and sympathy with the Imperial policy, to the familiar footing on which he was received in the stately house on the Esquiline. But the inspiration and art which enabled him to shape into lyric poetry the thoughts and impressions which he there received, came from his more peaceful home within the folds of the Sabine hills. He had acknowledged the happiness which he derived from this gift of his patron, in one of the Satires of the second book; but it was during the second period of his literary career that he most availed himself of the leisure and seclusion from the world which it afforded him. He tells us, both seriously in his Odes and playfully in his Epistles, that it is among the Sabine hills and in other beautiful spots in Italy that he feels his devotion to the Muses, and that life in Rome is incompatible with all poetical effort. Like Virgil he feels the power of poetry in association with the love of the woods and streams.

No more suitable home for an Italian poet can be imagined than the valley 'folded in Sabine recesses,' watered by the stream Digentia and crowned by Mount Lucretilis. It was within a few hours' drive from Tibur and so within easy access of the most refined and cultivated social life. But it afforded, if he chose, a complete retreat from all the distractions of society. He might live there alone, enjoying the companionship of the 'veterum libri' which he brought with him, or wandering, as some of his Odes indicate, in poetical mood, among woods and river banks, and lonely heights; or he might mix familiarly with his rustic neighbours, amuse them by sharing awkwardly in the work of the farm, and join, with the sympathy of a poet, himself country-bred, in the celebration of their rustic festivals. Or his lonely days of study and devotion to poetry might be varied by a visit from Maecenas or some of his literary friends, or from Tyndaris or Phyllis who might come to amuse him with their talk and song. Numerous passages in the Odes show the supreme contentment and happiness which he derived from his country home, and the charm which he found in its beauty. The expressions he applies to it show how absolutely his heart was satisfied. It was associated with the happiest hours of his life, the hours of inspiration and of fitting the thoughts and feelings of those hours to perfect words and music [1].

[1] The beauty of the scenery in the midst of which his farm lay and the happiness which he derived from it find their simplest expression in the line

Hae latebrae dulces etiam si credis amoenae.

There has been much controversy as to the actual position of his farm and country house in the valley of the Licenza, which runs at right angles from the road between Tivoli and Subiaco. The village which is passed on the left hand just before reaching the junction of the Digentia with the ancient Anio is Vico Varo, the Varia mentioned by Horace as the town to which the five farmers from his estate had been accustomed to repair for the transaction of the public business of the district. After entering the valley, which runs due north for four or five miles till it is stopped by a picturesque amphitheatre of mountains, rising to between 2000 and 4000 feet in height, the first conspicuous object is the village of Cantalupo Bardella, high up on the somewhat bare hill-face on the right, which represents both in name and in appearance the 'rugosus frigore pagus,' though the word 'pagus' properly denotes the whole country district—

Festus in pratis vacat otioso
Cum bove pagus—

not a particular village. About a mile up the valley, on the left hand, a steep rocky hill, on which stands the village Rocca Giovine, rises abruptly, and on it there are still found the remains of the old temple of Vacuna— 'fanum putre Vacunae'—with an inscription declaring that it had been restored by Vespasian. It is on a plateau at some considerable height above this ruin that M. Gaston Boissier and others place the country house and the 'aprica rura' of Horace. The late Mr. Justice Lawson in a letter in the *Times*, some years ago, gave convincing reasons for holding that the farm was higher up the valley, and situated not on the side of the mountain, but near the river, not far from where it is joined by the 'fons etiam rivo dare nomen idoneus' which it is natural to identify with the 'fons' to which Horace gives the name Bandusia. The writer points out that the lines in the Epistle to the Villicus—

Addit opus pigro rivus, si decidit imber
Multa mole docendus aprico parcere prato—

show clearly that the farm extended along the bank of the stream. He points out also that 'angulus iste' corresponds with the nook at the upper end of the valley.

On the identity of Bandusia with the 'fons' spoken of and not with the fonntain near Venusia, the writer says convincingly, 'Why should Horace celebrate in such beautiful strains a fountain at Venusia, which place there is no trace of his ever having re-visited after he came to Rome? Does not his description, and the intended sacrifice of a kid to dye its waters, import

The years which followed the publication of the Epodes and the second book of Satires, when he was between thirty-five and forty, during which he lived much in his Sabine farm, were the years of his purest inspiration and most sustained industry. During this time he concentrated himself entirely on his lyrical art. If he did not bring to his task the fresh enthusiasm of youth, he brought the wisdom and experience of his maturity; and by this predominance of reflexion over pure emotion, he may be said to have created a new type of lyrical art, which, while it brings back in the idealising light of retrospect the pleasures and amusements of youth, finds a poetical expression for the interests, the experience, and the convictions of maturer life. It was probably early in the year 23 B.C. that he gave to the world the three books which contain the results of the occasional lyrical inspiration of the years before the capture of Alexandria, and of his more continuous efforts between that year and the date of publication.

Our next knowledge of him is derived from the first book of the Epistles, published a few years later. Expressions in the dedicatory Epistle to Maecenas, such as 'Non eadem est aetas, non mens,' imply that an interval of some years had elapsed between the publication of the Odes and the composition of that Epistle. He professes in that Epistle to desire to withdraw altogether from poetry, and to devote himself to philosophical study and the realisation in practice of his contemplative ideal. From the Epistles contained in this book we learn that the taste for seclusion and for a more simple life grew on

a daily familiarity with it and an affection such as a poet would feel for a clear spring near his favourite haunts?'

The estate of Horace included woodland and pasture for goats, as well as meadow and ploughed land, and probably extended over a considerable part of the valley. There seems no ground for fixing the site of the house on so uncomfortable a position for a man of Horace's habits as a height rising steeply some hundred feet above the valley and the stream which gave him so much refreshment. There are still seen the remains of a tessellated pavement on the other site suggested, and though that is declared to be of later date than the Augustan age, it seems natural that the possessor of the estate in a later age should have built his more luxurious villa at or near the site which must have been made classic by its previous occupant.

him with advancing years. The delight which his Sabine home afforded him was strengthened by familiarity. He has celebrated its praises in his Satires and his Odes; but we learn even more in the Epistles of the restorative influence which it had on his whole nature. We learn also that the choice of a simpler and quieter life was forced upon him by some failure in health. During this decennium he had lost the beauty and gaiety of bearing which had characterised him in youth, had become prematurely grey, and had undergone that change of constitution which disposes a man to quiet contemplation rather than the energetic enjoyment of life. He found his companionship in books more than in society. We learn from the Odes that he varied his retreat to his Sabine citadel with residence at such health resorts as Tibur, Baiae, and Praeneste; and he speaks of himself as having passed his time at the last-named place in reading through the Iliad and Odyssey. We learn also that he was at this time a patient of the fashionable physician Antonius Musa, and that he was ordered by him to pass his winters at some place on the South Italian coast, such as Velia or Salernum. But, while living much away from Rome, he did not lose his hold on society. He combined his love of retirement with his love of social life by the new vehicle which he found for the expression of his thoughts, the poetical Epistle. This form of composition not only kept him in the minds of the men of his own generation, but enabled him to establish new bonds with the younger men who gave promise of distinction.

The date of the publication of the first book of the Epistles was probably 19 B.C. In the last poem of the series he tells us that he had completed his forty-fourth December in the consulship of Lepidus and Lollius, i.e. in the year 21 B.C. But he does not tell us whether that was the year immediately preceding the date of publication. A reference to the successes of Tiberius over the Armenians and of Agrippa over the Cantabrians indicates that the work was not given to the world, as it now stands, before 19 B.C. In any Epistle written after the September of that year, we might have expected to find some expression of sorrow for the premature death of Virgil, which must have been felt as a great national loss, and as a cause of personal grief to many in the circle of Horace's correspondents. It is probable that Horace and Virgil saw less of one another after Virgil's retirement to Naples; but the Ode addressed to him in 24 B.C. on the death of their common friend Quintilius, shows that there had arisen no coolness in his affection towards him; and, apart from personal feeling, Horace must have felt the profoundest literary interest in the progress of the Aeneid, to which many references are made in the fourth book of the Odes.

IV.

[Third Period: from 19 B.C. to 8 B.C.]

When Virgil died, Horace was recognised as the greatest living poet, certainly the greatest of those who made the serious interests of their own time the subject of their art. When Virgil turned his thoughts to epic poetry, Varius diverted his genius to tragedy, and produced the Thyestes, which Roman critics ranked with the master-pieces of the Attic stage. The art of Ovid was as yet limited to the celebration of his own pleasures in the Amores, and possibly re-awakening the romance of Greek mythology in some of the Heroides. At the celebration of the Secular Games in the year 17 B.C., Horace was called upon by Augustus to compose the Ode sung on that occasion. Two other Odes were composed by him three years later, also at the instance of the Emperor, in celebration of the victories gained by Drusus and Tiberius over the Vindelici and Rhaeti. These were published along with other Odes inspired by the state of public affairs, and a few others in his lighter vein, about the year 13 B.C. The long Epistle of the second book, in which he vindicates the literature of his own age, in answer to the admirers of the old Republican literature, was written also at the instance of, and was dedicated to, Augustus, and published along with an Epistle to one of his younger friends, Julius Florus. In it he gives a retrospect of his own literary career, and speaks of himself as having abandoned poetry to younger men, and as devoting himself henceforward to the study of the true harmonies of life. There is nothing which actually determines the date of this Epistle, but it is as likely to have been written after as before the publication of the fourth book of the Odes. He shows in it, as he does in the Epistles of the first book, and in the fourth book of the Odes, that he is interested in the work of the younger generation of poets, and he makes the results of his own experience and study available for the improvement of Roman poetry. A similar impulse directed him to the composition of the long Epistle to the Pisos, the didactic poem, known as the Ars Poetica, which has, until recent years, been accepted as his latest work, and has by some critics been supposed to have been left unfinished and given to the world after his death. Critics of distinction both in Germany and England have contended in favour of an earlier date, and assign its publication to the time between the publication of the three books of Odes and of the first book of Epistles [1].

---

[1] The grounds of their contention are that as the L. Calpurnius Piso to whom, in conjunction with his sons, the Epistle has been supposed to be addressed, must have been born not later than 49 B.C.—Tacitus in mentioning his death in 32 A.D. says that his life had extended to his eightieth year —he was not likely to have had two sons old enough to be addressed as 'iuvenes' in the year 8 or 9 B.C. They accordingly suppose that the person addressed is not this L. Calpurnius Piso, consul in 15 B.C., who returned to Rome in B.C. 11, after having obtained some important success in Thrace, but that he was Cn. Calpurnius Piso, consul in 23 B.C., whose son of the same name was consul in B.C. 7, and became so notorious in connexion with the death of Germanicus. It is said further that the Maecius Tarpa and the Cascellius who are spoken of as both alive at the time when the poem was written, are known from Cicero's correspondence and from a statement of Macrobius to have attained an established position—the one as what corresponds with the modern office of licenser of plays, the other as a 'iuris-consultus' in the years 55 B.C. and 56 B.C.— and thus were not likely to be actively engaged in life, if they were still alive, so late as 8 or 9 B.C. Further, it is stated that the reference to Quintilius Varus the critic, who died in 24 B.C., implies that he had been known to the young Pisos and was not long dead, and that the reference to Virgil and Varius indicates that they were both still living at the time of the publication of the poem. The time assigned for the composition of the

In contrast with all the other works of Horace, the Ars Poetica is singularly impersonal. It also has scarcely any reference to current events. The only allusion by which the date can in any sense be fixed is the mention of Quintilius as no longer alive; but there is really nothing in the way in which he is mentioned to suggest that he had been personally known, though he must have been known by reputation, to those to whom the Epistle is addressed. He is quoted simply as a candid and judicious critic whom Horace himself probably was in the way of consulting. Virgil and Varius are named together as representatives of the art and genius of the Augustan age, in contrast with Plautus and Caecilius, the representatives of the old Republican literature, just as they are mentioned together, as recipients of the favour of Augustus, in the first Epistle of the second book, written certainly after the death of one, and probably of the other. Cascellius may be mentioned in line 371 merely as the type of an eminent lawyer of a past age; but as men of quiet intellectual pursuits often lived and retained their faculties to a great age at Rome, there is no difficulty in supposing that he was known to fame in the year 56 B.C. and was still alive in the year 10 B.C. Trebatius must have been quite a young man when Cicero writes to Caesar that he is at the head of his profession—'familiam ducit'—as a lawyer. There is still less difficulty in supposing that the Maecius Tarpa of line 387 was a young man under thirty in the year 55, when he is mentioned by Cicero as superintending the choice of plays, or that he was still a hale veteran about the year 8, 9, or 10 B.C. Nor is there any great improbability in supposing that the L. Piso to whom ancient authorities tell us that this poem was dedicated, who is said himself to have been a poet, and who, as we gather from Tacitus, died in or after his 80th year in 32 A.D., should have had in the year 8 or even 10 B.C. two sons who

poem is thus some date between 24 B.C. and 19 B.C. A reference in Tacitus implies that Piso, the enemy of Germanicus, had entered on his public career in 26 B.C., so that he was not likely to have been so possessed by literary ambition five or six years later, as to be the subject of Horace's advice, which is evidently addressed to a young man just entering on life.

might be spoken of as 'iuvenes.' It was not uncommon for young Roman nobles (e. g. to take well-known instances, Julius Caesar, Pompey, Dolabella, and the young Marcellus) to be married before they were twenty. None of these considerations are sufficiently strong to invalidate the direct testimony of Porphyrion, that the father to whom the poem was dedicated was L. Calpurnius Piso, who was consul in 15 B.C. There is a much greater improbability in supposing that the whole current of Horace's thoughts and interests was changed in some short interval between the publication of the Odes and the composition of the Epistles of the first book. While the subjects treated of in those Epistles and the tone adopted are similar to the subject and tone of the Odes, especially of the third book, there is no relation whatever between either and the subject of the Ars Poetica. On the other hand, it seems quite natural that the bent to literary criticism, shown in the two Epistles of Book ii, should have continued after Horace had said all he had to say on the criticism of human life, and that it found systematic expression in the composition, during the last years of his life, of a didactic poem. The question put to Julius Florus in the third Epistle of Book i. about one of his young friends—

    An tragica desaevit et ampullatur in arte?—

and other similar references to the drama in Book ii, the publication about this time of the Medea of Ovid, and references made by him to the art of some of his contemporaries, show that during the last years of Horace's life an attempt was made to establish a classical Roman drama, which seems to have failed more from want of appreciativeness in the audience than want of art and genius in the writers. It would be entirely in accordance with the interest which Horace felt in bringing the national poetry to perfection, that after his own creative activity ceased—'nil scribens ipse'—he should give in didactic form the results of his Greek studies and of his own reflexion to the younger generation, who devoted themselves to the one form of serious art which might contend with the fashionable poetry of love, represented by Propertius and Ovid.

During all these later years of his life Horace stands in closer relations to Augustus and the members of the Imperial family, and to the favourites of the Court, than in the earlier period of his literary career. On the other hand the name of Maecenas, whose influence had during that period declined, occurs only once in the writings of the last decennium of his life. Disparagers of Horace, as being more of a courtier than a firm friend, may find in this silence a confirmation of their estimate of his character. But his silence may be explained on a more worthy supposition; that, as Maecenas could not occupy the first place in works commanded by Augustus, Horace did not care to assign him a secondary place; and this may have been in accordance with the wishes of Maecenas. The intimacy of Horace with Augustus was the result, not of time-serving on the part of the poet, but of repeated importunity on that of the Emperor. Yet Horace, notwithstanding this importunity, refused to quit the 'parasitica mensa' of Maecenas to fill the important office of the Emperor's private secretary. That his new relations to the Court produced no coolness between him and his old friend is proved by sufficient evidence. The whole motive of one of the lighter Odes of the fourth book, introduced among those celebrating the Imperial policy, appears to be the wish to express his undiminished affection for him to whom he had dedicated all the great works of his earlier years. The invitation to Phyllis—his latest love—

> meorum
> Finis amorum—

is pretty and graceful, like many of the lighter Odes of the earlier books; but it gains a serious interest from the stanza in which he tells her that the day for which she is invited is almost more sacred to him than his own birthday—

> quod ex hac
> Luce Maecenas meus affluentes
> Ordinat annos.

A still stronger testimony to their unbroken friendship is found in the words (already quoted) addressed in his will by Maecenas to the Emperor, 'Horati Flacci ut mei sis memor.' If the two friends were happy in their intercourse and true to one another in their lives, in their death they were not long divided. In the late autumn of the same year in which Maecenas died, 8 B.C., Horace was taken suddenly ill, and became rapidly so much worse that he had scarcely time to declare the man against whom he had fought in his youth his heir. Living in a changed world, he too had changed much, and had found his most cherished friends among those who had defeated the cause for which he had fought in his youth. Yet the last charge which can be justly made against him is that of being false either to his country or his friends. It might more justly be said that the supreme duties of life in Horace's eyes were patriotism and loyalty to friendship. The true test of the happy man is found in his willingness to die for his friends or his country—

> Non ille pro caris amicis
> Aut patria timidus perire.

V.

Personal Characteristics.

To most readers, the perfect frankness with which Horace reveals himself at once inspires confidence; and this confidence deepens into a strong conviction of the truth of his delineation of himself, or at least of his true self, which is really all that we need concern ourselves with in the lives of the great writers of a distant past. If we have to qualify by after reflexion the immediate impression of his temper and character, derived from his writings, it is by making it more favourable to him. The intellectual quality which distinguishes him above all his countrymen is his irony. 'Ut tu semper eris derisor' is a comment on himself which he attributes to one of the speakers in his Satires. This irony is as conspicuous in his judgments and statements about himself as about the world. He did not want to think himself, or to allow others to think him better than in his heart he knew himself to be.

We have to remember also that in his various works we have pictures of himself painted at different periods. And there is perhaps an apparent discrepancy between these pictures. We find a difficulty in realising that the author of some of the Epodes is the same man who wrote the first book of the Epistles. In trying to picture to ourselves his personal appearance, we must take into account not only his ironical self-depreciation, but the outward changes which time produced upon him. Thus, when he speaks of himself, at the age of forty or forty-five, as 'pinguem et nitidum bene curata cute' and as 'corporis exigui, praecanum,' and hints at his indolent and valetudinarian habits, we do not easily associate such a figure with the enthusiasm of a great lyrical poet, or with the wreaths of flowers which play so conspicuous a part in his convivial Odes. But we can correct this picture by glimpses which he affords us of his appearance in youth—of 'the black hair clustering round his narrow forehead' (a trait of beauty in a Roman, as their busts show that their foreheads were generally low and broad)—and by the thought of the days when his 'soft accents and graceful smile' were welcome at the banquet, and when it became him to 'wear a toga of delicate texture,' and to have 'his hair' (after the Roman fashion of the time) 'glistening with unguents.' We have to remember also that if it was not in his graceful youth that he sang of love and wine, it was then that he lived the life which he afterwards revived in his lyrical art.

At the stage when we know him best, that is, in the maturity of his productive powers, with the grace and adventurous activity of youth he had lost also much of its fire and passion; but he regarded the loss as well compensated by the philosophic mind which years had brought, and by the consciousness of becoming a kindlier and better man, 'lenior et melior.' It is at this stage of his career that we gain the best image of the man, though we can trace through all his career how he became what he then was.

His most marked characteristic is his self-dependence. He judged of things for himself, and refused to measure what was good or evil by the standards common among his countrymen (Ep. i. 1. 70, &c.). While he thankfully enjoyed all outward advantages, his aim was to be independent of them for his happiness. He desired to regulate his life by reason, to introduce consistency into his desires and pursuits, to know what he really cared for, and to limit his efforts to attaining it. To 'live for himself'—that is, not to live in selfish isolation, but to be true to his own nature, to be what he was meant to be, and not to try to be or seem anything else—and to be independent of fortune, is the sum of his philosophy. This doctrine was not learned from the schools, though it combined what was most real in the teaching of Epicureanism and Stoicism, but was gathered from reflexion on the experience of life. He learned something from the teaching of his father, from the example and precepts of such men as Ofellus. But the spirit of independence was inborn in him. We trace it in the account he gives of his way of life in Rome and in the country. We see it, combined with the poetic impulse, in his love for lonely rambles among the hills and woods, such as he describes in the twenty-second Ode of the first book and the twenty-fifth of the third. But, so far as his choice of a mode of life was influenced by books, it is to the record of his own life by Lucilius that we should ascribe one at least of the forces which moulded the character of Horace. The attraction which the satirist of the Republic had for the satirist of the Augustan age was personal as well as literary. There is a tone of sympathy with the man in those often-quoted lines,

> Ille velut fidis arcana sodalibus olim
> Credebat libris, &c.

All that is known of Lucilius from ancient testimony and from the fragments of his writings—his self-criticism, and his critical

attitude to the world around him, his intimacy with the best
men of his time, his love of independence, his enjoyment of
society, and the pleasure which he found in withdrawing himself into 'some quiet haven,' his contentment and love of simple
fare, his freedom from all pedantry and asceticism—seems to be
the counterpart of what Horace was in his ordinary prosaic
mood. When Horace says that he would not exchange his
independent ease for all the wealth of Arabia, he writes in the
spirit, almost the tone of Lucilius. Horace, indeed, had none
of the 'fierce indignation' of Lucilius, which reappeared long
afterwards, under different circumstances, in Juvenal. Nor had
Lucilius any of the 'ingeni benigna vena,' which was the chief
endowment of Horace. But in their ordinary tastes and habits
there was a real affinity between the 'vafer Flaccus,' the friend
of Maecenas, and the 'comis et urbanus Lucilius,' the friend of
Scipio and Laelius.

This resolute spirit of self-dependence influences his relation
to others and determines his deepest convictions. He maintains the attitude in presence of both Maecenas and Augustus,
though ungrudging in the expression of his gratitude to the one
and his loyal admiration for the other. It enabled him to live
on an intimate footing with many distinguished contemporaries
without being absorbed by any of them. While confessing, in
a vein of humorous exaggeration, to innumerable follies arising
from his love of pleasure, in the earlier part of his career, he
never, as Catullus, Tibullus and Propertius did, allows his
happiness and peace of mind to be at the mercy of any one.
In his attitude to the leaders of the philosophic schools, he does
not, like Lucretius, give way to any excess of hero-worship,
but acknowledges allegiance to no school or master. He judges
them all candidly, and can take from all of them what he finds
true in his own experience. But the only philosophical teacher
by whom he seems personally attracted is the Cyrenaic Aristippus.
He recognises in him that same detachment from alien influences
which he recognised in Lucilius, and which he cultivated in
himself. So too in his art, while knowing how to turn to the

best account the master-pieces of Greek lyrical poetry, he proclaims his own reliance on himself—

> Qui sibi fidit
> Dux regit examen.

His success is due to the union of absolute trust in his own powers with perfect knowledge of their limit. We see the same spirit manifesting itself in his contemplation of the ultimate mysteries of human life. He is as free as Lucretius from the superstitions which disturbed the peace of many of his contemporaries—

> Somnia, terrores magicos, miracula, sagas,
> Nocturnos lemures, portentaque Thessala.

He seems half to believe in a Power, uncontrollable by man, which determines the destinies of individuals, to which he gives the various names of Fortune, God, Jove,—a Power which gives and takes away the blessings of life according to its own will or caprice (for in different moods he regards it as a righteous will or a mocking caprice)—but even of this Power he claims to be independent, not indeed for external goods, but for his happiness—

> Sed satis est orare Iovem quae donat et aufert;
> Det vitam, det opes, aequum mi animum ipse parabo

In the midst of all his contentment with his lot, he never forgets the inevitable end. But he seeks no comfort outside himself. He does not, like Virgil, meet 'the thought of inexhaustible melancholy' with the vague hope of a spiritual life hereafter. He accepts it with a resignation calmer than, if not so lofty as that of Lucretius. Like Montaigne, he seems to feel that the way to 'fight death' is to 'disarm him of his novelty and strangeness, to converse and be familiar with him,' and that the 'premeditation of death is the premeditation of liberty.' He draws from this premeditation the lesson rightly to use and wisely to enjoy that which alone is at his command, the present hour.

This self-dependent attitude seems to be the central quality in the character of Horace, and the chief source of his intellectual and moral power. But this after all explains only one side of his nature. No one, of whom we know so much, seems to have combined in the same degree the capacity of being happy alone, with aptitude for and enjoyment of social life. While the first was the condition of his inspiration, of his meditative habit, and of his literary excellence, to the second he owed many of the materials of his art, and also the sanity of his genius, the moderation and truth of his judgment, his immunity from the weaknesses and extravagance of the literary temperament. His relations to society were determined by reflexion as much as by impulse. In his lonely musings he considered not only how he should be true to himself, but how he should be 'dulcis amicis.' His early admission into a social circle inheriting the traditions of a governing aristocracy, implies the possession of some great social charm; and the nature of that charm is indicated not only in the humour and gaiety of many of his writings, but in the manifold proofs which he gives in his Odes and Epistles of appreciation and consideration for others, and in the evidence which all his writings afford of tact and good sense, of freedom from vanity and self-assertion. His satire indeed made enemies, and he was feared and disliked by those who felt themselves to be exposed to it. But the exercise of this faculty was restrained in him by a high sense of honour. There is no charge which he repels with more grave earnestness than that of taking pleasure in hurting the feelings of others. There is no character which he describes with such concentrated scorn as that of the slanderer and backbiter—

> Absentem qui rodit amicum,
> Qui non defendit alio culpante, solutos
> Qui captat risus hominum famamque dicacis;
> Fingere qui non visa potest, commissa tacere
> Qui nequit; hic niger est, hunc tu, Romane, caveto.

Among the breaches of honour which he most strongly condemns is the betrayal of a secret, and among the qualities to which he assigns the highest place is faithful silence. He professes to use his satiric 'stilus' only in self-defence or

against the enemies and nuisances of society, Rufillus or
Gargonius. There is no doctrine which he preaches with more
sense and good feeling than that of charitable indulgence to the
faults of our friends. If it is safe to infer what his conduct was
from that which he fervently approves, we should conclude
that his relations with all those with whom he lived on terms
of intimacy—and they included all who were best worth
knowing in Roman society—were regulated like those of the
best men in our own day, by a high sense of honour, a tolerant
temper, and a kind heart. We find traces of the same temper
in his relations to slaves and social inferiors, as in the liberties
which he allows Davus to take with him, in the indulgence
which he shows to his overseer, his sympathy with the 'rustica
Phidyle,' who may have been his 'villica,' and the kindly
appreciation which he expresses for his country neighbours.
Yet while he was a true friend, we do not seem to recognise in
him that impulsively affectionate nature which is the great
attraction of Catullus. There is a certain degree, not of coldness
as in his love affairs, but of reserve, in his expression of feeling,
except towards one or two, notably Maecenas and Virgil. He
is more ready to sympathise with the signs of warm affection
bestowed on others than to claim them for himself. Thus, for
instance, the Ode on the return of Plotius Numida from Spain
naturally suggests a comparison with that of Catullus on the
return of Verannius. But while Catullus thinks of his own joy
in greeting his friend with the most unrestrained demonstrations
of affection—

> adplicansque collum
> Iucundum os oculosque suaviabor—

Horace pictures to himself those proofs of affection as bestowed
on a dearer friend and a younger man than himself—

> Caris multa sodalibus
> Nulli plura tamen dividit oscula
> Quam dulci Lamiae [1].

---

[1] From the fact that Aelius Lamia is mentioned in Tacitus as dying in
the last year of Tiberins (Annals, vi. 27), he must have been a considerably
younger man than Horace. The poem shows that sympathy which, like

So too in his sorrow for the loss of Quintilius, he thinks more of the pain which it will cause to Virgil, than of his own pain—

> Multis ille bonis flebilis occidit,
> Nulli flebilior quam tibi, Vergili.

Such expressions may be explained partly by his dislike to make any parade of his deepest feelings, but they may be due in part also to that spirit of renunciation which he shows in regard to worldly honours, to wealth, to life itself. As he held that most was to be got out of life by not valuing it too much, and most enjoyment from worldly goods by not calculating too absolutely on their permanence—

> Quanto quisque sibi plura negaverit
> A dis plura feret—

so even to the higher blessing of affection he did not abandon himself too unreservedly. He cultivated 'mediocritas' in feeling as he desired the 'aurea mediocritas' of station.

While he seems to attach more importance to the practical duties and the right management of life than to literary fame, yet he undoubtedly regards literature as the serious business of his life. The proudest feeling of his being expresses itself in the confident claim to immortality which he makes for his lyrical poetry. Of his Satires and Epistles, which have found nearly as much favour in modern times, he speaks almost slightingly as undeserving of the title of poetry, and as likely to be popular at Rome only so long as they are new—

> Carus eris Romae donec te deseret aetas.

Yet even in those works which he seems to regard as intended merely for the current age, and which seem to be the result of such natural and easy workmanship, he aims at correcting, both by precept and example, the fashion of careless composition which had come down from ruder times. But he undoubtedly felt that the great work of his life was to discover and make

Cicero, he always had with younger men, rather than his own feeling for the subject of it.

perfect the vehicle of expression for that vein of lyrical inspiration—'spiritum Graiae tenuem Camenae'—the first trace of which he finds in the poetic fancies of his childhood, and of which he must have become more fully conscious through the sympathetic study of the early Greek lyric poets. But a gift so delicate and rare could not be perfected, could indeed hardly be kept alive amid the bustle, distraction, and pleasures of Rome. By a man of Horace's social temperament the career of a lyrical poet could only be followed apart from the crowd and amid the peace and beauty of nature—

> me gelidum nemus
> Nympharumque leves cum Satyris chori
> Secernunt populo.

It is to the 'streams among the orchards of Tibur, and the thick foliage of the groves' that he attributes 'his distinction in Aeolian song.' It is around 'the groves and river banks of Tibur' that, 'like the Matine bee sipping the sweets of the wild thyme,' he, with unremitting toil and joy, moulded his thoughts and experience into form and melody. It is in the same place, or among the Sabine highlands, or in the cool mountain air of Praeneste, or beneath the clear skies of Baiae, that he is most conscious of his inspiration—

> Vester, Camenae, vester in arduos
> Tollor Sabinos.

That love of Nature which is one of the greatest charms in Horace's lyrical art may be said to be the condition of its existence.

The Augustan age and the age preceding it were times in which the Roman mind became eminently susceptible to the beauty of art, in the form of architecture, sculpture, gems, cups, pictures, furniture, &c. The desire to possess the most precious works of art became a strong passion among the richer classes, and the affectation of connoisseurship was apparently as common as in modern times. Horace hits at these weaknesses in his Satires, and professes his own indifference to the possession of those objects of desire, and his contentment with the plain furniture, the 'munda supellex,' which suited his tastes and means. But we need not in his case, any more than in Cicero's, who equally condemns the extravagant devotion to art, and whose early letters to Atticus attest his anxiety to adorn his villas with the works of Greek artists, take these expressions of Horace as indicative of any insensibility to the refining influence of the pleasure of the eye. In the license which he allows to Davus in the seventh Satire of the second book, he seems to admit the pleasure which he derived from the pictures of Pausias, who was famous for the minute perfection and delicacy of his workmanship. And passages both in his Odes and Epistles (e.g. Od. iv. 8, Ep. ii. 1) show his appreciation of these 'deliciae,' though he will not allow them to disturb the balance of his mind, nor allow that they have an equal claim with the work of the poet to perpetuate the great qualities of men. But the form and workmanship of his Odes are indirect testimonies to the power which art had over his taste and imagination. The mythology of his Odes seems in many cases to be transferred from the figures of the artist, and especially, as is remarked by Munro in his introduction to Mr. King's edition, from the engraving on gems, which probably had the same attraction for him as the minute art of Pausias. The finished form and delicate workmanship, and the clear impressions of the Odes, show a power of representation akin to that of those nameless artists whose works have come down to us. The power of musical sound, equally with the power of artistic form, has passed into his verse, and it is in their song and music that he finds the chief charm of Tyndaris and Phyllis when he invites them to his Sabine farm.

In his love of books Horace is a type of the finest culture of his own or any other age. If he appears to undervalue the older national literature, we must remember that he was almost alone fighting the cause of his contemporaries, Virgil, Varius, and the rest, against the critics who disparaged the present age as compared with the past. Yet he shows a true appreciation of the merits as well as of the faults of Ennius,

Accius, and Pacuvius; and his Satires and even his Odes show how deeply he was imbued with the style and sentiment of Terence as well as of his master Menander. If he does not name Lucretius or Cicero, he shows that he was a student of their philosophy and their style; and, notwithstanding his slight and apparently disparaging mention of Catullus, he shows his appreciation of him by not infrequent imitations of his language and tone. But it is his love of Greek literature that especially distinguishes him. In poetry, alone among his contemporaries, he disregards the Alexandrians, and goes back to the oldest and purest sources—the 'integri fontes'—Homer, Archilochus, and the whole range of Greek lyrical poets from Alcaeus and Sappho to Pindar and Simonides. As a satirist he was a student of the authors both of the old and the later Greek Comedy—Eupolis as well as Plato and Menander. In his studies of moral philosophy he seems to have also gone back to the older writers, and professes to be a disciple of Aristippus rather than of Epicurus: Chrysippus and Crantor, rather than the more recent representatives of the school, are quoted as the authorities on the philosophy of the Porch and the Academy. As a critic he seems to have attached himself to the Alexandrians, who were in that department as strong as they were weak in the province of creative literature.

Apart therefore altogether from the artistic charm of his works and their power of bringing back the life, and mind, and spirit of a great age in the history and the development of civilisation, the study of Horace brings before us a personality of a great human interest, which we can know as intimately as we can any man of letters of recent times, and a representative of the best and purest literary and artistic culture. It would be to run counter to the spirit in which he appeals to us, to make him out more perfect or more earnest in character than he has represented himself. But with all admission of some weakness, of a love of pleasure, of a love of the great world, which he does not profess to conceal, of some failure in the highest enthusiasm and of obvious limitations both of genius and spiritual life—if he shows neither the deep piety of Virgil, nor the superiority of Lucretius to all human weakness, nor the impulsive warmth of heart of Catullus, nor the wide human sympathy of Cicero—yet we feel that there is hardly any writer of any age of whom we seem to be able to make so familiar a friend, from whom we can learn so much in knowledge of the world, in manners, in culture, in good sense, in consideration for others, without feeling him too far removed from the sphere of our ordinary life and associations.

CHAPTER II.

THE SATIRES.

I.

HORACE is an instance of a kind of writer more common in modern than in ancient times, who was equally eminent as a satirist, moralist and critic, and as an idealising and creative poet. He combines, in a measure greater than any of his countrymen, the Italian practical understanding with the Italian receptivity of Greek art and culture. Had he lived in recent times he would probably have been as accomplished a writer of prose as of verse. The subjects of his Satires are essentially prosaic. They deal with the material of daily life in a style as nearly as possible approaching to the language of familiar conversation or correspondence.

The question might be asked whether the Odes or the familiar writings were the truer expression of the man. Was his habitual mood that of the shrewd and amused spectator, the moralist and critic of human life, or that of the lyrical artist and enthusiast? The review of his life shows that though the 'ingeni benigna vena' was never altogether dried up within him, yet it was not to him as it was to Virgil, the source which through all his life fed the main current of his thoughts. It was only in the meridian of his career that the pure poetical gift asserted itself as his master faculty. The work accomplished by him then demanded a laborious and sustained effort, and a frequent withdrawal from his ordinary interests and associations. The Satires on the other hand were the principal work of the first, the Epistles of the last ten years of his literary activity. They express his familiar moods, and the aspects of life habitually present to him, while living in the world, or while maintaining his relations with the world through the medium of correspondence. If we want to know how Horace regarded the actual world of business, of pleasure, of society, of literature, we turn to his Satires and Epistles. If we want to see what there was in his own life and in the life of those around him which he could invest with a more ideal grace, we turn to the Odes. In tracing the development of his character and opinions, we naturally read his various writings in the order in which they were written. In estimating his quality as a literary artist, we naturally consider together those which are of the same kind in form and manner; on the one side, the Satires and Epistles, the product of his critical faculty, on the other his lyrical art.

The object of Horace in his first literary adventure was to adapt the satire of Lucilius to the manners and taste of the Augustan age. Though one or two attempts had been made to revive it, this national form of literature, the one important literary invention of Rome, had fallen into abeyance. The lampoons of Catullus, Calvus and Bibaculus, in the previous generation, were as aggressively personal as anything in Lucilius; but in form, substance and spirit, they belonged to a different kind of literature. The Satires of Lucilius and of Horace belong to didactic, not to any kind of lyric or epigrammatic poetry, to which the iambics of Catullus and the Epodes of Horace belong. They had a practical purpose, that of reforming and regulating life, as well as the literary purpose of affording amusement. Personal criticism was made subsidiary to moral teaching and reflexion on life. Satire in the hands of Horace became associated with the new interest felt in moral philosophy. Among the literary influences affecting the substance of his satire, we should rank the more strictly ethical passages in Lucretius, and the ethical writings of Cicero, especially the Stoical Paradoxa. The more systematic reflexion on life introduced by Horace into his satire was certainly an advance on

Lucilius. As a form of literary art, satire, as treated by Horace, is still in process of development. It has not yet assumed the definite purpose of a systematic treatment of special vices, as it has in the hands of Juvenal. It still retains much of the character of the old 'medley.' It serves, as it did to Ennius and Lucilius, as a medium of personal communication between the poet and the outside world, and as a weapon of offence and of defence. By examining the Satires of Horace in the order of their composition, so far as that can be ascertained, we can follow the process of development from the more personal and desultory treatment of Lucilius to the more general didactic type which this form of writing ultimately assumes.

There is a considerable advance in literary form between the Satires of the first and those of the second book of Horace. The latter, though not formally didactic, are with the exception of the first, in which the use of satire is vindicated, intended to convey some lesson in manners or conduct, as well as to paint and comment on character. The aim of most of those in the first book is less definite. In some the object is merely to give amusement. One is apologetic, another polemical. One is almost purely autobiographical. Only two can be described as being of a general or reflective character. An advance may be noticed from the merely personal and polemical attitude which Horace at first assumes, to the more disinterested attitude of a spectator and critic of life. There is a marked advance also in urbanity of tone. There is a further advance from imitation and reproduction of Lucilius to greater independence of treatment.

II.

The Satires. Book I.

There is a general agreement that the earliest in date of the Satires of the first book is the seventh. This is a page out of Horace's earlier experience, while he served with Brutus in Asia. It probably was written at the time of the occurrence, and included in the collection as his earliest attempt in the manner of Lucilius. It represents a contest in wit between a scurrilous Italian, who is said to have offended Horace by sneering at his parentage, and a half-bred Greek, engaged in business transactions at the scene of the occurrence. The actors are real persons, introduced under their own names; and if the piece has any merit, it consists in the reproduction of their personal peculiarities. Similar encounters and similar presentation of character are found in the fragments of Lucilius. The scene witnessed by Horace probably recalled those passages of arms in the older satirist, and stimulated him to make his first essay after his manner. The Satire serves no other purpose than that of giving vent to the high spirits of young men, engaged in military or official duties, and finding amusement in the peculiarities of the civilians among whom they were quartered. In the mock heroics from line 11 to 17, there is a note of youth, not long emancipated from the schools; but there is also (as is pointed out by Mr. Palmer) in one line one of the few poetical touches in the Satires—

Flumen ut hibernum fertur quo rara securis—

one of those graphic touches, oftener found in the Odes or Epistles, by which the poetical features of some natural scene are condensed in a phrase.

Among the Satires written after his return to Rome the second was the earliest in date. In it the direct influence of Lucilius is still more marked. It is more aggressive in tone, and coarser in substance and expression, than any later Satire. In it he uses words only found in Lucilius. It has nothing of the kindly spirit or the delicate irony characteristic of the other familiar writings of Horace. The occasion which gives rise to it is the death of the Sardinian Tigellius, one of several personages who figure both in the Epistles of Cicero and the Satires of Horace. He is introduced as a special favourite with the 'Bohemians' of both sexes on account of his lavish prodigality. This trait suggests the contrast between the rake and the miser. The remainder of the Satire is an indictment of that extreme of character of which Tigellius is the type, and of which other instances are adduced among the adherents and personal friends of Caesar. One ancient tradition states that Maecenas, with whom Horace was not then acquainted, was sketched under the name of Malthinus; and Sallustius Crispus, who enjoyed a similar place in the later intimacy of Augustus to that enjoyed by Maecenas in the earlier, is introduced by his own name. In this Satire Horace shows familiarity with the coarser side of life; but the tone in which the scandals of the time are discussed is neither like that of Juvenal, one of indignant disgust, nor the ironical tone of the 'urbanus,' characteristic of Horace himself in his treatment of human weaknesses.

The fifth Satire is also one of the earliest, and one of those in which Horace most closely follows Lucilius. It answers more nearly to the original meaning of the word 'satura,' before it assumed the censorious character afterwards indicated by the word. It is simply a narrative of a journey to Brundisium, made in company with Maecenas, Virgil, Varius and other men eminent in the State and in literature. The idea of it is taken from a Satire of Lucilius, giving an account of a journey by land and water from Rome to the Sicilian Strait. With the exception of a few caustic remarks on some of the people encountered on the journey, there is nothing of a purely satiric, still less of an ethical character in the piece. Neither is there anything in it of striking incident or adventure; and in this respect it may have been less interesting than that of Lucilius, who, travelling a century earlier and by less frequented roads, had evidently found more difficulties and discomforts on his way, and had besides to encounter a dangerous storm at sea. It is a description of a pleasant holiday passed in the society of congenial and distinguished men, of which, however, only the outward incidents are briefly recorded. It brings back vividly a page from the actual experience of ancient civilisation, and has thus the same kind of interest as that possessed by a chapter in some of our older novels recording the humorous adventures and discomforts encountered in an ordinary journey. Among all the Satires of Horace it has most distinctly the character of the old Satura, as it had been transmitted by Ennius to Lucilius.

Another of a somewhat later date, the eighth, is written also in his earlier manner. So far as it serves any purpose beyond that of describing a ridiculous scene, it holds up to contempt the Canidia of the Epodes, and, indirectly, the class of women to which she belongs. As, near the end of the fifth Satire, he gave expression to the freethinking fashionable among the educated classes in the later years of the Republic, so in the lines near the beginning of this—

> Cum faber incertus scamnum faceretne Priapum
> Maluit esse deum—

he still more unmistakably scoffs at the popular beliefs; and as perhaps one object of the fifth Satire was to let the world know of his recently gained position among the friends of Maecenas, so the selection of the scene of the eighth may have been determined by the wish to draw attention to the great service rendered by his patron to the community, in changing the Esquiline from a burying-ground of the lowest classes into pleasure-grounds and a healthy habitable place.

In these four Satires Horace is an imitator of the coarser, lighter and less angry moods of Lucilius. He never aspired to reproduce his more vehement indignation against individuals and classes. But in the course of this book he follows the example of his prototype, in making his satire a medium of bringing himself into frank communication with his readers. Three of the Satires of this book, the fourth, sixth, and tenth, are distinctly apologetic in tone. In them he vindicates the quality of his satire as compatible with honour and kindly feeling, and asserts his own social and literary claims to consideration.

The fourth is an answer to the criticism excited by the censoriousness of his earlier Satires, especially (as appears from line 92) of the second. He appeals in his own justification to the license accorded to the poets of the old Comedy and to Lucilius. He shows that the ordinary detraction of society is more malignant than his satire. While disclaiming all back-biting, and professing to be restrained in all that he writes by the laws of social honour, he claims the liberty of commenting freely on the vices and follies of the world, and of illustrating his comments by living examples. He traces his habit of observing and judging the characters of men to the teaching and practice of his father, and shows how moral teaching becomes real by being thus brought into relation with actual life. Tacitus says that the great object of history, which in his hands assumes much of the character of satire, is to deter men from vices and to stimulate them to virtue by regard for the award of public opinion. A similar function is claimed by Horace for satire—

> Sic teneros animos aliena opprobria semper
> Absterrent vitiis.

In nearly every department of Roman literature the connexion between literature and morality was intimate, and the justification of personal criticism was that it acted on the lives of men through their sense of shame, and their fear of ridicule or reprobation. He professes to apply the same criticism to his own faults with a view to self-improvement. With his habitual tendency to disguise the seriousness of his purpose under a veil of irony, he concludes with the plea that to write in his style is at least a venial fault at a time when the majority of men were authors of some sort or other.

It is in this Satire that Horace first assumes the serious tone of a satirist, and clearly indicates both the kindly and tolerant view of life, and the sense of personal honour, which guided and restrained him in his comments on individuals and classes. But this apology gave offence to another class of critics, and as he defended himself in the fourth against those who objected to the writing of satire altogether, in the tenth he has to meet the opposition which his criticism on the literary merits of Lucilius excited among the admirers of the old writers. As in the fourth he defines the moral and social aim of his satire, in this he seeks to establish its literary position. With full appreciation of the boldness and caustic wit of the old satirist, he denies to him all claim to be a careful and finished writer, and at the same time states and exemplifies the conditions of style which the satirist of a polished age has to observe. He claims the same right of criticising Lucilius, while acknowledging his own inferiority to him, as Lucilius exercised in the case of Accius and Ennius. As in the fourth Satire he indicated the moral affinity of his position to that of Lucilius, in this he indicates his literary relation to, and divergence from him. Lucilius wrote carelessly and for an uncritical public. Horace writes with the conscious aim of perfecting the ruder workmanship of an earlier time, by which the circle of writers with whom he was associated—Varius and Virgil, Pollio and Fundanius—was animated. He desires to satisfy the taste of a 'fit audience' of men distinguished in the State and in literature. The disregard of vulgar opinion, expressed in more than one passage of his Odes, here finds vent in contemptuous phrases applied to the popular music-masters, Demetrius and Hermogenes Tigellius, and their apes and satellites. Thus, even in his satire, the least artistic of his works, Horace writes for the judgment of the few, and begins that warfare with the critics and poetasters of the time, Crispinus and the 'turgidus Alpinus,' which he continued to wage until the end of his career.

This Satire, as it stands last in the book, may probably have been one of the latest in order of composition. But it stands in immediate logical connexion with the fourth, which gave occasion to the criticism to which the tenth was a reply. From the connexion between the second, the fourth, and the tenth, we learn that whether or not each Satire was separately published immediately after it was written, it was at least widely circulated and discussed. Horace disliked the practice of public recitation, either as actor or listener, and he had no desire to have his books thumbed at the common book-stalls. Yet while he ironically complains that he finds few readers, the criticism which he answers in these Satires shows that they were not merely known to his friends, but were in some way or other circulated among the general reading public, before they were collected into one book.

His social advancement, and especially his intimacy with Maecenas, no less than his literary attitude, procured him enemies and detractors. The sixth Satire is his apology in answer to them. In it, more than in any of those of Book i, the satire of Horace fulfils the office of autobiography assigned to that of Lucilius in the familiar lines—

> Ille velut fidis arcana sodalibus olim, &c.

There is none of them which gives so full information about his early life and education, describes so vividly his habits and mode of life at the time when the Satire was written, and is so true an index of his character. He answers the sneers to which his birth exposed him, in such a way as to make out of this ground of obloquy his best claim to consideration. He shows unmistakably that his relation to his patron was one of mutual esteem, not of servile dependence. There is little of the caustic spirit of satire in this piece; but none of the Satires of the first book contained so true, and for Roman society, so new a lesson. He teaches the worth and the worthlessness of the claims of birth. They give, or at least they gave in an aristocratic Republic like Rome, a right to aspire to rank and office; they gave a man a certain prestige in popular estimation; but they made no difference in his real value or in the judgment which men of virtue and sense formed of him. Horace, in this vindication of himself, announced a great change in social opinion, which the Empire, as the great leveller of ranks, introduced. The extent of that change may be estimated by a comparison of the aggressive tone of the eighth Satire of Juvenal with the modest apology of Horace. In the favours and distinctions enjoyed by Virgil and Horace we see the best effects of this change of opinion; in the influence enjoyed by parasites and 'delatores' at the court of Nero and Domitian, and in the degradation of the representatives of the 'Fabii and Aemilii,' we see that extinction of ancient prejudice was not an unmixed gain.

While these three are mainly personal and apologetic, the ninth is the earliest and happiest specimen of Horace's dramatic manner. It brings a scene from actual life before us with the vividness of Catullus, and with even finer irony. It imitates the style of conversation with the vivacity, the grace, and the turns of expression of Terence. It sketches a common type of character with the keen observation of Martial, and with more truthful moderation. We seem to know the casual acquaintance of the Via Sacra more familiarly than we know the 'bellus homo' of Martial, and feel more certain that he is not a caricature. In none of his other Satires does Horace indicate more clearly his intellectual affinity to Addison. Although there is no direct teaching or reflexion on life in the treatment of the subject, yet it indirectly conveys a lesson on manners and on the essential difference between self-assertion and self-respect. In the part which Horace himself plays in this light comedy, he makes use of the ironical courtesy characteristic of the 'urbanus'; while in the other chief interlocutor he represents, to the life, the pushing and unscrupulous importunity of the kind of literary adventurer of whom a man of culture and honour is most reasonably intolerant.

The third and first approach more to the type which satire ultimately assumed. They have more of the character of a regular discourse on a definite subject. The word 'sermo,' applied by Horace to his Satires, may sometimes more appropriately be rendered 'conversation,' in other cases, as in these two, 'discourse,' although even in them the discussion is partly carried on in dialogue with an imaginary opponent. These are essentially didactic in tendency. They are part of that systematic ethical teaching introduced into Roman literature by Lucretius in verse and by Cicero in prose. In both of these Satires we recognise the influence of Lucretius in expression and thought, although the spirit in which Horace, in the Satires, regards life, is as far removed as possible from the passionate feeling of human dignity which animates the older poet. In the third Satire, the theme of which is the indulgence due to the faults of our friends, Horace, like Lucretius, takes up an attitude of antagonism to Stoicism, and appeals to the standard of utility against the paradox that all offences are equal. In the controversial tone which they adopt there is, however, the strongest contrast between the light irony of Horace and the polemical severity of Lucretius. While the contemplative Epicureanism of Lucretius appeals to higher elements in human nature, the practical Epicureanism of Horace appealed more effectually to the ordinary moods of his contemporaries. The admirable side of Epicureanism is conspicuous in the subject dealt with in this Satire, the duties, graces, and amenities of social intercourse. Friendliness was among the virtues, and friendship among the sources of happiness especially prized by the Epicureans. And no wiser teacher of the way to make the social relation of friends pleasant and permanent can well be found than Horace.

The first Satire, which serves as an introduction to all the others, is more purely an ethical discourse, illustrated by living examples and sketches of character, than any of the others of the first book. In it, as in the third, he shows by the choice of subject and by many expressions his relation both to Lucilius and Lucretius. In the general question which he raises, why the majority of men find no satisfaction in their lives, he is on the same ground as Lucretius. In the answer which he gives and which he reiterates in the Epistles and the Odes, he follows the more practical guidance of Lucilius. Lucretius answers from the contemplative point of view that the causes of human unhappiness are the fear of the gods and of death on the one hand, and the blindness and insatiable craving of human desires on the other; and he finds the only cure in the systematic study of philosophy. Horace finds the cause of the discontent which he witnessed, in what he regarded as the master-passion of his time, the desire to become rich and the sacrifice of the ends of life to an over-anxious care for the means of living; and he sought the cure in a practical appeal to men's common sense and their sense of ridicule. Lucilius had satirised the sordid saving and money-making of his day, and his fragments show that Horace makes frequent use of his language in this Satire; though it does not appear that Lucilius gave to this subject a greater prominence than to others. But the end of the civil wars and the loss of free political institutions gave a new impulse to all the modes of money-making, and brought the middle-classes, largely engaged in trade and money-dealing, into greater social prominence than at any previous time. In Horace's manner of dealing with the subject we recognise the weakness and strength of his method. He has no claim to be a systematic thinker. He forms a just judgment about the facts immediately before him, and arrives by a kind of intuition at general principles of conduct in conformity with common sense and human feeling. He has a true eye for character. But he neither tries to think out, nor is willing to accept any complete and connected theory of human life. In his treatment of his subject, he allows one thought to suggest another as it might in conversation or in quiet meditation. In the desultory, often inconsecutive way in which he discusses a question, we recognise his dislike of pretention and formality, which so often leads him to assume the mask of irony. But it is in keeping with his unsystematic way of observing life and drawing his lessons from it. One of the chief difficulties of his style arises from his mode of raising or meeting objections. We sometimes find ourselves at a loss to say whether he is speaking in his own name or that of an imaginary opponent. The same difficulty meets us in the interpretation of some of his Epistles.

Horace seems thus to have felt his way from the direct personality and scandals of the second Satire, to the more abstract and ethical type realised in the first and third. In all the Satires of this book he addresses the public in his own person. Yet he adheres to the original dramatic character of the Satura by frequently conducting his arguments by means of dialogue. He adheres to it in giving occasionally a narrative of some adventure or scene with no particular satirical or ethical tendency. He shows the direct influence of Lucilius in the personality of his attacks on well-known individuals, and in the exposure of a particular class of vices in the second Satire. In using his satire as a means of bringing himself into immediate relation with his reader, in answering criticism and justifying his position, and giving personal details of his mode of life and his tastes, he is also following the example of his model. In devoting separate Satires to his discussion and reproof of certain specific errors or vices as he does in the first, second, and third, he approaches that type of satire, latent in the original Satura and Fescennine verses, partially realised in several of the Satires of Lucilius, first fully realised in the Satires of the second book of Horace, and still more systematically in the Satires of Persius and Juvenal. The desultoriness of the original Satura still clings to these more reflective essays. In the first there are two distinct subjects, discontent and avarice, which find a not very satisfactory connexion at the end of the discussion. Human discontent is an excellent subject for a penetrating philosophical satire; avarice is one of the most common themes of social satire. But though in certain states of society the desire to be rich may be the prevalent cause of discontent, yet this affords an inadequate answer to the question propounded at the opening of the book—'Qui fit Maecenas,' &c. The common-place maxim that error lies in extremes has no logical connexion with the subject of the second Satire; nor does the exposure of inconsistencies of character in the person of Tigellius appear to be a logical prelude to the inculcation of charitable indulgence to the faults of our friends, and the refutation of the paradox that all faults are of equal magnitude.

III.

The Satires. Book II.

The second book of Satires appeared about six years after the first. The position of the poet had become, in the meantime, more firmly established. He had entered on possession of his Sabine farm, and was in the habit of dividing his time between the social pleasures and distractions of the town, and the simpler life and more studious leisure of the country. Though the Satires continue to be essentially the literature of the town, yet in this book may be traced the restorative effect which his genius and spirit derived from his frequent retreat to his Sabine citadel. He is now in sympathy with the new Government, and for the first time appears as the panegyrist of Caesar. The aggressive personality of some of his early Satires has given place to good-humoured raillery. While the tone of his satire is more kindly and genial, it is, at the same time, more serious. The pronounced Epicureanism of the first book is no longer apparent. The disciples of that school are satirised in the person of Catius, and the 'vitae praecepta beatae' are identified with the tenets of gastronomy, which, as we learn from Cicero's correspondence, had become a science and a fashionable pursuit among the disciples of Epicurus in the last years of the Republic. He shows at the same time a truer understanding of the attitude of Stoicism, though he still regards the personal peculiarities and literary pedantry of its professors as legitimate objects of satire. Thus, though he dissembles his serious meaning by attributing the moral teaching of the third and seventh Satires to a bankrupt connoisseur of art and antiquities, and to a slave, who profess to retail the teaching of two of the pedants of Stoicism, Stertinius and Crispinus, yet the first of these Satires is the most elaborate, the second the most searching, of all those in which he probes the diseases of human life.

There is a marked change in the literary form of the Satires of the second book. In those of the first book, though there is a frequent use of dialogue, Horace for the most part speaks in his own person. The Satires of the second book are, with scarcely any exception, dramatic. In one of them, the fifth, he does not appear at all; in the second and eighth he appears only as introducing the speaker or narrator; in the first, third, fourth, and seventh, he bears his part in the dialogue, but in all except the first he is rather a listener than a speaker. The sixth alone, in the earlier part, is directly personal and autobiographical. But the latter part of that Satire is a fable told in the form of dramatic dialogue; and the narrator of the fable is not Horace himself, but one of his country neighbours who was in the habit of dining with him at his Sabine farm.

One motive of Horace in adopting the form of dialogue was probably to make his satire less invidious, 'invidiam placare.' He avoids the pretentiousness of preaching to and reproving his neighbours by putting his censures into the mouth of Damasippus and Davus, and making himself the object of them. He probably felt also that the dramatic dialogue was a truer form of literary art, and more suited to his own ironical way of regarding the world, than the direct expression of opinion. While engaged in the composition of this book he was a student of the Greek comic poets—

> Quorsum pertinuit stipare Platona Menandro,
> Eupolin, Archilochum, comites educere tantos?—

and these studies must have strengthened his own dramatic tendency. The personages introduced by him are appropriate to the part they play, and play it consistently. We seem to know Trebatius, a hale veteran in his relation to Horace, as we know him some twenty-five years earlier in his relation to Cicero. We recognise some of the same traits in both representations of the famous lawyer, as his love of swimming and his love of wine. Ofellus and Servius are characteristic specimens of the Italian yeoman, shrewd and simple, serious and genial, thrifty and hospitable. Fundanius, the reviver of Roman comedy, is appropriately selected to rehearse the comedy from real life, known as the 'Banquet of Nasidienus.' In the Damasippus of the dialogue, who, like Trebatius, is one of the personages familiar to the readers of Cicero's letters, we have a specimen of the busy-body ('ardelio') and the collector of antiquities, whom we meet again in the Epigrams of Martial; and in the Davus of the seventh Satire we have a slave who speaks with even more freedom and a more satisfied sense of superiority than the slaves in Plautus and Terence assume to their masters. In the Catius of the fourth again, whether or not he is the Matius of Cicero's letters, we seem to recognise a real person, who treats the science of cookery with the gravity which its professors habitually assume; which meets us in the parasites of Plautus, and even in the fragments of the Hedyphagetica of Ennius, and in the irony of Cicero's concessions to the philosophy of Hirtius and the other Epicurean friends of Julius Caesar.

The first Satire is a prologue to the rest. In it Horace justifies his attacks on individuals by the example of Lucilius and the esteem in which he was held by the best men of his day. He professes to use his 'stilus' merely in self-defence, as the weapon with which nature provided him against his detractors and enemies. But by the words in which he characterises the attitude of Lucilius—

Scilicet uni aequus virtuti atque eius amicis—

he seems to indicate the moral purpose with which he wielded it. The true relation of Horace to his master in satire, the admiration which he felt for his genius and character, and his ambition to emulate him, are more agreeably indicated in this than in any of the other numerous passages in which Lucilius is spoken of.

Three out of the eight Satires of this book are devoted to the luxury of the table, a form of indulgence which was a common topic with Roman dramatists, satirists and moralists, from Plautus and Lucilius to Juvenal, Martial and Tacitus. The number of Latin words, such as 'lurco,' 'comedo,' 'helluo,' 'catillo,' 'popino,' denoting sots and gluttons, all used with a contemptuous application, indicate the Roman propensity to this form of indulgence, and the resistance which it met from the censorious spirit in the Roman character. The living examples which are found in satire, in Cicero's speeches, and in actual history, testify to the frequency of the vice and the moral reprobation awarded to it. There is no literature in which

> the virtue and the art,
> To live on little with a cheerful heart,

is so frequently inculcated. Lucilius, Lucretius, Virgil, Horace, Persius, Seneca, Juvenal, Tacitus, are all keenly conscious of the contrast between the luxury of the wealthier classes in Rome, and the ideal of 'plain living.' Horace, while often praising the 'dapes mensae brevis' which he says it is the office of the dramatic poet to recommend, admits, by the reproof which he allows his slave Davus to administer to him, his own liability to the common temptation.

Lucilius had lent authority to his discourse on this form of excess by putting it in the mouth of Laelius. The serious treatment of the subject enables Horace to introduce into the Satires one of his finest sketches of character, the yeoman Ofellus. But it is Horace himself who speaks to us by the voice of this

> Rusticus, abnormis sapiens, crassaque Minerva,

with all the manliness and good sense which he drew from his Apulian home. At the same time he avails himself of the language and illustrations of Lucilius, to describe the coarse profusion of Roman banquets. He holds up the standard of a refined simplicity—'mundus victus'—as the proper mean between a luxurious and a sordid style of living. An example of the serious tone which his satire occasionally assumes, and by which it almost rises into poetry, may be found in the lines 94 to 111, beginning 'Das aliquid famae,' and ending 'aptarit idonea bello.'

As he treats the subject in the graver relation to human life in the person of Ofellus, he treats it in the serio-comic view appropriate to gastronomy, regarded as a fine art, in the person of Catius. If Catius is the C. Matius who is one of the correspondents of Cicero, to whom Cicero attributes 'consilium, gravitas, constantia, tum lepos, humanitas, litterae,' we cannot recognise his identity with the professor of the art of good living, who enunciates the precepts of wisdom—

> qualia vincunt
> Pythagoran Anytique reum doctumque Platona—

as we recognise the identity of the Trebatius of the letters with Horace's legal adviser. But it is not unexampled to find men who in an earlier stage of their career give indication of much good feeling, good sense, and culture, and who in later life come to attach great importance to their reputation as 'Amphitryons,' and we may remember that Tacitus (Annals, xii. 60) speaks of the influential position enjoyed by the 'Matii and Vedii,' and (Annals, i. 10) speaks again of the luxury of Vedius as one of the chief scandals of the reign of Augustus.

The ridicule in this Satire is directed not against the precepts themselves, but against the importance attached to them. As he brings in Damasippus to enunciate, in the manner of the Stoical dialectics, serious truths about human life, so he brings in a Roman epicure to teach, with elaborate unction, how to make Roman banquets not only more luxurious but more refined and wholesome. The experience of Horace as the guest of Maecenas, and probably also of rich men such as Dellius and Sestius (the father of the latter, if we trust Catullus, had a reputation as a *bon vivant*[1]), might suggest to him the double object of giving such instructions to his generation, as Ennius did to his in his Saturae[2], and at the same time of satirising the extreme type of fashionable and exquisite Epicureanism, as he had satirised the extreme type of *gauche* and pedantic Stoicism. He himself holds the position of the man of sense who could enjoy the amenities and pleasures of social life without being a slave to them, as he could hold to a serious purpose in life without becoming an ascetic or recluse.

---

[1] Catullus, xliv. 7-10 ff.:
tussim
Non inmerenti quam mihi meus venter,
Dum sumptuosas adpeto, dedit, cenas;
Nam Sestianus dum volo esse conviva, &c.

[2] The Hedyphagetica most probably formed one of the Saturae.

As the fourth deals with the refined epicurism of the men of old-established wealth and station, who found in the luxury of their houses, gardens and entertainments, some compensation for the loss of a political career, the eighth gives a picture of the vulgar ostentation, extravagance, and meanness of one of those whom the rapid changes of a revolutionary time had raised from obscurity to wealth and position in the world of fashion. If under the name Nasidienus is disguised the person of Salvidienus Rufus, who was raised from a low station by Octavianus, and put to death for treachery in the year 40 B.C., Horace must in this Satire have recalled an incident of an earlier date than that of the time when the piece was written. But there is nothing in the sketch of Nasidienus to suggest the military adventurer; and between the time when Horace returned to Rome and the date of the death of Salvidienus, the latter was so constantly engaged in military command that it is difficult to see when he could have assumed the position of a fashionable entertainer at Rome. Perhaps the nickname of Nasidienus may first have been given to Salvidienus, and Horace may have applied that name to a notorious *parvenu* of a later date, just as he so often uses names borrowed from Lucilius to indicate some notorious person or some marked type of character in his own time. The type of character here held up to ridicule is common to the satirists of every age; but Roman society under the Empire was especially rich in specimens of it. The banquet of Nasidienus is a faint foreshadowing of the banquet of Trimalchio. There is no more common character in the Epigrams of Martial than that of the mean and ostentatious host. Nasidienus, like Catius, professed an elaborate and inventive skill in gastronomy, but made himself so intolerable by discoursing upon the subject, that the guests fled from the good things before them,

velut illis
Canidia adflasset peior serpentibus Afris.

Among other points of interest in this piece we see by the living examples of Porcius and Nomentanus on the one hand,

and Vibidius and Balatro on the other, the difference between the obsequious parasite, such as he appears in Greek Comedy, and the audacious 'scurra' who plays so large a part in Roman satire.

The most trenchant of all the Satires is the fifth. The weapon employed is not the genial irony of the fourth, but bitter sarcasm, 'rigidi censura cachinni.' It is not so much moral indignation, as intellectual scorn, which is expressed for a type of character,—known to all times, but especially common in Rome under the Empire—the fortune-hunter, or 'captator,' who rose to wealth by obsequious attention and base services to rich and childless old men and widows. Folly, vanity and meanness are the objects of his other Satires, and the tone in which these subjects are treated is that of serious remonstrance, good-humoured irony, or contemptuous ridicule. The subject of the dialogue between Tiresias and Ulysses is baseness, and the tone is one of restrained but incisive sarcasm. If Juvenal recognised any affinity between his own invective and the 'Venusina lucerna,' it must have been with the spirit of this Satire, and perhaps the second of Book i, that he found himself in sympathy.

As it is in the fifth that Horace shows himself in his most censorious temper and most observant of the viler side of life, so in the sixth, which with his artistic love of contrast he places beside it, we see him in his happiest mood, and turning his mind to that quarter which always restored him to his best self, 'the Sabine farm he loved so well,' and the homely virtues of the people living in that primitive district. This Satire, like the sixth in the first book, is a page of his autobiography. We learn from it that his town life had become a weariness to him. It no longer affords him that sense of independence and ease which he expressed in the former Satire by the words 'domesticus otior.' His intimacy with Maecenas lays upon him new responsibilities. He is no longer his own master. Hence arose the longing which he expresses here and in the Epistles, to escape from the distractions of the town to his 'citadel among the mountains.' His home among the Sabine highlands—the 'ardui Sabini'—was to him a source of inspiration, and that is its influence which is present in the Odes. But it was a place also which afforded the quiet and leisure needful for self-restoration, for 'keeping his soul alive,' and that is the influence which is present in this Satire and the Epistles. He could, when there, ask himself and discuss with his neighbours,

> Strong in sense and wise without the rules,

such questions as 'What makes men really happy?'—

> Quid pure tranquillet, honos an dulce lucellum,
> An secretum iter et fallentis semita vitae—

or, 'What is the true bond of friendship?'—such questions as Cicero represents the cultivated statesmen of his own and of an earlier time discussing in more academic fashion in the porticoes or walks in front of their country houses. In his happiest vein of irony he points the moral, that contentment is the ground of happiness, and that contentment is to be found in the simple fare and simple ways of the country, rather than in the glare and amid the luxury of the town, by the fable of 'The Town and Country Mouse,' which his neighbour Cervius is supposed to tell at one of the unceremonious dinners at which Horace entertained his country neighbours. This poem or discourse is really a peaceful idyll of rustic life embedded among the Satires dealing with the distractions, follies, vices, and characters of the town.

The third and seventh are serious ethical discussions, conducted with dramatic irony. They are based on the Stoical *Paradoxa* of Cicero, or on the authors whom Cicero used in the composition of that work. But the serious meaning of the discussions is partly disguised by the manner in which they are given to the world. In the one the spokesman is the bankrupt Damasippus, who repeats the teaching of Stertinius, a pedantic professor of the day, and discourses on the theme that all men are mad except the philosopher, in the abrupt dialectical fashion of the Stoics. The other expounds the thesis that the wise man alone is free; and the propounder of this thesis is the slave Davus, who professes to repeat what he had heard from the door-keeper of Crispinus, a voluminous pedant with whom Horace, in an earlier Satire, disclaimed rivalry. But while one object of these Satires is to criticise the personal and literary peculiarities of the Stoical teachers, in none is the ethical purpose of Horace—the wish to expose the moral waste of life—more evident.

In the third Satire the prevailing forms of human error are reviewed and illustrated by examples taken partly from actual life, partly, as was usual in Stoical dissertations, from the familiar personages of Greek legend and poetry. The prevailing forms of human error, discussed in order, are avarice, political and military ambition, luxury and extravagance, the passion of love, and superstition. These appear to Lucretius also the chief moral diseases of human life, but it is characteristic of the difference between the two men, and of the difference in the spirit of their age, that Horace, living in the world, at a time when political ambition was condemned to inaction, and when the energies of the middle-class were absorbed in money-making, and those of their sons and heirs in wasting money, should attach supreme importance to avarice and prodigality, and view superstition as a harmless folly; while Lucretius, the philosophic recluse, born and bred among the exclusive Roman aristocracy, the spectator of the fierce political passions through which the Republic perished, should see in superstition and the struggle for power the supreme evils under which humanity was crushed. The protest of Lucretius against the power of the various passions is uttered more with the zeal, the scorn, and the pathos of an inspired prophet, than with the calm conviction of a philosophic moralist. The protest of Horace is that of a man of sense and a man of the world, who sees that the happiness and dignity of life are sacrificed to an exaggerated care for the means of living, to false aims and infirmity of purpose, to the slavery of some ruling passion or appetite, or to intellectual weakness and fanaticism. He exposes these weaknesses from a real desire to cure them, as well as from the literary pleasure of moral analysis and representation. But he claims for himself no immunity from human infirmity. He allows his self-appointed mentor to charge him with indolence and irresolution, extravagance and social ambition, excessive love of pleasure, and a most irritable temper. Though his irony leads him to exaggerate his own faults, yet admissions in other places indicate that these, or some of these, were what he regarded as his besetting weaknesses.

The seventh Satire discusses the thesis that the wise man alone is free, and that all the rest of the world is mad. It is the same thesis as that discussed and illustrated in the fifth of Cicero's Paradoxa, and Horace shows his familiarity with the previous treatment of the topic by Cicero. The doctrine inculcated is the necessity of self-mastery and consistency of conduct. Consistency in vice is spoken of as less miserable than weakness and inability to resist temptation. The temptations which are treated of are the love of pleasure, the fashionable craze for pictures and other works of art, and the appetite for luxurious living. The nemesis of yielding to these temptations is the unrest and *ennui* which Lucretius had so powerfully described as one of the moral maladies of the previous generation, and which Horace himself in the Epistles and in the Odes regards as one of the chief diseases of his time. In this Satire Davus is allowed to make Horace himself the object of his caustic comment—

> Adde, quod idem
> Non horam tecum esse potes, non otia recte
> Ponere, teque ipsum vitas, fugitivus et erro,
> Iam vino quaerens, iam somno fallere curam:
> Frustra, nam comes atra premit sequiturque fugacem.

Horace may have realised enough of this condition in his own experience to make him better understand the lives of the idle and luxurious class of his day. But a comparison of this passage with other passages in the Odes and the Epistles, in which care is represented as the accompaniment of wealth and luxury, suggests the inference that, as in the Satires directed against avarice, he has the middle class, engaged in business, in his eye—the 'profanum vulgus,' the 'Philistines,' with whom he disclaims all sympathy—so in this analysis of the bondage to the pleasures of sense he has in view the rich, idle, and for the most part, noble classes, who formed the bulk of his readers, whose favour he enjoyed, and whom he did not care to offend. He avoids the invidiousness of appearing a censor of this class, by making himself the object of the Satire.

IV.

How far has Horace carried out his original purpose in writing satire, and how far has he introduced something new into literature? The older Augustan poets, in founding a new school of literature, did not wish to separate themselves abruptly from the past literature of their country. While expanding the national literature in different directions, they aimed at giving artistic shape and literary finish to the forms already established. Thus Varius aimed at reviving and perfecting the contemporary epic; Virgil ultimately gave the proportion and finish of a work of art to the national epic of Ennius; Pollio was a reviver and improver of Roman tragedy; Fundanius of comedy. Along with this restoration of the older forms, the most gifted of the new school aimed at conquering and reducing to the rule of Latium new provinces from the old domain of Greek art, in the spirit in which that had been done by the poets of the preceding generation. In this spirit Virgil produced his pastoral poems and Georgics. Horace, with apparently more conscious purpose than any of his contemporaries, desired both to improve an existing type of literature, and to expand the range of Latin letters in a new direction. He desired to be the Lucilius, as well as the Archilochus and Alcaeus, of his generation. In the Epistles he created for himself a new instrument.

In assuming the tone of the old popular national satirist, and in seeking to substitute artistic proportion and literary finish for the desultory treatment and rough workmanship of his predecessor, he recognised the new conditions imposed by the change of the times and by his own position. The motives which actuated Lucilius in writing satire were public spirit and political passion. He was as much a combatant in the warfare of politics as if he had been a tribune or censor. The essential condition of the 'virtue' which he upheld by his incessant attacks on vice and corruption is public spirit—

> Commoda praeterea patriae sibi prima putare.

The position secured to Lucilius by his birth, fortune, and intimacy with the best men in the State, and the republican freedom enjoyed in his time, enabled him to assail openly men in every grade of society and every sphere of political influence. In the stress which Horace lays on the relation of his predecessor to the writers of the old comedy, he indicates that his satire was primarily political, and that his most powerful weapon was direct personality—the boldness with which he stripped off the skin,

> nitidus qua quisque per ora
> Cederet, introrsum turpis.

From the whole field of political life—the greatest field for satire as for oratory—Horace was more absolutely debarred than any of the great satirists, ancient or modern. He found too, after his first experiment, that the temper of the society in which it was his ambition to live did not tolerate aggressive personalities on men of conspicuous station. The new satire, in so far as it was aggressive, had to limit itself to the field of social life, and to select its examples either from the notorious bores and nuisances of society, or from men of a past generation who had become notorious for their meanness or their prodigality. In so far as his satire is aggressive, it is limited to the general aspect of social life. And it is chiefly two extreme types of social life—the miser and usurer, Ummidius, Avidienus or Fufidius, and the *roué* and prodigal in his various gradations from the 'scurra Volanerius' to the son of Aesopus and the two sons of Arrius—that he has preserved from oblivion. Avarice and luxury are the chief offences denounced by him and exposed through living examples. These are the excesses which a prosperous and unrefined middle-class presents to a spectator regarding its members from the 'templa serena' of a polished and cultivated social circle. So far as his satire is aggressive his field is thus much more limited than that of either Lucilius or Juvenal.

The spirit in which Horace uses his satiric pen is different from that attributed to Lucilius and apparent in every line of Juvenal. Two opposite characteristics are attributed to Lucilius. All who speak of him agree in ascribing to him the greatest boldness and freedom of speech. But while to Horace and Cicero his urbanity and wit appear his chief qualities—'comis et urbanus' are the epithets applied to him by Horace, 'doctus et perurbanus' by Cicero—the fierceness of his indignation, the bitterness and vehemence of his invective, are those which attracted the satirists of the Empire to him. The fragments of Lucilius justify both views of his character. His spirit was as far as possible removed from that of a cynic, an ascetic, or a misanthrope. He appears to have been a man of the world, enjoying his life in manifold ways, laughing heartily at the follies of his contemporaries and not sparing his own, a genuine humourist not without a strong Rabelaisian vein in him. But he was also a man of great public spirit, a warm friend and a warm hater; the last more on public than on private and personal grounds. Patriotism, the basis of virtue, required him to be the enemy of bad men and bad morals—

<blockquote>Hostem esse atque inimicum hominum morumque malorum—</blockquote>

as well as to be the champion of the men and the morals through which the good of the State was promoted. His combative temper and keenness of intellect fitted him well for the part he had to play in the political and social warfare, so actively waged during the last thirty years of the second century B.C.

With this side of Lucilius the spirit of Juvenal was in thorough sympathy. Patriotism was to him too the basis of virtue; and his worst enemies would not refuse to him the title of a good hater. What roused his indignation to the utmost was the degeneracy from the old national standard of manliness and morality; and the men whom he most hated were the tyrant and his ministers to whose rule and influence he attributed much of this degeneracy. Horace had no such consuming passion. His Odes show that at a later time he was not wanting in the patriotism and public spirit evoked by the new Empire, and that he too cherished an ideal of the old national virtues. But at the time when the Satires were written there was no public virtue to which he could have appealed. The cause of the Republic, with which whatever remained of the old national spirit seemed to have been identified, was lost. The task which was left to the satirist was to make social life more pleasant, and the life of the individual more rational. The part which Horace had to perform was much the same as that which Macaulay attributes to Addison, in a time not unlike the early Augustan age, when a state of settled order and social respectability was beginning to succeed a time of revolution and of moral license. It was natural that he should find his relation to Lucilius, not in the vehemence and freedom of his invective, but in his irony, his knowledge of the world, and his tact in dealing with it.

But with another side of Lucilius Horace was more in sympathy than any other ancient writer. The satire of Lucilius, besides being aggressively critical on individuals and classes, was largely autobiographical. How this element was combined with the other elements in his satire must be matter of conjecture. It was probably, like the same element in Horace, partly fused through his general comments on the world, and partly the subject of separate episodes. His satire sometimes took the form of a narrative of adventures in which he had taken part, and a description of scenes of which he was a spectator. This, one of the original functions of satire, disappears from the type which it ultimately assumes in Juvenal. Scarcely any Roman writer tells us so little of himself, and is personally so much of an enigma, as the great satirist of the Empire. This personal element is the chief charm in the satire of Horace, as the relation established with the reader, by a real or assumed personality, is one of the greatest charms of the *Spectator*. It is through his social tact that Horace exercises a moral influence over others. He wants his reader to be in sympathy with him, and makes himself known to him in his habits and circumstances, thoughts and feelings, with good sense, good taste, perfect candour, and full reliance on being met with equal candour. As pure satirists, as masters of satiric invective or irony, others in ancient and modern times may claim a higher rank than Horace. They have written with more of passion and of the power imparted by passion, or with a more penetrating insight into the abysses of human nature. But Horace ranks among the foremost of those writers who have left a true record and picture of themselves to after times. Others have gained a permanent place in literature by the vivid memorials they have left, in the form of confessions, of the inward tragedy of their lives. Horace among the ancients, as Montaigne among the moderns, has made the record of his habitual moods profoundly interesting by the absolute candour and the self-knowledge of his revelation. He has done this also largely in his Odes and Epistles, yet it is to the Satires that we turn as our fullest and most authentic source of information about his actual life and habits. In the Odes we know him in the hours of inspiration; in the Epistles in his deeper thoughts and in his inner life; in the Satires in his daily life and habitual intercourse with men.

As in the Odes and Epistles, so too in the Satires, though he is there less formally didactic, Horace is a moralist. His work is positive as well as negative. His positive aim is to induce men to guide their lives by reason and common sense, to be consistent, to avoid extremes, and to be masters of their appetites. A definite purpose in life, and moderate wants, are the secret of contentment. But a man has to be not only at peace with himself, but on good terms with society—'dulcis amicis.' And nowhere is Horace more admirable than in inculcating charitable indulgence to the faults of our friends and courage in defending them. Nowhere is his satire more penetrating than in his exposure of the arts of slandering and backbiting. And while he directly inculcates the more serious duties of friendship, he indirectly, by the living representation of impudence and self-assertion, and the urbanity with which they are met, inculcates the minor duties of good manners in social intercourse.

One pervading quality of all Horace's satiric writing—of his reproof, his sketches of character, his narrative, his self-delineation, his positive teaching—is its truth and moderation. This is a ground of superiority over Juvenal and most satirists, ancient or modern. It is another point of resemblance between him and Addison. It was probably the recognition of a similar moderation and sobriety of treatment in the great master of irony and urbanity before his day, which explains the attraction that drew Horace to the comedies of Terence. Nowhere is the absence of these qualities more conspicuous than in Horace's great imitator Persius; and the contrast between the two satirists is especially marked in those passages in which the disciple has tried to improve on his master. This sobriety and truth to nature are especially admirable in his sketches of character. Roman society presented more extreme types of manners and character than modern society. But even such sketches as those of Avidienus, pouring his rancid oil drop by drop over his cabbage; of Tigellius praising the virtues of plain living and spending a million sesterces in a week; of Priscus, one day a rake in Rome, another a scholar in Athens; of the young prodigal, on the day of his accession to his fortune, summoning a council of the ministers of his extravagance, do not seem forced or caricatured. Often by a single trait, as that of the 'scurra Volanerius,' broken down by well-earned gout in the hands, and hiring a man to put the dice into the box for him, he suggests a whole career. If we have few elaborate and complete portraits such as those we find in Juvenal and Martial, we have suggestive glimpses of a great number of individuals and classes. Horace sketches character as he sketches outward nature, by seizing some vital characteristic of his object.

In estimating the literary value and originality of the Satires, we have to bear in mind the inartistic character of the older satire, and the aim which Horace set before himself in their composition. The merits of Lucilius, which Horace fully admits, were his freedom of speech, his wit, his vigorous understanding, his courage and manliness. But these qualities of a strong man and a good writer did not secure him from the careless execution which he shared with all the older writers, Terence alone excepted. The fragments of his Satires fully justify the criticism on his literary defects. Horace, while disclaiming for the satire either of his master or of himself the name of poetry, yet sets before the satirist a high standard of good writing—

> Est brevitate opus, ut currat sententia neu se
> Impediat verbis lassas onerantibus aures;
> Et sermone opus est modo tristi, saepe iocoso,
> Defendente vicem modo rhetoris atque poetae,
> Interdum urbani, parcentis viribus atque
> Extenuantis eas consulto—(Sat. i. 10. 9-14).

It is the part of the 'urbanus,' not of the poet or orator, that Horace habitually sustains.

In composition, diction, and rhythm, the Satires profess to be 'sermoni propiora.' They reproduce in a natural, familiar and varied manner the serious and humorous comments on life— illustrated by anecdotes, sketches of character, and personal criticism—and the frank confidences of a courteous and cultivated man of the world. They afford the same kind of entertainment as we derive from the reported 'table-talk' of remarkable men in modern times. They confirm what we should infer from many passages in his writings (e.g. Od. iii. 21, Ep. i. 5), that Horace had great enjoyment in conversation, and, as we should infer from his social popularity, that he was a great master of the art. There is no elaborate introduction or formal division of his subject, as in Juvenal, in whose satire successive paragraphs are marshalled in order, so as to work up to a prearranged effect. When he speaks in his own person he begins abruptly with some simple statement of fact, such as 'Ibam forte via sacra,' some general observation, such as ' Omnibus hoc vitium est cantoribus,' or some reference to a recent event, such as the death of the Sardinian Tigellius, in the natural, easy way in which men glide into conversation. And where the satire is dramatic, he allows Davus or Damasippus to begin without a prologue, or begins himself without one, as in the conversation with Catius, where he borrows the conversational manner of Plato. In the absence of formality with which he introduces his subject, he again reminds us of Addison and the other writers in the *Spectator*. Sometimes his transitions from one topic to another seem too abrupt, and sometimes two lines of thought seem to get entangled with one another. But even this seeming confusion adds to the impression of the easy, familiar, unsystematic teaching of the 'abnormis sapiens,' detesting all pedantry and pretention, and shrinking from nothing so much as from the infliction of weariness on himself and other people.

The style, as well as the method of treatment, is natural and familiar. It does not force attention, as that of Juvenal does, by perpetual point and emphasis. It rarely rises above the tone and pitch of animated conversation. In the graver passages he seems to aim at that excellence of style which Cicero (de Orat. i. 60) ascribes to the oratory of Scipio and Laelius, 'qui omnia sermone conficerent paullo intentiore.' In some of the lighter passages he reproduces the dramatic liveliness of Terence. In passages of broader humour, in which he is much less successful than in his finer irony, he allows himself, after the manner of Lucilius, the use of coarser words and turns of expression than Cicero would have written in his most unreserved correspondence. He might have treated his materials in prose, had he been master of a prose style, such as that into which Cicero seems occasionally to fall as it were by accident, such as French literature has had at all times, and such as English literature produced in the first half of the eighteenth century, before the influence of the pulpit, the senate, and the lecture-room had superseded

that of the social clubs in forming the manner of English prose
—a style absolutely unrhetorical, and combining the light touch,
the colloquial charm, the individuality of refined and lively
conversation with the studied grace and modulation of literary
expression.

But it was as great a triumph of art to bend the stately Latin
hexameter into a flexible instrument for the use of his 'Musa
pedestris,' as to have been the inventor of a prose style equal to
that of Addison or Montaigne. The metrical success which
Horace obtained in an attempt in which Lucilius absolutely
failed, is almost as remarkable as that obtained in his lyrical
metres, though of a quite different kind. To compare the hexameter of Horace, as employed in the Satires, to that of Lucretius
or Virgil, is to apply a false standard to it. Had he come nearer
to them he would have entirely failed in his object. He absolutely disclaims for himself the 'large utterance of the poet,' the
'os magna sonaturum.' The 'deep-chested music' of Lucretius,
the 'linked harmonies' of Virgil, are as alien to the mood in
which Horace writes his Satires, as the rhetorical pitch of
Juvenal. The 'magic spell,' the 'mira lenocinia,' which fascinated the few hearers to whom the music of Virgil's verse was
first revealed, would have been as misplaced in reading the
Satires, as the declamatory tones by which the verse of Lucan
and Juvenal awoke the applause of the recitation-rooms. To
impart measure and modulation to an idealised conversational
style was the use of the hexameter discovered by Horace, and
by him alone successfully applied. No later writers found the
secret of it, any more than of his lyrical metres; although
Martial, a successful imitator of the metres of Ovid and Catullus,
attempts, but soon abandons the attempt, to use the hexameter
for similar purposes. In one or two passages, as in the sixth
Satire of Book ii,—

> O rus, quando ego te adspiciam? quandoque licebit
> Nunc veterum libris, nunc somno et inertibus horis
> Ducere sollicitae iucunda oblivia vitae?—

where his feeling is deeper than usual, Horace imparts to his metre something of the smooth and liquid flow, though not the grander cadences of poetry. In the Epistles, in which the feeling is both graver and more tender than in the Satires, the musical effect is often more allied to that of poetry. He shows that the general effect aimed at is different from that of elevated poetry by the variation of his cadences when he aims at a mock-heroic effect, as by the coincidence of the metrical ictus with the accent in the last three feet in the line, in

> Rumperis et latras magnorum maxime regum,

or by the more artistic balance of dactyl and spondee in the lines

> fontes ut adire remotos
> Atque audire queam vitae praecepta beatae.

Generally the rhythm is more rapid than when used in graver poetry. The sense does not often end with the line, and, what is rare in other poets, there is not unfrequently a pause at the end of the fifth foot. The ordinary practice of making the accent and ictus coincide in the last two feet is often disregarded. The laws observed by severer poets as to the caesura are disregarded more frequently than in the Epistles. Generally the metre tends to produce the same effect of freedom, ease, and familiarity as is produced by the informal and unlaboured composition, and the natural and colloquial diction. The style and rhythm are less finished than the style and rhythm of Terence. They are thus better adapted to writings which contain an immediate copy from the humours of society and a direct expression of the comments of a spectator upon them, than to a work of art in which the comedy of life is shaped into a dramatic representation.

The Satires have thus the interest of marking an important stage in the development of Roman satire, the parent of the poetical satire of modern times. They give to Horace a place among Roman moralists, in company with the old dramatists, with Lucretius and Cicero, with Seneca, Persius and Juvenal.

They have preserved many sketches of individuals and classes, representative of contemporary social life. But their real originality and chief literary value consist in being the earliest and among the best specimens of a form of literature which sets before us the moods, experience and observation of ordinary life, through a natural, sober, familiar, truthful and yet artistic medium. Other poets we know in their 'singing robes.' Horace is one of the very few whom we know also 'discinctum'; in the seemingly careless but not unstudied undress of every day.

CHAPTER III.

HORACE AS A MORALIST.

Epistles. Book I.

THE Epistles belong essentially to the same branch of literature as the Satires. To both Horace applies the term 'sermones,' to distinguish them from the Odes, which he calls 'carmina.' They are both written in hexameter verse, in a style more akin to the urbanity and conversational ease of Terence, than to the tones of elevated poetry or high-pitched rhetoric. They make little demand on that pure but not very abundant spring of feeling and imagination, which seems to have flowed only scantily and intermittently during the years when the Satires were composed, and which Horace himself felt was becoming less active at the time when he wrote the dedicatory introduction to the first book of the Epistles. But the epistolary form gave a freer outlet than any other form adopted by him, to that observation of the ways and course of life, that constant reflexion on himself, that sympathy with and power of probing the inner life of others, that informal didactic tendency, which mingle with the social and personal criticism of the Satires, and are an important element in his lyrical poetry, but which formed the main current of his intellectual being at the time when the first book of the Epistles was composed.

While the Epistles are a new and more original product of the intellectual faculties which produced the Satires, they belong to a different stage in his intellectual development, and indicate a considerable change in his social relations, his literary position, his habits of life, his spirit and temper. He is no longer, as he appears in the earlier Satires, one among many rivals, struggling for his position in the world of letters, making enemies as well as friends in the struggle, having to defend every position by polemical criticism, finding out by tentative efforts the true bent of his own powers, living himself in the world and sharing in the follies which he criticises. He has now to complain more of servile imitation than of jealous rivalry. The ten years which intervened between the publication of the second book of the Satires and of the first book of the Epistles wrought a change in his whole view of life. The ordinary pleasures of life had lost much of their zest for him, but he had found ample compensation for them in the pleasures of the mind. Though still an amused spectator of life, he had outlived the animosities as well as the other passions of his earlier manhood. He had in the composition of the Odes of Books ii and iii assumed a higher position than that of negative criticism or indulgent toleration. Without falling into any ascetic extreme, he had realised by experience and reflexion that his own happiness and that of the cultivated classes, to whom his teaching is addressed, depended on a true understanding and wise direction of the inner life. He professes to regard even his lyrical art, in which he had found his happiness and his vocation, as a mere light amusement in comparison with the study how to regulate conduct and build up character.

What chiefly distinguishes the Epistles from the Satires is their more definite ethical purpose. They aim at effecting, not that mere reformation in outward life and manners which may be indirectly forwarded by acting on the sense of ridicule, but a change of heart, by acting on the higher nature, by substituting ' culture'—in the Latin, not the English, sense of the word— for the disorderly desires and passions of the natural man. In the Epistles Horace deals with the problems of life more searchingly than in the Satires, more systematically than in the Odes. Though not in form, they are in substance and spirit essentially didactic. To teach the true end and wise regulation of life, and to act on character from within, are the motives of the more formal and elaborate Epistles. And in those of a lighter and more purely personal meaning, which with his artistic love of variety he intermingles with those of a graver sort, by some incidental remark he seems to probe some weakness of character or to hint the way to a better and wiser life.

The epistolary form, while avoiding the pretention of a set philosophical discourse, is well suited to his object. It enables him to apply the different aspects of his philosophy to different circumstances and to individual cases; and at the same time to give expression to the feelings by which he was attached to many of his contemporaries, and the interest which he took in younger men entering upon life. It served as a medium for that frank communicativeness about his own tastes and habits which was seen to be one of the great literary charms of the Satires and the Odes. The original suggestion of the form may have been due to Archilochus; or perhaps to a still older poet, who in the lines addressed to Perses gave the first specimen of didactic poetry. Some of the Satires of Lucilius were written in the form of letters. There was, too, a still older instance of this form in Latin literature, the humorous verses addressed by Sp. Mummius to his friends at Rome during the siege of Corinth, which Cicero had often heard quoted by the grandson of Mummius. Two of the elegiac poems of Catullus are written in the form of letters to personal friends. Many of Horace's own Odes, expressing maxims of conduct and reflexions on life, are short lyrical epistles, addressed to persons whose position or character suggested the reflexions. The art of letter-writing was essentially Roman, not Greek, because to the Romans, constantly separated from their friends and from the chief centre of their interests by absence in distant provinces, it was a necessity of social and political life. The recent publication of the most interesting collection of letters in any language, the correspondence of Cicero, must have gained for the epistle recognition such as it had not hitherto enjoyed in literature. To a man of Horace's friendly and social temper, living, partly from taste, partly owing to failing health, on his Sabine farm or in such favourite resorts as Tibur and Tarentum[1], it was natural that he should wish to maintain his relations with his friends in Rome and with others engaged in business or official duties, or simply travelling for pleasure in the provinces. By using verse instead of prose as his vehicle, he was able to impart to the epistle a finer literary grace without sacrifice of the frankness and familiarity which give life to the 'colloquia absentium amicorum.' By the use of the epistolary form he adds human interest to his moral teaching, applying it to each individual whom he addresses and the circumstances in which he is placed. By acting on the principle that a different kind of admonition is suited to men in different circumstances and of different character, he can write without inconsistency, at one time in the spirit of a Stoic, inculcating independence of the world; at another in the spirit of a disciple of Aristippus, who understands from watching rather than from sharing in the game of life how to win or lose it; more often simply as a friend, expressing friendly sympathy, performing some friendly office, or offering friendly counsel. The Epistles thus combine the interest of unsystematic discourses or essays on the conduct of life by a man of much reading, observation, and reflexion, with the charm of a collection of actual letters, written to many persons, whose individual traits are indicated as those of Cicero's correspondents are in the letters addressed to them. They have thus a natural charm, entirely wanting to the formal ethical epistles of Seneca, in which only the individuality of the writer is present. These Epistles vary considerably in length and importance. A few extend to between ten and twenty lines only; a considerable number to between thirty and fifty; a few of those in which he is more expressly didactic from about seventy to about one hundred. The shortest among them is simply a letter of introduction

---

[1] Mihi iam non regia Roma,
Sed vacuum Tibur placet aut imbelle Tarentum.
Ep. i. 7. 44, 45.

similar to those of which we have so many in the thirteenth book of Cicero's correspondence. This letter is interesting as showing Horace's relation to the future Emperor Tiberius, then a young man beginning to gain that experience and distinction in military and diplomatic service which prepared him for the great position he had afterwards to fill. It is written in behalf of Septimius, for whom, if he is the Septimius of the Odes, Horace entertained an especial affection. It is in its tone—its tact, its self-depreciating yet self-respecting irony, and self-forgetful interest in his friends—an admirable specimen of his urbanity, and a model of what a letter of introduction to a social superior ought to be. Another short letter, in which his tact and irony are conspicuous, is the thirteenth, addressed to Vinius, to whom he had intrusted the three books of Odes ('signata volumina') to be conveyed to Augustus, then apparently absent from Italy[1].

The eighth is a short letter of congratulation addressed to Celsus Albinovanus, a young man on the staff of Tiberius, on his appointment as secretary. It is written apparently in bad health, and dissatisfaction with his own infirmity of purpose and restlessness of spirit. Here, as so often in the Satires, he admits his own liability to the moral maladies which his teaching is intended to heal. Perhaps his self-reproach was partly meant to soften the caustic admonition with which he concludes—one which successful young men at all times would do well to bear in mind—

> Ut tu fortunam, sic nos te, Celse, feremus.

The fifteenth is also written by Horace in bad health, but in

---

[1] 'Si denique poscet' seems to imply that Augustus was expecting to receive the poems. The directions given to Vinius imply a longer journey than from the Sabine farm to Rome, and Horace was more likely to have his copies of the work in Rome than at his Sabine farm. The words 'simul ac perveneris illuc' imply that the letter is supposed to be addressed to Vinius, at some intermediate place before he reached his destination. Augustus went to Sicily in B.C. 22; thence to the East, from which he did not return till 19 B.C. Thus this letter could not be written before the latter half of 22 B.C. Is it likely that the Odes had been given to the world some time before Horace ventured to send them to Augustus, or is it more natural to suppose that one of the earliest copies was sent to him?

a more genial vein. It is a letter of enquiry as to the relative advantages of Velia and Salernum as a winter residence, at a time when he was forbidden his usual course of baths at Baiae by Antonius Musa, the fashionable physician of the day, who cured the Emperor and may have killed his son-in-law by the cold-water treatment. In it he admits his liability to the common infirmity of valetudinarians—a difficulty in resisting the temptations of good living when they came in his way, though he could be independent of them when he had no opportunity of yielding to them. This self-criticism affords the opportunity of introducing in the person of Maenius the most finished and life-like picture of the 'scurra,' who plays a similar part in Roman satire to that played by the parasite in Greek comedy, though the Roman appears to be a more reckless and less inoffensive person than his Greek prototype usually is.

Other Epistles are written in the vein of some of the lighter Odes, and are addressed to some of the friends who are also addressed in the Odes. Thus the fourth is a letter to Tibullus, whom, under his gentile name of Albius, he consoles or rallies, in one of the Odes of Book i, on his desertion by his mistress. In this Epistle Tibullus is characterised as a poet and scholar, endowed with all personal advantages of mind, body and fortune, and cultivating his art or meditating on the wise conduct of life among the health-giving woods of his estate near Pedum. To one so blessed by fortune and so wise, the only lesson recommended is the Epicurean maxim which forms the burden of several of his Odes—

> Omnem crede diem tibi diluxisse supremum;
> Grata superveniet, quae non sperabitur, hora.

He concludes with an invitation couched in terms of ironical self-disparagement like those used in the Epistle to Vala—

> Me pinguem et nitidum bene curata cute vises,
> Cum ridere voles Epicuri de grege porcum.

The fifth, addressed to the same person as the seventh Ode of Book iv, a man of distinction and a rising advocate of the day, is in the form of an invitation to an entertainment, and enables us to judge of Horace in the character of a host. It shows the discrimination with which he chose his guests, his love of good conversation, and the importance he attaches to that article in the code of social honour, that the friendly conversation of the dining-room should not become a matter of gossip outside—

> ne fidos inter amicos
> Sit qui dicta foras eliminet.

Other letters intermingle hints on the conduct of life with words of friendly courtesy or good-humoured banter. Such are the Epistle to Iccius, the student of philosophy, whose new-born zeal for military adventure is the subject of raillery in one of the Odes; the Epistle to the friend to whom the 'Integer vitae' is addressed, Aristius Fuscus, in which he contrasts his own love of the country with the town-bred tastes of the critic and grammarian, in all other respects so completely his 'alter ego'; the letter to his steward, in which the charm of the country is contrasted with the pleasures of the town with still stronger emphasis; and the interesting letter to Bullatius, in which he questions him about his travels, and reminds him that the cure for restlessness and ennui—the common malady of the age—was to be sought, not in change of scene, but in change of heart and mind. The familiar quotation,

> Caelum non animum mutant qui trans mare currunt,

is what we so often find in the Epistles, a paraphrase of a thought expressed with lyrical fervour in the Odes—

> patriae quis exul
> Se quoque fugit?

In all of these the same lessons are taught or hinted at as in the Odes, the lessons of self-dependence, of simple living, of a love of nature and all natural pleasures, and of a grateful enjoyment of the present, undisturbed by any anxieties for the future. The wise enjoyment of life is the general lesson of these shorter Epistles, as the wise conduct of life is of those which are more formally didactic.

Among the most pleasing of those the interest of which

is chiefly personal, is that addressed to Julius Florus, while serving on the staff of Tiberius in the East, in which a friendly regard for the circle of young poets or aspirants to literary distinction, with which Tiberius had surrounded himself, is combined with candid counsel on the propriety of making up some quarrel with an old friend. The part of a mentor could not be filled with more tact or more consideration for the self-esteem of younger men. He touches lightly but impressively on the more serious teaching, which forms the main subject of his more elaborate Epistles; and happily indicates that the motive for the application of a rational philosophy to life is patriotism and self-approval—

> Hoc opus, hoc studium parvi properemus et ampli,
> Si patriae volumus, si nobis vivere cari.—(Ep. i. 3. 28, 29.)

So much of the teaching of the later Greek moralists and of the Romans who followed them, is directed to secure the happiness or the moral improvement of the individual, for his own sake, that it is interesting to note either in the Odes or the Epistles the recognition of that public virtue, which was the ideal entertained in the best days of the Greek and Roman republics.

Perhaps the gem of the whole collection is the seventh, the interest of which is almost exclusively personal. In it Horace with delicate courtesy and warm affection, but at the same time with frank independence of spirit, excuses himself for absence in the country during the whole month of August, after promising Maecenas to return to Rome within a week. In this Epistle, as in some others referred to, we find the note of the valetudinarian. No other passage, among the many in Odes, Satires, and Epistles which indicate the relation between Horace and his patron, gives a juster idea of what that relation was—not quite the friendship of social equals, but one of close intimacy and warm affection, of deference and gratitude, but tempered by self-respect, on the one side, and an affection springing from the need of sympathy and companionship, and tempered by courteous consideration, on the other. He soon relieves the strain of apology and self-vindication by an admirable story admirably told, illustrative of the relation of patron and client, the story of the well-to-do citizen who had been happy and cheerful in his own way, till he was taken up, partly from good nature, partly for amusement, by Philippus, the famous politician and advocate of the time of the Social war; who was encouraged and helped by him to buy a farm, and after being nearly ruined in consequence, came to his patron and begged to be replaced in his former condition. The account of this citizen, changed into a yeoman ('ex nitido rusticus'), and of his experience of the actual hardships and vicissitudes of a small farmer's life, is perhaps the best specimen of Horace's gift as a teller of stories ; a gift largely possessed by Italian writers ancient and modern. His frequent allusion to fables and anecdotes would lead us to suppose that he had, as other good talkers have had, a large store of them among the resources of his conversational powers.

In most of the longer Epistles—the first, second, sixth, sixteenth, seventeenth, eighteenth—to which may be added the latter part of the second of Book ii, the didactic spirit is more conspicuous ; the personal element, though not absent, is subsidiary. These Epistles present different aspects of his teaching. He seems aware of an apparent contradiction in professing at one time to uphold the tenets of Stoicism, and while entering in spirit into the duties of active life, and claiming to be independent of the outward conditions of happiness—

    Virtutis verae custos rigidusque satelles—

at another time to speak as the disciple of Aristippus, and, without becoming the slave of external conditions, to study how to make them most conducive to the enjoyment of life. As there is nothing on which he more insists than the necessity of consistency in conduct and opinion—

    Si curatus inaequali tonsore capillos
    Occurri, rides ; si forte subucula pexae
    Trita subest tunicae vel si toga dissidet impar,
    Rides ; quid mea cum pugnat sententia secum,
    Quod petiit spernit, repetit quod nuper omisit,
    Aestuat et vitae disconvenit ordine toto,
    Diruit, aedificat, mutat quadrata rotundis?—(Ep. i. 1. 94-100)

it appears, at first sight, difficult to understand his apparent adherence to irreconcilable philosophies. But, living among other men as well as meditating on the abstract tendency of things, he saw that human life was too complex to be reduced to any single rule. He felt the nobleness of an ideal of absolute superiority to the world; and he has expressed the power which this ideal had over the Roman imagination in passages of the Odes and Epistles with as much fervour as any Stoic. But he recognised also the necessity of living in the world, and, in some things, adapting oneself to its ways. Like Cicero, he regarded it as pedantry to apply an impracticable theory of perfection to the unimportant minutiae of life; and yet he knew how much of real well-being depended on these minutiae, what an important part pleasure played in life, and how much better it was to regulate than to eliminate it.

The first Epistle, addressed to Maecenas, is introductory to the rest, and is intended to show the efficacy of philosophic culture in subduing the lower nature—

> Invidus, iracundus, iners, vinosus, amator,
> Nemo adeo ferus est ut non mitescere possit,
> Si modo culturae patientem commodet aurem—

and to contrast the philosophic attitude of mind with the restless pursuit of wealth and pleasure, and the general dissatisfaction with the result, characteristic of Roman society at the time. Here, as in the introduction to the Satires, it is with the waste of human energy, the failure to attain satisfaction notwithstanding the eager pursuit of the means which each individual believes conduce to happiness, that he is most impressed. The spirit of his philosophy in this Epistle is more Stoical than Cyrenaic, as in the often-quoted text,

> Hic murus aëneus esto,
> Nil conscire sibi, nulla pallescere culpa.

But with a characteristic touch of irony, like that with which he concludes the second Epode, he sums up his doctrine with the Stoical paradox, which he ridicules in one of his earliest

Satires, that the wise man alone is rich, free, beautiful, a man of rank, a king of kings—

> Praecipue sanus, nisi cum pituita molesta est.

The second Epistle is also Stoical in its general scope. It is addressed to the son of one of the favourites of the Court, the Lollius of the ninth Ode of Book iv, and is an address on the formation of character through philosophic study and moral discipline. The advice is practical, given in the form of short gnomic sentences, many of which, such as 'ira furor brevis est,' 'semper avarus eget,' 'nocet empta dolore voluptas,' have become commonplaces. Here, too, he seems to disdain the pretentious attitude of a preacher by the irony of his conclusion—

> Quod si cessas aut strenuus anteis,
> Nec tardum opperior, nec praecedentibus insto.

The sixth,

> Nil admirari prope res est una, Numici,

is the most elaborate, the most enigmatical, and the most impersonal of all the ethical Epistles. It is difficult to follow his drift clearly and to distinguish between irony and earnest meaning. The 'nil admirari' of Horace is a translation of the ἀθαυμασία of the Cyrenaics, and does not differ much from the apathy of the Stoics. Cicero[1] uses the same phrase for the state of mind produced by a philosophic estimate of the true value of all worldly things, and speaks of 'these arms' as 'received from the Cyrenaics.' Probably Horace, in the abstract statement of the doctrine, may be following, as Cicero generally follows, a Greek original; while his practical applications of it are taken from his observation of Roman life. The maxim of perfection which he lays down as the supreme condition of happiness is that a man should moderate his desires by moderating his estimate of external things. But those who are incapable of this philosophic quietism and who follow the common objects of worldly desire—money, office, pleasure—are advised to follow

---

[1] Tusc. Disp. iii. 14 'nihil admirari quum acciderit.'

them with a will. Is this all irony, or serious advice? The terms in which the pursuit of money, of political influence, of pleasure, is spoken about, leave no doubt that to the moralist they are all irrational, and that in his eyes 'virtue' alone is able to secure happiness. Perhaps his doctrine is that for the majority of men it is best to make up their mind what they really want, and to follow that strenuously. He seems to imply that energy and consistency, even in the pursuit of fortune, ambition, or pleasure, is a less hopeless condition than weakness and indecision of character; but that the state of mind which cares for none of these things because it thoroughly understands their inadequacy to satisfy man's true nature, should be the aim of all who wish to lead a higher life.

The sixteenth has a special interest from its opening lines, which give a description of his Sabine valley, written with a quiet deep feeling of its peaceful beauty and its restorative influence on mind and body. The discourse which follows is on the difference between appearance and reality, true happiness and its outward semblance. The spirit is Stoical, though he holds that a man may still be of use to the world, even when he 'has quitted the post of honour,' and has become entirely absorbed in the pursuit of money. He can at least contribute to the material wants of other men—

> Naviget ac mediis hiemet mercator in undis;
> Annonae prosit; portet frumenta penusque.

The seventeenth and eighteenth are both in the vein of Aristippus, and give directions to two young men, Scaeva and Lollius, on the conduct necessary in their relations to the great men to whose fortunes they had attached themselves. Horace saw nothing degrading in a relation which, in the last century, was not held degrading by some of those who ultimately came to rank among the greatest of our countrymen—Swift and Burke, for instance. The common sense of the world, according to Horace, condemns the attitude of Cynicism, and approves that of Aristippus, who was at ease in any dress, at home in a palace or a cottage, who enjoyed but was not a slave to the comfort and amenities of others. In the letter to Scaeva there is an undertone of irony, like that in the Epistle to Celsus, a hint that if he wants to succeed in life he must not make his object too apparent. The letter to the younger Lollius, who seems to have been more likely to err on the side of rudeness than of humility, contains the advice of an older man, who, though not born in it, had lived much in the great world, to a young man just entering it. It contains admirable lessons on social tact, self-suppression, reticence, judgment of character, and care in the selection of associates. Near the end of the letter he passes into his more serious vein, and advises his young friend, while taking the means to succeed, to study at the same time the true end of life and the true means of securing inward peace—'quid te tibi reddat amicum.' He concludes with a charming reference to the restorative influence of his visits to his Sabine valley—

> Me quoties reficit gelidus Digentia rivus,
> Quem Mandela bibit, rugosus frigore pagus—

and of the sources of enjoyment which he still had and hoped to have for what remained of life—

> Sit bona librorum et provisae frugis in annum
> Copia, neu fluitem dubiae spe pendulus horae.

The last two Epistles have an autobiographical and literary rather than an ethical interest. The nineteenth, though in form a letter to Maecenas, is a Satire on his imitators, an assertion of his independent position in literature, and a vindication of himself against the spiteful attacks of the critics of the day—

> Non ego nobilium scriptorum auditor et ultor,
> Grammaticas ambire tribus et pulpita dignor.

The twentieth contains a modest appreciation of the work to which it serves as epilogue, and a brief summary of his own career, in which pride in his great rise from an obscure position and in the approval which he had gained from the foremost men of the time in war and peace, is tempered by ironical depreciation of his personal appearance and a candid admission of his besetting infirmity—

> Corporis exigui, praecanum, solibus aptum,
> Irasci celerem, tamen ut placabilis essem.

In the discussion which Horace raises as to the 'summum bonum,' we are sensible of the vagueness of all such ideals, and in the reliance which he seems to place on texts and moral maxims for its attainment, we feel the limitation of the Roman mind. But there is a charm and value in the first book of the Epistles independent of any claim to speculative originality. In the Epistles Horace performs the part of a physician, probing with delicate and kindly hand the causes of social and individual unhappiness and imperfection. He performs the same part for his age as Lucretius did for his, but in a less stern and uncompromising spirit. He does not, like Lucretius, resolve all the evils of life into superstition; but he sees in the morbid and misdirected activity, the 'strenua inertia' of all classes, the chief malady from which society was suffering. To each individual to whom he gives counsel, he seems with delicate irony to hint what is the matter with him; to

> lay his finger on the place,
> And say, thou ailest here, and here,

and at the same time to indicate the cure for his infirmity. And all this he does in the pleasantest manner, blending anecdotes and old fables, personal sketches and amusing social criticism, with the words of wisdom that fall from him.

But the crowning charm of the Epistles is the intimacy which he allows every reader to form with him, and the delightful impression of his natural disposition and settled character which that intimacy produces. The attempt to establish this confidential relation between the writer and the reader is common enough in modern literature. But it is rarely done with the same success. The pleasure of the relation is marred by some indication of egotism, of a bitter feeling against the world, of mortified vanity, or impertinent familiarity. In Horace, as in Cicero, the power of giving is as strong as the desire of receiving sympathy. And in him the sympathetic feeling is unmixed with the exacting vanity which, in the case of Cicero, partially alienates the affection due to his large humanity of nature. Horace has really a modest, though a just appreciation of himself. He knows his own superiority as a writer to the mass of his contemporaries; and in his Odes he shows a proud consciousness of his genius. But in presence of the great work of organising the Empire of the world in a shape to endure for centuries, he felt that all literary distinction was a secondary matter. Even as a poet he knew his inferiority to his Greek masters. He makes no demand on the reader of the Epistles for admiration or applause, but only for a just recognition on the ground of what he has done for Latin literature. He shows no personal animus against any one, and presents nothing but a friendly aspect to the world. He respects himself and his reader in the confidences which he makes to him. He never forgets the restraints of good sense, good feeling, and good taste; and his ironical humour is used quite as much in self-disparagement as in lowering the pretentions of others.

In speaking of his Epistles as 'sermones repentes per humum,' Horace seems to waive for them, as he does for the Satires, the claim to be ranked as poetry. Yet there is a considerable difference in poetical rhythm and expression between the Satires and the Epistles. The Satires, in point of style, scarcely ever deviate from a prosaic level; they are not animated by passion, nor raised above the tone of ordinary conversation, nor are they refined by imaginative reflexion. Their materials are not the

> 'thoughts that voluntary move
> Harmonious numbers.'

The Epistles, while never rising into powerful or impassioned poetry, maintain a modulated flow of thought, vivified and at the same time mellowed by feeling. As the prose writing of a poet, well practised in his art, retains the musical intonation, the vivid presentation of objects and ideas, and the subtle allusiveness of his greater style, so Horace, in returning to the manner and metre of his familiar writing, does not forget the mastery he has gained over the meaning and music of words. If the 'callida verborum iunctura' and the graphic conciseness of phrase do not arrest attention as perpetually as they do in the Odes, they yet add grace and power to the easy, familiar, yet serious and dignified style of the Epistles. There is absolutely no pretention in the style; nothing rhetorical, no undue emphasis, nothing formal or academic. Its character may be judged by comparison with the style of those passages in Lucretius in which he writes as a moralist, such as the introduction to the second and third books, and the conclusion of the third. From these passages it is clear that the habitual mood of Lucretius is that of a philosophic poet. He is possessed by the enthusiasm and the awe—the 'voluptas atque horror'—of an imaginative mind, to which the wonderful meaning of human life is newly revealed. In the style and rhythm of Lucretius we feel the pervading presence of the 'mens divinior,' through its natural accompaniment, the 'os magna sonaturum.' In reading Horace, we feel conscious of the pervading presence of a mind calmly contemplating the field of human life within its range, but not insensible to the mellowing light cast by imagination over its familiar aspect. Whatever enthusiasm there is, is the 'enthusiasm of moderation.' The style has been happily characterised as that of 'idealised common sense.' It is a better example of Roman urbanity than even the style of Terence. It is like the conversation of a man who, under the quietest demeanour, conceals much reflexion, feeling, and dignity of character. That it is the style of a poet also is apparent in many touches of description and harmonious effects of rhythm, to which there are only very rare parallels in the Satires. Such, for instance, are the lines lightly suggesting the different aspects of late autumn and early spring—

   Quod si bruma nives Albanis illinet agris,

and

      te, dulcis amice, reviset,
   Cum Zephyris, si concedes, et hirundine prima;

or those bringing before the mind a wide sea-view—

> Non locus effusi late maris arbiter,

and

> Oblitusque meorum obliviscendus et illis
> Neptunum procul e terra spectare furentem;

or those recalling by the sound no less than the scene the refreshment of a running brook—

> Purior in vicis aqua tendit rumpere plumbum,
> Quam quae per pronum trepidat cum murmure rivum,

and

> at ille
> Labitur et labetur in omne volubilis aevum;

or those in which the power of a few words to convey at once the charm of familiar associations and the outward aspect of a country district is felt—

> Me quoties reficit gelidus Digentia rivus,
> Quem Mandela bibit, rugosus frigore pagus.

And not only do we recognise the poetical eye for what is most characteristic of natural scenes, but the power of imagination penetrating into the secrets of human life, condensing into a single phrase some complex social condition, or deducing a kind of proverbial wisdom from some particular opportunity, as, for instance—

> Strenua nos exercet inertia,

and

> Vilis amicorum est annona, bonis ubi quid deest.

Again, we have an instance of deep feeling finding for itself expression and rhythm consonant to itself in the lines

> Me quamvis Lamiae pietas et cura moratur
> Fratrem maerentis, rapto de fratre dolentis
> Insolabiliter;

a reminiscence, probably, as has been pointed out by Munro, of the still more heartfelt words in which Catullus mourns for his brother's death.

Horace may not have cared to rank these Epistles as poetry,

because there was no recognised form of poetic art, Greek or Roman, other than the satura, to which they could be assigned. But they are a sufficient innovation on the Lucilian satire, to deserve to be regarded as an original addition to poetic forms; while in substance they seem to belong to a kind of borderland between the worlds of observation and of idealising reflexion.

CHAPTER IV.

HORACE AS A LITERARY CRITIC.

Epistles, Book II; Ars Poetica.

AFTER finishing the book of Moral Essays in verse, Horace seems to have published no important work for several years; for the Carmen Seculare cannot be called a work of high inspiration, nor, even to so slow and careful a writer as Horace, could it have involved much labour. He had the fastidiousness which shrank from giving to the world anything that was not wanted and anything that was not perfectly finished, and apparently also the dislike to fresh exertion, which is the accompaniment of such fastidiousness. He had produced his sketches and comments on society in his Satires; he had represented the more idealised aspect of his age and expressed its deeper and livelier feelings in the three books of his Odes; and he had summed up his maturer wisdom and reflexion on life in his moral Epistles. He may have felt that he had no new message to give to the world, till he received a command which could not be disregarded, to celebrate in lyrical poetry the victories gained by the stepson of the Emperor over the Alpine tribes of the Tyrol and the Grisons. This fresh call upon his powers proved to him that the fountain of his inspiration was not yet dry, and that he retained the old mastery over his art in which he had no rival or successor.

A year or two later, apparently, he was again called upon to revert to his more familiar style, and to include Augustus among those to whom his Epistles were addressed. Suetonius mentions that the Emperor, 'after reading certain of his discourses (sermones), complained that no mention was made of him in them.' He quotes the words of his letter:—'irasci me tibi scito, quod non in plerisque eiusmodi scriptis mecum potissimum loquaris.' The last words seem to imply that the 'sermones' are not the Satires, but the Epistles; and it is unlikely that Augustus, who so highly valued the writings of Horace—'scripta eius usque adeo probavit mansuraque perpetua opinatus est'—should not have become acquainted with the Satires till more than twenty years after their first appearance. But it is a question whether the Epistles referred to are those of the first book, or the two to Julius Florus and the Pisos. The word 'plerisque' seems clearly to show that he is speaking of more than two; but it is quite possible that these two may have been included among those which were read by Augustus and provoked his remonstrance. The evidence seems insufficient to determine with certainty whether the Epistles to Julius Florus and the Pisos were written at an earlier or later date than the Epistle to Augustus; and the opinions of the best recent critics and commentators are divided on the subject. All that can be said with anything like confidence is that they have a very close literary connexion with one another—just as the moral Epistles have with many of the Odes of the second and third books—and so may, with probability, be assigned to nearly the same period of their author's life.

In this new undertaking in a style which he had made peculiarly his own, Horace, more definitely than either in his Satires or in the first book of the Epistles, assumes the position of a literary critic and censor. The Epistle to Augustus is 'a defence of poetry,' and especially a vindication of the poets of his own time against the criticism that ranked the older poets above them. It affords him also the opportunity of celebrating the Emperor as a great ruler in more sober language than he has sometimes used on the same subject in the Odes, and of combining with his praises as a ruler a deserved eulogy on him as a patron of literature. In respect of its length and the systematic treatment of its materials, it holds a place intermediate between the earlier Epistles and the Ars Poetica.

The criticism of the old poets, contained in this Epistle, is sometimes censured as too depreciatory. The recognition of the merits of the old tragic poets in the line

<blockquote>Nam spirat tragicum satis et feliciter audet,</blockquote>

though probably just, seems cold when contrasted with the patriotic partiality of Cicero, who speaks of their works as if they were as well worth reading as those of Sophocles or Euripides. The disparaging tone used in regard to Ennius and Plautus is disappointing when compared with the enthusiasm of Lucretius and the calmer admiration expressed by Ovid for the former—'ingenio maximus'—or with Varro's praises of the style of Plautus. But we have to remember that Cicero's training and temperament inclined him to exaggerate, both in praise and blame, and that he had a national and personal pride in asserting the claims of Roman literature in answer to the exclusive pretentions of contemporary Greeks. Lucretius was a poet of exceptionally enthusiastic temperament; and Ovid wrote after the controversy was settled, when it was easy for a man of his candid nature to do justice to the rude genius of the father of Roman poetry, without disparagement of the art and genius of recent writers. Varro was probably regarded by the critics with whom Horace was at issue as their master. There were always two tendencies, supplementing and correcting one another, in Roman literature. There was the imitative tendency, which aimed at making Roman literature as nearly as possible a reproduction of the form and spirit of Greek literature. To this Rome owed her culture. This tendency culminated in the comedy of Terence, the artistic expression of the culture of the Scipionic circle. The national self-consciousness, gathering strength from the great part which Rome was playing in the world, also demanded an expression for itself; and was more anxious that that expression should be strong and genuine, than that it should conform to the canons of literary criticism. In Lucilius the national consciousness was exceptionally strong, and his culture was shown more in his knowledge of and insight into human nature, than in appreciation of literary form; and he, accordingly, made the course of the national literature return into its old and rougher channel. The nature of Lucretius was earnest and impassioned even more than it was artistic; he recognised in the genius of Ennius a force and power akin to his own, and felt a generous admiration for the pioneer who had first made smooth the rough places, 'avia Pieridum loca,' which he was himself traversing. But Horace was one who both in his life and art deliberately restrained enthusiasm, or at least made it subordinate to a cool judgment. He had the temper of a critic as well as the inspiration of a poet; and as he allowed no illusion about himself or others to disturb his judgment on life, so he allowed no patriotic illusion to disturb his literary judgment. He saw that fervour of feeling and a great spirit, which were the gifts of the old writers, were not enough to produce immortal works like those produced by the genius of Greece. He may moreover have had a defective sympathy with the vigorous vitality and irregular force of the old writers. These were not the gifts of himself or of the greatest among his contemporaries. The work which had to be done in his time could not be done by these powers alone. That work was to find, at last, the mastery of form, rhythm, and style, the proportion and moderation of workmanship, which would secure for the efforts of Roman genius as sure a passport to immortality as had been secured for the masterpieces of Greek literature. He saw that these qualities were not natural to the Romans, but were the birthright of the Greeks, the difference between whose artistic and speculative genius and the practical and didactic tendency of Rome he sums up admirably in the passage (Ep. ii. 1. 93-107)

Ut primum positis nugari Graecia bellis, &c.

These endowments could be acquired only by incessant study of Greek models and diligent labour in working after them.

He reviews the history of Roman literature from its origin in the rude Fescennine verses of the harvest home, and shows how it failed first owing to the coarseness inherent in the Italian temperament, and, after its second rise under the influence of the Greek theatre, owing to the rapid and careless composition of the writers; and again, in his own day, owing to the uneducated taste of the audiences. He then solicits the patronage of the Emperor for the writers of his own time, who wrote to be read, and not for the stage; and points to two representatives of the new literature, Virgil and Varius, who united Greek perfection of workmanship to a Roman spirit, as men who had both deserved and received the imperial favour. He imputes the failure of others to receive similar recognition to the sensitive vanity of the literary temperament. He concludes by pleading his own inability to celebrate adequately the great qualities of the Emperor and the great works accomplished in his reign.

Although there is much justice in the strictures on the careless workmanship of the older dramatic writers, and though Horace was right in calling attention to the cause of the failure of the Roman drama to maintain its ancient popularity, yet in this Epistle he shows himself a better critic of human nature than of particular writers. Here, as in the following Epistle, and in the nineteenth of Book i, he probes to the quick the besetting weaknesses and restless sensitiveness of the literary temperament. The lines

>   Cum laedimur, unum
> Si quis amicorum est ausus reprehendere versum;
> Cum loca iam recitata revolvimus irrevocati;
> Cum lamentamur non apparere labores
> Nostros et tenui deducta poemata filo:
> Cum speramus eo rem venturam ut, simul atque
> Carmina rescieris nos fingere, commodus ultro
> Arcessas et egere vetes et scribere cogas,

are as true for other times as for the Augustan age. But in this Epistle he does full justice also to the good qualities of the poetic character, the guileless simplicity, untainted by avarice or worldly ambition, which usually accompanies it, and calls attention to the good service which poetry renders to the State, from its humanising influence on the education of youth—

> Mox etiam pectus praeceptis format amicis,
> Asperitatis et invidiae corrector et irae,—

from its power of presenting the past so as to act on the heart and the imagination of each new generation, its consoling influence in poverty and sickness, and the religious function it performs in prayers and hymns to the Gods. We see in this defence of poetry how far removed the view of Horace is, notwithstanding the supreme importance he attaches to art, from the view of 'art for the sake of art,' so often expressed in recent times.

The second Epistle of this book is also largely occupied both with literary criticism and criticism of the literary character. It is difficult to determine whether it was written some years before the Epistle to Augustus or shortly after it. It seems certain that it was written either after Horace had permanently ceased to write lyrical poetry, or while his lyrical faculty was in abeyance[1]. These conditions would apply to any time between the publication of the three books of Odes, and the composition of the fourth—with the exception of the short interval given to the Carmen Seculare—or to any time between the publication of the fourth book and his death. On the one hand, the undoubted allusion to Propertius (91–101) seems to favour the earlier date; for we know that Propertius was alive and writing his Elegies in the year 16 B.C., and there is good reason for supposing that he did not long survive that date. But when we remember that Pope's famous lines on 'Atticus' were not given to the world till long after the death of Addison, we may suppose that Horace, in the same way, may have written this record of his uncongenial relations with the 'Roman Calli-

---

[1] Ep. ii. 2. 102–5:—
> Multa fero, ut placem genus irritabile vatum,
> Cum scribo et supplex populi suffragia capto,
> Idem, finitis studiis et mente recepta,
> Obturem patulas impune legentibus aures.

machus' after the death of the latter; or that having it already written—'membranis intus positis,'—he may have adapted it to an Epistle written some years afterwards. There is an apparent want of continuity in the way in which the passage is introduced—

> Frater erat Romae consulti rhetor—

which seems to support the latter supposition; nor is its connexion with the lines which follow—

> Ridentur mala qui componunt carmina—

very close. On the other hand, the tone in which Florus is addressed produces the impression that he was a considerably older and maturer man than when the third Epistle of Book i. was addressed to him. In that Epistle Horace is writing to one who was still a young man, in the spirit almost of a tutor to a pupil. In this latter Epistle he writes to him as an equal. In the earlier Epistle Florus is one of a number of young men, in all of whom Horace is interested, accompanying Tiberius on his first important diplomatic mission. In this he has become the confidential friend of the 'worthy and distinguished Nero.' The long apology which Horace makes for not having written to his correspondent since his departure from Rome, would have been quite uncalled for, if Florus was still engaged on the same mission as that referred to in the earlier Epistle. The words 'dixi me pigrum proficiscenti tibi' imply that Florus had in the meantime been back in Rome, and had again gone out on a new expedition with his old chief, of whom he had now become the attached friend. Further, this Epistle is nearly twice as long as the longest in Book i, and is not much shorter than the Epistle to Augustus. A sufficient motive for its composition might be the desire to extend that work to the dimensions of a moderately sized volume by the addition of another contribution to literary criticism, which now occupied much of his attention; while the mere desire to apologise for not having written sooner can hardly be regarded as a sufficient motive for its composition.

The poem has an autobiographical, a critical, and an ethical interest. We learn from it the motive to which he attributes his first essay in literature—

> paupertas impulit audax
> Ut versus facerem—

and the disinclination to resume his poetic task, which grew upon him in later years. This disinclination appears in marked contrast not only to the passionate delight which Lucretius, and the serener joy which Virgil found in this self-appointed task, but also to the pleasure which Horace himself derived from successful creation—

> Grata carpentis thyma per laborem
> Plurimum.

As he grew older he felt the decay of his creative power, along with the decay of some of those sensibilities which fed it—

> Singula de nobis anni praedantur euntes;
> Eripuere iocos, Venerem, convivia, ludum;
> Tendunt extorquere poemata.

He urges the impossibility of writing lyrical poetry amid the distractions of Roman life, and the rivalries and mutual flatteries of the literary cliques at Rome. But though his creative faculty had died out or was in abeyance, his critical faculty, matured by his creative experience, was still able to serve as a whetstone to the genius of others. He dwells especially on the need of a rigid self-criticism on the part of the poet, and of his sparing no pains in pruning all luxuriance, making smooth all roughness, bright all dullness, and strong all weakness of expression, so as to produce the impression of ease, spontaneity, and variety—

> Ludentis speciem dabit et torquebitur, ut qui
> Nunc Satyrum, nunc agrestem Cyclopa movetur.

The lines from 109 to 125 are not only as admirable practical advice on the cultivation of style as any ever given, but explain the secret of Horace's own 'ease in writing.'

In the last sixty lines of the poem he returns once more to the ethical teaching of the first book, and gives the final results of his silent meditations and self-colloquies—

> Quocirca mecum loquor haec tacitusque recordor—

on the true philosophy of life. It is characteristic that here in his latest Epistle, as in his earliest Satire, he regards the passion to become rich as the dominant disturbing element in life; and repeats, at considerable length, his somewhat conventional reasoning on the subject. But near the conclusion he rises from this trite discussion into a higher and purer strain than he has previously attained in his teaching on the conduct of life and the culture of character—

> Caret tibi pectus inani
> Ambitione? Caret mortis formidine et ira?
> Somnia, terrores magicos, miracula, sagas,
> Nocturnos lemures portentaque Thessala rides?
> Natales grate numeras? Ignoscis amicis?
> Lenior et melior fis accedente senecta?

He concludes in the solemn spirit of Lucretius, tempered somewhat by his own irony—

> Vivere si recte nescis, decede peritis.
> Lusisti satis, edisti satis atque bibisti;
> Tempus abire tibi est, ne potum largius aequo
> Rideat et pulset lasciva decentius aetas.

The last twelve lines of this Epistle are profoundly interesting, as the final message on the meaning of human life left by Horace to his generation. They are interesting as showing the refining of his nature, and the growth in gentleness and kindliness of the writer who began his literary career in angry criticism. They confirm also the impression produced by many of the Odes of the deep-seated melancholy underlying the outward geniality of his philosophy of life.

In the 'Ars Poetica' Horace assumes the office of a literary critic more formally than either in the Epistle to Augustus or in that to Florus. The epistolary has developed into the didactic form; or rather there is a kind of compromise between them. Three-fifths of the poem are almost purely didactic; the style in that part of the poem is more compact, sententious, and impersonal, than in any of the other Epistles; the irony and the conversational manner of his other Epistles are alike absent. This purely didactic part seems to be a *résumé* of Greek criticism on the drama, ultimately, perhaps, based on the doctrines of Aristotle; but, according to Porphyrion, really made up of selections from an Alexandrian critic, Neoptolemus of Parium. It contains general precepts applicable to all artistic creation, particularly to poetry as representative of action : and many technical directions, specially applicable to tragedy, are given. Attention is also drawn to the style suitable to the satyric drama. Though much of the illustration of this part of the poem is probably due to Horace himself, yet in the general principles which he lays down, he seems to be a mere exponent of the canons of Greek criticism. How far, besides being an exponent, he is also a translator, can only be conjectured, but certain phrases such as 'dominantia nomina,' and ' communia ' in the phrase ' difficile est proprie communia dicere,' look like translations; and the arrangement of the materials suggests the notion of a composition based on selections from a continuous work rather than of an organic whole, growing out of a definite conception of his subject and a definite plan of exposition. Perhaps we should not be wrong in referring the general principles applicable to all poetry, such as those on the paramount importance of the choice and conception of the subject, and on the dependence of the method of treatment on that conception—

> Cui lecta potenter erit res,
> Nec facundia deseret hunc, nec lucidus ordo—

as well as the technical precepts on the functions of the chorus, the division of the play into five acts, &c., to the Greek original; while the directions as to expression, where he reverts again to the old controversy on the relative merits of the new and old poets, may be regarded as Horace's own contribution to criticism, based on his own practice and that of the best of his contemporaries. In any case we have in the first part of the poem not indeed a methodical treatise on the art of poetry, nor a perfectly planned and articulated didactic poem, but a series of sound principles, on the conception of a dramatic action, the evolution of a plot, the consistent presentation of character, propriety and variety of style, regularity and variety of metrical effect, which might serve as a guide to those who were endeavouring to substitute for the old tragedy of Ennius and Accius a more legitimate drama, not servilely following, but more nearly conforming to the great models of the Attic stage. If the Roman drama was to rise to as high a degree of perfection as Roman epic and lyric poetry had attained in the Augustan age—and to enable it to attain that degree of perfection is the motive of the poem—it could only do so on the same conditions as those on which epic and lyric poetry had been perfected, by a thorough comprehension of and rigorous adherence to the methods of the Greek masters. In the Epistle to Augustus, Horace, while seeming to despair of a revival of the acted drama on the Roman stage, and while disclaiming for himself all thought of dramatic writing, yet assigns the very highest place in literature to the successful dramatist—

>   Ille per extentum funem mihi posse videtur
>   Ire poeta, meum qui pectus inaniter angit,
>   Irritat, mulcet, falsis terroribus implet,
>   Ut magus, et modo me Thebis, modo ponit Athenis.

The occasion of the young Piso following or aspiring to follow the fashion set by Pollio and Varius, prompts Horace to embody in a treatise written primarily for his guidance, the results of his reading and of his own reflexion on dramatic criticism; and he proceeds in the remainder of the poem, more in his own familiar, sometimes ironical, style, to offer advice which seems as much intended to dissuade him from as to encourage him in his task. He glides almost insensibly from the earlier to the latter part of his subject. Starting from a reference to the careless workmanship of Roman poets in their use of Greek metres, and the careless criticism of their audiences, he proceeds to show in his own language and from his own observation what goes to the making of a poet, and what constitutes good and bad taste—

> Unde parentur opes, quid alat formetque poetam,
> Quid deceat quid non, quo virtus quo ferat error.

It is in keeping with all the serious convictions of his later years that he bases all good writing on a true criticism of life in its ethical relations—

> Scribendi recte sapere est et principium et fons—

and that he ranks first in these relations the duties of patriotism and friendship—

> Qui didicit patriae quid debeat et quid amicis.

The poet's aim should be to combine pleasure with instruction. A few minor faults may be excused in a long poem, yet poetry is the one accomplishment in which mediocrity is intolerable. You are not called upon to be a poet, he says to Piso, and you have too much sense to undertake anything against the grain of your natural capacity—

> Tu nihil invita dices faciesve Minerva.

Yet if you do write submit your work to experienced critics, and 'keep it back for nine years' before publishing it. Poetry in days of old was purely a divine gift. It was by 'the sacred poet, the revealer of the will of the Gods,' that the elements of civilisation were introduced—

> Sic honor et nomen divinis vatibus atque
> Carminibus venit.

Next Homer and Tyrtaeus roused men by their verse to battles; then oracles were uttered in verse; finally lyrical poetry and the drama came as the solace of men resting from their labours. Genius, the divine gift, is thus the first condition of poetic success; but mere genius, without art, is ineffective—

> ego nec studium sine divite vena,
> Nec rude quid possit video ingenium.

Yet though success in every other accomplishment is sought by discipline, labour, and self-denial, men appear to think that they can write without taking any trouble. If any one read his poems to Quintilius, he frankly pointed out the faults, and urged correction of them. If the author defended his faults, he left him in his self-satisfaction and took no more interest in him. An honest critic will put a mark against lines that are lifeless, harsh, unpolished or obscure; and will insist on the pruning of all unnecessary ornament. He will become an Aristarchus, and will not fear giving offence to his friend. Sensible men do not like to have anything to do with poets who cannot submit to criticism. They let them go their own course and come to grief in their own way. The bad poet scares away the educated and uneducated alike by his persecution. If he does secure a listener, he sticks to him like a leech and bores him to death by his recitations—

> tenet occiditque legendo
> Non missura cutem, nisi plena cruoris, hirudo.

The work as a whole is hardly to be judged either as a systematic didactic poem, or as a familiar epistle. The one form imperceptibly passes into the other. It has sometimes been supposed that the work was left unfinished and published posthumously. There is no evidence to establish this conclusion. In point of execution the work is as finished as any in Latin literature. It is the maturest specimen of that style which Horace uses in serious discussion and exposition, but more compact and sententious than in the other literary Epistles. The doctrines themselves and their expression bear the mark of having been long weighed and considered. The expression of them has an authoritative, almost oracular character. The difficulty in tracing a connected line of argument or one definite aim in the poem, may be attributed rather to his love of conciseness and his preference of a familiar to a more formal style of exposition than to any want of completeness in working out his plan. Horace was not a systematic reasoner like Lucretius. It was a principle of art with him to avoid or make the most sparing use of those formulae, so largely used by Lucretius and after him by Virgil, by which the transitions from one line of thought to another are clearly marked. He may have begun the poem with the intention of writing a systematic didactic poem on tragedy. For this he found an example in the old national literature—the 'Didascalica' of Accius—and for some of his materials and method he may have had recourse to an Alexandrian model, as Virgil had to more than one in the composition of his didactic poem. But before completing more than half his task, he falls back, without ceasing to be didactic, into the more familiar attitude of one offering friendly advice, not based on books but on his own experience, to a particular person in whom he is interested. He knows perfectly well that genius and insight cannot be communicated by instruction. What can be done is to impress the necessity of avoiding the besetting sin of Roman authors, careless composition, and contentment with a low standard of good writing. This he had already urged in the Satires and in the Epistle to Augustus. Perfection of workmanship is what he inculcates by precept and example. If a man has neither genius nor taste, there is no call on him to write and become one of the nuisances of society. It is not so much by conformity to technical rules—though they have a negative value in the way of restraining extravagant conception and execution—as by having a high standard of accomplishment and sparing no pains to attain it, that the Roman drama may be raised to as high a pitch of perfection as other branches of literature. Genius is the indispensable condition of success; but genius is ineffective without culture, especially ethical culture, and without discipline, especially discipline in correcting errors, pruning redundancies, and remedying defects of style.

In the Epistles dealing with literary criticism there is a limitation of view, combined with a justice and sobriety of judgment, similar to the limitation and the justice of the criticisms on human life contained in the ethical Epistles. The ethical criticisms appear more trite and conventional, because the world has risen further above the age of Horace in the domain of action than of literature. Yet though Horace is dealing with the ancient drama and its relation to human life, and though he speaks of Sophocles and Aeschylus, there is nothing to indicate a true insight into their greatness. It is with the external conditions, not with the spiritual and ethical meaning of the Greek drama that he deals. Where his criticism is most admirable and valuable is in those passages in which he inculcates the necessity of careful writing, as in that passage of Ep. ii. 2. 109—

> At qui legitimum cupiet fecisse poema—

in which he shows how much an author can do to perfect his work by severe self-criticism and infinite pains in using all the resources of language—

> Vehemens et liquidus puroque simillimus amni
> Fundet opes Latiumque beabit divite lingua;
> Luxuriantia compescet, nimis aspera sano
> Levabit cultu, virtute carentia tollet,
> Ludentis speciem dabit et torquebitur, ut qui
> Nunc Satyrum, nunc agrestem Cyclopa movetur.

In much the same spirit he describes the functions of a true critic in the Ars Poetica, l. 445—

> Vir bonus et prudens versus reprehendet inertes,
> Culpabit duros, incomptis allinet atrum
> Transverso calamo signum, ambitiosa recidet
> Ornamenta, parum claris lucem dare coget,
> Arguet ambigue dictum, mutanda notabit.

These Epistles contain also much admirable criticism on human life, as in the account given in the Ars Poetica, ll. 161–174, of the characteristics of the various ages—

> Imberbis iuvenis tandem custode remoto, &c.

Where the criticism is most searching is in the truth of insight into the literary character both in its worth and its weakness. The style of these Epistles is more terse and compact than in the ethical Epistles. Occasionally it rises into genuine poetry, as in a passage which recalls the

> Vitaque mancipio nulli datur omnibus usu

of Lucretius, and Wordsworth's 'waves that own no curbing hand'—

> Sic quia perpetuus nulli datur usus, et heres
> Heredem alterius velut unda supervenit undam.

If the personal impression is less distinctly stamped upon them than on the ethical Epistles, it is of the same kind. There is the same stamp of sincerity, of good sense and good manners, of self-respect without self-assertion, and of considerate regard for the feelings of others.

CHAPTER V.

Horace as a Lyrical Poet.

The Epodes.

THE place of Horace among the great lyrical poets of the world is due to the four books of Odes, the fruit of his happiest years and maturest faculty. He anticipates immortality on the ground of having been the first

> Aeolium carmen ad Italos
> Deduxisse modos.

But he asserts another claim to consideration in the words

> Parios ego primus iambos
> Ostendi Latio.

Before becoming the Alcaeus of Rome, he made his first essay in lyrical poetry by imitating the metres and the manner and spirit of Archilochus. The realism and critical bent of his mind which attracted him to Lucilius, attracted him also to the old Greek poet, 'for whom rage had forged the weapon of the iambus.' Archilochus was not only the inventor of a new metre which a great destiny awaited, but the first poet who treated of the familiar matter of the day in the ordinary dialect of the day. He was the first also to make his verse the vehicle of his personal animosities; and he anticipated Lucilius, with whom he seems to have been a favourite, in the frankness of his personal confessions. It is probable that Horace became familiar with his writings during the time of his studies at Athens. The angry mood in which he returned to Rome after Philippi, and the 'recklessness of poverty' which first impelled him to write verses, naturally led him to make the old Parian poet his model. The popularity of the lampoons of Catullus, Calvus, and Bibaculus, assured him readers prepared to welcome verses written in a similar spirit, and in a metre only slightly different from that employed by the older writers. The 'Italum acetum,' the ebullitions of which had to be repressed by law four centuries previously, and which had found its chief outlet in the invective of the Forum and law-courts, had from the time of Naevius learned to concentrate itself in short and pithy epigrams, for which party-feeling and the scandals of private life supplied the material. If the state of public affairs no longer permitted lampoons to be written, as they had been between the years 60 and 50 B.C., on the masters of the Roman world, yet private scandals and animosities were sufficiently rife: and the position of Horace at that time, as a poor adventurer with a keen appetite for pleasure, a quick temper and a taste intolerant of uncongenial people, made him familiar with both. He was at that time of life when personal love and dislike—the 'odi et amo'—the original source of the lyrical poetry which springs out of private life, are strongest: and his love seems at this stage to have been more violent than fortunate, and not always distinguishable from his animosities.

In claiming to have been the first to introduce the Parian 'iambi' into Latin literature, he seems to forget the prior claim of Catullus and his contemporaries. The spirit of Archilochus is probably more truly represented in the iambics on Caesar and Mamurra, than in any verses of Horace. But Horace was the first to introduce, not the continuous iambics, but the ἐπῳδοί; i.e. the couplets in which the shorter verse is a kind of echo of the longer, of which several specimens are found among the fragments of Archilochus. To these poems Horace gives the name 'iambi.' Whether the title 'Epodon' was attached by himself to the volume containing them, or by some grammarian to a later edition, is uncertain. In the first ten poems the couplet is composed of an iambic trimeter followed by a dimeter. This combination is found again in a poem of the Catalepton attributed, probably untruly, to Virgil. It is employed also by Martial in a long poem which reproduces the idyllic character of the second Epode. In the eleventh Epode the first line is iambic, the second a hybrid between iambic and elegiac verse. In those from the twelfth to the sixteenth the couplet is formed by an hexameter, followed by an iambic trimeter or dimeter, or by the hybrid combination mentioned above. The seventeenth alone is in continuous iambics. Horace also used some varieties of the Archilochian couplets in some of his Odes, while he was still making experiments in metre, till he discovered that the stanza of four lines gave the true outlet to the deeper vein of his lyrical genius.

The composition of the Epodes was spread over the ten years that elapsed between the return of Horace to Rome and the battle of Actium, and nearly coincides with the time occupied by the composition of the Satires. The genuine spirit of satire is stronger in them than in most of the pieces written in the manner of Lucilius. They are more directly personal. They are in no sense didactic or reflective. Those of them in which the pure Archilochian spirit predominates are written, not from a desire to reform society, but from the impulse to give vent to personal feelings of dislike, disgust, or resentment. The passionate element in Horace's temperament, which he had learned to moderate before he came to the composition of the Odes, finds a free outlet in the Epodes. Two of these, the eleventh and the fifteenth, seem to be no idle play of fancy, but, like some of the utterances of Catullus, confessions into which he is hurried by violent gusts of passion. While the Odes present idealised pictures of the life of pleasure in the Augustan age, some of the Epodes throw an unpleasant light on the repellent aspects of the realism of that life, and are as unpleasant reading as anything in ancient literature. The reaction from the life of pleasure produces for a time in Horace, as perhaps also in Lucretius, a feeling of disgust, which finds expression in one or two pieces, as alien as anything well can be from his genial mood and good taste when, as soon happens, he is restored to his better and happier self. The poems of which Canidia is the subject, though not free from coarseness, are of a different stamp and are written with dramatic power and imaginative insight. In their union of humour and horror, and their grotesque combination of elements from the natural and supernatural world, though not conceived with equal vividness of fancy, they remind us of the witch scene in Burns's great poem. The lampoons directed against the male objects of his dislike, the fourth, sixth, and tenth, may have been prompted by a more respectable motive than personal animosity. Of these, the first is launched against a notorious person who had risen by a career of villany to wealth and importance; the second is a reprisal on a scurrilous writer who assailed inoffensive people; the third is a προπεμπτικόν invoking the horrors of a stormy passage across the Ionian Gulf on one who provoked even the mild spirit of Virgil to retaliate, and whose name in consequence, coupled with that of his associate Bavius, has been handed down as typical of an envious and spiteful poetaster. It seems a not unlikely conjecture that this poem may have suggested the προπεμπτικόν addressed to the ship which is to bear Virgil to the shores of Attica, and that that poem, instead of being the latest, may be one of the earliest in order of composition of the Odes in the first three books[1].

These poems seem to be vigorous exercises of the Archilochian 'stilus,' used, not against obscure and inoffensive people, but against the enemies of society, who constantly reappear and excite the strongest feelings of moral and literary antipathy. It is in these poems, not in the regular Satires, that Horace shows the spirit attributed to Lucilius in the lines of Persius—

secuit Lucilius urbem
Te Lupe, te Muci, et genuinum fregit in illis. (i. 114.)

With the subsiding of his warmer passions, and the growth of his lyrical and contemplative faculty, the Archilochian spirit passed almost entirely out of his nature and his writings.

---

[1] Cf. infra, p. 142.

There are some of the Epodes in which the spirit of indignation or disgust is combined with patriotic sentiment and serious political feeling. Of the earlier in date, the sixteenth is more of a dirge than a satire, and is an expression of despair over the ruin caused by the prolongation of the civil wars, and of a longing to find a new home among the fortunate isles of the Atlantic. There is a close parallel between the sentiment of this poem—the vague vision of a golden age and a land unvisited by the adventurous mariner—and that of the fourth Eclogue. The only difference is that Horace seems to express the feelings of the losing side before the peace of Brundisium; Virgil those of the winning side after its conclusion. This is the earliest manifestation of the political vein in Horace; in the vagueness of its idealising sentiment it is in marked contrast to the strong hold on reality characteristic of his later art. The only other poem of his pervaded by a similar vagueness of sentiment is the third Ode of Book i, addressed to the ship which is to bear Virgil to Attica, in which the old religious dread of the sea is the leading motive. In both poems may probably be traced the early influence of Horace's intercourse with Virgil, before he discovered the essential diversity of their genius, and consequently the different spheres marked out for each. The seventh Epode may probably have been written about the same time, and seems to be prompted by dread of a premature outbreak between the forces of Antony and Octavian, such as was generally apprehended during and immediately after the Perusian war, or perhaps by the renewal of the war with Sextus Pompeius after the short-lived peace of Misenum, B.C. 39. The fourteenth Ode of Book i. was probably written coincidently with this Epode. In neither of these poems, nor in the sixteenth Epode, is there indication of partisanship, which would certainly have appeared before the final conflict with Antony. On the other hand the words

          Parumne campis atque Neptuno super
          Fusum est Latini sanguinis

seem still more appropriate if written after the naval battles in the Sicilian Straits. The expression of alarm and dismay on the part of Horace might thus be referred to the same time as the concluding episode of Georgic i, before war between Caesar and Antony was actually declared. The mood expressed is simple weariness of the wars, and indignation against their guilt and madness. This was a state of feeling through which the remnant of the defeated party must have passed before they became finally reconciled to the rule of Caesar.

That stage, or at least the recognition of the truth that the cause of Caesar in the war against Antony and Cleopatra is the cause of Rome, is reached before the Epodes are concluded. The first Epode is called forth by anxiety for the safety of Maecenas, who was preparing to join Caesar on the expedition which ended in the battle of Actium. The contrast between the light Liburnian galleys of the Caesarians and the 'alta navium propugnacula' can only apply to this battle, and not to those fought on the shores of Sicily with Sextus Pompeius. Horace expressed his desire to accompany him, and according to one interpretation of the ninth Epode, which seems to give the feelings and impressions of an eye-witness, it is not impossible that he may have been present within view of the battle. If the usual interpretation of that poem is correct, and if the victor of Actium is celebrated as a greater general than Marius and the younger Scipio, Horace is not only reconciled to the supremacy of Caesar, but has, all at once, become his extravagant eulogist, and has fallen into the mistake, never afterwards repeated, of flattering him for qualities which he did not possess. Caesar had already proved himself a great statesman and a great ruler of men, but neither at Philippi nor in the battles in the Sicilian Straits had he shown military capacity; and the victory of Actium, like the final success over Sextus Pompeius, was due to Agrippa. But the interpretation of Plüss renders the poem more striking and more intelligible. He regards it not as a song of triumph, like the one written a year later, after the capture of Alexandria, but as an Archilochian invective against the foreign queen who had vowed the destruction of the Capitol. In the lines

> Io triumphe, nec Iugurthino parem
> Bello reportasti ducem,
> Neque Africano, cui super Carthaginem
> Virtus sepulcrum condidit

no comparison is intended between Caesar and the victors in the Jugurthine and the third Punic Wars, but between Cleopatra and the two generals, Jugurtha and Hasdrubal, who were brought back captives after those wars. Cleopatra combines the cruelty and treachery of Jugurtha with the cowardice of Hasdrubal. This general of the Carthaginians, after boasting that he would find his tomb in the ruins of Carthage, made ignominious terms with Scipio for his own safety, and had to bear the scornful reproaches of his wife, who sacrificed herself and her children among the ruins[1]. That the parallel between Cleopatra and Jugurtha was recognised is shown by the lines of Propertius, iv. 6. 65–66,

> Di melius! quantus mulier foret una triumphus,
> Ductus erat per quas ante Iugurtha vias.

That the threats of Cleopatra roused the bitterest sense of indignity is shown in the thirty-seventh Ode of Book i,—

> dum Capitolio
> Regina dementes ruinas
> Funus et imperio parabat—

and in Propertius, iii. 11. 45–46—

> Foedaque Tarpeio conopia tendere saxo,
> Iura dare et statuas inter et arma Mari.

In the grandeur of the pentameter there is surely a reminiscence of Marius as the conqueror of Jugurtha.

---

[1] Polybius, xxxix. frag. 3, ed. Dindorf. (Scipio speaks) οὗτός ἐστιν Ἀσδρούβας ὁ νεωστὶ πολλῶν αὐτῷ φιλανθρώπων προτεινομένων ὑφ' ἡμῶν ἀπαξιῶν, φάσκων δὲ κάλλιστον ἐντάφιον εἶναι τὴν πατρίδα καὶ τὸ ταύτης πῦρ, νῦν πάρεστι μετὰ στεμμάτων δεόμενος ἡμῶν τυχεῖν τῆς ζωῆς καὶ πάσας τὰς ἐλπίδας ἔχων ἐν ἡμῖν. This interpretation not only substitutes the force of scornful irony for the weakness of insincere compliment—and the spirit of the whole poem is very far from that of compliment and flattery—but affords the only rational explanation of the words
cui super Carthaginem
Virtus sepulcrum condidit.

The poem is the most powerful example of fierce sarcasm among all the imitations of Archilochus; and both the occasion and the person against whom it is directed impart dignity and seriousness to the employment of the weapon, as they do to its employment by Catullus against the father-in-law and son-in-law who were ruining the Commonwealth. The thirty-seventh Ode of Book i, while it is a song of triumph over the downfall of Cleopatra, is a partial retractation of the imputation of cowardice and dishonour. Neither poem could have been written by Horace, had he not felt himself thoroughly identified with the national cause as represented by Caesar.

A few of the poems, though written in Archilochian metre, have little if anything of the Archilochian spirit. They express moods and feelings which find their natural outlet in other forms of lyrical poetry. Thus, the first Epode, already referred to in its historical connexion, is a pure expression of Horace's affection and gratitude to Maecenas and of contentment with his own lot, such as we find in several of the Odes, Satires, and Epistles. The third Epode is of the slightest significance, except as it shows the relation of easy familiarity already established between the statesman and the poet, and intimates that when they chose 'discincti ludere,' their ideas of relaxation were not always very intellectual or very refined; perhaps not less so than those of Goethe and the Duke of Weimar, when they spent hours in cracking whips against one another in the market-place. The thirteenth is written rather in the vein of Alcaeus or Anacreon, than of Archilochus. It is a convivial Ode, in which the influence of wine is invoked to rouse the drooping spirits of himself and his comrades under the depressing influence of fortune and external nature. It may have been suggested by the disastrous results of Philippi. The inclement weather outside is symbolical of the inclemency of fortune. The only comfort is to be found in good wine—

> Tu vina Torquato move consule pressa meo.
> Cetera mitte loqui: deus haec fortasse benigna
> Reducet in sedem vice.

That the first hint of the poem is due to a Greek original may be inferred from the opening imagery, which recalls passages in the fragments both of Alcaeus and Anacreon, and from the concluding illustration in which Chiron mingles words of manly cheerfulness with the warning of his doom addressed to Achilles. In the older Greek poets wine and song were glorified as the restorers of life and spirit in trouble and danger—

> Deformis aegrimoniae dulcibus alloquiis.

In the Latin poets wine is glorified rather as a bond of companionship, and as affording relief from the monotony of existence; and the enjoyment of it is more often associated with bright weather and the grace and freshness of trees and running water than with rain and tempest.

The most poetical, and at the same time the most perplexing in its meaning of all the Epodes, is the second, in which the praises of a country life are put into the mouth of a notorious city usurer, a real, not a fictitious personage, whose whole soul is absorbed in laying out his money at interest on the Kalends of each month. Is the main purpose of the poem to ridicule this person and the inconsistency between his professions and his practice, and is his character dramatically sustained by slight touches, intentionally introduced into the body of the poem? Or does Horace intend to ridicule the insincere enthusiasm for the beauty of nature, which may have become fashionable then, as it perhaps is now[1]? Is the poem really a satire in the disguise of an idyll, or is it a genuine idyll, gathering into one picture the ideal charm of a country life, as it presented itself

---

[1] This is the view of M. Gaston Boissier: 'De toutes les raisons qu'on a données pour expliquer cette épode, il n'y en a qu'une qui me semble naturelle et vraisemblable. Il était impatienté de voir tant de gens admirer à froid la campagne; il voulait rire aux dépens de ceux qui n'ayant aucune opinion personnelle, croient devoir prendre tous les goûts de la mode, en les exagérant. Nous connaissons, nous aussi, ces prôneurs ennuyeux de la belle nature, qui vont visiter les glaciers et les montagnes uniquement parce qu'il est de bon ton de les avoir vus, et nous comprenons la mauvaise humeur que devait ressentir de ces enthousiasmes de commande un esprit juste et droit qui ne faisait cas que de la vérité.'—Nouvelles Promenades Archéologiques, pp. 17, 18.

to the Italian imagination, and as it may have been partially realised by the more fortunate yeomen in the Sabine or Apulian highlands, and by members of the cultivated classes who like Tibullus lived on and cultivated their own estates? Some lines in the poem suit best the ideal life of the Italian yeoman, as the

> Sabina qualis aut perusta solibus
>   Pernicis uxor Apuli,
> Sacrum vetustis exstruat lignis focum
>   Lassi sub adventum viri.

Others, suggestive of the more indolent pleasures of contemplation, and the final touch,

> Positosque vernas, ditis examen domus,
>   Circa renidentes Lares,

apply better to the refined and comparatively wealthy owners of large estates. The first impression which the poem must produce on every reader, till he is met by the surprise of the last four lines,

> Haec ubi locutus fenerator Alfius, &c.,

is that it is a sincere expression of the Italian love of nature and still more of the Italian delight in the labours of the field and their results, and also in the sports of the country—

> Aut trudit acres hinc et hinc multa cane
>   Apros in obstantes plagas.

This first impression is confirmed by the resemblance of the poem in tone and substance to the first Elegy of Tibullus, a poem written about the same time, and by its agreement in spirit with the ideal of such a life worked out in the fullest detail in the Georgics. It has been even suggested that Horace intended to parody the master-pieces of his friends. Certainly, if he did, never was art so well concealed. Why should he lavish so much serious poetical power, so many felicitous phrases, on a parody?—such, for instance, as

> Vel cum decorum mitibus pomis caput
>   Auctumnus agris extulit.

Horace would have left it to Bavius and Maevius to parody Virgil's art, and even if he had wished to parody Tibullus, the pleasure would have been denied to him, as the Elegy was not written till the year 22 B.C., after the Epodes had been published. It is much more likely that Tibullus took hints from Horace[1], as he did from the Georgics, than that Horace parodied either. All three deal with a subject which it was as natural for an Italian poet to treat as to sing of war or love. The enthusiasm of Horace, less heartfelt than that of Tibullus or Virgil, is rather of sympathy than of strong personal feeling. He often expresses other feelings also, as those of love and sorrow, through sympathy, rather than directly. The pleasure which he himself derives from his Sabine farm is not the pleasure here described, and this Epode may have been written before or soon after he entered on the possession of it. There is no feeling of personal longing, like that expressed even in the Satires. The art is purely objective. He writes, like Virgil, in sympathy with the labours associated with so much of the happiness and worth of the Italian race; he appreciates the spirit of thrift and industry, developed in such a life, and the material well-being, which are their result; and he realises the charm to eye and ear which the environment of such a life affords to the man of intellectual culture. The idyllic picture of virtuous and wholesome living is enhanced by contrast with the disorderly passions and luxurious banquets of the town—

> Quis non malarum, quas amor curas habet,
> Haec inter obliviscitur?

Though neither his own love of the country nor his true lyrical vein is yet fully developed[2], yet the poem appears to be an early and genuine expression of a poet's sympathy with a life which had great charms for the Italian imagination, and which, if Horace did not sympathise with it from his recollection of the

---

[1] The line in Tib. ii. 1. 23,
> Turbaque vernarum saturi bona signa coloni,
written some years later, seems a clear reminiscence of the
> Positosque vernas ditis examen domus.

[2] The profusion of detail is a sign of his earlier manner.

farm on the borders of Lucania and Apulia, he must have learned to appreciate from his intimate intercourse with the author of the Georgics. It is not likely that he found any suggestion of a similar feeling for the charm of a country life in his prototype, who denounces instead of glorifying the land in which his lot was cast. The only old Greek poet who realises the delight of such a life is Aristophanes, who describes its attractions in contrast to the hardships and discomforts of life in town during the Peloponnesian war. A passage (Pax, 569) in which this contrast is made is clearly imitated in the opening lines of the Epode.

What, then, is the meaning of the last four lines, in which all these fine sentiments are ascribed to the usurer Alfius? It is not enough to say, although it is true, that the charm of a country life is enhanced by contrast with the pleasures of making money by usury. But it is characteristic of Horace, when he is most in earnest, to check himself and bring himself back to the ordinary mood in which he meets society. To use a phrase of Mr. George Meredith's, he offers resistance 'to the invasion of the poetic' by means of 'the commonplace.' It was seen in the Satires and Epistles that he resists 'the invasion' of an over-earnest mood by satire directed against the paradoxes and the professors of Stoicism. Two of his noblest national Odes, where his feeling is most tragic or most elevated, end in a stanza of ironical self-depreciation. So he adds a satiric tag to this Epode, to prevent his being taken too seriously. The systematic enthusiasm with which he is carried away to celebrate the happiness of country life, partially checked in the course of the poem, is disclaimed with 'town-bred irony.' The poet, like some modern poets, may have prided himself at that stage of his career more on being a man of the world than on being a man of genius. Whether his art gains or loses most by this extreme self-consciousness, may be a matter of opinion.

The Epodes are, on the whole, the least interesting and satisfactory work of Horace. They are, indeed, important as revelations of the man and of a particular stage of contemporary society, which we do not get elsewhere. But they reveal chiefly the less genial side of his nature, his less happy experiences, and his antipathetic rather than his sympathetic relations to society. The impression we form from them must be corrected by that which we form from the Satires written at the same time. The difference between these impressions suggests a caution in judging of the character of a writer from single works or from the writings of a single period. It is from the totality of the impression produced by the works of his whole literary activity, that his nature and character should be judged. By this criterion there is no difficulty in deciding that there is more of the true Horace in the Satires than in the Epodes. The Satires deal absolutely with things as they are, the Epodes aim at a special artistic and imitated effect. The effect at which he aims in the Epodes is 'sal niger,' ill-natured sarcasm; but Horace's way of looking at life was humorous and genial, rather than ill-natured and sarcastic. The 'carmen maledicum,' as it gratifies the disinterested love of detraction common to all societies, enjoyed great temporary popularity in Greece and Rome; but to maintain its interest for after-times it seems to require not only some unusually pungent force of sarcasm, some force of finished expression, but some celebrity in the object to enable after-times to judge whether the satirist has hit his mark. The first condition of the effectiveness of all such literature is its sincerity. This is what imparts such pungency to the sarcasm of Catullus. His lampoons are perhaps the most powerful expression of concentrated scorn in any language. The objects of his invective—such as Clodia, Piso, Memmius, Mamurra, Caesar—were sufficiently eminent to redeem the attacks from that taint of ignobleness which sticks to the quarrels of obscurer people. In some of the objects of Horace's attack, there is nothing to clear it from this taint. The feeling by which he is moved seems sometimes that of the imitative artist rather than the man. In power of sarcastic expression, he is inferior to Catullus; in power of personal caricature, as in wit, he shows himself in the Epodes inferior to Martial: though the union of humour and grim horror in the representation of Canidia and her associates, male and female, is beyond the imagination of Martial to conceive. The poem in which the power of scornful sarcasm is most worthily employed in union with the vivid presentation of events, as if they were passing before the eyes of an interested and excited spectator, is the ninth, 'Quando repostum Caecubum.'

The Epodes have neither the musical charm and variety of the Odes nor their studied felicities of language. The iambic metre does not lend itself to the sonorous effects of the Alcaic stanza, the graceful vivacity of the Sapphic, nor the grave moderation characteristic of some varieties of the Asclepiadean. Horace cannot rival the charm of joyous speed imparted to the pure iambic by Catullus in 'Phaselus ille,' or the fiery force as of launched javelins[1] in 'Quis hoc potest videre.' But the metre of the earlier Epodes suits their terse epigrammatic style, in which each separate couplet is intended to leave its separate sting. Horace made himself master of this, as of all the other metres employed by him, and left a permanent impression of its power to utter a succession of stinging sentences, or to bring before the imagination a succession of peaceful sights and sounds from external nature. It was for this last purpose that it was reproduced by the great master of metrical effect in the first century of the Empire: Martial, at least, must have seen in the second Epode not a satire but an idyll.

[1] Cf. the phrase 'truces vibrare iambos.' Catull. xxxvi. 5.

CHAPTER VI.

HORACE AS A LYRICAL POET.

The Odes.

I.

IT is for his Odes that Horace claims immortality, and it is to them that he chiefly owes it. Scarcely any work in any literature has been so widely and so familiarly known. Almost from the time of their author's death, they became what they have been since the revival of letters, one of the chief instruments by which literary taste and a delicate sense of language have been educated. The music of their verse, the grace, lucidity, and terseness of their diction, the truth and, at the same time, the limitation of their thought, impress them on the memory; while their applicability to the ordinary experience of life has brought them more into the currency of quotation, in speech and writing, than the words of any other writer. Changes in literary taste and speculative thought do not seem to affect the estimation in which they are held. They gain and retain the ear of each generation from the perfection of their form and the importance of their meaning. No ancient writer has so much excited and so much baffled the ambition of translators; and scarcely any still continues to find so many critics and interpreters.

Yet among his professed admirers, the most opposite opinions appear to prevail as to the ground on which his distinction as a lyrical poet chiefly rests. He seems to speak to each reader in accordance with his prevailing mood. To one large class his message to his generation, commended by the perfection of form and melody in which it is conveyed, seems to be nothing more than to enjoy the present day and to be undisturbed about the future. To others he appears at his best as the interpreter of the greatness of the Roman Empire. Others again turn with most sympathy to the graver utterances and wiser lessons of his philosophy of life. One great authority on at least one part of his message finds his true nature, not in the 'gaiety and wit,' the 'easy mirth,' which inspired 'his social hours,' but in

> the humblest note of those sad strains
> Drawn forth by pressure of his gilded chains,
> As a chance sunbeam from his memory fell
> Upon the Sabine farm he loved so well,
> Or when the prattle of Bandusia's spring
> Haunted his ear, he only listening[1].

To one ingenious critic it appears that, while some of the Odes may be written in the vein of Anacreon, others in that of Alcaeus, others in that of Pindar, yet regarded as a whole, they are conceived rather in the spirit of 'the Simonidean dirge,' 'Ceae neniae,' and that their immediate motive was, first, to utter a lament over the tragedy of the civil wars, and, secondly, to point the moral of the tragic career of Licinius Murena.

This variety of impressions produced on different minds is a proof of the versatility of the poet and of the strong personal hold which he lays upon his readers. He has a very distinct individuality as a man and a writer; and it is one of the great charms of the Odes, as it was seen to be of the Satires and Epistles, that this individuality is vividly present in them. But he had also the emotional susceptibility of a true lyrical poet, and was thus able to throw himself with sympathetic feeling into the public and personal life of his age, to express with elevation what his fellow-countrymen felt in a great national crisis, and to make the thought, the culture, the ethical tendency, as well as the mirth and gaiety of a great

---

[1] Wordsworth, Liberty (1829).

epoch in civilisation, live for ever in the imagination of the world.

From the fact that Horace in various places, as in the Ode to Agrippa, the concluding stanzas of the Ode to Pollio, and of the third Ode of Book iii, speaks of his Muse as best fitted for the lighter themes of love and wine, the conclusion is sometimes drawn that, in his own opinion, to sing of these was his true function as a lyrical poet. But in the Ode to Agrippa he is merely expressing the same disinclination to describe, in elaborate poems, the military events of the day, which he had expressed in the dialogue with Trebatius in his Satires; and in the other places he checks himself, as he does habitually in the expression of his deeper feelings and higher enthusiasm, with the ironical urbanity of one who is, above all things, 'dissimulator opis propriae.' In other passages he claims to be the 'High Priest of the Muses,' the inspirer of loyalty and patriotism, and the teacher of public duty. He claims not only immortality for his own verse, but its power to crown with immortality the civic virtues of his contemporaries. In boasting that he has raised a monument more enduring than bronze, and in associating the eternity of his completed work with the eternity of Rome, he asserts a greater claim than that which in one of his earlier Odes he makes for the lighter songs of his idle hours—

> si quid vacui sub umbra
> Lusimus tecum, quod et hunc in annum
> Vivat et plures.

Thus if we are to judge Horace by his own estimate of his art, it is in its graver rather than its lighter tones that we should find the secret of its greatness.

In the Ode just quoted, and in a later one written after an escape from sudden death, in which he represents symbolically the enduring power of poetry, and seems to anticipate his own permanent rank among the great lyrical poets of the world, he indicates, as he does in both the first and second books of the Epistles, his wish to be regarded as the Alcaeus of Rome.

And of Alcaeus he speaks as the poet who sang of 'battles and banished tyrants' and also

>   inter arma
>   Sive iactatam religarat udo
>   Litore navim,
> · Liberum et Musas Veneremque et illi
>   Semper haerentem puerum canebat
>   Et Lycum nigris oculis nigroque
>   Crine decorum.

Had he regarded himself as specially the poet of pleasure, it is with the Teian Anacreon that he would have claimed kinship; or had he felt himself to be the poet of passionate love he would, like Catullus, have hinted at the relation of his own Muse to the Muse of Sappho. By claiming Alcaeus as his prototype he seems to imply that he regarded his lyre as equally tuned to the lighter pleasures and to the sterner and more dignified interests of life. At a later stage of his lyrical career, when called upon to celebrate the victories of Drusus and Tiberius, while he introduces himself as the poet who had sung and still was moved to sing in the vein of Alcaeus singing of Lycus, in the next Ode, while disclaiming all rivalry with Pindar, he yet indicates that it is in his spirit that he desires to accomplish his task. As his attitude to Greek systems of philosophy was that of an eclectic with apparently a preference for Aristippus, so he is somewhat of an eclectic in his attitude to the lyric poets of Greece. He seems to have wished not only to embody the spirit of Alcaeus and Pindar in his own lyrical expression, but to temper it with the spirit of Anacreon, with the sadder mood of Simonides, with some faint glow of the 'calores' of Sappho, and with much of the moral gravity which he attributes to Stesichorus. With the mobile temperament of true lyrical genius, and with the sympathy of a many-sided culture, he could enter into and reproduce the predominant moods of these various writers in accordance with the special occasion which moved him to write, and with the deepening and refining influence of time on his own nature.

If then we ask which was the predominant vein in him, it would seem natural to look for his gayer feeling in his earlier, and his graver tones in his later work. And this expectation is on the whole realised. But there is something exceptional in the part played by Horace, as at once the idealising lyrical poet of his age, the realistic author of the Satires, and the critic of the later Epistles. The double function of lyrical idealist and satiric realist may have been combined in Archilochus, among the ancients: and there are brilliant examples of the union of lyrical genius with the serious and humorous criticism of life and literature in modern times. But it is difficult to realise that the artistic idealist of the Odes is the same man who wrote the 'Journey to Brundisium' and the 'Banquet of Nasidienus.' Did Horace discover the true vein of his genius only after the age of passion and illusion had gone? This at least is certain; it was only after he had reached middle life that the richest vein of his lyrical genius revealed itself, and that he gained sufficient mastery over his art to express by its means the larger results of his own experience and observation. The Odes of the second and third books, which contain the maturest expression of his mind, belong probably without any exception to the years immediately following the battle of Actium. Several of those included in the first book (e.g. 24, 29, 31 and 37) fall in the same period. But a certain number of them belong to the years before that event, when the poet was still engaged in the composition of the Satires and Epodes; and some of them probably go back to the years immediately following his return to Rome after Philippi. Some (e.g. 4, 7, 28) are in form, though not in spirit, written after the model of Archilochus; and others, from the similarity of their substance, may be assumed to have been the product of the time during which he was engaged in the composition of the Epodes.

In the Odes of the first book there are clearer traces than in the later books of the imitative processes by which Horace formed his art. Thus Odes 9, 14, 18, and 37 all begin with lines translated or closely imitated from Alcaeus. The sixteenth appears to be immediately suggested by the palinode of Stesichorus. In some he seems to be merely reproducing the memories of Greek art and poetry, without associating them with anything in the public or private life of the day. The treatment of his subjects is more artificial and conventional; the tone is lighter and more careless; the substance slighter than in his later Odes. No deeper philosophy of life or higher teaching is found in them than that summed up in the maxim 'carpe diem.' About half of them are more or less connected with the pleasures of love and wine. Only five are inspired by serious interest in national affairs. In the note struck by the words

> Quid Tiridaten terreat, unice
> Securus,

he professes his own exceptional indifference to the public questions of the day; and although such Odes as 2, 12, 14, 35, 37, shew that in a serious crisis of the national fortunes he felt profoundly 'the grief and the alarm' which weighed on the Roman world in the troubled years between the death of Julius Caesar and the capture of Alexandria, yet the dominant note of the book is that indicated in the short Ode with which it concludes —'Persicos odi'—which is intended to relieve the severer strain of the thirty-fifth and thirty-seventh. If the spirit of the Odes is to be judged by the prevailing tone of those contained in the first book, composed for the most part apparently between the years 38 or 37 and 30 B.C., we should think of Horace, as he shows himself before the curtain falls on the first act of his lyrical representation, as the Anacreontic singer of the lighter joys of life—

> sub arta
> Vite bibentem.

Yet even in this book his gaiety is not so light-hearted as it appears. Often it seems to be a mood to which he gives way as a relief from painful memories or anxious forebodings. There is a ground tone of sadness under the graceful gaiety of his Epicurean maxims. He feels not only the inclemency of the times, and the vicissitudes in his own fortunes, but also the 'riddle of the painful earth.' But he early applied to himself and others the lesson expressed at a later time in the lines—

> Laetus in praesens animus, quod ultra est,
> Oderit curare et amara lento
> Temperet risu.

His gaiety is not the gaiety of the man of pleasure, following his natural bent without reflexion, as is that of Ovid and Catullus, but rather that of a man who fought against the melancholy suggestions of the times, of his own fortunes and his own temperament, and was able to rise buoyantly above them.

The dominant tone of the Odes in the second book is reflective and didactic; and the vein of melancholy latent in a few of the Odes of the first book comes out fully in several of those of the second. The Ode by which the book is introduced is the only one which deals with public affairs, and that not with their present, but with their past phase. The civil wars are looked upon as closed, and their tale is regarded as not indeed without elements of glory, but essentially sad and tragical, and still suggestive of forebodings for the future. The book is considerably shorter than either the first or the third book, and in the metres employed he adheres with only one exceptional experiment to the Sapphic, the Alcaic, and one variety of the Asclepiad; the Sapphic being used to express his lighter and happier, the Alcaic his more thoughtful and pensive mood. As in all three books, his gayer interchange with his graver or sadder tones. But in this book the latter predominate. His philosophy is no longer confined to the maxims of enjoyment, but extends to the wise conduct of life, and to the limitation of those desires which disturb its peace. He begins to speak in the tones of a censor, as in 18—'Non ebur neque aureum.' He is more serious and sympathetic in the expression of his personal feeling, as in 3 ('Aequam memento'), 6 ('Septimi Gades'), 9 ('Non semper imbres'), 13 ('Ille et nefasto'), 14 ('Eheu fugaces'), 17 ('Cur me querelis'), 20 ('Non usitata'). To all of these, as well as to 18, the thought of death and what comes after gives their pervading character. The theme is suggested not only by the thought which enters into all his meditations on life, but by danger apparently from failing health or accident threatening his own life, and by anxieties for one whose life was as dear to him as his own. The love poems, by which the prevailing tone of pensive melancholy is relieved, are absolutely free from any trace of personal passion. They are humorous and ironical, and composed in the spirit of one

> Cuius octavum trepidavit aetas
> Claudere lustrum,

and who finds amusement in contemplating the affairs of his younger associates. The general character of the book is marked by greater independence in his art, greater maturity of thought, and a deepening of seriousness in his personal relations and in the feeling with which he contemplates life.

> Non usitata nec tenui ferar
> Penna,

is the self-assertion of a poet who wished himself to be regarded as something more than the 'idle singer of an empty day.'

There is greater maturity of thought and feeling in the Odes of the third book; and still more prominence is given in them to the graver interests of life. He assumes in its opening stanza the office of the priest of the Muses, the prophetic teacher of the new generation. The world has entered on its new life. There are no longer regrets for the past, except in so far as the corruption of the age calls for a remedy. In this book he is, like Virgil, the national and religious poet of Imperial Rome. There is accordingly a severer tone in his moral teaching ('Intactis opulentior,' iii. 24), and a graver and more imaginative utterance of his philosophy of life ('Tyrrhena regum progenies,' iii. 29); yet in all his art, as in his life, he aims at tempering the grave interests of life with its gaiety and charm. In those which express this charm, whether in human and social relations, or in nature (as 7, 13, and 23), there is a purer and more disinterested feeling. He shows not only greater maturity of art, but is conscious of a more powerful inspiration ('Quo me, Bacche, rapis,' iii. 25). He is more proudly conscious of the greatness of his task, and of the success with which he has accomplished it. In his last poem he associates the eternity of his fame (as Virgil does in the ninth Aeneid) with the great symbol of the eternity of Rome—

> dum Capitolium
> Scandet cum tacita virgine pontifex.

The fourth book and the Carmen Seculare were tasks which he was called upon to perform on a great public occasion and in celebration of great victories. The serious and national tone is naturally that which predominates in them. The Odes inspired by public feeling are relieved by others, either the direct expression of personal feeling, or dealing with the old subjects of love and wine; but these are evidently subsidiary to those referring to public events.

The composition of his Odes may therefore be considered as having extended over nearly the whole of his literary career. But it was in the eight or ten years following the battle of Actium, when the national mind was most stirred, and the conditions of his own life were most favourable to lyrical inspiration, that his art was most mature. It is uncertain whether any of the Odes were in any way published at the time of their composition, and if so, what was the mode of their publication. In his Satires he declares his aversion to the practice of public recitation, but he was willing to gratify a select audience

> nobilium scriptorum auditor et ultor.

It is natural to suppose that the Odes addressed to individuals should have been sent to them, and should thus have obtained some currency before they were published collectively. It is possible also that there may have been some partial publication of some collection of his Odes before the completion of the first three books. But the Epilogue, when compared with the Prologue, shows that these three books were finally published as a collective whole, and were so regarded by the poet.

They were so arranged also as to give a different character to each of the three books, and to make them representative of the earlier, middle, and mature period of his lyrical activity. Yet this purpose is modified by his strong determination to avoid harping too long on the same string. Thus some of his slightest pieces, expressive of his most careless moods, are interspersed among the graver utterances of the third book. So, too, whilst the great mass of the Odes in the first book belong to his earliest period, one at least (i. 24), if we can trust the date given by Jerome for the death of Quintilius, must have been composed seven years after the battle of Actium. But there are several about which we can speak with considerable confidence as reflecting the public sentiment during particular phases of the national fortunes, or as representative of the poet's art at different stages of its maturity, and of his personal feelings at different stages of his career.

There is one of these (i. 3) the date of which has excited much controversy; as on the view taken of it depends the view taken of the date of the publication of the three books. Two views are held about this date: one that the poems were not given to the world in their present shape till about the middle of the year 19 B.C.; the other that they appeared some time in 23 B.C. The first opinion rests mainly on the opinion formed as to the occasion of the composition of the Ode, 'Sic te diva potens Cypri.' That Ode is addressed to the ship which was to bear Virgil on his voyage to Athens. We know that Virgil sailed to Athens in the spring of the year 19, and, on his return in September of the same year, died on landing at Brundisium. We know of no other voyage to Greece made or contemplated by him. But we know very little of the events of his life from the time that he retired to Naples about 37 B.C. We hear vaguely that he visited and lived for some time in Sicily; and passages in the third and fourth books of the Aeneid seem to reproduce the impressions of an eye-witness of the scenes there described. There is at least no improbability that Virgil made an earlier voyage to Greece, the impressions of which may perhaps be traced in the account of the voyage of Aeneas among the islands of the Aegean and past the shores of Epirus. If the Ode refers to his last voyage, it must have been composed immediately before the publication of the three books, which must then have taken place in the interval between the departure of Virgil and his death in the following September. The position assigned to it among Odes all referring to the earlier period of Horace's art, would in that case be very remarkable. It is urged that Horace wished to introduce his work to the world with Odes indicative of his relations to Maecenas, Augustus, and the greatest poet of the age. If it was intended to do special honour to Virgil by this juxtaposition, that purpose might have been served by placing there the twenty-fourth Ode, which is a truer tribute to his worth. If the poem were really written after the completion of the Georgics and Aeneid, we should have expected not only an expression of personal affection, but some reference to Virgil's pre-eminence as a poet. Different opinions may be formed as to the relative merits of the poem. It certainly shows imaginative power and concentrated energy of expression. But the thought is conventional and unreal. It is essentially the old theological thought of the sinfulness of human enterprise, to which Hesiod first gave expression, and which Virgil has himself reproduced in the fourth Eclogue—

> Pauca tamen suberunt priscae vestigia fraudis,
> Quae temptare Thetim ratibus, &c.

It is true that even in Horace's maturest art the thought is often obvious and commonplace. But then it is in accordance with fact, and is a comment on real experience. A somewhat similar thought is expressed in iii. 24—

> si neque fervidis
> Pars inclusa caloribus
>   Mundi nec Boreae finitimum latus
> Durataeque solo nives
>   Mercatorem abigunt, horrida callidi
> Vincunt aequora navitae.

There is solidity and reality in the thought that the stimulus to all the enterprise of the time is the passion for luxury. That an event so ordinary as a voyage from Brundisium to Greece should suggest the thought that the wickedness of man will not allow Jove to lay aside his angry thunderbolts, is so little in keeping with the moderation of Horace in the maturest period of his art, that it has been explained as irony. Yet it is still more improbable that in this Ode, bidding god-speed to the friend of whom he speaks as 'animae dimidium meae,' he is rallying him on his timidity.

The lines in ii. 9. 18–24

> et potius nova
> Cantemus Augusti tropaea,

have been thought to refer to the results obtained from the Parthians in the year 20 B.C. But a comparison of the stanza

> Medumque flumen gentibus additum
> Victis minores volvere vertices,
> Intraque praescriptum Gelonos
> Exiguis equitare campis,

with Virgil's description of Caesar's great triumph on his return from the East in 28 B.C. (Aen. viii. 725),

> Hic Lelegas Carasque sagittiferosque Gelonos
> Finxerat; Euphrates ibat iam mollior undis,

renders it much more probable that these lines refer to the events in the East following the capture of Alexandria, which produced a great impression at Rome; and that the poem was written in the year 27 B.C., immediately after Caesar received the title of Augustus. While therefore the evidence afforded in these two Odes does not require the date of publication to be deferred to the year 19 B.C., the evidence of the first book of the Epistles points to the conclusion that that book was given to the world not later than 19 B.C., and that it appeared at some considerable interval of time after the appearance of the Odes. In the first Epistle Horace speaks of himself as having laid aside 'versus et cetera ludicra.' He excuses himself to Maecenas, who wished him to resume his old task, with the plea,

> Non eadem est aetas, non mens.

The reference to Alcaeus in Ep. i. 19—

> Hunc ego non alio dictum prius ore Latinus
> Vulgavi fidicen—

and the following lines, prove that when that Epistle was written the Odes were generally known and criticised. The evidence of the Epistles is thus conclusive against assigning so late a date as 19 B.C. for the publication of the three books of the Odes. The other date generally assigned to the publication is the year 23 B.C., before the death of Marcellus, and the detection of Murena's conspiracy, which event took place in 22 B.C. It is urged with much force that it would have been inconsistent with the tact and good feeling of Horace to have sent forth the stanza

> Crescit occulto velut arbor aevo
> Fama Marcelli,

in which a stress is laid on the connexion of the house of Marcellus with the Imperial family, after the death of the young heir of the Empire had given to that connexion so painful a significance. It might perhaps be urged on the other hand, that it would have been even more marked to have omitted the stanza from an Ode written many years before the event and familiarly known: the stanza would still remain as a record not only of the old connexion formed by the union of Octavia with the father of the young Marcellus, but of the closer connexion created by his marriage with Julia. Still it would be remarkable that the lyrical poet of the Empire should have remained silent on an event which made so profound and lasting an impression on the Roman people[1], and which was lamented not only in the great epic poem of the age, but in the work of a poet almost entirely absorbed in his own passion, if it had occurred before the completion and publication of the three books of the Odes. The Ode iii. 19, in which it is not easy to find any other theme

---

[1] Cf. Tac. Annals, ii. 41: 'Sed suberat occulta formido reputantibus haud prosperum in Druso patre eius favorem vulgi, avunculum eiusdem Marcellum flagrantibus plebis studiis intra iuventam ereptum, breves et infaustos populi Romani amores.'

than that of a festive meeting held in honour of Murena, presents a similar difficulty. If the spirit of that Óde is entirely genial and friendly, it seems hardly possible that Horace would have published it after he knew of the punishment which had overtaken one so nearly connected with his friend and patron Maecenas. The answer given to this by Mr. Verrall is that the spirit is one not of friendly congratulation, but of mocking irony; and he finds the motive not only of that poem, but of the severest utterances and the most elaborate symbolism in the book (Od. iii. 4 and 24), in the painful feeling excited by the career of Murena. The nineteenth Ode is one of those in which Horace expresses himself not directly but dramatically, and this he does with an abruptness and apparent want of continuity to which there is scarcely any parallel. This at least appears, that neither this Ode nor ii. 10, directly addressed to the same person, implies that Horace had any strong personal regard for Murena. He might have still retained both Odes, even after Murena's disgrace and fall, as a record of warnings that had been delivered to him in the time of his prosperity, possibly at the instance of Maecenas himself, and as pointing the moral of a proud heart going before destruction. This we may regard as possible without assigning to the tragedy of Murena anything like the prominence which is given to it by Mr. Verrall. On such a supposition we might assign the publication of the Odes to the year 22, rather than 23. This would admit of that special reference to the riotous disturbance in the year 22, which Mr. Verrall, with his usual acuteness, finds in the lines (iii. 24. 25)

> O quisquis volet impias
>   Caedes et rabiem tollere civicam,
> Si quaeret PATER VRBIVM
>   Subscribi statuis, indomitam audeat
> Refrenare licentiam.

And this date seems to agree with the evidence of Ep. i. 13, in which Horace sends his Odes (*carmina*, not *sermones* or *satiras*) by the hands of Vinius to Augustus. He writes to Vinius, whom he supposes still on his journey, a letter recapitulating the instructions which he had given him at starting. He supposes that he has not yet reached his destination at the time the letter is written, and he urges him to press on.

per clivos, flumina, lamas.

This looks as if the Odes were sent to Augustus while absent from Italy; between the latter part of the year 22 and the latter part of 19 B.C. These considerations are insufficient to fix the date definitely; but they seem to limit it to the year 23 or 22 B.C., with a bias of probability in favour of the latter date.

The date of the Carmen Seculare is fixed for the year 17: the fourth book of the Odes after the year 15. There is a general but not absolute adherence to chronological order in the Odes written in connexion with public events. This chronological order is not necessarily that in which the poems were composed. Thus the second poem of Book i. may have been written after the twelfth, possibly after the thirty-seventh, and yet may be intended to give expression to the feelings of an earlier time.

II.

The first general impression we form of the Odes of Horace is that they are in form and expression the poetry of one who is emphatically an artist and a poet of culture, rather than of strong native inspiration. He does not, like some of the great lyrical poets of modern times, give back to his people their own joys and sorrows in their own language. He speaks through a Greek medium to a class of cultivated men and women, to whom Greek life and Greek art were thoroughly familiar. It was in the Augustan age that the genius of Italy was finally perfected by that union with the genius of Greece, still surviving in her art and literature, which had been becoming more and more close ever since the days of Ennius. And no one, not even Cicero in a previous age, nor Virgil in his own, felt more deeply the spirit of Greek culture than Horace. It had drawn him to Athens in his earliest youth; it had for a time almost induced him to forget his nationality, and, instead of making a new place for himself among the Roman poets, to 'attempt to add one more recruit to the mighty host of Greek bards'— 'magnas Graecorum implere catervas.' In one of the purest utterances of his personal feeling (ii. 6), his heart is touched by Greek associations, and his longing for Tibur and Tarentum seems to gather strength from the memories of their foundation by Greek settlers. But fortunately his national feeling and his common sense were stronger forces in him than his sympathetic culture. His ambition is to make the old art of Lesbos and Ionia live again in Italian measures, associated with the greatness of Rome, the varied beauty of Italy, and the interests of the hour, as Virgil had made the grace of the Sicilian pastoral live again in association with the beauty of his native district, and the vicissitudes of his personal fortunes. As the poet of culture, Horace sets before himself purer models than even Virgil had in his earlier works. He aspires to breathe the fresh air of the morning of Greek creation, and by the inspiration thus derived to glorify the realism of Roman public life and Roman pleasure, and his own relation to the world and to nature. What distinguishes him and Lucretius from all other Roman poets, is that they sought none but the 'integros fontes.' The absolute sincerity of the one, the faultless critical taste of the other, made them equally averse to re-echoing the Alexandrian echoes of a greater time. Yet the culture of the Roman world was more deeply steeped in Alexandrianism in the time of Horace than in that of Lucretius; and though Horace, for the form of his art, for something of his thought and much of his diction, goes back to Homer and the Greek lyric and tragic poets, yet in his use of Greek mythology as a kind of storehouse of romantic adventure, and in his numerous geographical allusions, we see that he is yielding to tastes formed and fostered by Alexandrian learning. But if we compare Horace in these respects with so thorough an Alexandrian as Propertius, we find that it is the personages and the tales of mythology familiar from Homer and Pindar and the Greek tragedians, not the obscurer beings and more artificial fancies of later creation, that live for us again in the Odes, and that his geographical allusions are not introduced as so much dead learning, but give new life to his subject by names which stirred the imagination in his own day with the thought of distant lands, or wild and wandering tribes on the confines of the Empire, or seas, suggestive of the enterprise of the present time and the memories of a more adventurous past.

This is the first impression we get from the Odes. We seem to be living in a kind of renaissance of Greek art and fancy. Perhaps it is a note of his wish to recall into life a Greek ideal, associated with poetry, that he begins his enumeration of the various ambitions of men with the lines 'Sunt quos curriculo pulverem Olympicum,' &c. There was in the age of Augustus a revival corresponding to the romantic revival, and one corresponding to the aesthetic revival of modern times. Virgil and Livy are the purest exponents of the first: Horace in his Odes of the second. But the time was also one of a great living movement, of a great revolution in human affairs, accompanied at first by a great disturbance in men's minds, afterwards by a settled determination of thought and feeling into new lines. It was a time by its sufferings and vicissitudes calculated to stimulate reflexion on the problems, the duties and interests of life. It was a time of great wealth and luxury, in which the refinement of pleasure afforded a piquant attraction to the senses, while the extravagance of luxury afforded an appropriate theme for satire to the moralist.

If Horace lived in imagination in the poetry of the past, he had lived his own life also; in the world of pleasure, and in retirement from the world, in active social intercourse with the men most eminent in literature and society, and in the most confidential intimacy with the man who was then the chief depositary of the secrets of state, and whose position called upon him to study and understand all the forces by which the new empire was consolidated. He felt, more than most poets, the two impulses spoken of by a poet of our own day, one driving him 'to the world without,' and 'one to solitude'; and in his solitude he shaped into artistic form and melody the thoughts and observations which came to him in the actual stir and hurry of life. If in his art and the mere ornament of his art no one is more of a Greek, no one is more essentially Roman in his sympathy with the great characteristics of his race and the dominant feeling of his time. Like Virgil he has an ideal Rome, glorified in his imagination; and of that Rome Augustus gradually becomes the representative. This ideal makes him more vividly conscious of the degeneracy and corruption of the actual Rome, and moves him to assume the function of a censor and reformer, as Lucretius is moved by his vivid consciousness of the difference between the ideal of life possible to man, and its actual condition. The great Roman qualities recognised in all the great representative Roman writers—in Ennius, Lucretius, and Virgil, as in Cicero, Livy, and Tacitus—the imperial feeling, the sense of the majesty of government, the moral fervour and gravity, have found a powerful voice in the light singer of pleasure and amusement. Even in expression he combines in a remarkable degree Roman strength and concentration with Greek grace and subtlety. He has also the special Italian susceptibility to pleasure, to social enjoyment, and to the enjoyment of nature. He has further the strong self-consciousness which gives such an interest to the 'confessions' of Catullus and Ovid. But the consciousness of Horace is more reflective. He not only receives vivid impressions from the world without and from the movement of his own spirit, but he meditates upon them; on the lessons they have to teach, and on the best mode in which they can be artistically represented. He does not, like Lucretius and Virgil, concentrate his thought for years on one great theme, so as to embody in one continuous work of art a great philosophy of nature and human life, or a great representative poem expressive of what Rome and Italy mean for all time; but, with the more mobile temperament of a lyrical poet, he keeps heart, mind, and imagination alive to all that can stir them; and thus in a series of short lyrical pieces, varying in length from two to twenty stanzas, and arranged with the intention of constantly varying their theme, and the mood in which they are to be received, he too has raised a 'monumentum aere perennius,' truly representative of the Augustan age, in its anxieties and alarms, its aspirations and exultations, its new faith and loyalty, its revived religion; in the lesson which its experience teaches, as well as in what was most vivid and piquant in social life, and what there was of purer and more refined enjoyment in the experience of its happiest and most gifted spirits.

It is an unprofitable question to ask whether Horace's true function was to be, what he sometimes is, the serious, national, religious and philosophical· representative of his age; or, as he often is, the ironical and yet not unsympathetic singer of its lighter moods; or the simple poet speaking from his own heart of what gave himself the purest pleasure. But to appreciate him through the whole range of his powers and susceptibilities, we may ask how he fulfils each of these functions. While the arrangement of his poems which he himself adopted must be borne in mind as indicating the artistic impression which he wished to produce, it is necessary to find some other principle of arrangement, so as to estimate fairly his varied gifts as a lyrical poet. Recognising the obvious fact that through all his poetic career he aims both at inspiring and teaching, and also at amusing his generation, that he uses his poetry both as an organ of impersonal feeling and thought, and as the outlet of his own personal experience and his own innermost feelings, we may try to estimate him first in his most serious and most impersonal vein, next in his mirth and gaiety, as the poet who reproduced to his own generation the ἐρωτικά and συμποτικά of Alcaeus, and lastly, as the poet who charms us by the revelation of himself. It is indeed a peculiarity of his art that he always makes us feel the presence of his own personality; but in some poems he is merely the sympathetic onlooker, or his own experience is appealed to as the witness of some impersonal truth; in others the expression of himself is the whole motive of the poem.

III.

In the first division we consider his national, religious, philosophical and ethical poems. Some careless utterances, such as the

> Mitte civiles super urbe curas, &c.

might to some readers suggest a doubt whether he was really deeply interested in the national fortunes, and whether all his expressions of public feeling are not more or less official. But the answer is that the various moods which he expresses are intended to heighten or to relieve one another. He acts on the principle he so well expresses in the words

> neque semper arcum
> Tendit Apollo.

There is a time to feel the strain of public anxiety, and a time to forget that and all other cares in social enjoyment. So, too, private griefs are to be forgotten in sympathy with national triumphs (ii. 9). He has the justest sense of the true proportions of things, and distinguishes sharply between the passing excitement raised by some rumour of distant trouble, and the real crises involving serious danger to the State. But in these, the great crises of the national fortunes, he feels and expresses the spirit which might animate a patriotic statesman, and during all the changing phases of the revolution which he witnessed, he seems to express, in his Odes, the deeper mood of the nation, from the anxiety verging on despair of the years between 40 and 30 B.C., to the deep security that followed it. He shares the patriotic sorrow and anxiety which all except the devotees of a lost cause must have felt during the final struggle between

Caesar and the remnants of the Pompeian faction. He recognises that the one need of the State is reconcilement, and acknowledges that the only ruler who can reconcile the Roman world is the man whose first duty was, as the avenger of Julius Caesar, to crush the remnants of the party for which Horace himself had fought (i. 2)[1]. After the defeat of Sextus and the crushing of Lepidus he finds in Caesar the only saviour of the State from disaster and anarchy, the man who has to do for Rome at that time what the united efforts of many national heroes, royal and republican, patrician and plebeian, had done through all the generations from the founding of Rome till the fall of the Republic (i. 12). At the great crisis of the national fortunes, the feeling of anxiety and self-reproach expressed in the pause before the outbreak of the great conflict between the powers of the West and the East—

> Eheu cicatricum et sceleris pudet
> Fratrumque (i. 35)—

gives way to a stern sense of triumph tempered by a reluctant admiration for the woman who had threatened to bring the Capitol to ruins (i. 37). When a new page seems to be turned over in the history of Rome, and the world is beginning to breathe again in peace, he cannot leave the past without writing a dirge over the civil strife of the thirty years from the consulship of Metellus (ii. 1), in which the sorrow for the national losses—

> Quis non Latino sanguine pinguior
> Campus—

does not restrain his tribute of admiration for the chiefs of the defeated cause—

> Non indecoro pulvere sordidos.

In the tones in which he records the national dishonour—

> auditumque Medis
> Hesperiae sonitum ruinae—

---

[1] 'Caesaris ultor,' seems to be the key-note of the poem.

we seem to find an anticipation of the solemn and dignified pathos of Tacitus.

It is in the remarkable series of Odes at the beginning of Book iii, all written in the Alcaic metre, and, unlike the great mass of poems in the other books, given to the world with no personal address prefixed to them, that he most distinctly comes forward as the poet of Rome and of the restored national life under the conditions of the new Empire. In them, more than any of the others, national is united to religious and ethical feeling. Their movement is grave and powerful. They are no expression of individual feeling, but the voice of the better genius of Rome, addressed to the generation which was entering on the duties of life in an altered world. Though no allusion marks the exact date of their composition[1], they are evidently written in the time of strongest national enthusiasm, between the years 27 and 23 B.C., when the hopes of the new Empire were highest and its aims most ideal, and while Horace himself was in the meridian of his lyrical inspiration. They are written and arranged with a distinct unity of purpose. The first two might be ranked also among the philosophical and ethical Odes, but they differ from such enunciations of his philosophy as that of iii. 29, or from the ethical Odes addressed to individuals, as inculcating, not the attitude towards life or the principles of conduct which best secure individual happiness, but the spirit of contentment and renunciation[2], and the training for public duty, which befit the subjects of the new Empire, in contrast to the struggle for personal aggrandisement and the pursuit of pleasure, characteristic of the last days of the Republic. They suggest also the qualities demanded for the governor of the new Empire—the heroic virtue which is independent of the popular caprice, which rises to Heaven by a way forbidden

---

[1] Unless 'Caelo tonantem' (iii. 5) is to be taken as referring to the dedication of the temple of Jupiter Tonans in 22 B.C.

[2] Cf. the spirit inculcated by Lucretius—

>   parere quietum
> Quam regere imperio res (v. 1127).

to common men, and raises the world along with it—and the virtue of trustworthiness which fitted a man to share in the counsels of the Empire—

> Est et fideli tuta silentio
> Merces[1].

These two Odes are introductory to the more sustained elevation of the third and fourth, in which the central feeling of the age, that which gave solidity and permanence to the new Empire, receives its most elaborate lyrical expression. They are inspired by the same sentiment and the same conviction as the national epic of Virgil. In the often-quoted lines with which the third Ode opens—

> Iustum et tenacem propositi virum—

we recognise no mere Stoical commonplace, but a tribute to the civic virtue and the strength of character which fitted Augustus to be the ruler of the world, and raised him to the level of the heroes of old,—who, themselves of divine origin, had by their services to the world obtained a place in 'the quiet ranks of the gods,'—and especially, of the great national hero and demigod Romulus. Then by the voice of the goddess Juno, the implacable enemy of Troy, he declares the great conquering and governing mission of Rome, in the spirit of Virgil's

> Tu regere imperio populos Romane memento,

and appeals to the Capitol as the symbol of the stability and the universality of her Empire. But he adds a warning, of which the true meaning is probably that suggested by Plüss. In the words

> ne nimium pii
> Rebusque fidentes avitae
> Tecta velint reparare Troiae,

we cannot regard the stern and impressive warning as mere rhetoric; nor can we suppose that Augustus or any one else seriously contemplated the transference of the seat of the Empire

---

[1] Cf. Propertius iii. 9, 34
> Maecenatis erunt vera tropaea fides.

from Rome to the site of ancient Troy, and that Horace was moved to make this patriotic protest against the design. But under the denunciation of any attempt to repair the dwelling of ancestral Troy, he may, without too direct a shock to old associations and sympathies, have wished to declare the impossibility of any return to the old forms of the Republic.

The third Ode inaugurates the new Empire, and assigns to it, as Virgil has throughout the Aeneid, a divine sanction. The fourth Ode completes, also with the aid of religious symbolism, the thought of the sanction on which the new Empire rests. The poem developes the idea of the divine favour and protection bestowed on genius, whether manifested in the art and inspiration of the poet, or in the art of governing men. As Jove with the aid of Pallas and Apollo, Juno and Vulcan (types of intelligence and light, of weight and dignity of character, and of skill exercised with patience and energy) crushed the rebellion of the Giants, so Augustus by wise counsels and the inspiration of genius triumphed over the anarchy and destructive forces, which, in the years that elapsed between the battle of Philippi and the capture of Alexandria, threatened the overthrow of civilisation.

In the fifth and sixth Odes the tone is no longer one of exultation, but of warning and reproof. Though Rome may have before it a future greater than its past, and though the man has appeared in whom her greatness is to be fulfilled, there still remain elements of evil which mar the fulfilment of the national mission. The object of these Odes is to rouse the public conscience to a recognition of these elements of evil, and so to remedy them. The first sign of degeneracy is tame acquiescence in the dishonour clinging to the Roman arms since the defeat of Crassus. The contrast is drawn between the spirit of the present and the spirit of the heroic age of the Republic. History is appealed to, to impress the old ideal of loyalty to duty on the imagination of the present generation. In the last of the series—

> Delicta maiorum immeritus lues—

the deeper source of national decline is traced to the neglect of religion and the corruption of family life. Again the memory of the stronger and nobler past is evoked in the lines

> Non his iuventus orta parentibus, &c.

And as in the former Ode the ideal appealed to is that of devotion to duty, the highest virtue of Rome in her best days, in this it is the ideal of purity and simplicity of life, which Roman writers represent as the special virtue of the Sabellian stock—

> Hanc olim veteres vitam coluere Sabini,
> Hanc Remus et frater, &c. (Georg. ii. 532).

In the twenty-fourth Ode the call is made in still sterner tones for a reformer to restrain and punish the two great evils, luxury and avarice, which Roman moralists regard as the two great causes of national decay. Here for once at least Horace looks on vice with the severity of Tacitus and Juvenal. It should be ranked rather with his ethical than his national Odes, but its motive is interest in the public weal, not in the character or fate of an individual.

The twenty-fifth Ode is one of those in which the poet glorifies his own inspiration; but the motive of the poem is the enthusiasm inspired by the revelation of the apotheosis of the Emperor. By the vividness with which he pictures the supernatural influence under which the Ode is composed, he seems to meet the 'incredulus odi' of the enlightened and sceptical class to which he himself belonged, regarding this new phase of supernaturalism.

The Odes of the fourth book, on the victories of Tiberius and Drusus which secured the communications of Italy with the lands north of the Alps, are Odes of triumph, appealing to the martial pride of the Romans, which since the restoration of the standards by the Parthians had again found a legitimate outlet. It is a tribute also to the greatness of the Emperor. The earlier books are full of vague alarms caused by the threatening attitude of the tribes and nations on the frontier; but now that three lustres had passed since the fall of Alexandria, all the peoples of the furthest East and West, all without the pale of Roman civilisation, had learned to fear and respect the power of Augustus. Two Odes of the same book, the fifth and fifteenth, sum up the glories of his reign, and record the fulfilment of what were only aspirations in the earlier books. The fifth, written as a pendant to the victory of Drusus, records in grave and quiet tones the sense of security which has succeeded to the long strain of anxiety, and the loyal enthusiasm of the people for the ruler to whom they owe the renewed fertility of their fields, the safe pursuit of commerce, the revival of honesty in trade, and of purity in the family. The idyllic picture presented in this Ode is to be looked at along with the contrast in iii. 24. These two Odes give the fullest expression to the moods of national despondency and of national contentment. They each tend to glorify the Emperor and to impress on the world the need of his absolute rule, and its efficacy. The fifteenth Ode, the pendant to the victory of Tiberius over the Rhaeti, might come as the inscription on some monument recording the sum of the whole glories of the reign of Augustus, in war and peace. The last tones we hear in the completed lyrical message of Horace testify to the lays and hymns sung in honour of Augustus as the descendant of Anchises and Venus.

During the twenty years over which the national lyrics of Horace extend, there is a great change in the aspect of the world, and a corresponding change in the public feeling of which Horace is the exponent. In the earlier Odes, Caesar is the hope of the Roman world in its hour of danger and distress. In the Odes of the third book he is the true representative of an ideal Rome, who is called upon, with the aid of Heaven, by the inspiration of his genius and his devotion to duty, to transform the actual Roman world, torn in pieces by civil wars, corrupted by private vices, false to the standard of national honour and manliness, to this new ideal, in which the great qualities of the past should be revived. The feeling expressed in these Odes is genuine and spontaneous. In the Odes of the fourth book the ideal is supposed to be realised; but there is less perhaps of the ring of genuine sincerity in the celebration of its triumph. The tone of the poet is more distinctly imperial than national. It is not Rome that is glorified, but the Emperor and the members of the imperial family. Even past history is pressed into this service, and it is as a glory of the Claudian family that the battle of the Metaurus is celebrated (iv. 4). The adulation which was the bane of the next century begins to be heard in such lines as

> Quo nihil maius meliusve terris
> Fata donavere bonique Divi (iv. 2).

The condition described by Tacitus—'ubi populum annona, *cunctos dulcedine otii pellexit*, insurgere paullatim, munia senatus magistratuum legum in se trahere'—has been already reached; and we understand how naturally that led to the later stage of acquiescence described in the words 'omnes exuta aequalitate jussa principis aspectare, nulla in praesens formidine,' till the suppression of all independence for a generation produces its natural result in the servile adulation of the next reign. Horace and Virgil cannot be cleared of all taint of this adulation. In Horace the 'dulcedo otii' and the desire to make all things pleasant impair his discernment. The publication of the Ars Amandi a few years later, and the career of the two Julias, afford an impressive commentary on the lines

> Nullis polluitur casta domus stupris, &c.

of Ode 5. The sterner picture in iii. 24 is nearer the truth than the vague optimism of the lines

> ordinem
> Rectum evaganti frena licentiae
> Iniecit emovitque culpas
> Et veteres revocavit artes (iv. 15).

The revival there spoken of could only have been a dream produced by the 'dulcedine otii,' which may have charmed the fancy or lulled the conscience of the world, but did not brace it to efforts to realise the ideal. At the best, the fancy shows that the purer aspirations of the Roman people were not as yet altogether extinct.

Horace is in his Odes the poet also of the religious revival which accompanied and was dependent on the revival of national feeling. And this religious revival, which was fostered by the policy and perhaps the personal belief of the Emperor, was partly ceremonial, partly aesthetic. More than at any earlier period the Gods of Rome and Italy became identified with the old Gods of Olympus, and all the associations of art and poetry were applied to reawaken, in the minds of the cultivated classes, the dormant faith in a divine presence in the world. It was in Virgil, brought up in the simpler beliefs and the household pieties of the Cisalpine province, that this revival found its sincerest and most reverential exponent. Horace, by education and by the critical temper of his mind, shared the free-thinking opinions of the cultivated classes in the last age of the Republic. In one of his earliest writings he uses the words of Lucretius to express his own disbelief in any supernatural action in the world. In the thirty-fourth Ode of the first book he gives what can hardly be taken as a serious account of his conversion from this 'insaniens sapientia,' and expresses a vague belief in a God, identified with the abstraction Fortuna which in more than one place he treats as a capricious power and invests with personal attributes. If there had been any real change in the personal convictions of Horace during the twenty years that elapsed between the journey to Brundisium and the composition of the Carmen Seculare, we should have found traces of it in the writings in which he expresses his innermost convictions on human life and conduct—the first book of the Epistles. The actual belief in the living presence of the Jove of the Capitol or the Gods of Olympus, in the efficacy of prayer to the Lares, or in the protection afforded to flocks and fields by the Italian Faunus, could not reassert itself in the mind of one educated in the school which had produced the *De Rerum Natura* of Lucretius, or even the *De Natura Deorum* of Cicero. But even Lucretius, in spite of his stern iconoclasm, could be moved to poetical sympathy with the religious fancies and symbolism which had been perpetuated from the ages of faith, in art, poetry, and external ceremonial. He could recognise a hidden omnipresent power pervading the universe, and could appeal to this power as a present help to his country in danger, and as the inspirer of his verse. Horace's grasp of speculative truth was neither so earnest nor so consistent; he wrote his Odes in an age of strong reaction from the destructive and disorganising forces of the preceding age; and, in this new age, he professed to revive the office of a Greek lyrical poet, one of whose functions was to compose hymns in honour of the Gods, and to tell the tale of their human adventures. It was natural that he should recognise in the religious forms and beliefs of the past a salutary power to heal some of the evils of the present, and also a material by which his lyrical art could move the deeper sympathies and charm the fancy of his contemporaries. Nor need we suppose the feeling, out of which his world of supernatural beings and agencies is recreated, altogether insincere. Though the actual course of his life may be regulated in accordance with the negative conclusions of the understanding, the imagination of a poet like Horace and Lucretius is moved to the recognition of some transcendent power and agency, hidden in the world, and yet sometimes apparent on the surface, which it associates with some concern for the course of nature and human affairs, and even of individual destiny. It is natural for the poet or artist to embody the suggestion of this mysterious feeling, which gives its transcendent quality to his poetry or art, in the forms of traditional belief, into which he breathes new life. If there is much that is artificial and conventional in the part played by the Gods of Olympus and by the fables of mythology in the Odes of Horace—and this is the element in his lyrical poetry which is regarded as most factitious—there is something of a true feeling after the divine and the ideal in these supernatural fancies.

It is in the Odes expressive of national and imperial sentiment, that we seem to find most of real meaning in the religious language of Horace. The analogy between Jove in Heaven and Augustus on earth is often hinted at; and the ground of this analogy is indicated by the emphatic stress laid on the triumph of Jove over the Giants

> Clari Giganteo triumpho (iii. 1).

It is the supremacy of order in the world of nature and human affairs which the imagination of Horace sees personified in that Jove

> Qui terram inertem, qui mare temperat
> Ventosum, et urbes regnaque tristia
> Divosque mortalesque turbas
> Imperio regit unus aequo (iii. 4).

Augustus is regarded as the minister and vicegerent on earth of this supreme power—

> Te minor laetum reget aequus orbem—

and it is on this ground that a divine function is attributed to him. The deification of the Emperor, originating in the superstitious idolatry of the Eastern provinces, thus receives its sanction in the lyrical as in the epic poetry of the age. The old Gods of Olympus are brought back, as in the Aeneid, blending with the lively personal attributes which the poetic fancy of Greece bestowed on them, the statelier characteristics of Roman life—

> Hinc avidus stetit
> Vulcanus, hinc matrona Juno, &c. (iii. 4).

But it is in the Carmen Seculare that the Gods of Rome and Italy appear in their strictly national character. Diana is there the Goddess of the Aventine and Mount Algidus, not, as in an earlier hymn, of Erymanthus and Cragus. Apollo is nearer to the Janus of old Italian worship than to the God of Delos and Patara. The Carmen Seculare is intended to be regarded not as a work of Greek art, but as a national hymn. The only reference to ancient story in it is one suggested not by the Iliad or Greek lyrical poetry, but by the new national poem, the Aeneid. The poem, in its antique prosaic phraseology and the literalness of its tone, presents a striking contrast to an Ode, written in connexion with the same subject, in which Horace in the character of a Greek lyrical poet addresses the same powers and recalls the artistic and poetical associations of the tales of Niobe, Tityos and Achilles. The one, in harmony with the formal utilitarian religion of Rome, clothes itself in language of studied plainness and even quaintness, and moves in verse which has little to satisfy the ear beyond formal correctness and regularity; while the other is bright with the vivid personality of the Gods of Greece, and moves with their nimble and graceful tread. This Ode—'Dive, quem proles Niobaea' (iv. 6)—and the earlier Ode to Mercury (i. 10), might be looked upon as mere imitative pieces unconnected with anything real in the age, did we not remember the aesthetic revival which in that age, as in recent times, accompanied the religious revival. The Odes of Horace in which Gods and Goddesses of Olympus reappear, surrounded with the associations of Greek art and poetry, are expressions of the same movement as led to the adornment of Rome in the Augustan age with Greek temples and statues, and induced Augustus himself, in a work of art still preserved to us, to be represented as blending the attributes of a Roman imperator with those of a Greek demigod[1].

But it is not only with the symbols of Roman belief or with this neo-Hellenic revival that Horace shews his poetical sympathy. Like Virgil and Tibullus he finds a charm in the observances and the beliefs of rustic Paganism. There is one at least of the Odes of Horace which may be called an expression of natural piety, that addressed to the peasant maid or housewife Phidyle (iii. 23), in which the pomp and state of the national ceremonial is contrasted with the humble prayer and simple offerings which ensure protection to vines, crops, and herds in the deadly autumn season. He feels the poetical beauty of the old rural festivals, bringing rest to man and beast, and giving scope to that gay social life in the open air which

[1] Cf. 'Virgil,' p. 19.

is so attractive to the temperament of the nations of Southern Europe—

> Ludit herboso pecus omne campo,
> Cum tibi Nonae redeunt Decembres;
> Festus in pratis vacat otioso
>   Cum bove pagus (iii. 18).

He peoples in fancy the romantic scenery of the valley among the Sabine hills with the presence of beings who lived an immortal life in the older poetry of Greece. He consecrates a pine overhanging his farm-house to Diana as the Goddess of the mountains and the groves (iii. 22). He sees Pan quitting the Arcadian Lycaeus and speeding in the form of the Italian Faunus to the lovely heights of Lucretilis (i. 17); he surprises Bacchus attended by Nymphs and Satyrs among its rocky solitudes, or follows him in rapt enthusiasm along the river banks and through silent woods. It was a great part of the charm which he found in his country life, to feel that it was in scenes like those in which he passed his daily life that the poets whom he loved had found the haunts of Pan, Dionysus, and Artemis, and to see in imagination those divinities coming back to earth to delight in the lonely and beautiful places of Italy, as they had of old in Arcadia and Caria. And it is not only on his fancy that the religious sentiment acts. It acts also on his affections. It deepens his sense of happiness and contentment with his own lot, and of the beauty and dignity of his own calling. In many passages which we cannot treat as merely conventional, he expresses a belief that he is a special object of divine protection, and this favour he attributes to the purifying influence of the love which he bears to the Muses—

> Di me tuentur, Dis pietas mea
> Et Musa cordi est.

Thus, though the Satires, Epistles, and Epodes present Horace to us as a man for whom any other world than that of ordinary experience had no existence, the Odes reveal him as a man moved by the idea of the majesty of Rome to the recognition of an infinite order and majesty supreme in the world, and one whose heart in realising its deepest happiness was not unmoved by natural piety. Through his patriotic sentiment and his love of Nature and poetry, the ironical singer of the lighter joys of life is capable of feeling something of the solemn enthusiasm and reverential piety of Virgil.

But if in certain moods he may seem to share in the religious feelings and beliefs of Virgil, in other moods he is nearer to the attitude of Lucretius. He, too, may claim a rank among philosophical poets, and the attitude towards human life which he maintains depends in a great degree on his philosophical conceptions. The Epistles present him to us rather as a man in search of a philosophical creed than, like Lucretius, the consistent and polemical upholder of a definite one. And it was natural that in his lyrical poetry he should let himself be swayed by conflicting sympathies, and see in opposite theories of life and actual ways of living some side of truth which moved his imagination or stirred his lighter fancy. There is a serious and impassioned side to his philosophy, in which we recognise the countryman of Lucretius, the inheritor of the masculine traditions of Rome. There is another side to it in which we seem to recognise the disciple of Aristippus, and the sympathetic student of Anacreon, Mimnermus and Menander. He was in contact with the life of his age at too many points to reduce it to a formula. As a poet he aims at vividly realising various situations in life; as a moralist he feels that the condition of happiness and consistency of character is to understand rightly each situation, and to meet it as it should be met. His philosophy is based on observation of life, more than on any speculative conception. But as Lucretius under the conception of 'Nature' declares his belief in the omnipotence of law in the world, and Virgil in personifying the Fates implies his belief in the firm decrees of Providence, the thought ever present to the mind of Horace is the uncertainty in human affairs, which he personifies under the name of Fortune, and the limit imposed on all effort and all enjoyment by the inevitable certainty of death, which he personifies as Necessitas. The aspect of irony in human affairs which Lucretius speaks of as the 'vis abdita quaedam[1],' and Tacitus as the 'ludibria rerum humanarum,' presents itself to the imagination of Horace as a personal power—

> Fortuna saevo laeta negotio.

In his conception of man's relation to this power there is an ethical grandeur in which he seems to rise to the level of Lucretius. Two lessons he learns from this aspect of life; the necessity of each man's absolute dependence on himself, and the necessity of limiting his desires. To be master of oneself, and to find happiness in simple pleasures, are the lessons which Horace draws from his philosophy. So far as there is any difference between Lucretius and Horace in the way in which these lessons are apprehended, they seem to come to the former like a new revelation, to the latter like old familiar truths. There is thus more of reverential awe in the tones of Lucretius, more of a stately calm in those of Horace. The sapphic stanza of Horace—

> Non enim gazae neque consularis
> Summovet lictor miseros tumultus
> Mentis et curas laqueata circum
> Tecta volantes (ii..16)—

can express the familiar thought of the impotence of pomp and state to secure peace of mind, with as much grandeur and elevation, if with less passionate vehemence, than the hexameters of Lucretius—

> Re veraque metus hominum curaeque sequaces
> Nec metuunt sonitus armorum nec fera tela (ii. 48).

In another place where Horace treads in the footsteps of Lucretius—

> Linquenda tellus et domus et placens
> Uxor,

---

[1] v. 1233: Usque adeo res humanas vis abdita quaedam
  Opterit, et pulchros fascis saevasque secures
  Proculcare ac ludibrio sibi habere videtur.

which may be compared with

> Iam iam non domus accipiet te laeta neque uxor
> Optima (iii. 892)—

there is a profounder pathos in the older poet, a calmer resignation in the younger. There is an austerer consolation also in Lucretius. He puts aside the fear of death by the power of thought, by the sense of reconcilement with the universal law of Nature. Horace, in one mood, draws from the thought of death the lesson to intensify the enjoyment of the present, almost in the spirit of those whose maxim, 'brevis hic est fructus homullis,' Lucretius treats with such austere scorn. But he approaches Lucretius in such passages as the

> Quod adest memento
> Componere aequus,

in which the same true and serious meaning may be read as in the lines

> Sed quia semper aves quod abest, praesentia temnis
> Imperfecta tibi elapsa est ingrataque vita (iii. 955).

Horace had a more real sympathy with the social and pleasure-loving side of Epicureanism than Lucretius. The sense of man's limitation tends, in Horace, to lower the higher energies of life—

> Quid brevi fortes iaculamur aevo
> Multa?—

while Lucretius holds that life with all its limitations and imperfections still affords sufficient scope 'dignam dis degere vitam.' Yet if we recognise in the philosophy of Lucretius a loftier power of contemplation, and a more austere courage resulting from it, the philosophy of Horace can invest the practical duties and the wise regulation of life with poetic charm and dignity. By being less consistent in his philosophy, Horace is truer to the conditions of human life. He has no rigid rule of logic to apply to the varying circumstances. A vein of natural Stoicism, inherited from the old Sabellian stock, and a sympathetic appreciation of the great practical qualities manifested in the best Roman statesmen and soldiers of all times, temper the Epicureanism natural to his social temper, his poetical tastes, and the pleasure which he found in nature, in human society, in art and poetry. His true ideal is not the Stoic, renouncing all the amenities, nor the Epicurean, renouncing the practical duties of life; not the contemplative thinker, nor the man who achieves success in the world of action, nor the man of pleasure, but the man who can temperately enjoy all the blessings of life and yet be independent of them, who performs public duties with capacity and integrity and yet is free from personal ambition, who is ready if called upon to sacrifice his life for his country and his friends. One of the latest utterances of his philosophy is in the Ode to Lollius, where, after paying a tribute to the supposed rectitude and capacity of the person addressed, he sketches an ideal in which the best qualities of the Epicurean and the Stoic are united to those of the patriot and the man of honour—

> Non possidentem multa vocaveris
> Recte beatum: rectius occupat
> Nomen beati, qui Deorum
> Muneribus sapienter uti
> Duramque callet pauperiem pati
> Peiusque leto flagitium timet,
> Non ille pro caris amicis
> Aut patria timidus perire (iv. 9).

He has that sense of the dignity of human life which is so marked a characteristic of Lucretius and Virgil, of Cicero and Tacitus, but he has a less profound sense of its pathos than either Lucretius or Virgil. With them the pathos of human life is felt in the severance of the ties of family affection; in Horace it is felt in the thought of the eternal banishment of each living individual from the scene of his transitory enjoyment—

> Omnes eodem cogimur, omnium
> Versatur urna serius ocius
> Sors exitura et nos in aeternum
> Exilium impositura cymbae (ii. 3).

Thus Horace represented in his poetry the graver interests of his time—the national sentiment in its most intense and exalted movement, the religious revival both in its national and its artistic significance, the serious thoughts on the conduct of life which the condition of society, the career of individuals, and his own experience and reflexion impressed upon him. Among Roman poets he holds a middle position between Virgil and Lucretius on the one hand, and the elegiac poets and Martial, whose poetry simply aims at giving pleasure, on the other. Horace ranks both among the 'sacri vates,' who interpret the deeper meaning of life, and among the poets who take the transient lights and shadows of their time as the theme of their art. If not the most representative poet of his country, for that title belongs to the author of the Georgics and the Aeneid, he is the most many-sided. It is not necessary to find with Mr. Verrall that his Melpomene is the Muse of Tragedy, to recognise that his great value among the poets of the world consists in the completeness and variety of his representation: and in this completeness and variety is included his capacity of interpreting the tragic element in national history and in the career of individuals, and his sense of whatever in the men of his own age or in the records and supernatural beliefs of the past added dignity and elevation to life, as well as the wit and gaiety with which he has idealised the 'fugitiva gaudia' of a refined society, loving pleasure both from natural temperament and as an escape from anxious cares and painful memories. There is a third function of his lyrical art, in which it becomes his own individual voice, expressing his sympathy with and appreciation of his friends, and giving utterance to what was deepest in his own personal feelings.

IV.

To a large class of his admirers Horace is best known as the Anacreontic singer of the pleasures of love and wine; and it is in the lighter poems dealing with these themes that they would find the truest expression of himself and the purest specimens of his art. The irony with which he sometimes seems to disclaim all higher purpose, and the enduring grace with which he can invest some transient phase of passion or sentiment, or of social gaiety, seem to afford some countenance to this view both of the man and of his art. But it is safer to look for the expression of his most real self in his familiar writings, and in the Odes to recognise him as the sympathetic artist, yielding to various and sometimes opposite moods, as they were fitted to call forth the graver or gayer tones of his lyre. Love and wine were favourite themes of his prototypes, the older Greek lyrical poets, as they have been of some of the greatest lyrical poets of modern times; and Horace, though neither an ardent lover nor an intemperate reveller, had in the memories of his youth and in the sympathetic observation of his maturer years the materials which his fancy could idealise in connexion with both of these subjects.

In his love poems he does not give utterance to the force of his personal passion, as Catullus does in the Lesbia poems, as tradition tells us that Sappho and Alcaeus did, and as Propertius and Tibullus did among his younger contemporaries. It is not in the Odes, but in one or two of the Epodes, that we find traces of personal passion in Horace—

> Cum tu magnorum numen laesura Deorum
> In verba iurabas mea,
> Artius atque hedera procera adstringitur ilex
> Lentis adhaerens brachiis.

The passionate sincerity of these words, uttered 'calida iuventa,' may be contrasted with the light-hearted irony with which he treats a similar experience in one of the most charming of his lighter Odes—

> Ulla si iuris tibi peierati
> Poena, Barine, nocuisset unquam.

The confessions of Horace seem to imply that he was too fickle or too self-possessed a lover ever to have been scathed by any 'grande passion' of which he would care to perpetuate the torment and the rapture as Catullus has done; nor did he ever allow this single feeling to gain such ascendency over him, and so to make the other interests of life indifferent to him, as was the case with Catullus, Propertius, and the other elegiac poets. His poems addressed to his many real or imaginary heroines are artistic studies in which he idealises and invests with the associations of Greek poetry, sometimes his own, but more frequently the lighter and more transient relations of the younger men of his day with the class in Rome who corresponded to the Glycerium or the Thais of Greek comedy. He sees them in the triumph of their dangerous fascination in such poems as

> Quis multa gracilis te puer in rosa (i. 5).
> Lydia, dic, per omnes (i. 8).
> Ulla si iuris tibi peierati (ii. 8).

He appreciates the humorous side which a sentimental affair with one of a lower degree presents to the associates of the lover, as in

> Ne sit ancillae tibi amor pudori (ii. 4).

He tells sympathetically a tale of true love in the 'Quid fles Asterie' (iii. 7), or dramatically varies the often-told story of 'amantium irae amoris integratio' in the 'Donec gratus eram tibi' (iii. 9). He reminds us of the influence of advancing years on the warmth of his feelings—

> Lenit albescens animos capillus;

and though he sometimes speaks of himself as burning with jealousy, he makes us think of him rather, to use his own words, as

> vacui, sive quid urimur
> Non praeter solitum leves,

singing the praises of Lalage in his Sabine wood, entertaining the accomplished Tyndaris in the beautiful valley crowned by Lucretilis, bidding a fatherly farewell to Galatea before she sails across the Adriatic—

> Sis licet felix ubicumque mavis,
> Et memor nostri, Galatea, vivas (iii. 27)—

or inviting Phyllis, the latest of all his loves, to come to his country house and entertain him with her music. It is not likely that these poems are mere literary studies dealing with purely imaginary situations and personages, nor that on the other hand they are a literal reproduction of actual circumstances. They are rather idyllic pictures suggested by or combined out of the ordinary experience of the time. So far as these heroines of Horace's Odes appear in his representation, they might be supposed to be refined and accomplished ladies leading a somewhat independent but quite decorous life. They appear to be well read in Greek poetry, and accomplished musicians. In addressing them he uses the stories of the Greek mythology as a literature of romance, as Ovid did later in the Heroides. Thus in the Galatea Ode he tells very charmingly the adventure of Europa—

> Nuper in pratis studiosa florum—

and in the 'Quid fles Asterie,' it is said of the agent who passes between Chloe and Gyges,

> peccare docentes
> Fallax historias movet.

In all of these poems he aims at introducing an ideal of Greek refinement and romance into the realism of Roman pleasure. But we have no pictures of Roman family life like that in the Epithalamium of Catullus—

> Torquatus volo parvulus—

nor do we find any noble picture of a Roman matron, like the Cornelia of Propertius. In general we find the lighter, brighter and more decorous phases of the love affairs and the life of pleasure of the time. Yet he reminds us also of the coarser and more reckless aspect of these affairs in the introduction of the 'Damalis multi meri' at the revels of young men, and he does not shrink, in two or three of his least agreeable Odes, from shewing us the other side of the picture—the hideousness of what remains of this life of pleasure after the charm of youth has passed. If we believed the motive of such Odes as i. 25,

iv. 13, to be bitter and vindictive, such a belief would seriously diminish the estimate we form both of the heart and of the taste of Horace. But we may look upon them rather as completing the artistic representation of this phase of life, shewing the life of pleasure in its decay as in its idyllic grace. And as all his representation seems intended also to point a moral, so the poems i. 25, iii. 15, iv. 13, impress the lesson which he applies to himself in the Epistles, that if there is a time when he can say 'non lusisse pudet,' the time also comes when it is imperative 'incidere ludum.'

Of all the poets of love, ancient or modern, Horace is perhaps the least serious. He is less serious even than Ovid, who at least in the Heroides shews occasionally a juster appreciation of the tenderness and constancy of a woman's heart. The tone of Horace is more that of persiflage than of either ardent passion or tender sentiment. He paints the piquant attraction of coyness or inconstancy, of waywardness or cruelty, in his Chloe or Pyrrha, his Glycera or Barine, but he regards the influence of woman, at the best, as ministering to the refined amusement of a man's lighter hours. He may sigh for the lot of those

>   Quos irrupta tenet copula, nec malis
>   Divulsus querimoniis
>   Suprema citius solvet amor die,

but he had soon for himself learned to lay aside the

>   Spes animi credula mutui.

We seldom if ever come upon that feeling of the union of heart with heart which is the secret of the charm of the 'Acmen Septimius suos amores' of Catullus. His song is nearer his own ironical description of it—

>   nos proelia virginum
>   Sectis in iuvenes unguibus acrium
>   Cantamus vacui.

Phrases here and there, such as

>   Nec tinctus viola pallor amantium,

or

>   Dum flagrantia detorquet ad oscula
>   Cervicem aut facili saevitia negat,

shew that he could note the signs of more powerful passion, but it did not come within the carefully meditated scope of his lyrical art to attempt any rivalry with Sappho or Catullus in a sphere in which they were unapproachable. His remonstrances with his brother poets, Tibullus and Valgius, imply a feeling that there is something unmanly in the complaints of lovers over the loss of the object of their affection through either inconstancy or death. It is especially in the treatment of this sentiment that the peculiar irony of Horace is shewn, and his frequent declaration that love is the one appropriate theme of his Muse might seem intended to disguise the prominence he elsewhere gives to the didactic office which his Muse fulfils or to her function in awaking national sentiment.

He is apparently more sincere in his praises of wine, though on this subject also we have to remember that he is following the example of the oldest lyric poets—

> Musa dedit fidibus Divos puerosque Deorum,
> Et pugilem victorem et equum certamine primum
> Et iuvenum curas et libera vina referre (A. P. 83–5).

The opening words of three of the poems in Book i—

> Vides, ut alta stet nive candidum
> Soracte—
> Nullam, Vare, sacra vite prius severis arborem—
> Nunc est bibendum, nunc pede libero—

remind us that in his praises of wine he was the artistic imitator of Alcaeus. But he writes also as a man to whom in his youth the pleasures of comradeship had been enhanced by wine—

> Cum quo morantem saepe diem mero
> Fregi coronatus nitentes
> Malobathro Syrio capillos (ii. 7)—

and who in his maturer years had no greater enjoyment than that of 'honest talk and wholesome wine' with an old friend, or with some of the intellectual leaders of the time. In his earlier poems on the subject—such as Epode 13, Odes i. 7, 9, 18, written probably in the time between the battle of Philippi and his subsequent prosperity—he celebrates wine as the alleviator of care and hardship—

> Quis post vina gravem militiam aut pauperiem crepat?

He brings out its soothing and cheering influence in contrast with the inclemency of Nature and of fortune, of which wild storms and the severity of wintry weather are the emblems. In later Odes written in his more prosperous days, he associates the pleasures of wine with other features of outward Nature, with the hospitable shade of the vast pine and the pale poplar, and with the brook fretting and hurrying along its winding channel in which the hot Falernian may be cooled (ii. 3). It is associated also with those peculiarly Roman tastes, the love of flowers worn as wreaths, and of perfumes. But he especially values the power of wine as breaking down the barriers to frank and friendly companionship, and as the promoter of good conversation—

> Tu lene tormentum ingenio admoves
> Plerumque duro; tu sapientium
>   Curas et arcanum iocoso
>   Consilium retegis Lyaeo (iii. 21).

On rare occasions of special festivity he may go beyond these more tranquil pleasures; and can say in his own name

> recepto
> Dulce mihi furere est amico (ii. 7),

or describe with Bacchanalian licence the revel to celebrate the bestowal of the augurate on Murena, or the return of Plotius Numida from Spain. But it is chiefly as enhancing the refined enjoyment of social life that he praises wine. He impresses on his friends the need that the Graces should be present at the feast, and make it a scene of harmony instead of brawling and discord. He reminds us also of a more subtle danger of intemperate revels—of the self-assertion, vanity, and boastfulness, the breaches of honour and reticence which are their accompaniment—

> quae subsequitur caecus amor sui
> Et tollens vacuum plus nimio gloria verticem
> Arcanique fides prodiga perlucidior vitro.

In his convivial songs, as in his love poems, Horace shews us everywhere the cool head judging the value of and assigning limits to the indulgence claimed by the genial temperament. He permits the freer indulgence of youth, though he would have that too regulated by good taste and cordial feeling, and while he appreciates the enhancement which wine could give to the more intellectual pleasure of the conversation of Maecenas or Messalla, he feels that it is only on rare occasions that this enhancement should be sought, and that the secret of such enjoyment consists in the simplicity of the daily life—

> Premant Calena falce quibus dedit
> Fortuna vitem—
>   —me pascunt olivae,
> Me cichorea levesque malvae (i. 31).

V.

In most of the Odes of Horace his own personality and his personal relations to many contemporaries are distinctly present. In his various writings, Satires, Epistles, and Odes, he seems to speak as an individual either opening his own mind to another individual, or winding into his confidence and extracting from him his secret by the force of personal sympathy. Many of his Odes, and especially those containing his maxims for the conduct of life, are of the same character as his Epistles; some of them addressed to men of social eminence, with whom his relations are more distant, others to men united to him by varying degrees of intimacy and affection. Some of these must have had more meaning for his contemporaries than they have for us. Some may have contained hints or warnings, or references to circumstances which with our limited knowledge of contemporary history cannot be fully ascertained. Horace shared the confidence of Maecenas. It was the special business of Maecenas to understand the characters of the leading members of society, and his position required him to exercise a constant vigilance over them, and to restrain ambitious designs in the quietest way. Thus, in what seem mere Odes of compliment to

Sestius, Munatius Plancus, Dellius, and others, it may be observed how an Epicurean acquiescence with the existing state of things is insinuated, and how they and others of their class are called upon to enjoy the wealth and high position which were still left to them. There is thus probably some political motive behind the exhortations to rich men to enjoy their riches. What is known of Licinius Murena leaves little doubt that the 'Rectius vives, Licini,' (ii. 10) was meant not only to inculcate the maxims of moderation, but to convey a warning; and the parallel pointed out by Mr. Verrall between the language and illustration of that Ode and Seneca's quotation from the 'Prometheus' of Maecenas would justify the opinion that the subject was one which Horace and Maecenas had discussed together. So in the Ode to Sallustius Crispus on the right use of wealth, we have to remember that it is addressed to one of the richest men of the day, and Mr. Verrall's remark perhaps applies to it, that it was a necessity of the Empire that these men should contribute to the needs of the State. Odes addressed to other members of the wealthy aristocracy, or favourites of the Court, such as Torquatus, Lollius, Censorinus, and men of more real distinction, such as Agrippa, Pollio, and Messalla, indicate the relation in which Horace stood to the great world. It was a source of pride to him that the rich man courted his society—

> pauperemque dives
> Me petit—

and that eminent men appreciated the compliment of having their names associated with his lyrical poetry. But if his Muse became something of a courtier, we have only to compare the way in which she plays that part in Statius and Martial with her attitude in the Odes of Horace, to feel how well he combined tact and urbanity with dignity and independence. If the deference which Horace pays to social distinction is to be condemned, he shares the reproach with one esteemed among the simplest and manliest of men of letters, Sir Walter Scott. Both lived at a time and in a state in which great stress was laid on such distinctions of rank. They might have rebelled against them, or kept themselves apart from the world in which they were encountered; they accepted them for what they were worth, neither envying them nor sacrificing their own natural life to them, but paying to them the outward deference which the usages of society made customary, and appreciating and profiting by whatever distinction of manner and dignity of character accompany such conditions. Horace uses his lyrical art to dignify and to warn the members of the aristocracy of the new Empire. He does not address them in the tones of an inferior towards a superior; but rather as Lucretius addresses Memmius, with the superiority of a wiser man, tempered by the urbanity of one who avoids making his superiority too apparent. Much of the personal influence exercised by Horace over modern readers is the influence of social manner; and it is in these personal addresses that the influence of his manner is perpetuated. There was no quality more cultivated by the Romans than urbanity, and the type of that quality in their literature is Horace himself. In his intercourse with the world, he studied to conform to its ways and to lay aside 'inhumanae senium Camenae.' On comparing him with Martial and Juvenal, we seem to apprehend some survival of the great and simple manner from the age of Scipio and Laelius to the men of finest culture, literary and social, of a later time.

But he understood too the wide difference between the courtesy imposed by this social relation, and his cordial bearing towards the friends of his choice; and it is in the Odes addressed to these that we feel most his social attraction. There is not, indeed, in the poems dedicated to friendship, the spontaneous expression of feeling in perfect forms of apparently unstudied art, such as there is in the poems of Catullus to Verannius and Licinius Calvus. Few poets have combined the warmth of heart and keen delight in friendship with the power of direct and simple expression given to Catullus. Horace wrote his Odes in middle life, when, though friendship is as firm, it is not so ardent as in early youth. He exercises more restraint in the expression of his feelings. His single friendship for Maecenas, like that of Cicero for Atticus, tended perhaps to make his other friendships less absorbing. He, however, like Cicero, was a man of largely diffused kindliness. In the poems addressed by him to Virgil, to Aelius Lamia, to Aristius Fuscus, to Septimius, to Pompeius, some shade of expression distinguishes the various modes of affection by which he was moved—a feeling of reverence for Virgil as one cherished in the inmost sanctuary of his heart; love for Lamia as one whose lighter and deeper joys he shared, as he shares in the Epistles his deeper sorrows; a confidence in the sympathy of Aristius Fuscus with the deeper intuitions of his meditative moods, as well as with his more playful fancies; towards Septimius a tender clinging in his own hour of anxiety and failing health—

> ibi tu calentem
> Debita sparges lacrima favillam
> Vatis amici—

to Pompeius the cordiality towards an old comrade with whom he had shared the pleasures as well as the hardships of the campaign under Brutus. Many of the friends to whom the Odes are dedicated appear again in the Satires and Epistles, and we seem from the terms of friendly raillery or discriminating appreciation applied to them to be able to reanimate that friendly circle of lively and cultivated men. With several of them—Aristius Fuscus, Valgius, Tibullus, Iccius—he was united by the bond of literary sympathy; and, as we learn from the Epistles, to some of them he was, as Cicero was to many of his correspondents, active in kindly offices. The clue to some of the lighter Odes addressed to his personal friends—e.g. 'Aeli vetusto nobilis ab Lamo' (iii. 17)—has been lost. Some slight occasion calls them forth; some slight verbal allusion would speak to the men of his circle of what is unintelligible to us. Yet such instances are rare; and, generally speaking, we learn from these Odes how frank and intimate the relations of Horace were to the men of culture in his time, and how largely these friendships contributed to the wisdom and happiness which he realised in life.

Yet, after all, it is not in the expression of his friendship, not even of his friendship for Maecenas, that Horace seems to speak most immediately from his heart. If we ask what was the secret of his deepest happiness, the answer which his Odes supply is that it was in his love of his Sabine farm and other favourite spots in Italy, and in the consciousness of inspiration and the practice of his art associated with them. It is in these themes that we find the purest expression of his personal feeling. The Satires and Epistles enable us to understand the actual happiness which he found in his Sabine retreat on the banks of the Digentia. In the Odes this valley becomes familiar to us, glorified by peaceful images of love and poetry, by the bright fancies of Greek mythology and the festive observances of the religion of Italy. He contrasts the peaceful life in this 'reducta valle,' not only with the smoke and wealth and bustling business, but with the violent pleasures and excitements of Rome :—

> nec Semeleius
> Cum Marte confundet Thyoneus
> Proelia.

It is in his lonely wanderings among its heights and woods that he is conscious of a more powerful inspiration: and it is there that he has a sense of peace and divine protection, arising from a consciousness of a heart free from guile or guilt. The idealising magic of his poetry, evoked by the pure affections of his heart, has added the names of Mount Lucretilis and the spring Bandusia to the names of Helicon and Parnassus, of Castalia and Aganippe, as consecrated to the genius of poetry. The rude mirth, on the festival of Faunus, of peasants who worked his fields, still lives in the

> Faune nympharum fugientum amator (iii. 18).

The source of his deepest contentment with his lot, of his

moral strength, and of his least artificial poetry, is to be sought in the

> Purae rivus aquae silvaque iugerum
> Paucorum (iii. 16),

the soothing and restorative power of which imparts something of an idyllic grace to the common sense of the Satires and Epistles, as well as to the purer inspiration of the Odes.

Besides the streams, mountains, and woods of the district of Mandela, the woods and waters around Tibur are associated for ever with the poetry of Horace. In one of the earliest of his Odes, written probably before he had received the gift of his Sabine farm, while still fresh from his travels in Greece and Asia Minor, he declares his preference for Tibur, with its varied beauty of grove and orchard, streams and waterfall, over the famous and beautiful cities and scenes of those favoured lands. In an Ode (ii. 6) in which he speaks most from his heart, written when weary and in weak health, and under some apprehension of the near approach of death, he expresses the wish that he might find at Tibur a place for his 'age to wear away in.' And again, in the last book of his Odes, it is around the groves and streams of Tibur that he describes himself as like the Matine bee, gathering honey industriously from the pleasant banks of thyme; and it is to the influence of the streams and thick foliage around Tibur that he ascribes the moulding of his lyrical faculty—

> Sed quae Tibur aquae fertile praefluunt
> Et spissae nemorum comae
> Fingent Aeolio carmine nobilem (iv. 3).

In Horace, the feeling inspired by Nature is not the contemplative enthusiasm of Lucretius, nor the sympathy with her manifold life which moved the poet of the Georgics, but rather the love for particular places—that which Cicero had for his 'ocelli Italiae'—as places of refuge from the distractions and pleasures of the city, as fosterers of meditation, and as giving a living impulse to his genius. Cicero finds in his country places the statesman's, Horace the poet's *otium*. The love of Nature in Horace is idyllic, not contemplative. He has in the highest degree the power of presenting distinct pictures of her various features to the imagination, and of marking the most characteristic signs of the various seasons. We seem, as we follow his guidance, to look on Soracte standing forth in his white robe, and the woods weighed down by snow, and the frozen streams; to feel the breezes of early spring rustling through the leaves, and filling the sails of the ships released from the inaction of winter; to see the silent river bank, in the heat of summer, unstirred by any wandering wind, and to mark the deeper hue of the ripening grape under the influence of autumn,

> Purpureo varius colore.

But it was in the living impulse given to his genius that he drew the chief nourishment from Nature. For it was in the consciousness and the active exercise of his genius that Horace, like Lucretius and Virgil, found his chief enjoyment. It was in living his highest life, keeping alive his purest susceptibilities of feeling, and shaping into artistic form the thoughts and images which Nature and meditation brought to him, that he was most truly himself. It is the consciousness of his inspiration, and the consciousness that he has done justice to his gift, that gave him his sense of distinction and of superiority to the more vulgar forms of ambition. One of his earliest expressions of personal feeling is in his prayer to Apollo at the dedication of his temple—

> nec turpem senectam
> Degere nec cithara carentem (i. 31).

One of his latest is his tribute of gratitude to the Muse for this gift of inspiration, and for the pleasure which through it he gave to the world—

> Quod spiro et placeo, si placeo, tuum est (iv. 3).

His absolute confidence in the immortality of his song deepens with the sense of his growth in power and with the greater seriousness of his art. In one of his earlier Odes (i. 32), in which he regards himself as a singer of the lighter pleasures of life—'lusimus'—he expresses the hope that his work might survive for some few years. At the end of the second book, under the figure of his change into a swan, he predicts his survival after death, and the wide diffusion of his fame and influence—

> Me Colchus et qui dissimulat metum
> Marsae cohortis Dacus et ultimi
>   Noscent Geloni, me peritus
>   Discet Hiber Rhodanique potor.

But it is not till the 'monumentum aere perennius' is completed by the great Odes of the third book, that he confidently proclaims the permanence of his work in words that are at this day fully realised—

> usque ego postera
> Crescam laude recens.

In his latest book he claims a place among the immortals with Pindar and Simonides, Alcaeus and Stesichorus, Sappho and Anacreon. So, too, he claims not only immortality for the poet, but the power of conferring immortality—

> Caelo Musa beat (iv. 8).

And this sense of living in the memory of future generations was to the Romans a reality. If the immediate motive to Horace to conquer his natural indolence and devote the best energies of the best years of his manhood to the perfecting of his art, was the 'sweet love of the Muses' which he shared with Lucretius and Virgil, his own words leave no doubt that the hope of living, as he has lived, in the life of future ages and among the future inheritors of civilisation who were then beyond its pale, was an elevating and sustaining influence in his life.

VI

Though neither by his practice nor his criticism does he proclaim himself one of those who value form above substance, yet it is to his careful art, as much as to the 'ingeni benigna vena,' that he owes his immortality. Each single Ode is, in itself, a work of art, producing a unity of impression, and, by its position, contributing to the complete and complex impression of the whole collection as an imaginative and artistic embodiment of the spirit of the age, and of the finer moments in the poet's life. In some Odes he expresses his own feelings and thoughts directly; in others in the form of a personal address, invitation, warning, or remonstrance; in others he describes some situation dramatically, allowing it to suggest its own story and its own lesson. In general, metre, diction, thought, imagery are so used as to convey and perpetuate various moods, happy or melancholy, light or elevated, through which a mind, in a high degree sensitive, but essentially sane and just, has passed, under various conditions of national and personal experience. He eliminates all that is alien from the real meaning of the situation, so as to leave only what has a universal and permanent significance. It would be too much to say that all the poems are equally perfect in form, for some of the Odes in Book i. (e. g. 7 and 28) suggest the inference that that improvement in concentration of effect and definiteness of purpose which the Odes shew in comparison with the Epodes, was not accomplished without much of the 'limae labor.' Whatever defects in form there may be among the later Odes seem to arise from excessive concentration. The transitions from one thought to another, or from one act in the drama to another, are too rapid and abrupt to be clearly intelligible. Instances of this kind of obscurity may be seen in the concluding stanzas of iii. 2, and in the account (iii. 19) of the revel held in celebration of the bestowal of the augurate on Murena. That poem may have the meaning which Mr. Verrall attributes to it, but it does not explain itself with the clearness of the drama where Asterie and Gyges, Chloe and Enipeus, play their part, in the light stanzas beginning 'Quid fles, Asterie.' Sometimes a seeming confusion in the thought or in the expression of it mars the harmonious development of the ideas, as in the sixth and seventh stanzas of i. 35—

> Te Spes et albo rara Fides colit
> Velata panno, etc.

But, generally speaking, the mastery of form was attained by him before the mastery over his materials, and that maturity of mind which ultimately made the graver predominate over the lighter products of his art. In the first book, it is in the poems of the simplest texture, in which a single thought or situation is presented, that we feel most the perfection of form, as in 5, 9, 14, 17, 31, 32. As he advances in his art, he still shews his consummate skill in expressing his mood of mind, or presenting some single phase of human life or nature to the imagination in a few stanzas, in which reflexion scarcely mingles with the pure or sparkling current of his feeling or fancy, as in ii. 6, 8, iii. 7, 9, 13, 18, iv. 3. But, at the same time, he has learned to combine thoughts, symbolism, and narrative into more complex harmonies, as in the first six Odes of Book iii. and the fourth and fourteenth of Book iv; to work some appropriate tale from Greek mythology into lines of kindly warning addressed to one of the heroines of his fancy; to express his philosophy of life in Odes of sustained dignity, as ii. 16, iii. 16, 29; or to utter the whole burden of the sins of the age in lines of continuous rebuke, each of which singly is incisive like the note of a Censor, as in iii. 24. In both the longer and the shorter poems, the fact or situation which gives rise to the poem is presented in the opening lines; then the feeling rises as it approaches the central fact or thought; and then for the most part dies away in lines that, while calming the emotion, deepen the impression of the whole; as, for instance, the majesty of the speech and bearing of Regulus gains a deeper impressiveness from the contrast suggested by the quiet ending—

> Tendens Venafranos in agros
> Aut Lacedaemonium Tarentum (iii. 5)[1].

The special excellence of the lyrical art of Horace is his mastery over his various metres, and his adaptation of them to express his various moods. The single word of recognition which his lyrical genius receives from any contemporary is the epithet 'numerosus,' applied to him by Ovid. His own claim to recognition is on the ground that he has made the music of the old lyrical metres of Greece live in the language of Italy. His first attempt to do this was in reproducing the recurring chime of the Parian iambics, which fitted the incisiveness and terseness of the Latin language, and proved itself an adequate vehicle for the biting satire of Italy and the sententiousness of the Roman mind. In the Epodes he makes experiments in other combinations of recurring lines, their characteristic being that the sense is generally completed in the couplet. In the first nine Odes of Book i, which are so arranged as to give specimens of all the most important metres, four are in couplets, four in stanzas of four lines of different structure, and one is composed in a verse of uniform structure, so arranged as generally to fall into strophes of four lines. Of the first class of metres, in which the couplet is used, only one—the third Asclepiad—was finally adopted by him as one of his regular metres, and it is so employed that two couplets are grouped together into one stanza; so that generally it may be said that the metres of the Odes are arranged in stanzas of four lines of limited variety of structure, in conformity with strict metrical laws. In the structure of each line and stanza, and in the tendency to complete the sense within the stanza, we recognise the distinction between the weighty and regular movement of the Latin language and the rapidity and free range of the Greek. By the recognition of this distinction Horace adapts the Aeolian melody

---

[1] This characteristic of the art of Horace is well brought out by Mr. Wickham in his notes on the Odes.

to the Latin tongue. Of the various metres which he adopted, five were found best suited to his purpose—The Sapphic, the Alcaic, and three varieties of the Asclepiad.

In the Sapphic, in which the trochee and the dactyl are the predominating feet, he brings out a light, graceful, and rapid movement, expressive either of gay or serious animation of feeling. Thus, in the 'Ne sit ancillae' and the 'Ulla si iuris tibi peierati,' the metre is the vehicle of his sprightliest raillery. In the 'Integer vitae' and the 'Septimi Gades,' it presents a transcript of the poet's mind in cheerful animation, or in the alternation between quiet hopefulness and pensive resignation. It moves with a stately and animated tread in the 'Otium divos' and in various poems as i. 2 and 12, which have the character of national hymns; while in iii. 11 and 27, it accompanies lively narrative used in connexion with a lively personal address. As an instrument of buoyant feeling, expressing itself by means of vivid and rapidly changing imagery, no Latin metre equals the Glyconics of Catullus; but that metre is not capable of the varied and more stately and concentrated effects of the Sapphics of Horace.

In the Alcaic, which he places last among the early specimens of the metres chiefly employed, as he places the Sapphic first, the power and impetus first imparted to it by its inventor are tempered by a weight and dignity of movement more accordant with the genius of the language, and the sustained elevation of feeling, the continuous volume of thought, action, and imagery, which it is generally used to convey. Perhaps Horace did not at first find out the true power and function of this metre. In the first book, the Sapphic is the metre employed in the earlier poems of national feeling, and it is only near the end of the book that he employs the Alcaic for sustained, powerful, and impassioned feeling. In the 'Vides ut alta,' the 'Velox amoenum saepe Lucretilem,' the 'Musis amicus,' the 'Quid dedicatum poscit Apollinem,' and others, he employs it on themes which did not call for the swelling and culminating effects which it produces in iii. 3, 4, 5, 6, iv. 4, 14, or the complex variations of iii.

29, or the dirgelike solemnity of 'Eheu fugaces,' and such stanzas as 'Quis non Latino sanguine pinguior' and 'Omnes eodem cogimur.' It is in the Odes of the second book that he first associates it with the grave or solemn movement of his spirit; yet to the end, whether from the desire to shew the versatility of his instrument, or to avoid the impression of monotony of effect, he from time to time, as in 'O nate mecum consule Manlio' and 'Vixi puellis nuper idoneus,' reverts to the practice of its inventor, who, 'amid the respites from battle or the perils of shipwreck, sang of Bacchus and the Muses, of Venus and the boy who never leaves her side, and of the beauty of the dark eyes and dark locks of Lycus.'

In short Odes characterised by Greek grace and subtlety of feeling and observation rather than Roman dignity and elevation, or Italian sprightliness and animation, there is no metre which he employs with more charm than the combination of two Asclepiads with one Pherecratean and one Glyconic, generally called the fifth Asclepiad. The mood expressed in it may be sombre or bright, but it is one that comes and passes more lightly than that expressed either in the Alcaic stanza or in other combinations of the Asclepiad. The Pherecratean, following on the two longer lines, breaks the monotony of mood, while the light and rapid Glyconic at the end of the stanza seems to allow the mood to pass away, leaving no feeling of satiety, but either a happy memory, or a blending of buoyant hopefulness with some feeling of regret or alarm over which the mind does not care to brood. Among the happiest applications of this metre are the 'Quis multa gracilis,' the 'O navis referent in mare te novi,' the 'O fons Bandusiae,' and the 'Quid fles, Asterie,'—all among the most perfect in form of the shorter pieces of Horace. In the first, the mood expressed is that of a light regret lightly passing and losing itself in the artistic pleasure of looking on a graceful and piquant picture. In the second the regret is deeper, and the thought accompanying it is graver, but it is one on which the poet will not let his fancy dwell, and the buoyancy of the metre suggests the hope that the ship which the poet is watching with alarm and anxiety, will avoid the 'dangerous seas among the shining Cyclades.' In 'O fons Bandusiae,' he has arrested and perpetuated the joy of a happy hour spent among the Sabine hills, looking on and listening to the clear waters of Bandusia, springing from the ilex-crowned rock, and hurrying to join the larger stream of the Digentia; while the picture is completed by the graceful life of the young kid

> cui frons turgida cornibus
> Primis et Venerem et proelia destinat.

In 'Quid fles, Asterie,' the metre tells a love story, full of life and graceful movement, in the fewest possible words. The mood is that of passing trouble and anxiety, but with the light of hope and ultimate happiness breaking through and banishing the clouds. It is also, as in the 'Quis multa gracilis,' the mood of a disinterested spectator, in whom the drama passing before his imagination rather stimulates a sympathetic curiosity than arouses any deeper emotion. To the 'Vitas hinnuleo me similis, Chloe,' a sense of the young life of spring is imparted, in accord with the young life of the person addressed; but the tone of the Ode shews that in the transient interest with which Chloe inspires him, the poet is 'non praeter solitum levis,' and that while his fancy is charmed his heart is untouched. There is a similar buoyancy of feeling in the hymn to Diana (i. 21) as the goddess of streams, groves, and mountains, and the concluding stanza— 'Hic bellum lacrimosum'—suggests the passing away of the cloud of foreboding which may have given occasion to the hymn, if, as is probable, it was sung on some public occasion. It is perhaps a matter of regret that he should once have associated this, the most graceful and charming of his metres, with the least pleasing of all the subjects of his art, in 'Audivere, Lyce.' But as, in the most conventional of his Odes, there is always some touch of nature which keeps them alive, so, in the least pleasing of his poems, in those of which the general effect is repulsive, there are images of grace and beauty. And so in the lines—

> quid habes illius, illius,
> Quae spirabat amores,
> Quae me surpuerat mihi,
> Felix post Cinaram, notaque et artium
> Grataram facies?—

there lives a feeling of regret for the spell once exercised over him, in contrast to the indifference with which he now can contemplate the 'dilapsam in cineres facem.' Rapid transition is the note of the poem, the change from vehement passion to vehement scorn. The graceful beauty of the past forces on the mind the thought of the hideousness of the present, but he does not care to dwell on the thought. The object of this invective passes from his mind, as she passes from the sphere of her fascination. But he proves the metre an apt instrument for the vein of Archilochian mockery in his temper, as for his finer fancies.

He has used more frequently other combinations of the Asclepiad with the Glyconic—the three Asclepiads followed by the one Glyconic, and the couplet consisting of the Glyconic followed by the Asclepiad. The effect of the first is to express gravity, moderation, and sobriety of feeling, whether of happiness or sorrow. In iii. 16, 'Inclusam Danaen turris aēnea,' the feeling expressed is that of calm and temperate contentment; of the happiness procured by simple pleasures and few wants, contrasted with the pomp and vanity of great wealth. In iv. 5 the metre seems to be the very echo of the feeling which he desires to express, a mood not of enthusiasm or elevation, but calm and sober happiness secured by the rule of Augustus—

> Tutus bos etenim rura perambulat,
> Nutrit rura Ceres almaque Faustitas,
> Pacatum volitant per mare navitae,
> Culpari metuit Fides.

In 'Scriberis Vario' there is the sobriety of tone of one disclaiming all lofty ambition. Regret and longing, made calm by resignation and the appreciation of the quiet and chastened graces of character, have found no utterance in any language more in harmony with the mood expressed than in 'Quis desiderio sit pudor aut modus.' In poems connected with love—'Albi ne doleas plus nimio' or 'Extremum Tanain'—there is the tone of one complaining over faithlessness or hardheartedness, not of passionate or indignant remonstrance. In 'Iam veris comites' (iv. 12) there is present a sense of idyllic quiet, combined with the elegiac feeling awakened by the thought of death; while in i. 15 — 'Pastor cum traheret' — there is a grave inexorable denunciation of doom, uttered with no violence or anger, but with a calm certitude.

The couplet formed by the Glyconic and the Asclepiadean dimeter has a somewhat different effect from the couplets used in the Epodes. The metre is less epigrammatic, but it has an incisive, definite, sententious and even abrupt character, resembling the Epode. It presents a series of thoughts, images, and feelings, succeeding one another with rapid transition, rather than the continuous swelling and subsiding of some simple mood. This seems to be the character of i. 3—'Sic te diva potens Cypri.' The thought or sight of the ship which is to bear Virgil on his voyage suggests the old 'reverential fear' of the sea. The images—the 'monstra natantia,' the 'mare turgidum,' the 'infames scopulos Acroceraunia'—and the thoughts of the impiety of man's enterprise, of the old fraud of Prometheus and of its consequences, follow one another in rapid and abrupt transition, till they conclude with the

>   Nil mortalibus ardui est:
>   Caelum ipsum petimus stultitia, neque
>   Per nostrum patimur scelus
>   Iracunda Iovem ponere fulmina.

In iii. 24—'Intactis opulentior'—a succession of thoughts is presented with the incisiveness of Archilochian satire, and the gravity and sternness of censorial rebuke. In iii. 19—'Quantum distet ab Inacho'—the metre expresses abrupt transition of scene and thought, combined with excited feeling. In iii. 25—'Quo me Bacche'—the mind passes rapidly from the scene before the eye to the inward thought and feeling, from the vision of the God, swaying the Bacchantes, uprooting the tall ashes, to the sense of inspiration expressed in

> Nil parvum aut humili modo,
> Nil mortale loquar.

The metre is employed also in two Odes in which the poet exercises his most subtle and delicate gift—in 'Donec gratus eram tibi' and 'Quem tu Melpomene semel.' The terseness of the Latin language, and the power of the metre to concentrate in a few short stanzas a whole drama of the abrupt and capricious moods of lovers, and of 'a woman's last word,' are exemplified in the first. The second is perhaps the most perfect specimen of Horace's most delicate manner, and another example of how much can be done in the fewest words. The note of the metre is that thought and feeling do not seem to pass into one another by logical transition, as in the Alcaic, Sapphic, and the other combinations of the Asclepiadean, but to stand apart, suggesting a vivid contrast, the link of connexion between them being supplied by the mind. This adds to the vivid impression which each individual thought or picture makes.

The simple Asclepiadean dimeter, with its unimpassioned rhythm, is employed, with admirable tact, to claim for his own art a place among the various aims and pursuits to which men devote their lives, and to declare the reality of the success which he has achieved. A few other metres are employed once or twice in the collection, and give variety to it. But he did not find them equally suited either to his subjects or to the genius of the Latin language. It is to be observed that he does not use the metres which Catullus had naturalised in Latium—the hendecasyllable, the pure iambic or the scazon. Perhaps he did not care to tread on ground already appropriated :

> Libera per vacuum posui vestigia primus,
> Non aliena meo pressi pede (Ep. i. 19. 21).

But, apart from this desire not to appear among the servile ranks of imitators, he must have felt that, though these metres had been proved to be suited to the genius of the Latin language as a direct medium for the utterance of simple or impassioned feelings, they were not the true expression of the more varied and more reflective movements of his own mind. He adopted the Sapphic stanza, although that had been employed by Catullus with a power more approaching to that of its passionate inventor; but in adopting it he entirely altered its character. He made it more regular in movement and calmer in tone than it is either in Catullus or in the extant specimens of Sappho. He twice uses the Asclepiad trimeter—employed by Catullus for tender remonstrance—but as an instrument of sententious rather than emotional expression. The metres which he first employed he made absolutely his own. As Munro has said of them, the secret of their music was lost with its inventor. Seneca has made a mechanical reproduction of his Asclepiads and Sapphics in the choral odes of his tragedies; and in the Silvae of Statius there is one specimen of a Sapphic ode, no better or worse than some of the innumerable exercises in Sapphic verse, written for two centuries in our English schools. The only true master of metre who flourished under the Empire, Martial, while he adopts with success the metres of Catullus and Ovid, has limited his ambition to the use of one of the metres employed by Horace in his Epodes, that of the 'Beatus ille qui procul negotiis.'

The great success of Horace is in eliciting new musical effects from the Latin language, in accordance with the grave, powerful, and commanding tones which made it the organ of Roman law and empire, with the terseness and incisiveness which have made it the language of inscriptions, epitaphs, and epigrams, and with the softer and livelier tones responding to the Italian sensuousness, vivacity, and emotional susceptibility, which already appear, though without poetic grace, in the cantica of Plautus, and have survived as the dominant characteristics of the modern Italian tongue. It is essentially a 'carmen Latinum' to which his lyre is attuned. The music, though caught from the old Aeolian melodies, is generally Roman or Italian.

But if the first note of his lyrical art is the musical power which

Ovid recognises in applying to him the epithet 'numerosus,' the second, and one inseparable from his music, is the power characterised by the 'arbiter elegantiarum' of the reign of Nero as the 'curiosa felicitas' of his language—a felicity shewn as much in the arrangement and combination, as in the choice of his words. This gift, like his power over metre, is partly the result of his Greek studies, partly of his Roman nurture and Italian birth. He was thoroughly steeped in the language of Homer and of the old lyric poets and apparently also of the tragic poets. In adapting Greek phraseology to Latin, he studies the genius of his own language more closely than the older Roman poets. He avoids such novel word-formations as 'silvicultrix,' 'silvifragus,' etc., which Catullus and Lucretius perpetrated after the example of the older poets, and of which there are traces in Virgil, and, later, in the Metamorphoses of Ovid. Except where the thing of which he speaks is Greek, as for instance 'melos,' 'barbiton,' etc., he uses Latin words to render the phrases which he imitates, and Latin phrases to render the compound words to which the more plastic nature of the Greek language gave birth[1]. He shews how his genius has assimilated the Greek influence in his avoidance of that exaggerative tendency which their rhetorical training developed in Roman poets, and from which not even Virgil is exempt. He can convey much feeling and meaning by use of the simplest and commonest words, such as 'brevis,' 'vacuus,' 'integer,' 'improbus,' 'vagus.' This Greek moderation of expression is conspicuous in his frequent employment of the figures of speech known to grammarians as litotes and oxymoron, e.g. 'non hoc pollicitus tuae,' 'splendide mendax,' 'grata protervitas,' and the like. It is conspicuous also in the emphasis which he gives by such juxtaposition of discordant qualities as in 'tenues grandia,' 'dulcia barbare,' 'credulus aurea,' 'perfidus hospitium.' He avails himself of Greek constructions to compress the greatest amount of

---

[1] E.g. the periphrasis for χαλκεοθώρηξ—'tunica tectum adamantina' (i. 6. 13).

meaning and feeling into the fewest possible words. This new power over language was not gained without some sacrifice of the purity of the Latin idiom. And this sacrifice is especially apparent in the prose style of the historian Tacitus, who, as an imitator of Horace and Virgil, availed himself of the same aid to terseness and condensation.

But, while the language of many of the Odes, especially those of which the subject has an affinity to Greek thought and feeling, reproduces the subtle moderation and grace of Greek diction, no writer can be more truly Roman in his phraseology and constructions. In his purely Roman Odes he employs the plainest and most prosaic phrases, terms associated with Roman life, and adds dignity to his subject by their employment. Such phrases as these—

> Motum ex Metello consule civicum (ii. 1)—
>
> neque consularis
> Summovet lictor miseros tumultus
> Mentis (ii. 16)—
> Descendit in campum petitor (iii. 1)—
> Nec sumit aut ponit secures (iii. 2)—
> ut capitis minor (iii. 5)—

and many others, appealed powerfully to the Roman imagination in their plain and direct realism. Occasionally, but very rarely, this Roman realism betrays him into some coarser or more grotesque phrase, more suited to the mood in which the Satires are written than to the delicate art of the Odes. The realistic and concrete force of Latin is seen also in the use of the participle of verbs instead of some abstract substantive, as in

> Desiderantem quod satis est,
> Quod si dolentem nec Phrygius lapis,
> Multa petentibus desunt multa.

In the plain directness of such maxims or generalisations as

> Bene est cui deus obtulit
> Parca, quod satis est, manu,

or

> Quod adest memento
> Componere aequus,

it is not the Greek artist but the Roman moralist to whom we are listening. The Roman 'vates,' moved by the sense of doom, seems to speak in such powerful expressions of national grief as

> auditumque Medis
> Hesperiae sonitum ruinae,

or inspired by the vision of triumph in

> stet Capitolium
> Fulgens triumphatisque possit
> Roma ferox dare iura Medis.

Horace is able, in the fewest words, to present outward scenes and processes of Nature to the inward eye, as in

> —rura quae Liris quieta
> Mordet aqua taciturnus amnis,

or

> —positas ut glaciet nives
> Puro numine Iuppiter.

A similar power of condensation of language is seen in the graphic touches by which a scene from life is called up at a single stroke—

> Nunc et latentis proditor intimo
> Gratus puellae risus ab angulo,

or some record of human experience crystallises in a phrase—'Arcanique fides prodiga,' 'Spes animi credula mutui.' The more imaginative and figurative use of language is seen in many of the epithets he applies to the sea, such as 'aequor imperiosius,' 'mare tumultuosum,' 'dux inquieti turbidus Hadriae,' or in such phrases as 'ventos aequore deproeliantes.' The same descriptive power, combined with the imaginative gift of seeing analogies between natural and moral phenomena, is more fully shewn in the few longer similes which he employs. There is poetic enthusiasm as well as vigour in the comparison of himself, hurried along through silent woods, to the Bacchante

> Hebrum prospiciens et nive candidam
> Thracen ac pede barbaro
> Lustratam Rhodopen (iii. 25).

In the Odes in celebration of the victories of Drusus and

Tiberius, there is Pindaric vigour, if not novelty, in the comparison of Drusus, descending suddenly on the Rhaeti, to the eaglet swooping down (iv. 4), and of the havoc made by Tiberius on the barbarous hosts to that made by the impetuous Aufidus,

>Cum saevit horrendamque cultis
>   Diluviem meditatur agris (iv. 14).

So too, in the common comparison of the course of life to the course of a river—

>   cetera fluminis
>Ritu feruntur nunc medio alveo
>   Cum pace delabentis Etruscum
>   In mare, nunc lapides adesos
>Stirpesque raptas et pecus et domos
>Volventis una non sine montium
>   Clamore vicinaeque silvae,
>   Cum fera diluvies quietos
>Irritat amnes (iii. 29)—

we feel, as we feel in reading Lucretius and Virgil, that the poet had often watched such a spectacle, and reflected on its significance.

Horace belongs to that class of lyrical poets in whom impulse and enthusiasm are subordinate to, and controlled by reflexion. Wherever we can compare him with Catullus, we feel his inferiority in spontaneity, in ardour of feeling, in direct presentation of his object. It would be unfair to compare their love-poetry, in which Catullus is at his best, and Horace hardly professes to be serious. But even in the expression of affection for friends, in which both are excellent, and, still more, of hatred or scorn of enemies, Catullus is the greater. It was seen in an earlier chapter how much colder the verses are in which Horace celebrates the return of Numida from Spain than the outburst of joy with which Catullus greets the return of Verannius—

>Venistine domum ad tuos Penates
>Fratresque unanimos anumque matrem?
>Venisti, O mihi nuntii beati!

And the unpleasing bitterness of the twenty-fifth Ode of Book i.

—'Parcius iunctas'—is tame indeed compared with the scathing scorn of the stanzas to Furius and Aurelius—

> Cum suis vivat valeatque moechis.

Horace avoids fastidiously those diminutives of which Catullus, like the old Comic poets, makes such prodigal use as terms of endearment. It is by the use of the simplest and quietest words, or by the emphasis given by the position of a word, as in the 'care Maecenas eques,' in 'necte meo Lamiae coronam,' 'animae dimidium meae,' 'vatis amici,' that Horace signifies the presence of his personal feelings. Horace writes with a manly affection and esteem for his friends, and an artificial hatred and more real disdain for his enemies, but never with the passionate love and passionate scorn which live for ever in the burning and the biting lines of Catullus. In other poems which we can compare, as for instance the 'Dianae sumus in fide' and the 'Dianam tenerae dicite virgines,' we feel the difference between the vivid visions of a poet of the 'first intention,' and an artist reshaping the fancies of earlier poets. The feeling of the new life of the world, and the new joy in the heart of man which comes with it, is more vividly present in 'Iam ver egelidos refert tepores' than in 'Iam veris comites quae mare temperant.' Horace nowhere reaches such heights of creative imagination as Catullus reaches in the Attis, nor is he capable of the sustained union of vivid feeling with vivid imagery which we find in the Epithalamium in honour of Manlius and Vinia. The deepest springs of personal joy and sorrow are not among the forces of his lyrical poetry, any more than the awe of the supernatural world or the spirit of adventure in action and in speculation. If it were necessary to award poetic supremacy to either, it would be right to bear in mind the short time allowed for the genius of Catullus to mature, and the mellowing wisdom which the last twenty years of his life brought to Horace. Had he died at the age when Catullus died, he would have been either altogether forgotten, or known only as the author of a few Satires, and these not his

best. Where he is superior to Catullus is in the wider range
and the greater dignity of his art. He is in sympathy with
human life in many more of its relations. It is permissible to
think that Catullus had a stronger and more vivid nature, and
yet to hold that the work of Horace, even if limited to the Odes,
is a more important contribution to Roman literature, that it is
more truly representative of the idea of Rome than any other
work except the Aeneid, and that it bears the stamp of immortality—artistic perfection—more surely than any work except
the Georgics. If his was not so purely a poetic nature as that
of Catullus, he was a man much more complete. While as free
from austerity, he was much more serious, much more capable
of appreciating the true proportions of things, and his own
claims on life. The work accomplished by him is thus much
more complete, more equable, more solid. His apparent want
of spontaneity, his occasional conventionality, the obviousness of
his thought, are compensated by the art which lends a charm
even to these limitations of his spirit. No one knew better the
impossibility, without the natural gift, of producing poetry that
could please and live—

> Quod spiro et placeo, si placeo, tuum est—

but no one realised more truly how much industry and method
and critical insight could do, to draw forth and shape into
perfect form the rough ore of genius. His spiritual gift was
able to render its fullest service to the world by becoming
obedient to his intellectual power and critical judgment.

THE ELEGIAC POETS

THE ELEGIAC POETS

CHAPTER I.

Roman Elegy.

It was seen in a former chapter that Horace, as the literary lawgiver of his age, encouraged the cultivation of the great forms of poetry, especially of the tragic drama, with the view apparently of imparting to it an artistic perfection equal to that attained by epic, didactic, and lyrical poetry. The substance of poetry was to be sought in a true criticism of life. The great Greek writers were still to be followed as models of artistic execution; and it was accepted as an article of critical faith that the older Greek writers were the best—

> Si quia Graecorum sunt antiquissima quaeque
> Scripta vel optima, &c. (Hor. Ep. ii. 1. 28).

He, alone among his contemporaries, will have nothing to do with the Alexandrian poets. He came more and more to regard the function of the poet as, in the main, an ethical one, and to demand that above all things he should be of use to his generation. He evidently thought little of the art of those among his younger contemporaries who alone produced works which still live. He speaks disparagingly of the form and substance of elegiac poetry. To the metre he applies the epithet 'trifling,' *exiguus*. While to the hexameter he assigns the sphere of war and heroic deeds, to the iambic that of dramatic action and dialogue, to lyrical measures that of celebrating the praise of gods, heroes, or victors in the games, and the loves and gaiety of youth, he limits the function of the elegiac metre to the expression of sorrow, and to inscriptions on votive offerings—

> Versibus impariter iunctis querimonia primum,
> Post etiam inclusa est voti sententia compos (A. P. 75).

In accordance with this view of the primary function of the elegy, he applies the epithet 'miserabileś' to the elegies of Tibullus; and uses the terms 'flebiles modi' and 'molles querellae' of the verses of Valgius, a poet of the circle to which Tibullus belonged.

The name of elegy is so much associated, in all literature, with the idea of a lament, that it is natural to accept this account of its origin, which probably rests on some Greek authority. The word ἔλεγος, as is remarked by K. O. Müller, is used by Euripides (Iph. Taur. 1091) of the lament of Alcyone for her husband Ceyx, and in Aristophanes (Av. 218) for the lament of the nightingale over Itys. The word ἐλεγεῖον is applied by Thucydides (i. 132) to the inscription on the votive tripod raised by the Greeks in Delphi from the spoils of the Persian war. It is clear that the metre at an early stage of its development was recognised as suitable for two functions which it afterwards fulfilled, that of a lament and that of an epigram. But the earliest extant specimens of the metre in Greek, the appeals of Callinus to his countrymen and of Tyrtaeus to the Spartans, are conceived in a spirit the very opposite of that of the 'imbelles elegi' of the Roman poets, and presumably of the Greek poets whom they followed. The political manifestoes of Solon, the gnomic maxims of Theognis, and the convivial ditties of Phocylides and others are equally remote from the purely personal, unreflective, sentimental utterances of the Latin elegy. The elegiac metre, a development of the epic hexameter by a weakening process, was used in the great era of Greek literature for a more simple and less impassioned expression of personal feeling and reflexion than that of lyrical poetry. But that it was regarded as allied to this latter form may be inferred from the musical accompaniment with which it was presented.

Among the early elegiac poets the name of Mimnermus alone is associated with love. He seems to have treated the subject in a spirit somewhat resembling that occasionally found in Tibullus; and as the art of Tibullus is comparatively free from Alexandrian tendencies, it is not unlikely that he, like Horace, drew from older and purer sources of inspiration than his contemporaries. Mimnermus flourished in the latter part of the 7th century B.C. Though there is the breath of battle and of patriotism in some of his fragments, yet the prevailing tone of them is the lament of the individual for the loss of youth and its pleasures. That the line

> τίς δὲ βίος, τί δὲ τερπνὸν ἄτερ χρυσέης Ἀφροδίτης;

is the key-note of his poetry, as it is of the Latin elegiac poetry, may be inferred from the manner in which he is spoken of by the Latin poets who had all his writings in their hands. Propertius and Horace adduce him as the prototype of those who made love the chief theme of their verse and the chief pursuit of their lives.

> Plus in amore valet Mimnermi versus Homero

is the language of Propertius, who is represented by Horace (Ep. ii. 2. 100) as thinking it a finer compliment to be compared to Mimnermus than to the Alexandrian Callimachus. Horace, who gratifies Propertius by this comparison, quotes Mimnermus as the authority by whom a life of gaiety and pleasure is justified—

> Si, Mimnermus uti censet, sine amore iocisque
> Nil est iucundum, vivas in amore iocisque (Ep. i. 6. 65).

An Alexandrian poet, Hermesianax of Colophon, speaks of him as burning with love for Nanno, and finding a vent for his feelings 'in the breath of the soft pentameter.' But it was first by the Alexandrian poets themselves that the elegiac metre became identified with the poetry of pleasure. Love as a passion had found its most ardent expression in the lyric poetry of

Sappho; as a pastime it had been treated in graceful and lively tones by Anacreon. The part which it plays in the tragedy of human life had found its representative poet in Euripides; and its part in the comedy had found a poet in Menander—

<blockquote>Fabula iucundi nulla est sine amore Menandri.</blockquote>

But as it was in Ionia, after the martial and enterprising spirit of her cities had begun to decay, that the spirit of the erotic elegy was first displayed, so it was after the decay of Greek enterprise and creative genius, in an age of luxury and learned leisure, that the love of the poet for his mistress became the principal motive of the poetry which drew its material from actual life. Even the revival of the romance of the past, to which much of the literary activity of the Alexandrian poets was devoted, was largely influenced by the desire to idealise the pleasure that enlivened their own days. For the expression of that sentiment the elegiac metre by its gentle and languid movement commended itself as the fittest vehicle; and the form and composition of the poems in which it was employed were elaborated with studious art.

Before what is strictly called the Alexandrian age, Antimachus of Colophon had composed certain books of elegies, to which he gave the name of his mistress, 'Lyde.' Ovid mentions her along with the heroine of the elegies of Philetas—

<blockquote>Nec tantum Clario Lyde dilecta poetae,
Nec tantum Coo Bittis amata suo est (Trist. i. 6. 1).</blockquote>

The idea of Antimachus which naturally occurs to the readers of Latin poetry is that suggested by Catullus in comparing him with the author who gave his name to the 'Annals of Volusius'—

<blockquote>At populus tumido gaudeat Antimacho.</blockquote>

But the author who seems to have first limited the scope of the elegy to the love of the poet for his mistress was Philetas of Cos, of whose art and genius a more favourable opinion may be formed from the admiration frequently expressed by Propertius, and the allusions to him in Ovid; and from the more convincing evidence of the contemporary poet, Theocritus, who regarded him as his master :—

> οὔτε τὸν ἐσθλὸν
> Σικελίδαν νίκημι τὸν ἐκ Σάμω οὔτε Φιλητᾶν
> ἀείδων, βάτραχος δέ ποτ' ἀκρίδας ὥς τις ἐρίσδω

Other Alexandrian poets also wrote of their loves in elegies, as Hermesianax and Euphorion, the latter of whom was a popular author among the younger poets of the last days of the Republic, and was regarded by Cicero as the corrupter of their taste.

Of the Alexandrian spirit and culture Callimachus was the recognised representative. The line by which Ovid characterises him—

> Quamvis ingenio non valet, arte valet—

is probably as true as that where the father of Roman poetry is characterised in exactly opposite terms,

> Ennius, ingenio maximus, arte rudis.

Some idea of his culture and talent, as shewn in the elegies, which are lost, may be formed from the translation by Catullus of his 'Coma Berenices,' a poem of no spontaneity but of elaborate composition, and from what is probably an imitation of his manner, the elegy addressed by Catullus to Allius, in which the love story of Protesilaus and Laodamia is artificially worked into the personal expression of the poet's most ardent passion and his deepest sorrow. But besides this tribute from Catullus, the claim made by Propertius to be the Roman Callimachus, the imitation by Ovid of his 'Ibis,' and apparently his adoption of the idea of the Αἴτια of Callimachus in the Fasti, and his mention of him after Homer and Hesiod and along with Sophocles and Menander among the poets whose words would live for ever—

> Battiades semper toto cantabitur orbe—

imply that the Roman elegiac poets regarded him as specially their model and master. Quintilian assigns to him the first place among the Greek elegiac poets, awarding the second to Philetas.

These Alexandrian poets not only revived the use of the elegiac metre, largely employed for the expression of personal feelings in the earlier era of Greek poetry, but formed elegiac poetry into a new branch of literary art, as pastoral poetry was formed by Theocritus and his successors. The motive of this poetry was the sentiment and passion, the pleasure and the pain of love. The substance of it was largely taken from actual life. But the romance of older love stories, belonging to a brighter and more adventurous time, was revived to glorify the realism of the present. From the spirit in which their love is treated by Tibullus and Propertius, and from the impression given in the tenth Eclogue of Virgil of the treatment of the subject by Gallus[1], it may be conjectured that the Alexandrian elegy, like the Roman based upon it, conformed to the original idea of the elegy, and bore to a large extent the character of a 'querimonia,' either a complaint of the faithlessness or caprice of a mistress, or an expression of that luxury of melancholy so often associated with the sentiment.

The elegiac metre has a history in Roman poetry before it becomes the instrument by which the later Augustan poets give vent to their tender or impassioned feelings. It had been first used by Ennius for one of the purposes to which it was applied in Greek poetry, that of inscriptions and short epigrams. Lucilius also employed it in one book of his Satires, of which so little is left that it is impossible to say to what purpose the metre was applied by him. From the character of the man it is most improbable that he wrote anything in the vein of Philetas or Callimachus. It is more likely that he used the metre more in the vein of Theognis, and may have imparted to it something of a gnomic character analogous to its later employment in the satiric epigram. Early in the first century B.C. it was employed by Q. Catulus and Valerius Aedituus for short erotic pieces

---

[1] The lines of Propertius (ii. 34. 91)—
    Et modo formosa quam multa Lycoride Gallus
    Mortuus inferna vulnera lavit aqua—
fully confirm this impression.

which may have been written in imitation of the school of poetry to which many of the writers in the Greek Anthology belong. The poems of Meleager, who was nearly contemporary with them, were certainly familiar to the later elegiac poets. Catullus seems to have been the first Roman poet who made a large and varied use of the metre. He anticipated the later elegiac poets in using it both in a tender and a bitter spirit for the relations of lovers[1]; he anticipated Martial in using it to give point to the sting of the epigram. But his most perfect elegies are those which are the expression of his personal sorrow. In the employment of the metre Catullus did not attain the same perfection of rhythm as in his phalaecians, scazons, and pure iambics; nor the same smoothness as in the pure hexameter. Still, his execution is unequal rather than barbarous. He brought the metre more nearly to the state to which Lucretius brought the hexameter, than to that in which Ennius left that measure. It was probably also the metre in which Calvus lamented the death of Quintilia, and it may have been that in which Varro Atacinus celebrated the praises of Leucadia. Specimens of it are still extant in the compositions of the writers of the Augustan age, other than the pure elegiac poets. The most remarkable of these is the 'Copa,' marked by great freedom and energy of movement, quite unlike the smooth liquid flow of Tibullus. There are also one or two short poems, of the character of epigrams, ascribed, and probably rightly, to Virgil. Even these lead to the conclusion that the task of perfecting the metre was reserved for Tibullus, as that of perfecting the hexameter had been reserved for Virgil.

These instances shew that the metre was originally employed by the Latin poets as much for the epigram and for various other purposes, as for the poetry of love. What distinguishes the elegiac poets of the Augustan age from those who employed the metre before them was not only that they brought it to as high perfection as that to which the hexameter and the various

[1] Compare the 'Ianua' with Propertius i. 16, and the elegies in Ovid and Propertius which express the feelings of the lover towards the 'lena.'

lyric measures were brought by the older poets, but that they assigned to the elegy the special province of expressing the sentiment and passion of love. They nationalised the Alexandrian elegy of Philetas and Callimachus, as Virgil had nationalised the Sicilian pastoral of Theocritus. The passion of love as the most absorbing of all the personal emotions and the most capable of idealistic treatment became the paramount motive of poetry, both in Greece and Rome, in the decay of national and public feeling. As the elegies of the Alexandrian poets are lost, it is in the Roman elegiac poets that we find the chief record of the power of this passion over the life and art of men of genius and culture in an age of the greatest material civilisation and refinement. The subject had indeed largely entered into the earlier Roman literature. The liaisons and intrigues of the 'amantis ephebi' had supplied their chief material to Plautus, Terence, and the older comic poets. Lucilius had devoted one book of his Satires to his mistress. Whether this was of the nature of a satire or a chapter of his autobiography we have no means of determining. The long passage at the end of the fourth book of Lucretius is a vividly realistic satire, written, as it were, in anticipation of the torments and raptures, the weakness and the illusions, which filled so large a place in the life and art of the poets of the following generation. Catullus, himself the greatest poet of love, addresses a poem to his friend Caecilius as 'poetae tenero'; and speaks of their common love of poetry as a bond of sympathy between him and his mistress. The apology of Ovid addressed to Augustus from the place of his exile mentions the names of orators and politicians, as well as of poets and men of letters, among those who had been guilty of an offence, if it were an offence, against morality, similar to that for which he suffered. Among them, besides the greater names of Catullus and Calvus which are mentioned by him with a tender feeling of appreciation, are those of Hortensius and Memmius, of Cinna and Anser, of Cornificius and the grammarian Cato, belonging to the last age of the Republic, and of Gallus, Varro, and Tibullus in the early Augustan age.

There is mention also of what must have been a book of elegies under the name of Perilla, of which a Metella was the heroine and Ticida the author. Propertius (ii. 34), not to vindicate, but to magnify his art, adds to the names of Calvus and Catullus, Virgil the poet of the Bucolics, Varro the poet of the Argonautics—

> Haec quoque perfecto ludebat Iasone Varro,
> Varro Leucadiae maxima flamma suae—

and Gallus the poet of Lycoris, among those who had earned by their amatory verses renown as great as that bestowed on more serious writings. It is curious that Horace, notwithstanding his own profession of being the poet of love, and the fame he has bestowed on many heroines, real or fictitious, is not mentioned in either of these passages or in that of the third book of the Ars Amandi in which Ovid prescribes Callimachus and Philetas, Sappho, Anacreon and Menander, Gallus, Tibullus, Propertius, and Varro, as reading for women who desire to charm and retain their lovers. Is this omission to be explained by the alienation of Horace from these younger poets, or does it imply a consciousness that his treatment of the subject was mere irony and persiflage? It certainly did not proceed from ignorance, as there are many clear traces of the study of the Odes in both Ovid and Propertius.

Although so many other poets of the last years of the Republic and the early part of the Augustan age obtained renown or notoriety as amatory poets, yet only four—Gallus, Tibullus, Propertius, and Ovid—are ranked among the genuine elegiac poets of Rome. These are mentioned in order of succession by Ovid, and the list of elegiac poets is limited to them by Quintilian. It may be that most of the other poets who wrote of love did not confine themselves to the elegiac metre, but like Catullus and one of the oldest among the amatory poets, Laevius, author of the Erotopaegnia, used a variety of lyrical measures as well. The Leucadia of Varro and the Perilla of Ticida probably belonged to the same class as the Cynthia and Delia elegies of Propertius and Tibullus, and the Amores of Ovid; but they cannot have established or long retained their claim to rank with them. Their existence, however, proves how close was the relation between the life of pleasure and the cultivation of poetry among contemporary writers.

The one new work which remained to be done when Tibullus, Propertius, and Ovid began their literary career was to bring the form and metre of the elegy to the perfection attained in didactic, pastoral, epic, and various kinds of lyric poetry. They—or at least Ovid and Propertius—felt most powerfully attracted to those later Greek poets who had been most like themselves in their lives, tastes, and circumstances. They were impelled to write of what immediately interested themselves and what was likely to interest the society in which they moved, the passion and romance of their own lives. They were all young men, born in a good position, of means sufficient to procure for them the best culture of the day and to enable them to enter without restraint on the life of pleasure. Their career began after peace and prosperity were secure, and during the first revulsion of feeling from the wars which had deluged the world with the blood of Roman citizens. They lived their lives, loved their loves, and wrote their poems in the full enjoyment of that 'dulcedo otii' which was the forerunner of the corruption of the Empire. They did not, like the writers of the Republic, appeal to the traditions and the higher mood of a great governing class; nor did they set before themselves, like Virgil and Horace, the aim of reconciling that class to changed conditions and of rousing a new enthusiasm in favour of the Empire. Art became with them—certainly with the youngest of them—simply the minister of pleasure. It was chiefly the expression of personal feeling, the outlet in literature of the emotional and sensuous element in the Italian temperament. Even when it becomes objective, as in the Epistles and narrative poetry of Ovid, it addresses itself chiefly to the prevailing taste and to a light curiosity, rather than to a strong human interest about the past as a field of heroic action or tragic passion. The age came more and more to resemble the Alexandrian age, and the fashionable movement in literature was to carry out to their perfection the Alexandrian tendencies, which had been carried a certain length by Catullus and his contemporaries. That it was a sound instinct which led them to draw the materials of their poetry from what was most vivid in their own experience, rather than to attempt an artificial restoration of a nobler past, may be inferred from the failure of the restorers of tragedy, among whom was the most versatile and brilliant of their number. The artistic representation of the grander passions on the stage might have interested a small and cultivated audience; it could have been nothing but weariness to the ordinary spectator of the mimes and other scenic entertainments which had superseded the tragedy and comedy of the Republic. The elegiac poets, like the authors of the mimes, though with a refinement and decorum altogether unknown to them, find in the intrigues of private life the chief motive of their art. It is no object of theirs to combine the 'utile' with the 'dulce,' except in so far as they yield to the didactic tendency natural to the Roman character, and write an Art of Love.

Poetry was no longer mainly addressed to men. Women played a more important part in society than at any previous time. At no time probably, except perhaps in the age of Pericles, has the class to which belong the Cynthia and Delia of Propertius and Tibullus, the Neobule and Galatea, the Phyllis and Glycera of Horace's fancy, combined so much literary and artistic accomplishment with personal fascination. It is not probable that they belonged universally to the class of freedwomen. Cynthia, granddaughter of the poet Hostius, cannot have belonged to that class. Ovid distinctly mentions that Corinna was 'ingenua.' Horace speaks of his temporary liaison with Myrtale—

> Libertina, fretis acrior Hadriae—

as something exceptional. But the taste for pleasure and the poetry of pleasure was not confined to the class either of freedwomen or of those who conformed to their ways. Notwithstanding Ovid's protestations that his poem which taught the art of love was not meant for those who wore the 'vitta,' it must have found many readers who were separated from the class openly devoted to a life of pleasure more by social station than by the severity of their morals. We might almost fancy that we have a survival of the beauty and intelligence, combined with a free, bright, and benignant spirit, which presided over the pleasure-loving society of Rome between the years 20 and 2 B.C. in the bust of the elder Julia, preserved in the gallery of the Uffizi in Florence. The lover of Iulus Antonius was not likely to have left the poetry of Ovid and Propertius unread.

The poetry addressed to a society for which pleasure had not yet lost its bloom naturally did not seek to express itself in the old Roman tones. Its aim was to act on the tender emotions by the luxurious softness of its melody, or to quicken the spirit of gaiety by its brilliance and vivacity. As the form of metrical and poetical art latest brought to perfection, the elegy was able, more than any other form of poetry, to avail itself of the resources of imaginative diction and rhythmical effect developed in the Latin language by the efforts of several generations of poets. The result is, with Ovid and Tibullus, the most popular representatives of the Roman elegy, a facility, a lucidity of language, an unimpeded smoothness of rhythm, and, in the case of Ovid, a rapidity of movement, unequalled in any other branch of Roman poetry. The aim of the art of Tibullus and Ovid is to produce as little sense of effort as possible. Propertius indeed has imparted a different movement to his verse, suited to the deeper, more powerful, and more turbid movement of his own feelings, and the more thoughtful workmanship and recondite suggestiveness of his imagination. But his style is exceptional and peculiar to himself. The true character assumed by the Latin elegy, in ancient times and in its modern imitations, is the liquid smoothness of Tibullus or the buoyant and sparkling rapidity of Ovid. The delight of the ear entered at all times largely into the Roman enjoyment of oratory and poetry; and that was now diverted from the larger and more sonorous utterances of great orators to the recitation or chanting of those smooth-flowing couplets, falling pleasantly on the sense of hearing and immediately suggestive of luxurious sentiment or vivid pleasure. Education, more than at any other time, prepared men and women for this kind of literature. The authors studied were almost exclusively poets, and to a large extent those who treated of love. Even the training of an orator was more poetical than strictly oratorical. Little interest was felt in history and philosophy or severer studies and pursuits of any kind. The great literary teachers of the previous generation, Greek and Latin, Parthenius and Cato, had been themselves poets; and, by the character of their compositions, a guide to the younger generation of poets towards paths on which poetry now entered.

This tendency in literature was opposed to that encouraged by Maecenas and Augustus, of which Horace was the chief exponent, which aimed at strengthening and elevating the national character, as well as refining and giving zest to life. It was fostered along with other tastes in the literary circle of Messalla, which, without being in active opposition to the new régime, did not concern itself with the policy of the Empire. The influence exercised by Messalla, as a patron of letters, could not have been so powerful as that exercised by Maecenas, yet if judged by the simplicity and refinement of the art of his devoted friend and admirer Tibullus, it must have been in a high degree genial and beneficent. The character of Messalla is perhaps the most attractive of any of those known to us as playing an active part in the crisis of the Republic, and during the first establishment of the Empire. The praise bestowed on him by Octavianus after Actium, that after having been a most formidable enemy at Philippi he had rendered him the greatest service at Actium, is an ample testimony to his military capacity; and the answer attributed to Messalla, that he had on both occasions fought on the right side, is all that befitted an honourable man and patriotic citizen. The historian Appian pays a rare tribute to his character. After mentioning that he had been one of those who were proscribed by the Triumvirs, and recounting the service rendered by him in the Sicilian war, he adds that he records as a tribute to the virtue of the Romans the occasion on which Messalla, when the man who had proscribed him was involved in disaster and cut off from aid, yet proved loyal to him as his sovereign, and saved him from his peril. He continued to perform important services as a soldier, a diplomatist, and a public official, but he never identified himself, as Maecenas and Agrippa did, with the fortunes of the Emperor, nor did he in any way profit by them. He gained a lasting reputation as one of the two greatest orators of the day, and according to the evidence of Horace, whose talent he was one of the first to recognise (Sat. i. 10. 85) and who has associated his name with one of the most genial of his convivial Odes, he was deeply imbued with the teaching of the noblest school of Greek philosophy[1]. The feelings of friendship and admiration entertained for him by Tibullus are as loyal as those of Horace towards Maecenas. Ovid tells us that Messalla was the first to recognise and foster his genius, and in the time of his exile the poet turns to the sons of his patron as among the great friends on whose sympathy and advocacy he most relies, in consequence of his intimacy with them from their earliest years. The love story of his niece Sulpicia, which has been saved from oblivion partly in her own verses, attests the literary refinement and the freedom from conventionality of the circle by which he was surrounded. The glimpses afforded of his family life in the poetry of Tibullus are suggestive of a genial and united household. He was certainly no severe censor of morals; yet the poetry which flourished under his fostering favour has nothing either of the reckless or of the licentious spirit present in the other

---

[1] Non ille quanquam Socraticis madet
Sermonibus te negleget horridus (Od. iii. 21. 9).

elegiac poets. Tender affection, tinged with melancholy, is the note of the love of which Tibullus and Lygdamus sing, as ardent passion is of that of Propertius, and mere pleasure, made more piquant by intrigue and more entertaining by all the resources of gallantry, is of that of Ovid.

The publication of his first book, the 'Cynthia Monobiblos,' secured for Propertius the patronage of Maecenas. Yet this influence had very little effect on his art, though it diverts him from time to time to express the feeling excited by some of the striking or tragic events which happened in his day. The elegies of Propertius afford a graphic delineation of an exceptional experience and individuality rather than an image of the society of his time. He stands apart from the other poets of the day, almost as much as Lucretius stands apart from all other poets. He is absolutely absorbed in himself and his passion, as Lucretius is in his thought. The power of passion over the southern temperament and the weakness of character to control it, vivid imagination and a great effort to prove himself a poet, combined with some failure in the power of beating his music out completely and of attaining the simple manner of perfect art, are what we chiefly recognise in him.

The very seriousness of his art and the originality of his conception unfitted Propertius to be the favourite poet of a lively and frivolous generation. That position was undoubtedly due to and was enjoyed by Ovid. He did not need the fostering patronage of Messalla or Maecenas. His patrons were the whole fashionable and cultivated society of the day. The publication of the work with which his name is most associated, and which many critics regard as his master-piece, almost coincidently with his disgrace, is the culmination of the reckless licentiousness of the age. From that time the elegy had to change its note, like the Fescennine license of an earlier time,

> Ad bene dicendum delectandumque redacta,

and to awaken an interest in the rites and ceremonies and legends of ancient Rome. In its latest note of all, it becomes in him who was the light-hearted poet of pleasure truly a 'querimonia,' but at the same time it loses much of its old artistic excellence. The distinction between the treatment of the sentiment and passion and pursuit of love by these poets and that of older poets, Greek and Roman, is that with these love is exclusive of all other interests in life. It is accepted by the more serious among them as a bondage, and one which brings more pain than happiness. All other objects of ambition are to be sacrificed to it. In many ways the love idealised by these poets is of a lower quality than that idealised in English poetry; but in none more markedly than in this forgetfulness of all other claims which life has upon them. The sentiment of these poets of pleasure is not only unlike but is absolutely antagonistic to that of our own Cavalier poets, as we find it, for example, expressed in the familiar lines—

> I could not love thee, dear, so much
> Loved I not honour more.

The words

> But am I not the nobler through thy love?

would have been quite unmeaning to Ovid and Propertius, though perhaps not altogether to Tibullus. 'Laus in amore mori' is the highest ideal to which its most passionate exponent can rise. Nothing can be less Roman than the spirit in which these poets glory in their unfitness to encounter the perils and hardships of war, though Tibullus, under the influence of friendship, bore his part honourably in one campaign. This feeling may indeed be partly explained by the dislike, often enhanced by jealousy, entertained by men of taste and refinement for the military adventurer who returned to Rome enriched by the spoils of war, but it is significant also of a decay of fibre not only in the individual poet, but in the society which he addressed.

In the poets of an earlier time, Ennius and Lucretius and Catullus, and in the greatest of the contemporary poets, Virgil and Horace, the Roman governing spirit or the spirit of Republican freedom is, if not predominant, yet blended in due proportion with Italian impressibility. In the elegiac poets the Italian 'mollitia' is present to the exclusion of the strong Roman fibre, and the power of reflexion which goes along with strength of character. And this 'mollitia' does not show itself as sympathetic humanity of feeling, as it does in the great prose-writers no less than in the poets of Rome, but in its best side as a susceptibility to beauty in art and nature, in its weakest as a mere love of pleasure—'the spirit of lubricity,' as it has been named by a recent poet and moralist. The races of Italy which had been longest united with Rome and had played a part, though a secondary part, in her career of conquest, seem to have felt the spell of her greatness less than the races further removed from her immediate attraction. Virgil and Livy have even more, or at least a higher kind, of the Italian 'mollitia' than any of the Italian elegiac poets: but they are as sensible as the proudest Roman could be of the grandeur of the Roman character and institutions. The elegiac poets are indeed sensible of the wonderful spectacle presented by Rome as the capital of the Empire, and still more as the capital of pleasure. They have nothing in common with that grand representation of Roman character—

Moribus antiquis stat res Romana virisque.

In Ovid, the truest representative of the spirit of his time, the sentiment of Rome is merged in adulation of the imperial family. Reverence and seriousness of spirit were among the best elements in the Roman character, and among those that most conduced to the stability of Roman power. These are not wanting in Tibullus, though hardly of the Roman stamp. In Propertius they are replaced by a superstitious and sombre gloom. The tone of Ovid is the utter negation of all reverence and seriousness. The art and literature of pleasure, as they appear in his writings, show more than any other ancient writings the bloom which precedes decay. They mark the beginning of that degeneracy in the men and women of the old governing families which we read of in the account given by

Tacitus of the following reigns. They are the antecedent condition of the state of morals which has been described once for all in the satire of Juvenal. The spectacle of that life of pleasure in its later stage is the best commentary on the spectacle it presents in its bloom.

But apart from the ethical significance of their writings as a picture of the individual and social life of their day, and a record of the spirit in which that life was lived, these poets have an artistic value, not indeed equal to that of the greatest among their predecessors, but sufficient to admit them into the company of the renowned poets of the world. Their works are the last original expression of the Italian Camenae, and the last conquest of Roman culture in the domain of Greek art ; a conquest under which the province apparently became much richer than it ever had been under its original occupants. This superiority of the Roman poets to those whom they imitated, testified to in the moderate language of so impartial a critic as Quintilian, was due to the greater vitality of a younger race, to the fresher charm of the Italian life, to the more splendid and piquant spectacle presented by Rome in the Augustan age as the capital of government and pleasure, and to the superiority of the still unexhausted forces of the Latin language over an artificial literary diction connected by no near relation with the active intercourse of life. The elegiac poets of Rome have found a fresh and living and yet idealised expression for whatever there was in the old Italian temperament of tender emotion, of ardent passion, of vivid sensibility to pleasure. This sensibility of feeling, allied to a susceptibility to beauty in art and nature, awoke a new interest in the mythology and legendary story of early Greece, regarded as an age of romance, but an age of romance enlivened by the love adventures of gods and demigods and youthful heroes with nymphs of the woods and fountains, or mortal maidens. This, the dominant character given to Greek mythology by the poets of the Augustan age, and probably largely suggested by the contemporary pictorial art presented to the eye in temples and the porticoes of private houses—for painting then and previously had become subservient to the same kind of taste as poetry—was that conception of the subject which passed into the imagination of the painters and poets of the Renaissance.

The personality of the poet has been seen to be an element of interest in all Roman poetry more than in Greek or in most of the poetry of modern nations. The Roman elegy presents this element of personal feeling and experience unmixed with general reflexion. The individualities of Tibullus, Propertius, and Ovid are very distinct from one another, and are all vividly present in their poetry. Of Ovid we have two different pictures painted by himself, one in the days of his light-hearted gaiety, the other in the misery of his exile. Yet they produce the impression of the same personality though under very different conditions. None of the three is so interesting as a man or so great in genius as Horace or Catullus, Virgil or Lucretius: yet with the exception of Catullus, Cicero, Horace, and perhaps Martial, there are no Roman authors to whose life we are able to come so near. Though endowed with much more vivid sensibility and adorned with much finer artistic accomplishment than average men and average writers, they are not raised above them by force of character or range of intellect. Our intimate knowledge of them thus enlarges our knowledge of the ancient Italian nature, and also enables us better to understand 'the passionate heart' allied to the artistic temperament of youth, in other times and among other nations.

Another reason which justifies the interest felt in them, and the time devoted to their study, is the new power of melody, and of direct, sensuous, and emotional expression, which they elicited from the Latin language. The efficacy of their metre as the simplest poetical instrument for the greatest variety of purposes is shewn in its large employment by the scholars and poets of the Renaissance and more recent times. It is indeed sometimes a matter of complaint that its superiority as a vehicle of sentiment and epigram over any form struck out in the vernacular literature delayed the development of the vernacular literature, and has denied to the scholars who employed it the poetic fame to which their natural genius entitled them. It was by Martial that the metre was finally adapted to the epigram. But Ovid was his master, and it cannot be doubted that he is the master of all who in modern times have employed it to utter their sentiment, or wit, or sorrow, or for the description of nature or the interchange of friendly feeling. The hexameter, like the English blank verse, though the most perfect of all metres when employed by the greatest masters and in works of sustained elevation, is heavy, laboured, and pedantic—except indeed in the hands of Horace—when employed on subjects of trivial interest. It lends itself to indignant declamation, as in Juvenal, but to be impressive it must be the organ either of sustained elevation or powerful rhetoric. The lyric metres of Horace, light and grave, do not adapt themselves to the expression of modern moods with the same versatility and success as the elegiac. The elegiac metre, as the last to be brought to perfection by the ancient Latin poets, became the smoothest and most facile of all employed by them. It is the only one which conveys its meaning immediately and without the necessity of thought or close attention. It could thus produce the sense of spontaneity even when employed by those to whom it came as a foreign instrument of expression.

The works of the elegiac poets, though they may not have much in their substance to say to our own time, yet deserve study as masterpieces of art, and as records of personal experience and feeling bringing vividly back a page from the history of ancient civilisation. They cannot be neglected in any comprehensive study of literature.

CHAPTER II.

GALLUS, TIBULLUS, LYGDAMUS, SULPICIA.

I.

THE earliest in point of time of the four principal elegiac poets of Rome was Cornelius Gallus. He was distinguished, like Asinius Pollio, in the military and political, as well as the literary history of his age. As his works are lost, we can judge of the share he had in shaping the Roman elegy, and of the quality of his poetical art and genius, only from the impression he has left on the writings of contemporary poets and later critics of literature.

The outward facts of his life are briefly these. He was born at Forum Julii in Gallia Norbonensis in 69 B.C. In the year 41 B.C. he was, along with Pollio and Varius, one of the three commissioners engaged in the division of the lands in the neighbourhood of Mantua. Ten years later he highly distinguished himself in the siege and capture of Alexandria, and was appointed the first Prefect of Egypt. He was deprived of his government in consequence of his self-assertion and disloyalty; and being accused among other things of speaking disrespectfully of Augustus, he fell into disgrace, was put under a social ban, and committed suicide in the year 26 B.C. His literary reputation was made before the time of his greatness and fall, first by a translation of some work of Euphorion, 'the Chalcidian Shepherd,' as Virgil calls him in the Eclogues; later by four books of elegies, under the name of 'Lycoris.' In these he bewailed his desertion by Cytheris, the famous actress, the mistress of Antony and several others, who is mentioned by Cicero in one of his letters (Fam. ix. 26) as being present at an entertainment given by P. Volumnius Eutrapelus where Cicero was a guest. Gallus may have been one of the new school of young poets, the 'cantores Euphorionis,' whom Cicero, in the Tusculan Disputations, written in B.C. 44, speaks of as slighting Ennius for the more artistic and effeminate strains of Euphorion.

The loss of his poems is probably to be regretted more on account of the interest of his personality than of their artistic excellence. That he had the gift of winning the affections as well as moving the imagination of his contemporaries may be inferred from the tone of the sixth and tenth Eclogues of Virgil, and especially from the lines—

> Gallo cuius amor tantum mihi crescit in horas
> Quantum vere novo viridis se subicit alnus.

No sufficient reason has been shewn for doubting the statement of Servius, that the Georgics originally ended with a panegyric of his services in Egypt, for which the fine but irrelevant story of the shepherd Aristaeus was afterwards substituted. The original passage formed a natural conclusion to the last book of the poem, the first book of which ends with the apprehension of the outbreak of hostilities between the great Western and Eastern provinces. Propertius and Ovid allude with sympathy to the fate of Gallus, especially the latter, who introduces him, along with Calvus and Catullus, as prepared to meet the shade of Tibullus in Elysium—

> Tu quoque, si falsum est temerati crimen amici,
> Sanguinis atque animae prodige, Galle, tuae.

In his apology to Augustus, Ovid says that his disgrace was not due to his celebration of Lycoris, but to speaking indiscreetly over his cups—

> Nec fuit opprobrio celebrare Lycorida Gallo,
> Sed linguam nimio non tenuisse mero (Trist. ii. 445).

His more adventurous disposition, higher spirit, and greater capacity for affairs distinguish him from the other elegiac poets, whom he resembles in his love of poetry and of pleasure, in the subjects which he chose for his art and his manner of treating them. Like theirs, his poetry also was the poetry of youth, and addressed to the young.

In the later development of personal ambition and vanity we recognise a likeness to the career of Licinius Murena, rather than to that of Pollio. It would have been interesting to possess a self-portraiture of the poet, soldier, and restless politician similar to that which we have of the peaceful unadventurous poet by whom the elegy was perfected. That Gallus was the first to form the elegy into a distinct province of art is a proof of his originality; that he was ranked along with the other three implies literary distinction; that his works have perished while theirs still live may be an accident—for those of Catullus and Propertius narrowly escaped the same fate—or may be due to that defect in his style which Quintilian indicates in applying to it the epithet 'durior.' He failed in that quality which was the essential charm of the Roman elegy.

II.

Albius Tibullus, the next to Gallus in order of time, was a considerably younger man, although the exact date of his birth is uncertain. The evidence of his epitaph by Domitius Marsus—

> Te quoque Vergilio comitem non aequa Tibulle
>   Mors iuvenem campos misit in Elysios,
> Ne foret aut elegis molles qui fleret amores
>   Aut caneret forti regia bella pede—

shows that he died, while still a young man, shortly after the death of Virgil, who died late in the year 19 B.C. This is certainly the interpretation put on the word *iuvenem* by the author of the short life of him, most probably based on that of Suetonius, to which this epigram is prefixed. The words with which the life ends are 'obiit *adolescens*, ut indicat epigramma supra positum.' The lament of Ovid (Amores iii. 9) is a testimony to the affection and admiration which he inspired in younger men of genius, and the whole tone of that elegy, as of the epigram, implies that he died prematurely. Ovid mentions the presence of his mother at his death and funeral; he compares the sorrow for his death to that of Aurora for her son Memnon, of Thetis for Achilles, and of Venus for the young Adonis; and he represents him as met in the valley of Elysium by 'Catullus with his youthful temples bound with ivy.' The earliest fact known about him from external testimony and from his own writings is that he accompanied Messalla in his Aquitanian campaign, the date of which is probably 30 B.C. It is nearly certain that he was not born before the year 54 B.C., the year which the latest critics assign to his birth, though the date is put five years earlier by Dissen, who supposes that his first military service was in 42 B.C.

The life referred to above is comprised in five or six lines, and in these five lines there are at least two serious corruptions of the text. It is to this effect: 'Albius Tibullus, a Roman knight, a man singularly handsome, and remarkable for the care he bestowed on the adornment of his person, was the devoted friend of Corvinus Messalla the orator, and was a member of his staff in the Aquitanian war, and received orders of distinction for his services. In the opinion of many he holds the first place among the elegiac poets. His amatory epistles, although short, are quite "utiles." He died a young man, as the epigram quoted above indicates.' The two corruptions of the text are the words 'regalis' after 'eques,' and 'originem' after 'Messallam.' These had been corrected into 'Romanus' and 'oratorem.' But Baehrens (Tibullische Blätter) points out, with force, that these words are too remote from the words in the text to admit of their having been corrupted into them. He proposes to read *eques R.* (i.e. Romanus) *e Gabis = Gabiis*, and for '*originem*' '*ob ingenium.*' He also suggests 'dulces' instead of 'utiles,' as the epithet applied to the 'epistolae amatoriae.' The only change of importance is the *e Gabis*. In the Augustan age Gabii is spoken of as a typical instance of a town almost deserted[1]. It may, however, still have been the most important place in that part of Latium and have given its name to the district round about it. Horace, in the epistle addressed to Albius, writes to him, as living on his country estate, 'in regione Pedana.' The old towns of Pedum and Gabii were within a short distance of one another; and the home of Tibullus may have been somewhere in the district lying between them.

A much more important question is whether the poet Tibullus is the Albius addressed by Horace in the thirty-third Ode of Book i—

> Albi ne doleas plus nimio memor
> Immitis Glycerae—

and of the fourth Epistle of Book i. From the time of the scholiast Porphyrion and the old grammarian Diomedes[2], this identity has hardly been doubted till quite recently. But it is argued by Baehrens[3] that the language both of the Ode and the Epistle is irreconcilable with what is known of Tibullus from his own writings, and must have been addressed to another Albius, also an author of love-elegies. He argues that the words of the Ode do not apply to Tibullus, who complains, not of the infidelity of an 'ungentle Glycera,' but of Delia and Nemesis, and who nowhere hints that a younger rival was preferred to him—

> neu miserabiles
> Decantes elegos cur tibi iunior
> Laesa praeniteat fide.

This difficulty has occurred to others, and it has been conjectured that Tibullus had another mistress named Glycera, on whom he wrote elegies which have been lost; or that

---
[1] Gabiis desertior atque Fidenis vicus (Hor. Ep. i. 11. 7).
[2] Cui opinioni consentire videtur Horatius, cum ad Albium Tibullum elegiarum auctorem scribens, etc.
[3] Tibullische Blätter, pp. 7-11.

Horace substitutes the name Glycera for Nemesis, as (for instance) he substitutes Licymnia for Terentia. To this the answer is that Ovid when he wrote his elegy on the death of Tibullus knew only of Delia and Nemesis; that there could be no reason in the case of Nemesis for the adoption of a false name; and further, that the word Glycera would not in every position in a line—e. g. when the next word began with a consonant—fulfil the conditions as to the quantity of the syllables forming the name which are invariably observed when one name is substituted for another by the poets. The Ode must have been written before the connexion between Tibullus and Nemesis, which did not exist till the last years of the poet's life.

Further, Tibullus makes no complaint of younger, but only of richer rivals. But, it may be asked, is there any reason to suppose that Horace, in rallying his friends on their love affairs, adheres more closely to actual facts or to the actual names of their mistresses, than he does in writing of his own? The heroines of his Odes are more or less imaginary beings, idealised under some Greek name, suggestive of some characteristic charm of beauty or grace, of nature or manner. Glycera is a name used by him of one of the many objects of his own volatile attachments. In the combination of the words 'immitis Glycerae,' 'the ungentle sweet one,' do we not recognise his partiality for the figure oxymoron? The Ode probably was written—as nearly all of those in the first book were—before the publication of the Elegies on Delia. Horace may not have known or cared to know—or, if he knew, to reveal—the circumstances of the relation of Tibullus to Delia. He rallies him on treating too seriously the faithlessness of a mistress. The moral of the poem is that all love should be regarded as pastime and as a matter of caprice over which no man has any control, 'the sport of Venus'—

> cui placet impares
> Formas atque animos sub iuga aënea
> Saevo mittere cum ioco.

A similar remonstrance, though written with more serious

sympathy, is addressed to another elegiac poet belonging to the circle of Messalla, Valgius, who is exhorted to cease lamenting his lost Mystes and to rouse himself to sing of the fresh trophies of Augustus. The one thing clear about the Albius addressed in the thirty-third Ode of Book i. is that he was a poet who wrote love-elegies on his mistress.

It may be assumed that the Albius of the Odes is the same as the Albius of the Epistles, and it is objected that the latter is, in his personal attributes and circumstances, unlike the Tibullus known to us in the elegies; and further, that he is not recognised by Horace as the accomplished poet that his works and the reputation which he enjoyed in antiquity prove him to have been. Horace applies to him the words

> Curantem quicquid dignum sapiente bonoque;

and certainly the characteristic of the poetry of Tibullus is not philosophical reflexion. The wealth and health and capacity for enjoyment attributed to him—

> Di tibi divitias dederunt artemque fruendi—

appear to be contradicted by statements of his own regarding his circumstances and by the plaintive tone of his elegies. It is but a poor compliment to say of the author of the elegies on Delia that he may be engaged in writing something superior to the 'opuscula' of Cassius of Parma, which were so insignificant that nothing more is known of them. Further, Cassius is known as the author of tragedies, not of elegies. Had Horace been writing to the well-known elegiac poet Tibullus, he would, it is urged, have hinted at his superiority not to Cassius of Parma, but to Cornelius Gallus [1].

These considerations, suggesting further doubt as to the identity of the poet with the friend addressed by Horace, are not convincing. Horace does not say that he was a philosopher, but that he was leading a good and philosophic life. In the mood in which Horace wrote the Epistles he would regard one

---

[1] Cf. Baehrens, Tibullische Blätter, pp. 10-11.

who was so indifferent to wealth and ambition, who loved the country and lived simply, as one who understood the secret of a philosophic life; and as his object in the Epistles was to uphold this philosophic ideal, he draws attention to it, in connexion with Tibullus, in that work; as in the Odes, which reproduce the emotional side of life, he writes of him as a lover and poet. We need not suppose that we find the whole nature of Tibullus expressed in his Elegies. In them he dwells on the two aspects of his life that gave it an ideal charm for himself, his love for Delia and Nemesis, and the deep enjoyment which he derived from his home in the country. To Horace, who does not appear to be especially intimate with him, he would naturally be best known as a refined and cultivated gentleman, living on his hereditary estate. Though Tibullus says that he no longer enjoys the large estates of his ancestors, and complains that he is supplanted by a richer rival, yet he adds that he has enough for his wants—

> ego composito securus acervo,
> Despiciam dites despiciamque famem—

and that he has learned or is rapidly learning 'contentus vivere parvo.' He speaks of receiving Messalla as an honoured guest, and of producing old Falernian and Chian wine on festive occasions. The whole tone of the first elegy of Book ii, and especially the lines

> Turbaque vernarum, saturi bona signa coloni,
> Ludet et ex virgis exstruet ante casas,

is that of a fairly prosperous man, living on the proceeds of his estate, and with many people dependent upon him. This statement of his position exactly corresponds with the

> mundus victus, non deficiente crumena

ascribed to him; and it is a doctrine of Horace, inculcated in Odes, Satires, and Epistles, almost to satiety, that the truly rich man is he whose wants are moderate and who has enough to satisfy them. It is true that the cloud of impending death seems to cast a shadow over his happiness, though not the deep gloom which it casts over that of Propertius. His reference to his 'slight limbs' and 'tender hands' (ii. 3. 9) may be suggestive rather of the beauty attributed to him than of robust health; and his serious illness at Corcyra and his premature death may confirm what we should infer from the gentle strain of his verse, that he was not endowed with that vigorous vitality which beats in every line of Ovid. Yet we must remember that it is part of the delicate art of Horace, in the Epistles, to play the part of a physician and to hint to each person what is the matter with him; and as we saw how he did this to those whom he deemed too easily satisfied with themselves, so he would address words of cheering to such as may have seemed to him too prone to despondency. The words 'silvas inter reptare salubres' and the concluding advice as to the secret of true enjoyment,

> Omnem crede diem tibi diluxisse supremam:
> Grata superveniet quae non sperabitur hora,

may have been intended as hints to one who appeared to him, as he himself may have appeared to others, over-regardful of his health and over-apprehensive of death[1]. His intimacy with Maecenas made Horace too familiar with such a state of mind. Other expressions in the Epistles correspond with the impression which we derive of Tibullus from his poems. The 'regio Pedana,' a district in Latium, between Praeneste and Tibur, where the Campagna rises up towards the Sabine and Æquian hills, suits exactly the notion we form of the estate of Tibullus, as one adapted for flocks and herds, as well as corn-crops and vineyards: and the ceremony of purifying the fields, described in the first elegy of Book ii, is an old rite of the Latin husbandmen. In the line

> An tacitum silvas inter reptare salubres,

the word 'reptare' is suggestive of the gentle nature of the man, in contrast to the excitability of Propertius and the pleasure-

---

[1] This remark and one or two others in this examination of the Epistle were suggested by Kiessling's notes on the passage: 'aber Tibull ist Hypochonder und quält sich mit Todesgedanken.'

loving vivacity of Ovid. We may compare the epithet 'tacitum,' and the reference to his 'facundia,' his 'gift of expression,' in the words 'fari quae sentiat,' to the words in which Martial (viii. 70) characterises Nerva, whom he calls the Tibullus of his time—

> Quanta quies placidi, tanta est facundia Nervae.

The 'gratia' attributed to him applies well to the favoured friend of Messalla.

Even the slight allusion to his literary work is appropriate to the writer of elegies or epigrams. Horace could not have applied the term 'opuscula' to the tragedies of Cassius, but his use of the word indicates the same feeling which suggests the epithet 'exiguos' applied to the elegies in the 'Ars Poetica.' This Epistle may have been written before the first book of Elegies was published, and Horace may have known by report only of Tibullus as a writer of elegies. He addresses him as the 'candid critic of his Satires.' Had the Odes been given to the world when the Epistle was written, he would certainly have valued his favourable opinion of them more than of his 'sermones.' It was natural that Horace, writing perhaps about the year 25 or 26 B.C., should avoid the name of Gallus, who had so recently fallen into disgrace. It is somewhat remarkable that among the names of those who are mentioned by him in the tenth Satire of Book i. as the critics for whose favour he wrote, almost every name eminent in the literature of the age is mentioned, except that of Gallus. After his career in Egypt, Gallus must have been an especial object of suspicion to Maecenas, whose position required him to observe and watch all who might be dangerous to the Empire. Dion (liii. 24) records as a signal proof of the disgrace of Gallus, the disgust which Proculeius, so intimately connected with Maecenas, and mentioned by Horace as a type of all that was most respectable in that age, shewed when he met him. Cassius of Parma had been a leading man in the army of Brutus and Cassius, and may thus have been known to Horace personally. If it is necessary to account for the omission of the name of Gallus and the presence of that of Cassius of Parma, explanations may be given quite consistent with the identity of Albius with the author of the Elegies.

There seems therefore no reason to doubt that Albius, the friend of Horace, is Albius Tibullus the poet. The gentleness and loyalty of the cultivated friend of Messalla would naturally attract Horace, as the vanity and self-assertion of the unwelcome intruder into the circle of Maecenas repelled him. The pictures of the two contemporary elegiac poets, Tibullus and Propertius, as they are painted in the first and second books of the Epistles, bear the test of a close comparison with the impression of themselves unconsciously left by those authors on their works, and confirm the opinion that in his Epistles Horace is a true and subtle, if not always indulgent discerner of character. The picture of Tibullus not only confirms but completes our knowledge of the man, and makes us better understand how worthy he was to be the comrade and friend of Messalla, the lover of philosophy no less than of literature.

But for all the details of the circumstances, tastes, interests of the poet, we must trust to the small volume which has reached us under his name. Of the three or, according to a division adopted in modern times, four books, contained in the volume, the first two only, those of which the prominent motive is the love of Delia and of Nemesis, can with certainty be ascribed to him. It is most likely that the first book only, consisting of ten elegies, was given to the world by the author, probably about 25 or 26 B.C., and that the second, consisting of six elegies, one of which is only twenty-two lines in length, was left incomplete, not finally revised by the author, and published soon after his death by some of the members of the circle of Messalla.

The first six elegies of the third book are the work of Lygdamus, a younger poet, and an evident imitator not only of Tibullus but of Ovid and Propertius[1]. The hexameter

---

[1] As Lygdamus is not mentioned by Ovid or any of the ancients among the poets of the Augustan age, it is supposed by Birt ('Das antike Buch-

poem, a panegyric on Messalla written in the year of his Consulship, 31 B.C., which intervenes between the elegies of Lygdamus and the concluding elegies of the book, is the composition of some member of the same literary circle. Most of the remaining elegies are devoted to the love-story of Sulpicia and an otherwise unknown Cerinthus. The last six of these are the composition of Sulpicia herself. The earlier elegies, introducing these, are not unworthy of Tibullus, and may have been written by him in sympathy with a daughter of the house, who from her intellectual gifts no less than her personal charms (iii. 8) may well have excited a warm and kindly interest in all the members of the circle, from her guardian Messalla to the poets and other friends who frequented his house.

The main story of the life of Tibullus, and the record of his feelings which is the most interesting part of it, are to be gathered from a rapid survey of the elegies composing the first two books. He was born about the year 54 B.C. (more probably after than before that date) and died still a young man in the year 18 B.C. He was of equestrian rank, and belonged to an old Latin family, settled in the neighbourhood of the towns of Pedum and Gabii. His estate had been handed down to him through a long line of ancestors (ii. 1. 2), but had since their time been much diminished (i. 1. 19–22). It is generally supposed that, as in the case of Virgil, Horace, and Propertius, his losses were due to the confiscations that followed the battle of Philippi. But Tibullus does not, as he might naturally have done, assign this as the cause of his losses; and landed property is diminished by other causes besides confiscation, acting through several generations. No town in Latium is mentioned by Appian among those whose lands were assigned for that purpose. Tibullus was born into the position, the most fortunate in that age for a man of culture, of the inheritor of a country

wesen') that his elegies were at an early period comprised in one volume with the short second book of Tibullus, and that thus they came to be cited in the middle ages as from the second book of Tibullus. No third or fourth book is referred to in the anthologies which existed in the middle ages.

estate, endeared to him by old family memories and associations, and, though much reduced from its ancient dimensions, yet sufficient to give him all the really desirable advantages of life.

He is first introduced to us as living in his country-house, where he had lived happily as a child (i. 10. 15)—

> Sed patrii servate lares: aluistis et idem
> Cursarem vestros cum tener ante pedes—

and where his ancestors had lived from immemorial times; and contemplating with strong reluctance and some natural fears the prospect of his first campaign. That was probably in the year 30 or 29 B.C., when he shared the tent and served on the staff of Messalla, in his Aquitanian campaign. He is said to have gained 'orders of distinction,' 'militaria dona,' by his services; and he gained the more solid advantage of the permanent friendship of his chief. In the poem referred to above, probably his earliest, though he indicates his susceptibility to love, he hints at no definite attachment rendering him more reluctant to incur the dangers of the expedition, as his attachment to Delia a year or two later makes him reluctant to accompany Messalla again on his mission to the East.

Probably in the winter following his return from the Aquitanian campaign he became the lover of Plania, who, under the name of Delia, is the heroine of his first book of Elegies. Her position is ambiguous. He speaks of her as if she were a married woman, whose husband was absent as a soldier in Cilicia, but he says also that she did not wear the 'head-dress' or the 'long robe' characteristic of a Roman matron; and in a later poem he speaks of a 'lena' who was the agent of her later intrigues[1]. Probably she was united to her *vir* by some of the less binding relations which did not entitle her to wear the 'vitta.' She is a more shadowy personage than the Cynthia of Propertius, but

---

[1] Haec nocuere mihi quod adest huic dives amator:
    Venit in exitium callida lena meum (i. 5. 47).
He proceeds to denounce the 'lena' in terms that recall, though there is no touch of humour in them, Horace's denunciations of Canidia.

there can be no doubt that in the first three Elegies of the book we are reading a genuine story of mutual love, probably the first deep affection of both their lives. Five poems only, out of the ten composing the first book, are devoted to the love of Delia. The second appears to be the earliest in date, and is in the form of a παρακλαυσίθυρον, a complaint uttered before her closed door. It is evidently written in Rome, and in the winter succeeding the Aquitanian campaign—

> Non mihi pigra nocent hibernae frigora noctis,
> Non mihi cum multa decidit imber aqua—

but while still in Rome, he longs to be in the country with Delia, tending his flocks on the familiar hill:

> Ipse boves mea si tecum modo Delia possim
> Iungere, et in solito pascere monte pecus.

In the first Elegy the love of his home is as prominent a motive as the love of Delia. It is written to excuse himself to Messalla for not again accompanying him on foreign service. He urges that he has no need nor wish to enrich himself, and that he cannot tear himself from the 'formosae vincla puellae.' The line

> Et sedeo duras ianitor ante fores

and the lines

> Nunc levis est tractanda Venus, dum frangere postes
> Non pudet et rixas inseruisse iuvat,

indicate, what we should not have supposed from the thoroughly idyllic character of the first half of the poem, that it was probably written in the city, though under the influence of the quieter thoughts of his country home.

The third Elegy, written later in the same year, informs us that he had started with Messalla on his mission to the East. It represents Tibullus as detained in Corcyra by a dangerous illness, from which he is still suffering or just recovering. After expressing in the two opening lines his affection for Messalla and his comrades, he devotes the rest of his poem to the longing for Delia and for his home, and to the thoughts suggested by his recent danger. None of his poems is so full of tender beauty as this. His whole feeling is exalted and purified by absence and the prospect of death. There are few passages in ancient poetry so perfect as a picture from life and an expression of feeling as the lines in which he anticipates his unexpected and unannounced arrival before Delia, engaged with her handmaids on their evening tasks:

> Tunc veniam subito nec quisquam nuntiet ante,
> Sed videar caelo missus adesse tibi:
> Tunc mihi, qualis eris, longos turbata capillos,
> Obvia nudato, Delia, curre pede.

His return, however, did not fulfil his hopes. In the fifth poem he appears again in Rome. Delia had been dangerously ill; and Tibullus believes that he has saved her life by his prayers and ceremonial observances. He had dreamed of a happy life in which he should share with her the congenial labours of the farm. But she is no longer unsophisticated as when he parted from her. She has applied the arts of intrigue, which he reproaches himself with having taught her, and through the agency of a 'lena' has sold herself to a richer lover. In the following poem the husband has returned from the wars. Tibullus appeals to him to guard Delia from his rival. He appeals to her old mother, who had always favoured their love; he entreats Delia to be chaste, not from fear, 'sed mente fideli,' and ends with the prayer,

> nos Delia amoris
> Exemplum cana simus uterque fide.

If it is true that the love of Cynthia made Propertius a poet, the love of Delia inspires the happiest poetry of Tibullus. Fortunately we know this passion only in its short-lived bloom, and not, like that of Propertius, also in its decay, and through the stormy seasons preceding its decay. Though her infidelity produced its natural effect in separation, he allows no words of scorn or coldness to mar the beauty of his past.

Three other poems of this book, the fourth, the eighth, and the ninth, are of a sentimental character, of a much less pleasing sort. The subject of them is a beautiful youth, Marathus; and they indicate at least a sympathy with that aberration of feeling which is the chief stain on ancient civilisation. It is generally assumed that these poems are later than those written in connexion with Delia. But there is no evidence for this presumption. It is as likely that they are the record of an earlier state of feeling, before his deeper nature was stirred by his love for Delia and his friendship for Messalla. The tone of these poems is less gentle and kindly than in his other elegies[1]. They not only show little of his purer affection, but they bear no traces, or only the faintest, of his life in his country estate, or of his devotion to Messalla.

One poem, the seventh, not yet noticed, gives the worthiest expression to these feelings of devotion to his friend. It was written in honour of the birthday of Messalla, which happened to be the anniversary of his great victory on the river Atax, and celebrates at the same time the triumph awarded to him in the year 27 B.C. It recalls the memory of the campaign in which he himself had borne his part, and gives a rapid survey of the wonders of the lands which Messalla visited in the course of his Eastern mission. The tone of the whole poem is thoroughly genial, and the concluding lines bring Messalla before us, as happy in his family life, and as beneficent in the works of peace, as he had been distinguished in war.

Several years must have elapsed between the composition of the Elegies of the first and those of the second book. He seems to have been roused to write only when under the influence of some strong attachment; and his love for Nemesis, which is the principal subject of this book, belongs to the last years of his life[2]. That book was left unfinished and must have been published after his death. The fifth poem certainly could not

---

[1] Cf. especially 9. 45-76.
[2] Cf. ii. 5. 109-112—
    iaceo cum saucius annum,
 Et faveo morbo, cum iuvat ipse dolor,
Usque cano Nemesim sine qua versus mihi nullus
 Verba potest iustos aut reperire pedes.

Ovid writes as if the love of Tibullus for Nemesis had endured till his death. This poem was written in 18 B.C.

have obtained the final revision of the author. This book brings him before us in the same relations as the earlier book,—as a lover, and the poet of love, as living happily on his estate, feeling a lively sympathy with the homely pursuits and joys of the country people, and with the ancient ceremonies of rural life; and as the friend of Messalla devoting his art to celebrate the entrance of Messalla's son on public duties, and led on by this new theme, to find, like the other elegiac poets, inspiration for the last effort of his genius in the ancient memories of Rome.

The love for Nemesis has more the nature of a 'bondage' than that for Delia. She seems to exercise over him something of the spell which Cynthia exercises over Propertius. She tortures him by her infidelities, and threatens to ruin him by her rapacity. He even faces the contingency of having to part with his old home, the source of so much of his happiness and inspiration:

> Quin etiam sedes iubeat si vendere avitas,
> Ite sub imperium sub titulumque, Lares (ii. 4. 53).

These are the slight and simple materials out of which the texture of his poems is woven. Love is the chief inspirer and the chief motive of his poetry:

> Ad dominam faciles aditus per carmina quaero:
> Ite procul Musae si nihil ista valent (ii. 4; 19).

He is as indifferent to fame as to wealth:

> Non ego laudari cupio, mea Delia; tecum
> Dum modo sim, quaeso segnis inersque vocer (i. 1. 57–58).

If his love has less ardour than that of Propertius, it has more tenderness and self-abnegation. Virgil alone among ancient poets is capable of such feeling and such sympathy with feeling as that expressed in the line,

> Non ego sum tanti ploret ut illa semel;

and of the self-forgetfulness of

> At iuvet in tota me nihil esse domo.

He feels strongly the sanctity of love, and says of him who violates it,

> e caelo deripit ille deos.

As Virgil finds a place for 'pii vates' and 'casti sacerdotes' in Elysium, Tibullus finds there a place for faithful and gentle lovers. His ideal of happiness is a permanent union ending only with death, of which the pain should be mitigated by the sympathy of the loved object—

> Te teneam moriens deficiente manu.

Affection and dependence on affection, tinged with melancholy, are the predominant sentiments in his love for Delia and Nemesis. He expresses also affection for those nearly connected with them, as in his grateful remembrance of her mother after Delia had proved faithless—

> Vive diu mihi dulcis anus: proprios ego tecum,
>   Sit modo fas, annos contribuisse velim:
> Te semper natamque tuam te propter amabo:
>   Quidquid agit, sanguis est tamen illa tuus (i. 6. 63)—

and in his tender recollection of the young sister of Nemesis—

> Parce per immatura tuae precor ossa sororis:
>   Sic bene sub tenera parva quiescat humo.
> Illa mihi sancta est, illius dona sepulcro
>   Et madefacta meis serta feram lacrimis:
> Illius ad tumulum fugiam supplexque sedebo,
>   Et mea cum muto fata querar cinere (ii. 6. 29).

His elegy is the true elegy of love, expressive of its sorrows rather than its joys, sorrows arising from separation and desertion, and, even when the happiness is most complete—'in ipsis floribus'—from the sense of its transitoriness. No poet has given more refined expression to the charm of youth and beauty and to the speed with which it passes away. The lesson which he draws is that drawn, lightly or sadly, by so many other Epicurean singers of the joys of life:

> Interea dum fata sinunt iungamus amores:
> Iam veniet tenebris mors adoperta caput.

Love with him, as with Catullus and other poets, ancient and modern, 'spices his fair banquet with the dust of death.'

If the sentimental mood of Tibullus appears alien to the more masculine Roman temper, no other poet, with the exception of Virgil, is so possessed by the spirit of Italy, the love of the country and of the labour of the fields, and the piety associated with that sentiment. To the life of the country and the teaching of the rural gods he attributes the origin of civilisation, of poetry and of love, and it is in the actual labours of the field, not in the 'latis otia fundis,' that he finds the chief charm of country life. Like Virgil, he associates this charm with the love of Rome and all the homely joys of life, the joys of the poor no less than those of his own condition:

> Quam potius laudandus hic est, quem prole parata
>   Occupat in parva pigra senecta casa:
> Ipse suas sectatur oves, at filius agnos,
>   Et calidam fesso comparat uxor aquam (i. 10. 39).

Part of the horror of death is to pass from the sight of cornfields and vineyards to 'the sunless land' where

> Non seges est infra, non vinea culta (i. 10. 35).

He remembers and acts on the precept

> Imprimis venerare deos,

and believes that all the success of his labours is due to his reverence for the ancient objects and ceremonials of religion (i. 1. 9–14). In one of the latest passages which he wrote, he associates the rude mirth of the shepherds' festival with the genial influence of family affection:

> Et fetus matrona dabit, natusque parenti
>   Oscula comprensis auribus eripiet,
> Nec taedebit avum parvo advigilare nepoti
>   Balbaque cum puero dicere verba senem (ii. 5. 91).

As in Virgil, the love of the country creates an idealising longing for the restoration of the innocence and happiness of the Saturnian age (i. 3. 35). While he writes in the spirit of the Georgics, and must have deeply felt the influence of that poem, which was first given to the world about the time when he was composing his Elegies, he is no servile copyist of it. None perhaps of his contemporaries was so well fitted by his life and tastes to assimilate all the feeling with which that poem is saturated. Yet both in his art and in his love of the country Tibullus is quite independent. The expression of his feeling is more purely idyllic, less tinged with reflexion, than that of Virgil. The large admixture of an idyllic element in his elegies distinguishes Tibullus from his more powerful and more brilliant rivals in elegiac poetry, who are essentially poets of the passions and pleasures of the town.

Closely connected with his love of home and the country is his love of peace. He writes under the influence of a strong reaction which followed the thirty years of civil strife, dating from the consulship of Metellus. He does not, like the poets of the circle of Maecenas, express his sympathy with the success of the national cause in the war against Antony and Cleopatra, nor any interest in the later wars carried on for the consolidation and security of the Empire, except in so far as they brought distinction to Messalla. He thinks about war as affecting individual happiness; and idealises peace as the fosterer of love and the homely joys of life (i. 10. 49 ff.). His horror of war is enhanced by his melancholy foreboding of death:

> Quis furor est atram bellis arcessere mortem?
> Imminet et tacito clam venit illa pede (ibid. 33).

The thought has not for him the grim fascination which it has for the imagination of Propertius; he does not fight against it by familiarising himself with it as Horace does; still less does he encounter it with the austere submission of Lucretius. As Virgil seeks his consolation in the vague hopes of a spiritual philosophy, so Tibullus finds his in the vague fancies of the perpetuation in a purified and exalted state of what was to him the chief poetic charm of this life (i. 3. 57–66).

He is also the idealising poet of a friendship as loyal as that of Horace for Maecenas, as fervent as that of Catullus for Calvus and Verannius. His affection for Messalla mingles with all his joys, interests, and cares. In his dream of happiness when he thinks of Delia living with him, and sharing the pleasant toils of the farm, the crowning joy was to be the visits of Messalla—

> Huc veniet Messalla meus, cui dulcia poma
>   Delia selectis detrahat arboribus;
> Et tantum venerata virum, hunc sedula curet,
>   Huic paret atque epulas ipsa ministra gerat.
> Haec mihi fingebam quae nunc Eurusque Notusque
>   Iactat odoratos vota per Armenios (i. 5. 31).

In the festival of the purification of the fields it is to the health of Messalla that every one is called to drink (ii. 1. 31–32). In anticipation of death he desires that this shall be inscribed on his tomb:

> Hic iacet immiti consumptus morte Tibullus
>   Messallam terra dum sequiturque mari (i. 3. 55).

He is moved by the military and civil distinctions of Messalla, but above all his sympathies with him are roused on the occasion of the assumption of the first public duties by his son Messalinus, and he anticipates the pride which the father will feel in the triumphs which await his future career:

> Tunc Messalla meus pia det spectacula turbae
>   Et plaudat curru praetereunte pater (ii. 5. 119).

The public office bestowed on the young Messalinus was that of one of the Quindecemviri who had charge of the Sibylline books; and the poem was apparently composed in connexion with the festival of Apollo, preceding the celebration of the Secular Games, for which Horace also composed the sixth Ode of the fourth book. Through his interest in the function performed by Messalinus, the voice of Tibullus becomes for the moment the organ of national feeling, and gives picturesque expression to the contrast between the magnificence of Rome in the Augustan Age and the pastoral loneliness of the seven hills in early times:

> Carpite nunc tauri de septem montibus herbas.

From this he passes by natural transition to the thought of the imperial mission of Rome:

> Roma, tuum nomen terris fatale regendis,
>   Qua sua de caelo prospicit arva Ceres.

There is no mention of, nor apparently any allusion to Augustus in this expression of national feeling. But his silence on an occasion which might almost seem to have demanded an expression of sympathy with the dominant sentiment of the hour, need not be attributed to antagonism to the court. It is rather indicative of one who lived much apart from the world, indifferent to favour, popularity, and advancement, and acting consistently on the principle involved in the line

> Nec vixit male qui moriens natusque fefellit.

But though there is no recognition of the dominant sentiment of the hour, there are clear traces of the influence of the great poem which is its monumental embodiment. In earlier poems we are reminded of the sentiment and language of the Bucolics and the Georgics; in the references to Aeneas and to Turnus we feel the immediate presence of the Aeneid. The only poet between whom and Tibullus we can trace a distinct affinity is Virgil. They are alike in their human affection and their piety, in their capacity of tender and self-forgetful love, in their delight in the labours of the field, and their sympathy with the herdsman and the objects of his care. They have the same delicate sense of art and cultivated fastidiousness of expression. Tibullus does not profess to make any Greek poet his model: nor does his culture display itself in recondite allusions to Greek mythology, although he varies his idyllic pictures of natural scenes and of incidents in human life with one or two reproductions of the stories more familiar to art and poetry, such as that of Apollo feeding the flocks of Admetus. Neither does he make such use of Greek idioms and modes of expression as Virgil and Horace. That he was familiar with the Alexandrians may be assumed; but the influence of their art, as it appears in their professed imitator Propertius, and their translator Catullus, is not distinctly traceable in his elegies. Too little is known of Philetas to justify any judgment on the relation of Tibullus to him. From the similarity of sentiment in passages in which Tibullus laments the transitoriness of youth and beauty, to some of the fragments of Mimnermus[1], it seems not unlikely that Tibullus may, like Horace, have drawn from the older sources of Greek poetry, rather than the Alexandrian reservoirs. His own vein, though not abundant, is thoroughly 'ingenuus,' thoroughly his own. He guides it carefully but never exhausts it. He is satisfied with the one channel that was fitted to convey his moods of peaceful happiness or pensive melancholy, and has no need for the more varied outlets demanded by the more mobile temperament and active intellect of Horace.

That he profited by the advance made in composition, metre, and diction by his predecessors in elegiac poetry may be assumed: but to him belongs the distinction of having given artistic perfection to the Roman elegy. The structure of the several elegies exemplifies that delicate art which conceals the labour and thought bestowed upon it. There is at once unity and variety in every elegy—the unity of a dominant sentiment, the variety of thoughts and pictures in keeping with it, arranged in groups corresponding with one another, and succeeding one another by gentle and natural transition. Thus the third poem is written to give utterance to his feelings when lying ill of fever and apprehensive of death in Corcyra. What gives unity to the poem is his memory of the love of Delia in the past, and his longing for her in the immediate future. But with this feeling is blended his love of home; and a vivid contrast is drawn between the perils of war and foreign adventure, and the ideal happiness of the Saturnian age. From these perils he passes to the thought of his own imminent danger, and from that to describe the joys of the blessed in Elysium and the tortures of the damned in Tartarus: among them he mentions last the punishment of the daughters of Danaus, 'Danai proles Veneris quae numina laesit.' This thought leads him back by the force of contrast to the brightest picture which his imagination can paint in the world of the living, that of Delia spinning among her handmaids and of his own

[1] Noticed by Gruppe and referred to by M. Plessis.

unexpected return. There is no mechanical arrangement, but rather a harmonious combination of his materials, their succession being regulated sometimes by the suggestions of similarity, sometimes of contrast. The peaceful joys of the country are, in many of the elegies, set over against the dangers and the rough life of the soldier, and the joy of youth and love is made more intense by the thought of death. There is nothing forced or strained in his manner of treatment; no undue emphasis or exaggeration of colouring. He is impressive by the truth and simplicity of his separate pictures, and their harmony with the moods to which he wishes to give expression.

As he was the first to perfect the form of the elegy, he was the first also to impart to the elegiac metre that smooth and liquid flow which Virgil imparted to the hexameter in his pastoral poetry, the charm of sound that befits the 'Muses who delight in the country' as well as the Muse of tender emotion. He avoids altogether the long continuous passages without any break in the sense, and the long compound sentences out of which the more elaborate elegies of Catullus are composed. The sense of each distich is complete in itself. The clauses are direct and simple, expressive often of a wish or prayer, or making a plain statement of fact; and follow each other, either without any connecting word, or with a conjunction co-ordinating them with one another, or more rarely marking the dependence of one thought on another. The connexion between one distich and another is felt but seldom expressed. Sometimes emphasis is given to it by repeating the word which is the key to the thought in the previous line, or more usually, by placing first in the couplet the word that indicates the connexion. There is an equable rise and fall in the metre; an equable balance between the hexameter and the pentameter, and between the first and second half of the pentameter. Yet he avoids the extreme monotony of movement which would result from a uniformity of pause at the end of the first line, as is the case with the English decasyllabic couplet. There is frequently more than one pause in the couplet. Sometimes the principal pause is in the middle of the fourth foot of the hexameter; more frequently at the end of the first foot of the pentameter. The balance between the two halves of the pentameter is often maintained by the position of an epithet at the end of the first half and of the substantive which it qualifies at the end of the second half, as

> Et teneat culti iugera multa soli.

He varies the ordinary iambic ending of the pentameter by occasional but not too frequent trisyllabic or quadrisyllabic endings. To a modern ear the movement of the verse is smoother than that of the Ovidian elegiac with its rapid succession of epigrammatic antithesis: while it never leaves the impression of strain and labour, as if the single lines and couplets were beat out by separate efforts, which is often left by the metre of Propertius. As in the structure of the whole poem there is an equable and varied onward movement, so the rise and fall in the metre is at once equable and varied. He fully recognises its limits, and its inadequacy to the expression of consecutive thought. Poetry with him returns to something like its original function before it was used as the organ of action and thought. It becomes in a great measure again the simple expression of feeling in the form of a prayer, a wish, or a regret.

There is great beauty and delicacy also in his diction. It has not the vivacity and sparkling wit of that of Ovid: neither is it boldly inventive and creative like that of Propertius. But it is never forced or artificial, and, though always simple, it is never trivial nor superfluous. The active power of his imagination is perceptible rather in the collocation of his words than in figures of speech, as in the line which vividly contrasts the steadfast agency by which ships are guided in their course with their own instability—

> Ducunt instabiles sidera certa rates.

Much oftener he produces his effects by the natural use of the simplest words, as for instance in

or
> Sic bene sub tenera parva quiescat humo—

or
> Non ego sum tanti ploret ut illa semel—

> Te teneam moriens deficiente manu.

The often expressed contrast between past happiness and present pain is brought out, partly by the position of the two epithets in the hexameter, partly by the direct simplicity of the last words of the pentameter, in the lines

> Saepe ego cum dominae dulces a limine duro
> Agnosco voces, haec negat esse domi.

He has, like most of the Latin poets, the power of moving feeling by the vague suggestions of musical sound in his language, as in the lines

> Haec mihi fingebam, quae nunc Eurusque Notusque
> Iactat odoratos vota per Armenios.

All the charm of youth lingers in the movement as in the meaning of the line

> Solis aeterna est Baccho Phoeboque iuventas;

and the pathos of the transitoriness of all beautiful things is profoundly felt in the movement and meaning of these:

> Quam cito purpureos deperdit terra colores,
> Quam cito formosas populus alta comas.

There is no laborious search for mythological parallels, no facile enumeration of obvious generalisations from the processes of nature or the operations of human industry, as in Propertius and Ovid, to adorn or illustrate his subject. Picturesque and beautiful forms and scenes from human life and outward nature present themselves to his imagination, in perfect harmony with the feeling that moves him. Such is the picture already referred to of Delia running to meet him on his unexpected return:

> Tunc mihi qualis eris, longos turbata capillos,
> Obvia nudato Delia curre pede.

Such is that of the maid, going through the darkness to meet her lover:

> Et pedibus praetemptat iter suspensa timore,
> Explorat caecas cui manus ante vias.

Such is that of the soldier, telling his battles over again—

> Ut mihi potanti possit sua dicere facta
> Miles, et in mensa pingere castra mero—

and this, which along with its playfulness mingles some of the tenderness of the most pathetic passage in Lucretius,

> natusque parenti
> Oscula comprensis auribus eripiet.

The sight of corn-fields and vineyards, of hills and plains, with the added charm of animal life, gives him the pleasure which it gives to Virgil and Lucretius, and to Horace in his more idyllic moods; and the elegies abound with evidence that those were the sights most constantly before him, and those which sank into his heart. Other aspects of nature which move the imagination more powerfully are also to be found in these elegies. Such is that, in the account of the purification of the fields, of the night succeeding the evening mirth and festivities, which followed the celebration of the religious rite:

> Ludite: iam nox iungit equos, currumque sequuntur
> Matris lascivo sidera fulva choro;
> Postque venit tacitus fuscis circumdatus alis
> Somnus et incerto somnia nigra pede.

Though he missed seeing the strange Eastern lands through which Messalla's mission led him, he yet realises in imagination the natural and historic wonder of the prospect from the place where

> maris vastum prospectet turribus aequor
> Prima ratem ventis credere docta Tyros.

Tibullus is one of those poets who inspire affection by the personal impression which they have left stamped on their writings, an affection rising from the recognition of a simple, tender, and loyal nature, free from all taint of vanity, envy, or malevolence. That this was the feeling inspired in his lifetime may be inferred from the qualities which Horace attributes to him: it might be inferred from his friendship with one of the most loyal and high-minded gentlemen whom Rome at the epoch of her highest social civilisation produced. The epigram of Domitius Marsus indicates that the sorrow felt for his premature death was like that felt for the loss of Virgil. The elegy in which Ovid, whose best quality is the candour of his appreciation of other poets, utters not so much his own sorrow as the sorrow of the whole world of culture for his loss, almost redeems the levity of the three books of the Amores. If he seems deficient in sympathy with the public virtue or the martial spirit of Rome, except in so far as he recognises their union in his friend Messalla, this may be attributed possibly to his sympathies with the Republic and to his own choice of the 'secretum iter,' apart from any contact with public affairs, and to the character of the wars waged in his day. The battle of Actium was indeed able to arouse all that still remained of patriotic enthusiasm, as it does in Virgil, Horace, and Propertius, and to reconcile the old adherents of the Republic, as it did Messalla, to the Empire. But the wars preceding it, in which Tibullus was too young to have borne his part, though he was not too young to bear a lasting impression of them, were such as to leave on the imagination a vivid sense of all the horror and misery, and none of the glory and greatness of war. And those which immediately followed it, though necessary to the security and consolidation of the Empire, were to the individual rather a field for adventure and for booty than a call to patriotism, and could excite enthusiasm only in those who felt themselves identified with the success of the Empire. Tibullus alone among the poets of the age not only abstains from any words of flattery, but makes no acknowledgment of the real beneficence of the rule of Augustus. His feeling towards Messalla is the feeling of one cultivated gentleman towards another, to whom he is attached by a lifelong friendship, based on admiration for his great qualities of heart, and intellect, and character.

He had no ambition to advance himself by his art, nor does he seek to impress the world by his originality. A delicate fastidiousness, like that of the poet Gray, made him write little and give the world only of his best. He shows no great intellectual power or large range of imagination, no recondite learning or intuitions into secrets of nature or human life which he alone is able to reveal. He holds a place, far indeed from the highest, among those poets who please every generation of readers by the attraction of their personality, the purity of their taste, the sincerity of their feeling, the music of their diction, and the adequacy of their genius to body forth pleasing pictures from nature and human life in keeping with the movement of their spirit. If he is less Roman in his moods than most of the other poets of Rome, he is thoroughly Latin in the sobriety and sanity of his imagination. By the soundest criticism of antiquity he was regarded as the greatest master of the Roman elegy. The criticism of Quintilian is: 'In elegy also we rival the Greeks, of which Tibullus appears to me the purest and finest representative. Some indeed prefer Propertius to him. Ovid is more licentious than either, as Gallus is harsher.' The prodigal creativeness of his imagination has gained for the poems of Ovid a greater fortune in modern times. In the present day the comparative novelty of Propertius, his irregular and daring force of conception and expression, and the ardour of his temperament, have altered the balance of admiration in his favour; still, among scholars and lovers of literature there may yet be found those who would say of themselves 'sunt qui Tibullum malint.' In elegiac poetry, the most subjective of all the forms of poetry, it is impossible to separate sharply the impression produced by qualities of heart and character in the writer from the effect produced by his art. The personality of Tibullus is much the most attractive, much the most admirable of the three. In his art he is the most faultless, the most perfectly harmonious.

III.

The other poems which have reached us in the same volume as the genuine poems of Tibullus appear in the MSS. as composing one book, but in most editions as Books iii. and iv. They are divided into three parts, and are to be assigned probably to four different authors. Their bond of union is that they emanate from the circle of Messalla. So far as they are written in elegiac verse, the influence of the art of Tibullus is predominant in their style and sentiment, though they bear traces of imitation of the language of Ovid, Propertius, and Horace. The first section, printed as Book iii. and consisting of six elegies, much inferior to those of Tibullus, is professedly the work of Lygdamus. Of him we know nothing, except what he tells us of himself. No ancient writer quotes him by name or speaks of him as an elegiac poet. The name is Greek, and occurs in Propertius as that of a slave of Cynthia. It appears to be formed from the Greek word λύγδος, a white stone or marble, and has been supposed to have been assumed as an equivalent of the Latin Albius. It is certain from the statements which the author makes about himself, and as certain as any such inference can be from the inferiority of his art, that he cannot be Tibullus. There is no ground for supposing that he was a Greek or a freedman. He writes of himself as a man of good social standing; and in the directions which he gives as to the disposal of his remains after death, he begs that his bones may be placed in a marble tomb, or urn—

> Atque in marmorea ponere sicca domo.

The name Lygdamus is probably not the true name of the author. If his real name was Albius, and if he was, as has been conjectured, a younger kinsman of the poet, a sufficient motive for the assumption of the name would be the wish to mark the distinction between himself and the greater poet who bore the same gentile name. The writer fixes the date of his birth in a line which occurs also in the Tristia (iv. 10. 42)—

> Natalem primo nostrum videre parentes
> Cum cecidit fato consul uterque pari.

The two following lines—

> Quid fraudare iuvat vitem crescentibus uvis
> Et modo nata mala vellere poma manu—

are nearly identical with two lines from the Amores of Ovid (Am. ii. 14. 43–44). It is natural to assume that in both cases the inferior poet has been the plagiarist, especially as in the latter of the two quotations the thought is both more perfectly expressed and suits the context better in Ovid than in Lygdamus. Neither author, however, could cast a stone at the other in respect to borrowing from other writers; the chief difference between them being that Ovid made more thoroughly his own and often improved what he borrowed. As the first edition of the Amores probably appeared before the poems of Lygdamus, it may be assumed that Lygdamus is the plagiarist in the two latter lines. But it is different with the line marking the date of birth. If Lygdamus did not write these lines till the fourth book of the Tristia appeared in 12 A.D. he must have been well on to the age of sixty at the time of the composition of his elegies. But he writes of himself as a young lover, and the two immediately preceding lines (in the latter of which another resemblance to Ovid is found—A. A. ii. 670) are

> Et nondum cani nigros laesere capillos
> Nec venit tardo curva senecta pede.

How then are we to account for the identity of the line

> Cum cecidit fato consul uterque pari

in both writers? If Lygdamus borrowed it from the Tristia, we must suppose that his elegies are the reminiscences of a love of his youth recalled in imagination by the poet when advanced in years, a possible though not probable supposition. Or, again, he and Ovid being exactly of the same age, living in the same circle, may have read their verses to one another, and Ovid may have made the line long before he used it for his own autobiography, or it may have lingered unconsciously in his memory, if read to him by Lygdamus. Or (as is suggested by Mr. Postgate) both may have taken it from a common and forgotten source. The line may, like the line of Ennius,

> Unus homo nobis cunctando restituit rem,

or like the

> Fato Metelli Romae fiunt consules,

attributed to Naevius, have passed into common use, as marking emphatically the date of the fall of the Republic.

The subject of the poems of Lygdamus is his love for Neaera. There is a difficulty in understanding his exact relation to her. She is evidently a lady of good position, the daughter of honourable parents, and belonging to a cultivated household:

> Nec te conceptam saeva leaena tulit,
> Barbara nec Scythiae tellus horrendave Syrtis
>   Sed culta et duris non habitanda domus,
> Et longe ante alias omnes mitissima mater
>   Isque pater quo non alter amabilior.

The poet writes as if he were married or betrothed to her, and as if she were his cousin, 'soror patruelis.' In sending her a poem on the first of March, the Matronalia, he writes,

> Haec tibi vir quondam, nunc frater, casta Neaera,
>   Mittit et accipias munera parva rogat,
> Teque suis iurat caram magis esse medullis
>   Sive sibi coniunx sive futura soror;
> Sed potius coniunx.

In expressing (after Tibullus) the wish that Neaera should attend his funeral, he uses the words,

> Sed veniat carae matris comitata dolore;
>   Maereat haec genero, maereat illa viro.

Ultimately she refuses to be re-united to him and deserts him, and he finds what consolation he can with his boon companions.

These poems are the utterance of a gentle cultivated youth, of modest temperament and chivalrous nature, imbued with the poetry of the day, but with no original genius. He moulded himself apparently in character and tastes as well as in his art on Tibullus, and it is a tempting conjecture that he may have been a younger brother or near relation of the poet. He shows the same gentleness and self-depreciation, the same craving for affection.

Though the diction of the poems has almost the appearance of being a cento from various authors, including Catullus and Horace as well as Ovid and Propertius, the imitations of Tibullus are much more frequent than those of any other poet. We find similar references to the favour of Bacchus and Apollo as bestowed on poets, to the cult of Apollo, and to the myth of his feeding the flocks of Admetus; a similar expression of indifference to wealth, a belief in the imminence of death and in the Elysian fields after death, and the prayer that Neaera ' longos incompta capillos ' should weep over his tomb. We find the same common-place thoughts about the winds dissipating his idle fancies—

> venti temeraria vota
> Aeriae et nubes diripienda ferant—

and about the impossibility of the tender spirit of his mistress having anything in common with the cruel forces of nature—

> Nam te nec vasti genuerunt aequora ponti.

In his rhythm and diction he tries to reproduce the effect of Tibullus, as in the emphasis imparted to the contrast between the charm of voice and manner of the speaker and the melancholy purport of his message in the words

> Edidit haec dulci tristia verba sono.

IV.

The panegyric on Messalla, written in hexameter verse, is by another young member of the circle, of even less genius and mastery of his instrument than Lygdamus. It is impossible to imagine it a youthful production of Tibullus. With no hint of his artistic excellence in rhythm or diction, it shows more than any other extant Latin work the faults most alien to his art, of irrelevant learning and exaggerated rhetoric. The poem has a certain value, as reflecting the culture of the day. We learn from it as we do from the greater writers, that a knowledge of Homer was essential to a liberal education. We find, as we do in Virgil, Horace, and Ovid, indications of the interest taken in remote and partially known lands and tribes, and we realise the different effects produced by the unimaginative intrusion of dead knowledge and by the imaginative suggestion of vivid wonder of which such allusions are capable. We note also, as we do in Virgil, Ovid, and Propertius, evidence of the surviving influence of Lucretius in the references to cosmogony, and we apprehend the difference between the prosaic and the poetical treatment of the subject. We feel also how dull and unmusical an instrument the hexameter became in the hands of inferior artists, and what a gain the elegiac metre was for the 'opuscula' of minor poets. The prosaic treatment of the prosaic details of castrametation and other military functions enables us to realise the loss which the literature of an age incurs when the balance between prose and poetry is not rightly adjusted, and especially when verse intrudes into the province of the historian. The complaint of Horace of the misdirected energy of his age—

> Mutavit mentem populus levis, et calet uno
> Scribendi studio: pueri patresque severi
> Fronde comas vincti cenant et carmina dictant—

gains confirmation from the accidental preservation of this and some other of the minor poems of the age.

The poem also adds something to our knowledge of Messalla and his circle, and confirms the general pleasing impression which we form of both. The panegyric though exaggerated has not the air of insincerity. The tribute to the eloquence of Messalla as a political and forensic orator, and the comparison of him to Nestor and Ulysses—

> Nam seu diversi fremat inconstantia vulgi,
> Non alius sedare queat; seu iudicis ira
> Sit placanda, tuis poterit mitescere verbis—

confirm the impression we form of his 'mitis sapientia.' The tribute to his military capacity implies the solid rather than the brilliant qualities of a good soldier. We learn that Valgius was looked on in the circle as the great poet of epic song, and from the language applied to him—

> aeterno propior non alter Homero—

we may infer that the circle was one of mutual admiration, a more amiable if intellectually less stimulating bond of union than mutual detraction.

The writer of the panegyric is modest about his own claims as he is appreciative of the genius and capacity of others. He complains of the loss of his estates—the only point of analogy between him and Tibullus—but unlike Tibullus he has no inclination for a life of ease and country pursuits, and is ready to accompany Messalla over the sea in the wildest storms of winter, to stand alone in his defence against hostile squadrons, and to cast his 'small body' into the flame of Etna on his behalf. An allusion to the consulship of Messalla shows that the poem was written in the year 31 B.C. It is impossible that the author of the Delia elegies could have written in this 'Ercles vein' at any stage even of his boyhood, still less within a year or two of his finest workmanship. The poem is to be regarded as a strange specimen of a fly preserved in amber.

V.

A much more interesting and attractive member of the circle is brought before us in the concluding elegies of the book. Sulpicia, daughter of Servius Sulpicius (a son probably of Cicero's friend) and of Valeria, sister of Messalla, springs from two of the oldest and noblest patrician houses of Rome; she adorns her high birth by beauty and accomplishment, and the attraction of a frank, lively and ardent nature—too frank, perhaps, and ardent, according to old Roman ideas. In these eleven short poems are preserved a few pages from a true love-story in the Augustan Age, told partly by a sympathetic poet, partly by the lady herself in short letters, as genuine and full of feeling as any letters of the present day, and more graceful than most of those which have the good or bad fortune to obtain publicity. There is nothing to determine who the poet is who writes the first pages of her romance. It has been conjectured that it may have been Messalla himself. If it was, the world has lost in him a true poet. But the tone of the poems is more that of a younger and sympathetic admirer, though not a lover, than of a kind and careful guardian, who may not altogether have approved of 'Sulpicia the daughter of Servius,' as she proudly calls herself, throwing herself away on the young Greek Cerinthus.

Though the art is not like that of Tibullus, it is not unworthy of him, and the art of a poet dealing objectively and somewhat playfully with a love with which he sympathises as a spectator, naturally differs from that in which he utters his own feelings. Whoever was the author, he speaks, in the earlier poems of the series, at one time in his own person, at another dramatically in that of Sulpicia. The last six are apparently the composition of Sulpicia herself. The first poem is a letter of compliment sent to her on the first of March, the Matronalia, when gifts or compliments were sent to matrons or maidens. It is a genuine tribute to the 'infinite variety' of her charms—

> Illam quidquid agit, quoquo vestigia movit
> Componit furtim subsequiturque decor—

and like the Odes of Horace it expresses in the language of gallantry a feeling no warmer than disinterested admiration. The second poem, full of tenderness, not without a slight tinge of jealousy, is a complaint of Sulpicia on the absence of Cerinthus on a hunting-party. The third is a prayer to Apollo to restore Sulpicia from a dangerous illness, and is written to comfort Cerinthus, who is suffering the torment of a devoted lover:

> Pone metum Cerinthe; deus non laedit amantes:
> Tu modo semper ama; salva puella tibi est.

'It will be a day of pride and joy to Phoebus, when both pay their vows at his altar for her recovery':

> Tunc te felicem dicet pia turba deorum,
> Optabunt artes et sibi quisque tuas.

The next two poems are birthday addresses, the one in the name of Sulpicia to the genius of Cerinthus, the other an address by the poet to Juno, as presiding over the birthday. Sulpicia is represented as adorning herself in honour of the goddess, but at the same time having some one else in her mind whom she wishes to please:

> Est tamen, occulte cui placuisse velit.

Her mother in her anxiety for her welfare may try to direct her prayers, but she, feeling herself her own mistress, asks in her secret heart for something else.

Six short poems follow, extending in all to forty lines. They are notes in elegiac verse written by Sulpicia to Cerinthus. In the first she declares herself tired of keeping up appearances, and takes pride in the open avowal of her love:

> vultus componere famae
> Taedet: cum digno digna fuisse ferar.

In the next she complains that Messalla, with too great solicitude, has invited her to pass her birthday at his country house near Arretium, instead of allowing her to remain in town with Cerinthus. The next is a short note to say that she is allowed to stay. In the next there is the first little rift in her happiness, an expression of her jealous fear lest some unworthy object was for the moment of more interest to him than 'Sulpicia the daughter of Servius'; and she reminds him that others are jealous on her behalf. The next is a note of gentle reproach for his supposed indifference while she is suffering from fever. In the last she writes to express her repentance for an appearance of coldness, prompted by the wish to hide the warmth of her feelings—

> Ardorem cupiens dissimulare meum.

What was the end of this love-story, nearly twenty centuries old, we have no means of knowing. It is difficult to imagine the frank and natural girl developing into the conventional Roman matron, nor is there any ground for thinking that one so true in her first love and so resolute in clinging to it in the face of discouragement, should have conformed to the fashionable immorality of the time when Julia was the queen of Roman society and the 'Ars Amandi' the manual of conduct. As a specimen of the direct simplicity, the grace and warmth of natural feeling, not without a piquant admixture of the 'grata protervitas' by which the fancy of Horace was attracted, the poem in which she expresses her unwillingness to leave Rome on her birthday may be quoted:

> Invisus natalis adest, qui rure molesto
>   Et sine Cerintho tristis agendus erit.
> Dulcius urbe quid est? an villa sit apta puellae
>   Atque Arretino frigidus amnis agro?
> Iam nimium Messalla mei studiose quiescas,
>   Neu tempestivae perge monere viae.
> Hic animum sensusque meos abducta relinquo,
>   Arbitrio quamvis non sinis esse meo.

There remains one other short poem, claiming to be the work of Tibullus, and one epigram. Two poems in honour of the garden god have also been attributed to him, similar to those of which many were written in the Augustan Age. None of these in any way add to his reputation, and the first, in which, contrary to the practice of the real Tibullus, the writer speaks of himself by name, is, as Mr. Postgate has shown, almost certainly a forgery. Some of the lines, as noticed by Dissen, are not without power and beauty: but after the elegies of Tibullus and Propertius had taught the secret, any one could catch the trick of writing a few lines in elegiac tones. If these lines can be supposed to have been some composition of Tibullus, written in a careless or conventional mood—and either mood seems incompatible with all we know of him— which accidentally got preserved among other poems written by members of the circle, he certainly attached no importance to them or they would have found a place in the two books, which he and he only could have written. There seems no more reason to attribute the Priapea and the epigram to him, than the panegyric in hexameter verse. Whether he had any share in the Sulpicia poems we do not know. They are not unworthy of his art and genius, though they would imply a different application of them from that which we find in the two books of elegies. Whoever is their author, they have a real value as poetry, and a unique value as a most interesting page from the active life of the time.

CHAPTER III

Propertius: Life and Personal Characteristics

THERE is a greater difference of opinion about the literary position of Propertius than about that of any other Roman poet. The place of Lucretius and Virgil, of Horace and Catullus, in the first rank of Latin authors and among the great poets of the world, has been generally conceded. A similar position would have been allowed to Ovid in any century before the present. The rank of Tibullus as a classic of the second order is also undisputed. Propertius, on the other hand, has, within the present generation, emerged from comparative neglect to the place of chief favourite among the elegiac poets. Quintilian informs us that he had, in the ancient Roman world, his admirers who preferred him to Tibullus and Ovid; and the younger Pliny, in speaking of a poet of his day who claimed to be descended from him, writes appreciatively of him. Ovid, a just as well as a generous critic of his contemporaries and predecessors, by the words 'ignes' and 'blandique Propertius oris' shows his appreciation of the ardour as well as the musical charm of his verse. Martial includes the 'Cynthia Monobiblos' among the gift-books for which he wrote inscriptions, and Juvenal mentions Cynthia along with her

> cuius
> Turbavit nitidos exstinctus passer ocellos

as an instance of the degeneracy of Roman morals from the old Sabellian ideal. Statius also includes him in a common appreciative notice with Philetas and Callimachus, Ovid and Tibullus. But there is no indication that in ancient times he enjoyed the popularity of Tibullus, or exercised the same influence on later literature as was exercised by Ovid.

The imperfection of the text, and the late era to which the MSS., with perhaps one exception, belong, may, in the absence of any notices of the knowledge of his writings, be taken as evidence that Propertius was not much read between the fall of the Roman Empire in the West and the revival of letters. With the recovery of ancient literature, his poems attracted the attention of scholars and were for a time imitated by the modern writers of Latin verse in Italy: but from that time till about the middle of the present century, though not altogether neglected, they do not seem to have been held in high esteem. He was for a long time spoken of as a writer whose poetry was overlaid and whose passion was chilled by a pedantic display of learning. Gibbon in the last century, the late Professor W. Ramsay and Dean Merivale in the present, may be taken as fair representatives of the opinion of scholars on his merits. More sympathetic readers in recent times who recognise the desperate sincerity and intensity of his passion, the penetrating and creative force of his imagination, and the new and more distinctively Roman movement which he has imparted to his metre, are repelled by the abnormal difficulty of his style, and by the monotony with which he harps on the single theme which through the best part of his poetical activity absorbed all his thought and passion, and constituted all the joy and all the torment of his life. Though love is one of the perennial sources of poetry, the interest of its poetical treatment depends not solely on the sincerity and intensity of the feeling, or the imaginative power with which it is presented, but to some extent on the personal impression made by the writer and on the ideal charm with which he has invested the object of it. Among the more sympathetic students of Propertius in the present day some perhaps might be willing to address him in his own line—

    Ardoris nostri magne poeta iaces.

Other admirers of his genius, who feel neither his own personality nor that which he has imparted to Cynthia very congenial, and that it is possible to have too much of the 'amantium irae' and the 'amoris integratio,' may be more inclined to apply to the record of his sorrows another motto from his own verses,

> Maxima de nihilo nascitur historia.

Even those who may regard him as at least potentially one of the greatest of Roman poets, may still think that if Cynthia first awakened his poetical faculty, she also did much to mar its full development. Like some modern poets, he enjoys rather the devotion of a few warm admirers, to whom his talent has revealed itself as something new and unexpected in ancient literature, than the position of a great classic whose thought and experience have 'enriched the blood of the world.' Perhaps he gains more by the novelty of the impression which he produces, and by his freedom from the conventional associations of classical literature, than he loses by the demand which he makes for a serious effort to penetrate to his meaning.

For the circumstances of his life, and his personal characteristics, we depend almost solely on the evidence of his own writings; and his style of writing is often so indirect and allusive, that we have to be satisfied with more or less doubtful inferences on some important points, such as the date of his birth, his exact birthplace, the time of the publication of his various books, and the duration of his liaison with Cynthia. Of his relations to his more eminent contemporaries, we learn from Ovid that a bond of comradeship existed between the two poets, but Ovid tells us nothing to confirm or modify the impression of his personal qualities derived from what he consciously or unconsciously reveals of himself. Perhaps the silence of Ovid, in general so appreciative of the personal as well as the literary qualities of others, may be regarded as a confirmation of the impression produced by the manner of Propertius in writing to and of his associates, that he was too much absorbed in himself and his passion either to form warm attachments to other men, or to attach them to himself by strong bonds of sympathy. That his society was uncongenial to one eminent contemporary seems certain from the passage in the second Epistle of the second book of Horace, which is as palpably a stricture on the vanity and self-assertion of the 'Roman Callimachus,' as the fourth Epistle of the first book is a tribute to the gentle and modest character of Tibullus.

The name by which he speaks of himself, and which is applied to him by Ovid, Statius, Pliny, and Martial, is simply Propertius, without the adjunct of *praenomen* or *cognomen*. That his *praenomen* was Sextus rests on the evidence of the grammarian Donatus. The additional names of Aurelius Nauta, which appear in the old editions of the poet, are now universally rejected.

The dates of his birth and of the composition of the various books into which his poems are divided have to be determined by internal evidence, and have been much disputed. Editors are divided in opinion also as to whether the number of books left by him was four or five. As this latter question has no bearing on the enquiry as to the circumstances of his life or personal characteristics, any reference to it may be left till the consideration of the artistic composition of his poems is reached. In the meantime it is only necessary to state that in references to passages quoted from the poems the division into four books is presupposed. A question as interesting though perhaps not so important as that of the date of the poet's birth and of the composition of his works, is that of his birthplace, about which an old controversy, which appeared to have died out, has been recently revived by Sr. Giulio Urbini in his treatise on 'La Patria di Propertio.' Though it can make no difference in our estimate of the man or our enjoyment of his poetry to know whether he was born at Spello or Assisi, yet an attempt to solve the question by a comparison of the sites of these towns with the three passages in which the poet describes or alludes to his birthplace will bring us into the presence of scenes of natural beauty and places of historic interest which were familiar to him both in his childhood and in his later life, and may thus help us to realise some of the influences which acted on his imagination.

The passage of Ovid already referred to (Trist. iv. 10) as mentioning the four recognised elegiac poets in their order, establishes the fact that Propertius came after Tibullus and before Ovid in the list. Does this necessarily imply that his elegies appeared later than those of Tibullus, or only that he was a younger man? The evidence of his poems clearly establishes the latter point: it leaves it doubtful whether, though the earlier elegies of Tibullus were written two or three years before the earlier ones of Propertius, the first book of Propertius may not have appeared either before or not long after the elegies of the first book of Tibullus were collected and published together. In their first works neither poet can be shown to have influenced the other, nor is there any evidence that they were acquainted with one another. Tibullus was apparently a man 'paucorum hominum,' and though it may be assumed that he did not leave the 'Cynthia Monobiblos' unread and unappreciated, he was probably not intimate with Propertius any more than with his younger contemporary Ovid, whom he may have met occasionally in the circle of Messalla.

Propertius tells us that his love for Cynthia, his first and only serious passion, was preceded by a liaison with Lycinna, apparently her slave, which began shortly after his assumption of the toga virilis. His relations with Cynthia may thus be assumed to have begun when he was about eighteen or nineteen years of age. The first book was finished about a year and a half or two years after the commencement of the liaison, during a time of estrangement which, from the evidence of a later passage (iii. 16. 9), is inferred to have lasted a year.

Propertius, in his opening poem, written in a state of extreme despondency, and probably after the composition of all the other elegies in the book, says of his passion, or the reckless condition to which it reduced him,

> Et mihi iam toto furor hic non deficit anno,
> Cum tamen adversos cogor habere deos.

Does 'hic furor' refer to the whole period of his passion for Cynthia, the time of rapture as well as of torment, preceding the date of the composition of this poem? Or is it limited to that phase of it when owing to her cruelty he lived this reckless and disorderly life? The last is the view generally adopted, though the words *hic furor* might perfectly apply to the happy as well as the unhappy stage of his infatuation. The only year to which the words

> Peccaram semel et totum sum pulsus in annum

seem applicable is that during which this and some of the other elegies of Book i. were written. It may therefore be taken as probable that when Book i. was finished a period of at least a year and a half had elapsed since the beginning of his connexion with Cynthia, and of not more than three years since his assumption of the toga virilis. If that was assumed about the age of seventeen, he was probably in his twentieth or twenty-first year when the book was finished. If we could determine the date when the first book was finished we should be able to fix the date of Propertius' birth approximately to about twenty years earlier. There is only one poem, the sixth in the first book, to which a possible date can be attached. The Tullus who is represented as inviting Propertius to accompany him to the Province of Asia, and to whom the words

> Tu patrui meritas conare anteire secures,
> Et vetera oblitis iura refer sociis

are addressed, is supposed to be a nephew of L. Volcatius Tullus, who having been Consul in 33 B.C. might in accordance with the *Lex Pompeia* be entering on his proconsular government of Asia in 27 B.C. but not earlier. If this were accepted as the date of the poem, and if the year of estrangement after that date is allowed for, the book would have been finished and given to the world probably in 26 B.C., and this seems to fit in with the allusions contained in the later books, with one important exception. The thirty-first poem of the second book describes the opening of the temple of the Palatine Apollo in the latter

part of 28 B.C. This at first sight suggests the inference that
the first book was finished and given to the world before that
date. But the poem may well have been written in the earlier
stage of the liaison, and may not have been included in the
series selected to form the 'Cynthia Monobiblos,' as not being
in harmony with the dominant mood of which that book is
a record. Or it may have been written some considerable time
after the event referred to. The only motive of it is to give
a description of the artistic beauties of the portico. It has
really nothing to do with the love of Cynthia, and its tone
is more disinterested and unimpassioned than that of any poem
referring to the earlier phases of his love. Two other dates
may be fixed approximately in connexion with Book ii. The
seventh poem speaks of a repeal of one of the laws, enacted in
the year B.C. 28, by which Augustus endeavoured to force
marriage on the wealthier celibates. The law was repealed
shortly after its enactment, probably within a year or two,
i.e. about 27 or 26 B.C. In the tenth poem Caesar is spoken
of by the name Augustus; first bestowed on him in 27 B.C., and
is represented as contemplating an expedition to the East to
avenge the defeat of Crassus. The line

> Et domus intactae te tremit Arabiae

marks the period referred to as anterior to the unfortunate
expedition of Aelius Gallus in 24 B.C. The conclusion of
M. Plessis that the year 25 B.C. is the year indicated seems
as nearly certain as any such conclusions can be. The poems
of Book ii. would therefore seem to range over a period of
about two years, or two years and a half, either between 28 B.C.
and the beginning of 25 B.C. or more probably from the
beginning of 26 till the end of 24 B.C. During all that time
the relation to Cynthia—which is indeed the burden of the
whole book, with the single exception of the tenth poem—
went on. In Book iii. one definite date is fixed to the latter
part of the year 23 B.C. by the eighteenth elegy, which is a
lament over the death of the young Marcellus. But there is

nothing in the poem to imply that the poet's relation to Cynthia still continued. Another poem, the fourth, is written in immediate anticipation of an Eastern expedition, and is referred to the year 22 B.C., when preparations were made for the expedition which brought about the restoration of the standards by the Parthians. There is no word of Cynthia in the poem, though in anticipation of the future triumph the poet writes,

> Inque sinu carae nixus spectare puellae
> Incipiam, et titulis oppida capta legam.

If the 'puella' there spoken of is Cynthia, the only conclusion we can come to is that after what seemed a final renunciation, declared in poems 24 and 25, the poet had again renewed his relations with his first love, and the evidence of Book iv. renders that not improbable. But though the word 'puella' when used by Propertius during the continuation of his liaison can only refer to Cynthia, there is no need so to limit its use after their rupture. The most important statement of all for determining the dates relating to the life of Propertius occurs in iii. 25, in which he seems finally to renounce his mistress, in the line

> Quinque tibi potui servire fideliter annos.

He had been her faithful slave for five years. But here again a question is raised. Do these five years include or exclude the years of estrangement? Do they begin with the actual origin of his passion, or with the renewal of the intimacy after an estrangement of a year? The conclusion of M. Plessis here also is probably right; that the five years are meant to include the whole period from the first awakening of his love till his renunciation of it. He was still her faithful slave during all the year of her estrangement.

The poems of Book iii. seem to embrace the time from about 24 to 22 or 21 B.C. One year may be allowed for the poems of this book written before the renunciation, two years and a half for those contained in Book ii, one year and a half for those in Book i. The time of his liaison with Cynthia, the one important event in the life of Propertius, may be thus approximately fixed either to the years between 29 and 25 B.C. (inclusive) or more probably to those between 27 and 23 B.C. Assuming that it began about a year or a year and a half after his assumption of the toga virilis, the birth of the poet may be brought back to some time between the years 48 and 46 B.C. The completion of Book i. may be assigned with most probability to the early part or middle of 26 B.C. when the poet could not have been more than twenty years of age. One date in his life can be fixed with certainty. The eleventh poem of Book iv. proves that he lived and wrote in the year 16 B.C., the year in which a Cornelius Scipio, brother of the Cornelia in honour of whom the poem is composed, was Consul.

The next point to determine is what is the particular town or place in Umbria which Propertius designates as his home or birth-place.

The three well-known passages in which the riddle is proposed are: (1) the short epilogue subjoined to the book by which Propertius first introduced himself to the world; and (2 and 3) two passages from the long introductory poem to the fourth book, in the first of which (iv. 1. 65–66), in his own name, he describes in two lines the characteristic features of his native town, in the second of which (iv. 1. 121–6), by the voice of the astrologer Horos, he repeats, with a slight alteration, that description, and adds two lines introducing two familiar landmarks visible from or in the immediate neighbourhood of the town.

The first passage, which professes to be an answer to the enquiries of his friend or patron Tullus, to whom the book is dedicated, determines the locality only by its neighbourhood to Perusia, a town only too well known as associated with the most tragic events of the Civil Wars. The lines

> Proxima supposito contingens Umbria campo
> Me genuit, terris fertilis uberibus

define the 'patria' of Propertius as a town the territory of which lay beneath it, and extended to the border of the territory of

Perusia. This passage, if taken alone, might suggest the inference that he was born in a country-house situated in the rich plain, extending from the foot of the mountain-range, on two spurs of which Assisi and Spello are built, to the Tiber, forming the boundary between Umbria and Etruria. If Assisi possessed any territory at all it is difficult to conceive where it could have been, if it was not part of this plain extending in the direction of Perusia till it met the river.

The second passage (iv. 1. 63–66)—

> Ut nostris tumefacta superbiat Umbria libris,
> Umbria Romani patria Callimachi,
> Scandentes quisquis cernit de vallibus arces,
> Ingenio muros aestimet ille meo—

associates his poetic fame more definitely with a town of Umbria, situated on a steep height. There are two ambiguities of expression in line 65. Are we to translate 'arces' 'heights' or 'battlements'? and are we to take 'de vallibus' after 'cernit' or after 'scandentes'? Is the whole passage to be translated 'Whoever marks the battlements (or heights) climbing up steeply from the valleys,' or is it 'Whoever from the valleys beneath marks the battlements (or heights) towering upwards'? The position of the words does not determine which interpretation is right. Reasons will be given later for holding that the latter is required by the only locality to which the words can apply.

In the next passage the town is still more definitely marked by its neighbourhood to two places, one of which at least is perfectly well known—

> Umbria te notis antiqua Penatibus edit.
> Mentior? an patriae tangitur ora tuae,
> Qua nebulosa cavo rorat Mevania campo,
> Et lacus aestivis intepet Umber aquis,
> Scandentisque Asis (arcis?) consurgit vertice murus,
> Murus ab ingenio notior ille tuo?

In this passage there are more serious uncertainties both of interpretation and reading.

Do the words *noti Penates* apply to the family residence of

Propertius or to his native town? It is argued that they cannot apply to the former because Propertius tells us that he was neither of noble birth nor of a particularly rich family (non ita dives). But 'noti' does not mean either 'rich' or 'noble,' but 'respectable'; and that is exactly what the parentage of Propertius was. He was not of knightly birth like Tibullus and Ovid, but he was a member of a good provincial family possessing a considerable estate—

> Nam tua cum multi versarent rura iuvenci,
> Abstulit excultas pertica tristis opes.

Penates might be used of his native town, but not necessarily or even naturally. When Catullus writes to Verannius

> Venistine domum ad tuos Penates?

we do not naturally think of Rome, or any town of Italy, which may have been the home of Verannius. This point is of some importance, as one of the chief arguments urged in favour of Spello is that Hispellum was, or became after it was turned into a military colony, a much more important place than Assisium. But even if we were constrained to regard *Penates* as indicative of the town, though Hispellum may have been more famous, Assisium may yet have enjoyed a certain repute which would justify the use of the word *noti*. Had he meant to imply any greater distinction the poet would probably have used some such word as *clari* or *insignes*.

What, next, is the meaning of 'patriae tangitur ora tuae'? Does Propertius mean to define the exact boundaries of the territory attached to his native town as being Mevania on the one side and the 'lacus Umber' on the other? Or is it sufficient to regard these two places, the 'Umbrian lake' and Mevania in its low-lying plain, with the mists from the Clitumnus rising over it, as conspicuous landmarks in the neighbourhood? This question becomes of great importance if the ordinary interpretation of the words 'lacus Umber' is accepted. The territory lying between Bevagna and the sources of the Clitumnus may have formed part of the territory of Spello, but it could not possibly have been that of Assisi, nor could it in any sense be described as the part of Umbria nearest to Perusia. But Sr. Urbini raises here an important question, his answer to which really *seems* to tell against his own contention in favour of Spello. Is the interpretation of 'lacus Umber' as 'the broad pool formed by the sources of the Clitumnus' really right? It is said that a scholiast on Virgil (Georgics ii. 147) applies the word *lacus* to the Clitumnus, and Pliny, in the well-known passage of his Letters in which he gives an account of his visit to its sources, describes the pool of running water in which these various sources meet as 'gurgitem qui lato gremio patescit.' But does not the word 'gurges' almost exclude the notion of a lake in the natural sense of the word, and still more of a lake to which the words 'aestivis intepet aquis' are applied? But the characteristic of the water at and near these sources to which Pliny and other ancient writers draw emphatic attention is their extreme coldness, and the truth of their statement may be verified by any one who visits them in the present day[1]. If this 'gurges' ever extended to the dimensions of a lake, it has now shrunk to the dimensions of a moderately sized pool, overgrown with weeds, through which however the 'divini fontes' still flow in a clear stream, 'splendidior vitro.' It is impossible to conceive a description less applicable in every way than the line

Et lacus aestivis intepet Umber aquis

to the clear-flowing cold stream of the Clitumnus, of which the charm was so great in the eyes of those accustomed to the muddy streams of central Italy as to be deemed worthy of a temple to mark the sanctity attached to it. How then is the line to be explained? The words point to a sheet of water of considerable size, which would be a conspicuous object from the town, whether it was Hispellum or Assisium. But no such lake is visible in the neighbourhood of Perugia, Assisi, or Spello,

---

[1] The waters were found to be pleasantly cold both to the taste and touch in a hot day of May, 1890.

nor indeed anywhere in what was the ancient territory of Umbria. It seems to follow that either the text is corrupt—and that has been suggested, though on no sufficient grounds—or that what was once a lake has disappeared and become part of the rich flat plain which stretches between the Tiber and the hill on which Assisi is built. Sr. Urbini states that in a medieval document the modern Bastia, which is the first station after crossing the Tiber on the railway between Perugia and Assisi, is spoken of as an island[1], and its inhabitants are called 'Isolani[2].' Bastia is situated at the confluence of two considerable streams, the Chiascio and the Tescio, which flow into the Popino, of which the Clitumnus also is an affluent: and their united waters empty themselves into the Tiber about fifteen miles from Perugia. The flat plain above and below Bastia looks as if it might have been at no very distant date covered by the waters of a shallow lake, to which the two streams mentioned above may have contributed their waters. From its vicinity to the frontier it might naturally receive the general name of the 'Umbrian lake,' not being of sufficient size or importance to receive a distinctive name, like the Thrasimene lake, the lake Vadimon, or the lake Velinus. The disappearance of a shallow sheet of water, by natural causes or by drainage, in a well-cultivated territory, is not an unusual occurrence. Thus, for instance, the waters of the 'Nor-loch,' familiar to readers of the 'Fortunes of Nigel,' have been replaced within recent memory by the Princes Street Gardens that separate the old and new town of Edinburgh. The existence of such a lake in the neighbourhood of Bastia can, of course, only be a matter of more or less probable conjecture, based partly on the fact that the land on which it stands was at one time known as 'the island' and its inhabitants as 'the islanders,'

---

[1] He quotes from a document of the twelfth century: 'Una petia de terra cum vinea quae posita est infra comitatum Assisinatum in loco qui dicitur de insula Romanesca.'

[2] 'Nel 1053, ch' è, per quanto si sappia, la più antica data sotto cui se ne faccin ricordo, gli abitanti erano chiamati, per la natura del luogo, *isolani* semplicemente.'

and partly on the appearance of the district. There is certainly no such difficulty in admitting this conjecture as there is in supposing that Propertius, or any other poet, or any person of sane judgment, should have selected the 'steaming warmth of its summer waves' as the special characteristic of the pool of clear, cold, running water, in which the sources of the Clitumnus meet, a few feet below the spot where they issue 'ab Umbro tramite[1].'

It remains to ask which of the two walls or walled towns

---

[1] Propert. iii. 22. 23-4:
> Hic Anio Tiburne fluis, Clitumnus *ab Umbro Tramite*.

Compare i. 18. 27-8:
> Pro quo divini fontes et frigida rupes
> Et datur *inculto tramite* dura quies.

The use of the word *tramite* in both these passages suggests that the 'divini fontes' are the sources of the Clitumnus, and that the 'deserta loca et taciturna querenti,' to which Propertius retired in his despair, are the same scene as that which he describes in a happier mood in ii. 19, where he proposes joining Cynthia in a few days, and enjoying such field sports as he was capable of—
> Qua formosa suo Clitumnus flumina luco
> Integit, et niveos abluit unda boves.

The lines
> Sola eris et solos spectabis Cynthia montes
> Et pecus et fines pauperis agricolae

will at once occur to any reader of Propertius as he looks towards the amphitheatre of hills immediately to the south of the sources. But what is the exact meaning of *tramite* in these two passages and in iii. 13. 43-4—
> Et leporem, quicunque venis, venaberis hospes,
> Et si forte meo *tramite* quaeris avem?

Hertzberg points out that these last two lines are a translation of two Greek lines of Leonidas of Tarentum—
> Εὐάγρει λαγόθηρα, καὶ εἰ πετεεινὰ διώκων
> Ἰξευτὴς ἥκεις τοιθ' ὑπὸ δισσὸν ὄρος.

Propertius seems thus to use *trames* in the same sense as the Greek ὄρος. Can we translate, in i. 18. 28, 'inculto tramite' 'wild hill-side,' like 'the cold hill-side' in Keats's 'La belle Dame sans Merci,' a poem expressive of a mood not remote from the mood of this, one of the grandest of all the Elegies of Propertius? In Virgil's
> Ecce supercilio clivosi *tramitis* (Georg. i. 108)

the word must be used in the same sense as in Propertius. Dr. Kennedy translates it 'from the brow of a cross-lying slope,' and in all these passages something much nearer the notion of a 'hill' than a 'channel' or 'cross-way' is wanted. The bare range or hill-side at the foot of which, close to the road, the Clitumnus rises, runs across and forms one boundary of the plain, through which the stream flows in a northerly direction.

described as 'climbing up a steep height' answers best to the description given in

> Scandentes quisquis cernit de vallibus arces,

and

> Scandentisque Asis (arcis?) consurgit vertice murus.

Assisi and Spello are situated on two spurs, which jut out into the plain at each extremity of the long range of Subasio, a bare mountain running in a direction from north to south, and rising to a height of about 3600 feet. These spurs are about six miles from one another. Assisi is on the northern, that nearest to Perugia. The height on which Spello is built is considerably smaller and lower than that occupied by Assisi. The modern town of Spello rises at once out of the plain and climbs up the face and two sides of a kind of promontory, sufficiently detached to have the appearance of a separate hill, though connected with the main range by a narrow ridge. Assisi, on the other hand, does not rise out of the plain, but begins about half-way up the height, and the town does not rise on any side to the top of this height. It is to be noted that in both the passages Propertius fixes our attention not on the towns themselves but on their walls:—

> Ingenio muros aestimet ille meo.—
> Murus ab ingenio notior ille tuo.—

Sr. Urbini remarks that as the wall of Assisi does not begin to rise out of the plain, while that of Spello does, the description can only apply to the latter. But can 'de vallibus' possibly mean the same thing as 'de campo'? There are no valleys nor any single valley lying below the height on which Spello is built; unless those words can be intended to denote the whole of the broad plain lying between the Monte Subasio— the name given to the whole range rising above both Assisi and Spello—and the low range which separates the waters of the Clitumnus and the Popino from the valley of the Tiber. Professor Ramsay decides that the town meant cannot be Assisi, because it is situated not on the top (vertice) but on the side of the height. To any one looking at Assisi in front, from the 'campo supposito,' or walking through the town itself, there is nothing within sight to correspond with either the 'valleys' or with 'the wall rising on the summit of the height.' The first impression of any one looking at the two places will be that on the whole Spello deviates less from the actual description given. But if he climbs up to what was the old citadel and returns by the back of the hill, on which there are no houses built, the two conspicuous objects which fix his attention, as he makes his way to the town gate, are the turns and windings of the deep valley of the Tescio below him, and the great ancient wall which climbs up from that part of the hill on which the church of St. Francis is built, past the gate which rises above and to the right of the church, till it reaches the citadel and then continues to run along the summit of the ridge, by which the Monte Subasio joins the outlying spur on which the town is built. The wall, though not so ancient as that running up the height on which Cortona stands, has all the appearance of the workmanship of the old Roman times. If then we translate the first passage 'whoever from the valleys below observes the battlements rising one above the other,' and the second 'and a wall rises up along the summit of the steep height,' or 'the steep Asis,' we shall find no difficulty in identifying the description with what any one may see who goes out of the gate, above and to the right of the famous church, and walks along the hill at the back of the town till he reaches the old citadel. The distinct statement of Propertius that his native district was that part of Umbria nearest to Perusia is thus confirmed by his description of striking characteristics of the site of the town to which that territory was attached. The number of inscriptions of the Propertii found at or near Assisi affords confirmation of this. If 'Asis' is the reading in line 125, it is difficult to see how it can apply to Spello. Sr. Urbini supposes that this was the name for the whole range of Monte Subasio. But in that case he is obliged to translate 'vertice' not 'the summit,' but 'a height,' certainly an unusual use of the word. If the 'lacus Umber' is to be sought in the neighbourhood of Bastia, it was within a short distance of Assisi, and may have formed one boundary of its territory. The neighbourhood of Mevania may have formed its southern extremity. In any case the town of Mevania, which was a much more considerable place in ancient than in modern times[1]—as is testified by the remains of an amphitheatre—and the mists rising over it from the valley of the Clitumnus, would be conspicuous objects from the heights on which Assisi is built. In the opposite direction the most conspicuous objects were the hill and town of Perusia, so fraught with tragic memories for Propertius.

The conclusion therefore to which we come is that Propertius was born about the year 46 B.C., either in the town of Assisi, or possibly in a country house in the territory attached to it. He belonged to a good though not a noble or equestrian family, which, as we learn on the authority of the younger Pliny, continued to be connected with that district for more than a century afterwards. He lost his father in his childhood, and about the same time was reduced to poverty by the assignment of part or the whole of his lands to the soldiers of Octavianus:

> Ossaque legisti non illa aetate legenda
>   Patris, et in tenues cogeris ipse Lares:
> Nam tua cum multi versarent rura iuvenci,
>   Abstulit excultas pertica tristis opes (iv. 1. 127).

The territory of the neighbouring town of Hispellum was enlarged in the interests of the military colony settled there, and it is natural to infer that what Hispellum gained in territory, Assisi lost. There is nothing to indicate that Propertius retained any part of his hereditary estate; but there are passages (i. 18, ii. 19) in his poems which show that he returned, at least on two occasions, to some place in the neighbourhood of the sources of the Clitumnus.

The event which made the deepest impression on his imagina-

[1] Mentioned in Tacitus, Histories iii. 59, as evidently a place of importance: 'Ut terrorem Italiae possessa Mevania ac velut renatum ex integro bellum intulerat.'

tion while he was still a child was the siege of Perusia in the year 41 B.C., with all its accompanying horrors. This impression has stamped itself on various passages of his poems, but especially on the two short and closely connected pieces which form the epilogue of Book i. His sombre and melancholy temper, perhaps too the precocity with which his nature and talent developed themselves, may have owed their origin to the experiences of his childhood, as the melancholy of Lucretius may have been partly induced by his experiences during the reign of terror established by Marius and Cinna. The horrors of the siege followed immediately after the miseries of the confiscations; and one near kinsman, who may not improbably have been his mother's brother, and his own natural guardian [1], took part in the siege, and after making his escape through the Caesarian lines, perished by the hands of brigands. Among the many vivid pictures painted by the imagination of Propertius, none arrests the attention more forcibly than that of the dying Gallus giving his last message to the wounded soldier to bear the tidings of his death to his sister:

> Tu qui consortem properas evadere casum
>   Miles ab Etruscis saucius aggeribus
>   Quid nostro gemitu turgentia lumina torques?

Not only was this incident stamped on his imagination as he may have heard it told by the wounded soldier himself, or as it may have been brought home to him by the grief of his mother, but it sank deeply into his heart. The solemnity and pathos of his reference to his loss in the following poem—

> Si Perusina tibi patriae sunt nota sepulcra,
>   Italiae duris funera temporibus,
> Cum Romana suos egit discordia cives—
>   Sit mihi praecipue, pulvis Etrusca, dolor:
> Tu proiecta mei perpessa es membra propinqui
>   Tu nullo miseri contegis ossa solo—

---

[1] Cf. i. 21. 6:
   Haec soror acta tuis sentiat e lacrimis.
The dying Gallus sends his last message specially to his sister. This would have made a vivid impression on the memory and heart of the child if that sister of Gallus was his own mother.

show that the memory of this early sorrow was a lasting one. Virgil, Horace, and even Tibullus had a sterner experience in their earlier manhood than anything which Propertius had to encounter. But no other Roman poet, except perhaps Lucretius, had, in the impressible years of childhood, been so powerfully and deeply affected by the sufferings and tragedies of the civil wars.

After the loss of his lands he seems to have been taken to Rome by his mother, with what still remained of his inheritance—

> Aspice me cui parva domi fortuna relicta est (ii. 34. 55)—

and educated under the grammarians and teachers of literature there. He remained under his mother's charge till he entered on manhood:

> Matris et ante deos libera sumpta toga (iv. 1. 132).

She was still alive when the eleventh poem of the first book was written (i. 11. 21), but had died before the composition of the twentieth poem of the second book (ii. 20. 15). On the rare occasions in which he mentions her, he does so with the piety habitual to an Italian. We hear of no other members of his family, but he speaks of 'friends of his father[1],' who took an interest in his career, and did what they could to divert him from his fatal passion. His boyhood must have been unusually studious : in the beginning of his poetic career, which commenced soon after the assumption of the toga virilis, he shows not only extraordinary precocity of talent, but a remarkable familiarity with the Alexandrian literature. The words in which he describes himself before his passion for Cynthia changed his nature—

> Tum mihi constantis deiecit lumina fastus,
> Et caput impositis pressit Amor pedibus (i. 1. 3)—

are indicative of a virtuous and somewhat secluded training; and the ardour and unrestraint with which he yielded to his

---

[1] Was his father the Sextius Propertius mentioned by Cicero, pro Domo sua 19?

passion are suggestive of that inexperience of the world and want of other interests in life natural to a home-bred poet, absorbed in himself and in the study of a literature which supplied few subjects of thought, but fed the natural inflammability of his temperament. On entering on manhood he, like Ovid, determined to have nothing to do with the uncongenial career of an advocate, but to devote himself to poetry:

> Mox ubi bulla rudi dimissa est aurea collo,
> Matris et ante deos libera sumpta toga,
> Tum tibi pauca suo de carmine dictat Apollo,
> Et vetat insano verba tonare foro.

Among the friends of his youth, the one whom he seems to have valued most and to whom his first book is dedicated is Tullus, a nephew apparently of Volcatius Tullus, consul in 33 B.C. He was a man of wealth (i. 14) as well as noble birth, and is commended by Propertius for his devotion to the service of his country, and his indifference to the life of pleasure, followed so generally by the youth of Rome:

> Nam tua non aetas umquam cessavit amori,
> Semper at armatae cura fuit patriae.
> . . . .
> Me sine quem semper voluit fortuna iacere
> Hanc animam extremae reddere nequitiae (i. 6. 21, 25).

Tullus was anxious to take him abroad with him, but he was unable to detach him from his 'bondage' to Cynthia. Propertius feels the intellectual attraction of the cities of Greece and Asia by which Catullus, Cicero, Virgil, Horace, and Ovid were at different stages of their career drawn to visit them, but whether fortunately or unfortunately for the full development of his genius, his intellectual ambition at this period of his career was too feeble to resist the more immediate claims of passion:

> An mihi sit tanti doctas cognoscere Athenas
> Atque Asiae veteres cernere divitias,
> Ut mihi deducta faciat convicia puppi
> Cynthia et insanis ora notet manibus? (i. 6. 13).

That he was not unmoved by this ambition may be inferred from a later poem (iii. 21), written apparently just after the spell is broken, when he proposes, as the only means of escape, to repair to Athens and devote himself to the study of the great masters of philosophy, of oratory, and of wise and witty intercourse with the world:

> Illic aut studiis animum emendare Platonis
> Incipiam aut hortis, docte Epicure, tuis:
> Persequar aut studium linguae, Demosthenis arma,
> Librorumque tuos, docte Menandre, sales.

If, as he so often tells us, Propertius was fitted by nature only to be the poet of love, it may be that his genius would never have received its first powerful impulse had he sacrificed the ardours of his early passion to a larger and more liberal culture, and to that wider knowledge of men which a more ambitious career would have opened up to him. But if, as some of his poems indicate, he had capacities and aspirations which never obtained their full realisation, the doubt may at least suggest itself whether the world would not have had in him a more complete poet had the studies of his boyhood been crowned by the philosophical culture of Athens, and his character disciplined and strengthened by some larger contact with life.

His other friends in Rome of whom we read were young men devoted to poetry, Bassus and Lynceus, writers of tragedy, and Ponticus, who was engaged on an epic poem on the war of Thebes; his kinsman Gallus, and Paetus a young merchant, whose untimely death he laments in a later elegy. Propertius does not seem to have had for them the cordial appreciation which Catullus and Horace feel for their friends. He writes of them or characterises them in the critical and captious spirit of one asserting his superiority, with nothing of the *bonhomie* with which Ovid treats everyone, or the affection and tenderness with which Tibullus writes of Cornutus and Macer. The not unfrequent notices of Bacchanalian indulgences bear no record of lively or genial boon-companionship. Though the life of Propertius is almost entirely passed in Rome, we hear scarcely anything of the open air life and sports of the Campus

Martius[1], which were part of the training as well as the pleasure of Roman youth. His extreme paleness and the slightness of his figure—

> Nec iam pallorem totiens mirabere nostrum
> Aut cur sim toto corpore nullus ego (i. 5. 21)—

were the signs of a constitution unfitting, or at least disinclining him for any of the more manly amusements of youth. He prides himself on his effeminacy and on his unfitness for anything else except to love Cynthia and gain her favour by his poetry. He thinks it worth recording that he gave much thought to the adornment of his person, and affected a stately and leisurely mode of walking:

> Nequiquam perfusa meis unguenta capillis,
> Ibat et expenso planta morata gradu (ii. 4. 5).

All other interests in life, except the art which celebrated and ministered to his passion, were sacrificed to it during the longest and most active part of his poetical career.

The heroine of the love poetry of Propertius is no idealised creation of his fancy, or typical representative of the class to which she belonged. She has a very real and marked individuality, which her lover is constrained to describe, as he describes his own weakness and infatuation, with the desperate sincerity and truthfulness of a man making the full confession of his life to the world. On the same authority as that from which we learn that Lesbia was Clodia, and that the true name of Delia was Plania, we learn that the real name of Cynthia was Hostia. There is no reason to suppose that she was a freedwoman, though she belonged to the class which was largely recruited from freedwomen; nor any ground for doubting that, in the line (iii. 20. 8),

> Splendidaque a docto fama refulget avo,

Hostius, one of the early annalistic poets in the style of Ennius,

---

[1] Cf. ii. 16. 33:
> Tot iam abiere dies cum me nec cura theatri
> Nec tetigit campi nec mea musa iuvat.

who wrote on the Istrian war, is referred to as her grandfather. Her original home was Tibur; and she was buried in the Tiburtine territory, near the banks of the Anio. When she appears to Propertius after death, she is represented as asking to have this inscription engraved on a column raised above her tomb:

> Hic Tiburtina iacet aurea Cynthia terra:
> Accessit ripae laus, Aniene, tuae (iv. 7. 85).

We hear of her being at Tibur on one occasion during her lifetime, and summoning Propertius to come and see her there. Her house in Rome was in the Subura; and at the time of her death she appears to have had a considerable establishment of slaves in her household.

Among the many lovers who supplied the means for her extravagance, we hear more than once of a praetor, whom, in a very early stage of her liaison with Propertius, she is preparing to accompany to his province of Illyria. She is finally induced to stay 'not by gold nor precious gifts,' but 'by the soft persuasive influence of poetry,' 'blandi carminis obsequio.' It is probable that she was considerably older than Propertius, as after their relations had lasted for some three or four years he reminds her that she will at no distant date be an old woman:

> At tu etiam iuvenem odisti me, perfida, cum sis
> Ipsa anus haut longa curva futura die (ii. 18. 19).

He tells us that the first advances came from her—

> Cum te tam multi peterent, tu me una petisti (ii. 20. 27);

and, as in the case of Catullus and Clodia, they were drawn together by literary sympathy. He often speaks of her devotion to poetry—

> Carmina tam sancte nulla puella colit (ii. 26. 26).

She admired his elegies and was proud to be their theme—

> Gaudet laudatis ire superba comis (ii. i. 8).

The thought which after death moves her spirit to forgive his coldness is of the proud place which she had held in his poetry:

> Longa mea in libris regna fuere tuis (iv. 7. 50).

She was not only appreciative of genius, but was herself an accomplished poetess, and claimed to rival the Greek Corinna. Propertius describes her beauty and accomplishments in many passages. He compares her on the ground of her personal attractions to the early heroines; and in a different mood and on other grounds, to the Lais, the Thais, and the Phryne of later Greek story. He ascribes to her the dark auburn hair, so much admired by Roman poets and Venetian painters; dark and glowing eyes, which in one of his happier moods he describes as

> geminae, sidera nostra, faces;

a complexion which he compares to 'rose leaves floating in milk,' but which in a less flattering mood, when his illusion was passing away, he declares was not 'ingenuus,' but artificial:

> Et color est totiens roseo collatus Eoo
>   Cum tibi quaesitus candor in ore foret (iii. 24. 7).

He records also the charm of her long hands, of her tall and Juno-like figure, and her stately movements:

> Fulva coma est longaeque manus et maxima toto
>   Corpore et incedit vel Iove digna soror (ii. 2. 5).

He praises her accomplishments as much as her gifts of personal beauty. She was a graceful dancer and a skilful musician, and her conversation had a singular charm:

> Unica nec desit iucundis gratia verbis (i. 2. 29).

She had not only all the graces, but also skill in the useful arts cultivated by women in ancient times:

> Omnia quaeque Venus quaeque Minerva probat (i. 2. 30).

The intellectual gifts and accomplishments attributed to her explain how members of the class to which she belonged enjoyed so much distinction and played so important a part in Greek and Roman life. The attributes of character with which he endows her are drawn with evidently more truthfulness than flattery; and they help to explain the domination she exercised over him. That domination was the action of a strong and imperious on a weak and submissive nature, which she alternately fascinated by capricious fondness, and drove to despair by hardness and inconstancy. He stands in awe of her even after death; and the words of tenderness, which in imagination he hears her ghost address to him, are mixed with others which show her angry spirit still untamed by the funeral fires.

The part played by Propertius in this tragi-comedy seems to realise that attributed to the lover in Roman comedy and satire. Like Phaedria in the Eunuchus he vows repeatedly that he will break the spell, and as often breaks the vow[1]. He too experiences the 'amari aliquid' in the thought that the wit exercised by his mistress was at his expense:

> Quin etiam multo duxistis pocula risu,
> Forsitan et de me verba fuere mala (ii. 9. 21).

The passion of Propertius for Cynthia is more interesting as a psychological study than as a romance of love. It has not the charm of the earlier phase of the love of Catullus and Lesbia, or the love of Tibullus and Delia, or Sulpicia and Cerinthus. It would be difficult even if it were worth while to follow him closely through all its vicissitudes. But it is necessary for the right understanding of his poetry to keep in mind the main outlines of the story, if that can be called a story which is often a mere alternation of passionate moods. Yet a certain though irregular movement may be traced in the process of change from the 'ardours' of the first book, through the tumults of the second to the comparative indifference of the third, till the final stage of disillusion is reached at the close of that book.

The first book exhibits two distinct stages in the develop-

---

[1] Cf. ii. 5. 9:
> Nunc est ira recens, nunc est discedere tempus:
> Si dolor abfuerit, crede, redibit amor.

ment of his passion. The elegies from 2 to 10 represent him as during the first months of their union happy and elated by this new experience in his life, boasting of it to his friends who endeavoured to detach him from it, but at the same time yielding to that luxurious sense of pain—the 'dolor' following the 'gravis ardor' of which Catullus speaks—which is a condition of violent emotion:

> Me dolor et lacrimae merito fecere peritum:
> Atque utinam posito dicar amore rudis (i. 9. 7).

The first sign of any serious rift in his happiness is in the eleventh poem, addressed to Cynthia, who had quitted Rome for Baiae; but it is not till the seventeenth and eighteenth poems that the signs of serious estrangement appear. What the cause of the estrangement was is not directly stated. In a poem written long afterwards (iii. 16), when he is hesitating whether he should obey her summons to Tibur, he uses the words

> Peccaram semel, et totum sum pulsus in annum,

and in the introductory elegy he describes himself as having been unhappy in his love, and driven by his unhappiness to reckless courses during a whole year:

> Et mihi iam toto furor hic non deficit anno
> Cum tamen adversos cogor habere deos (i. 1. 7).

In the fifteenth poem he writes as if he were contemplating a voyage, and reproaches Cynthia for her indifference to the danger which he might have to encounter. The seventeenth poem describes vividly a scene in which he appears in actual danger of shipwreck; and in that poem he reproaches himself for having left her. The poem begins abruptly with the line

> Et merito quoniam potui fugisse puellam.

Whether this intended voyage was the cause or the consequence of the quarrel is not stated. But the eighteenth, one of the finest of all the elegies of Propertius, is a true love elegy written in the deepest despair among the solitudes by the sources of the Clitumnus. His comparison in the first elegy of his own sufferings to those of Milanion among the caverns and rocks of Arcadia leads us to think that he may have retired for some time to the neighbourhood of his first home, and there finished and arranged for publication the elegies of the first book, to which he gave the title of 'Cynthia.' In the first line of the introductory poem,

> Cynthia prima suis *miserum* me cepit ocellis,

he strikes the key-note not only of this book, but of nearly all the poems of which Cynthia is the subject. He is a born self-tormentor, and even in the poem which he long afterwards recurs to as a record of his happiest time—

> Quid iuvat ornato procedere, vita, capillo? (i. 2. 1: cf. iv. 5. 55)—

there is a note of discontent.

The publication of this book at once established his fame. It procured him the favour of Maecenas. It effected his reconciliation with Cynthia, who, if she was tired of his reproaches and self-tormentings, was proud of gaining celebrity through his poetry. Within a month of the publication of his first book he was writing some of the elegies of the second:

> Vix unum potes infelix requiescere mensem,
> Et turpis de te iam liber alter erit (ii. 3. 3).

In the third poem of the new series he tells us that he had hoped to cure his passion and to devote himself to serious study, 'studiis vigilare severis,' but that after he had made his peace with Cynthia his infatuation returned with greater force than ever. The thirty-four poems of this book are with scarcely an exception devoted to the record of the next stage in the development of his passion. Raptures and reproaches, protestations of his own devotion and complaints of her infidelities, follow one another with irregular alternations. Cynthia acts according to her *métier*; is sometimes kind and gracious, more often hard and faithless. He compares the number of her lovers to those of Lais or Phryne. At last he learns the lesson that it is best to wink at her infidelities as 'the way of the world:'

> Qui quaerit Tatios veteres durosque Sabinos,
> Hic posuit nostra nuper in urbe pedem (ii. 32. 47).

The third book represents his gradual disillusion, ending in renunciation. The happiest poems in connexion with Cynthia are those which are the record of past, not of present emotion. He is able to devote himself to other subjects. He is more possessed with the thought of his art and his fame, of the crowd of poets who imitate, and of maids who admire him, than with his passion. The motive of his writing is no longer the desire to gain the favour of Cynthia, but the hope that his book may be the favourite reading of every lady waiting for her lover:

> Ut tuus in scamno iactetur saepe libellus
> Quem legat exspectans sola puella virum (iii. 3. 19).

He contemplates devoting his future years to the great subjects which Lucretius had treated before him; and proposes to make a voyage to Athens to complete that literary education which had been interrupted by his career of passion. The two latest poems proclaim his disillusion and emancipation. He anticipates for Cynthia the future which Horace anticipates for Lydia, and saw realised in Lyce. The unlovely severance of a not very lovely union is proclaimed in the last lines of the book:

> Has tibi fatalis cecinit mea pagina diras,
> Eventum formae disce timere tuae.

But were these not very chivalrous words the end of the story? The last two poems of the book indicate a permanent change of feeling, and they seem to hint that the advancing years of Cynthia had something to do with the change. But the opening poem of the fourth book, in which by the voice of the astrologer Horos he gives an outline of his own career, hints that though the illusion was over the old domination was resumed:

> Et bene cum fixum mento discusseris uncum,
> Nil erit hoc; rostro te premet ansa suo.

In the poem in which Cynthia's ghost appears before him soon after her burial (iv. 7) he introduces himself as bewailing his now lonely life—

> Et quererer lecti frigida regna mei—

U

and the commands which Cynthia lays upon him imply that he exercised the rights of a master over her household. The following poem, a light comedy succeeding the tragedy of the seventh, could hardly have been written during the continuance of the serious passion. It seems to be a record of a time when she still exercised a sway over him, but when he could think of her imperious and violent temper as a subject for amusement rather than for tears. The passion which begins with joy, not unmixed with morbid complaints and repinings, runs its troubled course, growing gradually quieter and colder, till it disappears for a time, reveals itself again for a moment in the record of a disorderly debauch, and re-asserts its original intensity in the tragic sense of remorse and awe with which he recalls the memory of her who had been, as he so often calls her, his 'life,' and in a sense also his death; who, if she first inspired his poetry, marred the full development of his nature and genius.

In the poem written after the death of Cynthia he anticipates that his own end is near at hand. The elegy on Cornelia, the last poem of Book iv and probably the last finished by Propertius, proves that he lived till the year 16 B.C., but there are no grounds for supposing that he long survived that year. All through his poems, from first to last, he writes as if anticipating an early death. The passionate excitability of his temperament, so unlike the healthy sensuousness of Ovid, the extreme paleness, 'pallor amantium,' the index of that excitability, and the slightness of frame suggested in such phrases as 'exiles tenuatus in artus' (ii. 22. 21), point to a constitution not naturally fit to cope successfully with the vehement pleasures and pains of his existence. His last book was probably left unfinished at his death. The second book also gives the impression that, in its present shape at least, it was not finally arranged by himself. The passages in Pliny (Ep. vi. 15, ix. 22) which speak of the elegiac poet who claimed descent from him, leave a doubt whether, after his rupture with Cynthia and the passing of the *lex Iulia de maritandis ordinibus,*—the law characterised by

Horace in the prosaic phraseology of the Carmen Seculare as 'prolis novae feraci'—he did not marry and leave descendants. Though the words 'inter majores numerat' might perhaps be used by one who counted him as a kinsman, the phrase 'a quo genus ducit,' seems to point to direct descent.

The only passion which vies in intensity with his love for Cynthia is his passion for fame as a poet. The two passions feed one another. The greatness of his love gives life to his poetry: through the power of his poetry he hopes to win and keep the favour of his mistress. No Roman poet is more self-conscious, and none is more confident of his immortality. He anticipates his renown before he is known to the world:

> Tum me non humilem mirabere saepe poetam:
> Tunc ego Romanis praeferar ingeniis (i. 7. 21).

After the publication of his first book, he writes of his glory as

> ad hibernos lata Borysthenidas (ii. 7. 18).

He is the high priest initiated in the rites of Philetas and Callimachus, whose triumphal car is to be followed by all the other poets of love. As the fame of Homer has grown with years, so will his own fame gather strength from time:

> Meque inter seros laudabit Roma nepotes:
> Illum post cineres auguror ipse diem (iii. 1. 35).

It is the proud boast of Umbria that it has given birth to him; and even the wall that climbs up along the hill on which his native town is built has derived new renown from his genius. It is not by the delight in his art, 'the sweet love of the Muses,' but by the desire of recognition, that he professes to be influenced.

He expresses a genuine admiration for Virgil, but though he has some words of recognition for his predecessors in amatory poetry, Varro, Catullus, Calvus and Gallus, he has none for his eminent contemporaries, Tibullus and Ovid, with the latter of whom at least he was united by literary sympathy. He is preoccupied with his own eminence in the field which he has selected. Neither does Propertius make any allusion to Horace, though in the second poem of Book iii he has imitated more than one passage in the Odes. Horace however has left us a study of him, which, whether true or, not, is not flattering. The lines of the second epistle of Book ii. 91-101,

> Carmina compono, hic elegos, &c.

are clearly written in reference to him. Mr. Postgate has pointed out how such phrases in this passage as 'caelatumque novem Musis opus,' 'quanto cum fastu quanto molimine,' 'vacuam Romanis vatibus aedem,' are characteristic of the straining after strong expression, the self-consciousness and self-assertion of him who regarded it as the chief honour of his native district that it gave birth to the Roman Callimachus, and who proclaims that Mimnermus is a greater master in love than Homer:

> Plus in amore valet Mimnermi versus Homero.

The admiration expressed by Propertius for Virgil has a genuine ring; but the compliment paid to a contemporary poet, Ponticus—

> Primo contendis Homero (i. 7. 3)—

if it is not ironical, can only be attributed to that insatiable love of praise which Horace notes among the characteristics of the mutual admiration cliques of the day. As Propertius more than realises the weakness of the lover satirised by Horace, so too he is a living embodiment of the sensitive vanity of the poet, which the satirist has drawn from life in his Epistles. There is no ground for imputing to Horace any jealousy of the favour bestowed on a rival poet by Maecenas. The language of Propertius, though it testifies to the kindliness of the great patron of literature, to his appreciation of genius and his desire to give it a worthy direction, implies that he himself was not within the inner circle of his intimate friends, as Horace was and as Virgil and Varius had been. But though Horace may not have been of a jealous, he was of a quietly disdainful temper; and as we can understand how Tibullus, the gentle friend and comrade of the cultivated and high-minded Messalla, was attractive to Horace by his personal and social qualities, so we can understand how both the character and the art of Propertius were distasteful to him, especially after his adoption of the ideal of a philosophic attitude towards life, and after he came to regard the wise understanding of life as the true foundation of the highest literary art. He never seems to have lost his interest in or sympathy with younger men who combined gracefully a love of pleasure with a love of literature; but Propertius was not one who could take his pleasure lightly in the spirit of Horace's earlier maxims,

> nec dulces amores
> Sperne puer, neque tu choreas.

As the chief representative of Alexandrianism, he must have been antagonistic to the taste of Horace for the older masters; and the admiration for his poems must have run counter to the direction into which Horace wished to guide the taste of his contemporaries. Even the exceptional and irregular force of expression in Propertius, and the vividness of his imagination, were not likely to be appreciated by so consistent a follower of the rule of moderation in art as in conduct.

While therefore attaching its proper weight to the contemporary testimony of Horace as to the personality of Propertius, we have to qualify it by a consideration of the temper of the critic and the probable grounds of the antagonism between the two poets. The offence given to Horace's common sense and social tact as a man of the world probably made him less just in his appreciation of the genius of Propertius, than he was to the young men on the staff of Tiberius. Yet the fact that Propertius is singled out for the encounter of wit and ironical compliment, seems to be a recognition that he occupies, in Horace's view, a different position from the mere herd of imitators who both irritated and amused him.

The secret of the weakness and unhappiness of Propertius, and partly also of the imperfection of his art, was that his imagination was so much stronger and more elevated than his character. An ideal of an intenser love, a more intellectual life, a happier realisation of the pleasures of art and imagination, is always conflicting with and marred by the actual disorder of his career. The exceptional precocity of his genius, and the early age at which his great passion began, have also to be taken into account in estimating the work which he produced. He began writing before he had any knowledge of life except that taught him by his passion; and he never afterwards succeeded in rising permanently out of the narrow groove of interests in which his life first ran. It is his concentrated devotion to Cynthia through the long period of his 'bondage' which gives a kind of unity and consistency both to his career and his art. His premature death prevented him from fully accomplishing what his genius was capable of, after the horizon of his intellectual interests was widened. His work remains as evidence how passionately, how blindly, and how unhappily an Italian of that age could love, and sacrifice all other claims and interests of life to that absorbing emotion.

CHAPTER IV.

THE ART AND GENIUS OF PROPERTIUS.

PROPERTIUS, in the opening poem of the third book, claims to be 'a high priest from a pure source of poetry, who first bore the sacred symbols of Italy through the movements of the Greek dance.' In language less strained, he claims to be the first interpreter of the passions of Italy in the forms of Greek art. In making this boast he seems to forget the claims of Calvus and Catullus, of Varro and Gallus, which he had just conceded in the last poem of the second book. He is here consciously or unconsciously repeating the claim expressed by Horace in simpler language—

> carmina non prius
> Audita Musarum sacerdos
> Virginibus puerisque canto—

as in the following poem he recalls more than one thought of the 'Exegi monumentum.' But the claim made by Horace is better warranted than that of Propertius. Not only had those four poets celebrated their loves in Greek forms and metres, but the contemporary poet Tibullus had at least an equal claim with Propertius to have brought the elegy to perfection. The words of Propertius, taken along with his claim to be the Roman Callimachus, and with the two opening lines of this poem—

> Callimachi Manes et Coi sacra Philetae,
> In vestrum, quaeso, me sinite ire nemus—

are to be interpreted as meaning that he was the first Roman poet who reproduced the art of Alexandria in Latin literature.

The claim is justifiable to this extent, that he was probably a much closer imitator of the manner and matter of his originals than any of the other elegiac poets. But as these originals are lost we can only form vague inferences as to their art. All evidence points to the supreme importance which they attached not only to diction and metrical effect, but to the composition of their separate pieces, and also to the arrangement of the several pieces in each book so as to produce the impression of an artistic whole; 'simplex et unum[1].'

How far has their professed imitator followed their example in the arrangement of the several books, so as to produce in each a distinct unity of impression? The answer to this question is that this object seems to have been prominently before his mind; that he has completely realised it in the first book; partially, if not completely, in the third; that for some reason or other the second book fails to produce the impression of completeness or arrangement on any principle; and that in the fourth book, there are two independent currents of interest, which were probably never intended to form one continuous stream.

The first book, which was known and prized in later times as a separate work under the name of 'Cynthia Monobiblos,' brings before us, with no more intrusion of alien themes than is sufficient at once to vary and deepen the impression of the whole, the two earliest phases of his passion, the one of the brightest sunshine, the other of the deepest gloom. The opening poem, written in the darkest night of his trouble, but just before a new and more stormy day broke on him, indicates the dominant spirit in which his passion is treated by Propertius. The elegy is with him, even more than with Tibullus, a 'querimonia.' 'Flere' is used by him as equivalent to 'canere,' and

---

[1] The importance attached to the arrangement of the different pieces so as to produce the impression at once of unity and variety, is a marked feature in the Eclogues of Virgil, the Odes of Horace (who to this extent was an Alexandrian), the Elegies of Tibullus, the Amores of Ovid, and also, though the traces are more difficult to follow, in the collected poems of Catullus.

'lacrimae' to 'carmina.' This introductory poem is immediately followed by the brightest in the whole series, full of the 'new life' which this 'new love' brought into his existence. In this poem alone his happiness appears almost unmixed with any feeling of regret or self-reproach, of gratified vanity or querulous complaint. From the second to the tenth, the poems are so arranged as to bring out the pride which, under the plea of justifying his love, moves him to boast of it, and the joy which enables him to sympathise with a similar joy of one of his friends. The little rift which declares itself first in the eighth poem, ends before the poem is completed in a more tumultuous 'amoris integratio.' From the eleventh to the fifteenth, supposed to be written during Cynthia's absence in Baiae, the feeling is more troubled and anxious, and his sympathy with his friend's amour is changed to a complaint of his heartless indifference. The fourteenth poem, addressed to Tullus, which introduces a pause into the development of the story, is, in the main, bright and cheerful. The fifteenth is written with forebodings of the approaching estrangement. The sixteenth, which in its subject recalls the 'Ianua' of Catullus—a common theme of elegiac satire—adds nothing to the development of the situation, but serves as a pause before the feelings of desolation expressed in the two most powerful poems of the book, the seventeenth and eighteenth, and the more melancholy resignation in the nineteenth—states of mind apparently leading to that year of reckless irregularity of which the first poem bears evidence. The twentieth is a poem of more disinterested art than any other in the book, and, though the tone of it is plaintive, serves to relieve the gloom by presenting outward nature and a story of the Greek mythology in their most picturesque combination. The dominant note of melancholy in the two short poems which form the epilogue of the whole book, especially that vivid reproduction in the twenty-first of a tragic scene stamped on his childish imagination, seems an augury of the gloom and trouble of the passion which consumed his life.

It may be said therefore that the first book, finished before he was much past twenty years of age, shews artistic composition and arrangement, unity of subject, variety of treatment, and deepening impressiveness. Had this been the only record of the passion of Propertius, the artistic excellence of his work would have been more generally acknowledged, and he would have left a happier impression of himself as a man and a lover.

Editors from the time of Lachmann have been about equally divided in opinion as to whether that which in the MSS. is numbered Book ii originally formed one or two books, and should be printed as ii, or as ii and iii. The arguments urged in favour of the subdivision into two books are based on the unusual length of the book; the appearance of a new beginning in the tenth poem—

> Sed tempus lustrare aliis Helicona choreis—

and the lines (13. 25–26) written, like so many others, in anticipation of death—

> Sat mea sat magna est si tres sint pompa libelli,
> Quos ego Persephonae maxima dona feram.

There is no reason to suppose that Book iii, which belongs to a later stage in his liaison, was either composed or in his thoughts when that line was written. Still, in a book bearing the marks of so much incompleteness and irregularity, both as a collected whole and in its several elegies, it would be unsafe, on the strength of a single passage, to accept this conclusion against the evidence of the MSS. If it were not for the existence of the more orderly third book, it would be difficult to resist Munro's conclusion, to which M. Plessis indicates his adherence, that the first book alone was published in a finished shape by Propertius. It is difficult to believe that so careful an artist as the author of the 'Cynthia Monobiblos' could have regarded the arrangement of the poems in Book ii as final. They are not arranged according to chronological order. Thus the thirty-first poem refers to an event of the year 28 B.C., which took place either immediately after or possibly a year before the publication of Book i. The poem or series of poems (28 *a*, *b*, *c*) referring to the dangerous illness of Cynthia must have been written before the ninth, in which Propertius recalls his vows for her recovery. And if there is nothing like chronological order observed, it is difficult to detect any other principle of artistic arrangement. Attempts to re-arrange the book, like most of the attempts to re-arrange single poems, succeed only in satisfying the artistic sense of the restorer, and leave on other editors or critics the sense of deepened confusion. Another possible explanation of the condition in which the book is left suggests itself—that there may have been originally two books referring to this phase of the liaison, but that Propertius contemplated recasting them and reducing them to one, as Ovid recast and reduced his five books of Amores to three, and that death overtook him while his task was still incomplete. It is certainly desirable, for purposes of reference, that editors should come to an agreement on the subject.

The thirty-four poems of this book, with scarcely any exception, represent the alternations of experience and feeling during the years which followed the renewal of his passion. A fit motto for the book, and for the life of the poet at the time when the elegies composing it were written, might be taken from the twelfth poem, in which, guided by the teaching of his own experience, he analyses the meaning of the painter who represented the god of love as a winged boy:

> Scilicet alterna quoniam iactamur in unda,
> Nostraque non ullis permanet aura locis.

The fluctuations of passion, between joy, despair, and anger, follow one another without an indication of any change of circumstances to account for them. The disorder of the book is a symbol of the agitation under which it was composed. He seems to have written under the impulse of the moment, and never afterwards to have been able to shape the record of his varying moods into a coherent whole. A certain change in the development of his humour may indeed be traced towards the end of the book. Two of the least moody poems in the book are the nineteenth—'Etsi me invito discedis, Cynthia, Roma'—

and the thirty-second—'Qui videt, is peccat.' In the first he is fully conscious of Cynthia's frequent infidelities: in the second he is reconciled to them. The first and the last poems serve as a prologue and epilogue to the book. They are both apologies for his art, and are interesting as expressive of his just appreciation of the character of Maecenas and of the genius of Virgil.

The third book, though it also brings before us violent alternations of mood, dependent on the capricious favours, the imperious exactions, and the frequent infidelities of Cynthia, and repeated struggles to emancipate himself and to rise into a higher range of intellectual life, has more the character of a consistent whole. The opening poems, in which he invokes the shade of Callimachus and the sacred relics of Philetas, indicate a change of mood, and a mind more occupied with his fame than with his past or present miseries. His love is now more a theme for his art than the torment of his life. He can deal with it in an easier style, as in the sixth poem, in which he questions her slave Lygdamus about his mistress's feelings towards him, and he is more inspired by the memories of past favours, as in the poem on the 'lost tablets,' and that in which he begs Cynthia to wear the dress in which she first captivated him. He deals with his passion more as an artist than a lover. The most serious expression of his personal feelings is in the two final poems in which he renounces his love. The poems of which Cynthia is the theme alternate with others dealing with the interests of public and private life. The spell which she had exercised over him reminds him now not only of some of the famous heroines of old, but of one who has become a heroine to modern poets, the 'incesti meretrix regina Canopi,' whose ambitious hopes and tragic end he has described with more power than any other Roman poet. In another he expresses the hope that under the patronage of Maecenas his genius may gather strength to celebrate the beginnings of Rome, and the great events of contemporary history. He writes, too, in anticipation of the triumph of the expedition to the East, meditated by Augustus on leaving Rome in the year 22 B.C. He deals also with the passion of love in a more disinterested spirit, and presents a worthier ideal of it than that realised in his own troubled experience, in his remonstrance with Postumus (12) for leaving his bride Galla to follow the arms of Augustus. In the following poem, the love of luxury and rage for wealth, the motive both of the soldier's and the merchant's career, are contrasted with an ideal of a primitive life when the Gods of the country mingled freely and genially among men, a note of the survival of that purer and more tranquil ideal of life which was realised by Tibullus, and which agitated Propertius and made him, unlike Ovid, restless and unhappy amid the constant excitements and pleasures of the town. It is apparently the secret longing for rest to his restless spirit, that makes the thought of death so vividly present in all his poetry. In this book the thought is not associated solely with himself, but is vividly brought home to him by the shipwreck in which his young and adventurous friend Paetus perished (7), and by the great national calamity of the untimely death of the young Marcellus (18).

If the first book is most artistic in its treatment of the chief phases of the poet's passion, the third has the advantage of greater variety of subject and a more disinterested treatment. Even the poems inspired by Cynthia gain artistically as being the record of emotions recalled by the imagination after the passion has cooled, instead of being the immediate outpouring of the turmoil of incongruous emotions. No irregularity or disorder is apparent in the composition of this book. Except for the inexplicable condition in which the second book has been left, there would be no reason to doubt that the third was given to the world in its present shape about the year 21 B.C., and helped to enhance the poet's claim to be the Roman Callimachus.

There appear to be two incongruous motives in the fourth book. The original intention, as indicated in the introductory poem, was to carry out the idea already hinted at (iii. 9) of a series of poems on the origins and antiquities of Rome and on Roman rites and customs, suggested apparently by the Αἴτια of Callimachus. But in this introductory poem, of which the most interesting parts are the notices of his life already discussed, he describes a struggle in his mind between the ambition to write of this subject in the spirit of Ennius, and what he knew to be his true calling, which is declared to him in the words of the astrologer Horos—

> At tu finge elegos, fallax opus, haec tua castra,
> Scribat ut exemplo cetera turba tuo.

Poems 2, 4, 9, and 10 are written on the plan contemplated in the first poem. It is obvious that he either did not live to complete the plan, or that, like Virgil with the subject of the 'Alban kings,' he became 'offensus materia.' Some editors have supposed that these poems were his earliest compositions. But the evidence of the former books proves that Cynthia was the first inspirer of his elegy. The lines in iii. 9. 49–52,

> Celsaque Romanis decerpta Palatia tauris
> Ordiar et caeso moenia firma Remo,
> Eductosque pares silvestri ex ubere reges,
> Crescet et ingenium sub tua iussa meum,

imply that this was a later enterprise urged on him by Maecenas. Even the vanity of Propertius could scarcely have claimed that the wall around his native town had become more famous owing to his genius, before the composition of the Cynthia poems. And the words of Horos (iv. 1. 137–144) can only refer to the love for Cynthia and the poems commemorating it. Further, the technical structure of the verse, in which the disyllabic ending of the pentameter is nearly as uniform as in Ovid, leaves no doubt that these poems are in his later manner.

The other seven poems of the book are elegies unconnected with one another, on various subjects of personal, private, and public interest, and all are among the most powerful products of his art and genius. Two are on the old subject of Cynthia, but written no longer under the spell of her visible fascination. In the first of these, the two most potent influences of his poetry, love and death, are united in the most tragic association. The remorse for his past coldness, and that foreboding of early death to which, in the reaction from the feverish excitement of his life, he was so liable, are both aroused by a vivid vision of the ghost of Cynthia appearing to him immediately after her burial. The following poem betrays not only the levity which so strangely intermingles with the sombre gloom of his temperament, but also an unexpected vein of humour in recalling the violent temper and capricious imperiousness of the former object of his idolatry. It could only have been written after his imagination was completely disillusioned. The sanity and vivid realism with which the situation is presented confirms the impression derived from some other poems of this book, that he would have been a more attractive poet if he could more frequently have assumed a more objective and less impassioned attitude to his own experience, or to the personages and incidents which moved his imagination in the art and poetry of the past. A third poem, in the vein of Archilochus rather than Mimnermus, addressed to a 'lena,' shows that in the ashes of his extinct love there survived the hate of the agent of her infidelities. A happier and more disinterested utterance of the Muse who inspires the poetry of love is recognised in the epistle of Arethusa to Lycotas, which may have first suggested the epistolary form of Ovid, as the poems on Roman rites and the legends connected with them may have suggested the subject of the Fasti. This epistle is more interesting than any of the Heroides, as its substance is taken not from remote legends, but from the real experience of the Augustan age. It is interesting as presenting a purer ideal of womanhood than is usual in the elegiac poets; and, further, as evidence how the love of adventure or the hope of booty acted even on the effeminate spirits of the time—

> Dic mihi, num teneros urit lorica lacertos?
> Num gravis imbelles atterit hasta manus?

The sixth poem was written for a public occasion, the celebration of the games which commemorated the victory of Actium.

The terror and hatred inspired by Cleopatra add a new testimony to the dangerous fascination exercised by woman in that age, of which the earlier books of Propertius afford the most living record. The last poem of the series, probably the last written by Propertius, is, if not the most inspired and spontaneous, certainly the noblest of his elegiacs. It reminds us that if there was a Cleopatra, whose fascination and ambition brought about one of the great decisive struggles of the world, and if there were many Cynthias, by whom private lives were wrecked, the ideal of Roman matronhood still survived, and was sometimes realised amid the general corruption. The elegy professes to be the 'apology for her life,' uttered by Cornelia, a member of the great house of Scipio, connected with the imperial family through her mother Scribonia, and the wife of Paullus Aemilius Lepidus. The image presented of her may be more a creature of the imagination than a true likeness, but it is a high ideal of the dignity of manner, the greatness of sentiment, and the loyalty of womanhood, realised in some of the women of the great Roman families, of which traces survive in some of the busts which have come down from the earliest and best years of the Empire. It is an ideal not only of a great Roman lady, ennobled by the memories of her own family and of that into which she had married, so closely connected with her own in the day when each produced its greatest men, but also of a loyal and devoted wife, a pious and devoted mother. From this poem, the latest impression we form of Propertius is of capacities unused and latent through the long years of his entanglement. It adds to the regret that after having sufficiently sung of his love, he did not live to produce more mature work, bearing testimony to his appreciation of the enduring nobleness in Roman life.

The union of two incongruous objects in this book suggests the inference that the poet was carrying on two separate works at the same time, that neither was left complete, and that his friends after his death published what they found in his 'scrinia' in what seemed to them the order most conducive to variety of interest. As to his first design, the astrologer was probably a true prophet, in indicating that the rôle of Ennius could not be taken up by him in elegiac verse. Nor had he, as Ovid had, the lightness of touch required to make tales of romance or amusing adventure out of the aetiological myths associated with ancient temples and ritual. There is an element of pedantry in the way in which Propertius deals with Roman antiquities, as there sometimes is in the way in which he deals with Greek mythology. The other subjects are sufficiently varied between those purely personal and those of general human interest. The tone also is sufficiently varied from tragedy to comedy, from indignation to tenderness or noble pathos, to make us feel that, under other conditions, his art might have vied with that of Horace in its power of finding shape and expression for the imaginative sentiment of the time, and that he was even capable of striking a more powerful note than any struck by Horace. Though by the loss of any considerable portion of his work, we should have been in danger of losing some of his most sincere and passionate utterances, yet perhaps he would have been more popular as a poet, and ranked more highly as an artist, if we had possessed only the 'Cynthia Monobiblos,' a very few of the poems of the second book, nearly the whole of the third book, and of the fourth book all except those in which he attempts to elicit a spring of poetry out of the dryness of aetiological myths. We should thus have been spared much of the iteration, the sense of unrelieved misery and weakness, the pedantry, the obscurity and confusion, which mar the pleasure of reading Propertius as a whole.

The structure of the single elegies is different in Propertius from what it is in the other elegiac poets. We feel in him the impulsive rush of passion, not the rise and fall of tender sentiment as in Tibullus, or the lively movement of fancy and curiosity as in Ovid. He often, as is remarked by M. Plessis, begins abruptly, as if after long brooding the expression of what was uppermost in his mind at the moment was forced

from him. Instances of this startling abruptness are seen in
i. 17:
> Et merito, quoniam potui fugisse puellam;

i. 18:
> Haec certe deserta loca et taciturna querenti;

i. 21:
> Tu qui consortem properas evadere casum;

iii. 7:
> Ergo sollicitae tu causa, pecunia, vitae.

In most of the elegies the passion appears immediately in its utmost intensity, but does not maintain itself at the same pitch. The feeling seems to burst forth without warning and to force a way for itself, but as it advances it seems to check itself, and follow the guidance of a fancy overladen with mythological learning, till it cannot recover its first impetuous speed. One striking instance of this is iii. 12—

> Postume, plorantem potuisti linquere Gallam—

where the tender beauty of the first twenty-two lines, ending

> Pendebit collo Galla pudica tuo,

is certainly not enhanced by the sixteen lines which give a summary of the adventures of Ulysses to prove that

> Vincet Penelopes Aelia Galla fidem.

The charm even of i. 2, which grows in intensity till line 14 by all the illustrations of the unadorned beauty of natural things, seems to fade away in the irrelevant learning of lines 15–20. In some of the finest elegies of Book i, as 17 and 18, the flow of feeling knows no check; and one cause of the greater artistic charm of the first book is that the poems in it do not exceed the length during which one strong emotion is able to run without impediment.

The passion and feeling of the moment seems to force out and shape the language and metre suitable for the expression of his thought. He is always striving to vivify the objects of nature of which he speaks, and to present his thought in some picture or image. Often his figures of speech seem to be suggested by works of art, such as pictures or other artistic representations of the God of Love. The strange and almost grotesque phrase,

> Itala per Graios orgia ferre choros,

recalls those works of art in which Apollo is represented as joining with the Muses in their sacred dance. He frequently strikes out new Latin combinations of words as the equivalents of striking phrases in the Greek authors whom he studied, Philetas and Callimachus, Theocritus, Apollonius, Meleager, and Leonidas of Tarentum. Possibly if we possessed the lost elegies of the Alexandrians, we should understand better much that seems forced and unidiomatic in the diction of Propertius. Occasionally we are reminded of native poets, Catullus, Virgil, and Horace—more however in the sentiment and thought than in the diction—but on the whole no poet seems to have kept himself more free from the facile abuse of the conventional language of poetry. Each single phrase seems the mintage of his own mind, and it is the endeavour to make his language independent of the ordinary repertory of poetical art, that makes it often forced and obscure. We feel always the presence of an energetic 'forgetive' mind in his diction. We feel it in his novel word-formations, as in

> Cogar et undisonos nunc prece adire deos (iii. 21. 18);

in such revivals of archaic words as in

> Illa mihi totis argutat noctibus ignes (i. 6. 7);

in the transitive meaning given to intransitive verbs, as in

> Frigidaque Eoo me dolet aura gelu (i. 16. 24);

in the attribution of a living personality to natural objects—

> et invito gurgite fecit iter (i. 17. 14).

He forces the Latin language from its ordinary sobriety of phrase and ordinary obedience to grammatical law to be the medium of an imagination working powerfully, incessantly, and irregularly under the influence of powerful, unceasing, and irregular emotion. The language of Propertius is the idealised monologue of an introspective mind, making its meaning vividly present to itself, as that of Ovid is the language of idealised conversation addressed to a pleasure-loving, refined, and quick-witted society. Propertius is seldom gay, natural, easy and familiar, as Ovid always is. There are few continuous passages of six or eight lines in which the diction is simple and direct, as it is for instance in the passage i. 2. 9–14—

> Aspice, quos summittat humus, &c.

In the thirteenth line the word *persuadent*, for which no tolerable substitute has been suggested, cannot be said to convey the idea corresponding to it simply or naturally. It is very seldom that we come on even four lines together, in which we detect so little sign of effort, of that straining for success which Horace indicates in the word *torquebitur*, as in the lines 1. 11. 23–26—

> Tu mihi sola domus, tu, Cynthia, sola parentes,
> Omnia tu nostrae tempora laetitiae.
> Seu tristis veniam seu contra laetus amicis,
> Quidquid ero, dicam: Cynthia causa fuit.

The most powerful effects of the language of Propertius are associated with his power over his metre. The energy of his imagination shows itself in the vividness and novelty of the imagery by which he symbolises his thought: his capacity of imaginative feeling shows itself in his susceptibility to the grander or more solemn and to the more soothing and voluptuous effects of the sound of words and their combinations. In his metre also we seem to feel as if the music of single lines and couplets was slowly beat out by conscious effort. The lines seem intended to be dwelt on singly, and to bring out their full musical effect they have to be read with a certain 'lenocinium' of the voice. The lines and couplets arrest the attention and sink deeply into the mind; but no single poem of Propertius carries us on with the facile flow of Ovid or the equable movement of Tibullus. In Tibullus and Ovid we find a continuous and connected movement of thoughts, each complete in the couplet, and either passing into one another by gentle transition, or indicating their relation to one another by a rapid and perpetual flow of lively and witty antithesis. In Propertius we find long continuous passages, in which there is scarcely any pause, and in which the sense frequently runs on into the third line. But the great difference in their rhythmical movement is that in Ovid and Tibullus the rise of the feeling in the first line is followed by its 'falling in melody back' in the second; in Propertius there is more frequently a culminating than a subsiding effect in the second line of the couplet. The pentameter instead of being a weaker echo of the hexameter is the stronger line of the two, and has a weightier movement. In Ovid the dactylic movement predominates in the first as in the second half of the pentameter. In Propertius two spondees in the first half of the line are more common than two dactyls. He is fond of the long vowel sound of *o* and *u* in his pentameters:

Quam cito de tanto nomine rumor eris (i. 5. 26).

In the first book Propertius adhered to the old Greek practice of ending the pentameter with words of three, four, and five syllables. In the later books he yielded to the new taste fostered by Ovid for a uniform disyllabic ending. It may be doubted whether he did not lose more by thus limiting the range of his instrument, than he gained in smoothness. Horace in his employment of the Sapphic metre, beginning with a strict uniformity of movement, seems to have felt its monotony and tameness, and reverted to the freer movement of the Greeks; and in this he seems to have been more happily guided. The elision of final syllables is more frequent in Propertius, and this sometimes produces a sense of crude harshness in his lines, as in

Quaerere: non impune illa rogata venit (i. 5. 32).

Sometimes, however, a kind of rugged grandeur, harmonising with the thought, is thus imparted to a line, as in

Nunc tibi pro tumulo Carpathium omne mare est (iii. 7. 12).

The effect of the verse and diction of Propertius is especially manifest in their power of vaguely impressing the imagination and awakening emotions of awe and solemnity. The power of the pentameter in evoking the solemn feelings associated with death (with a similar effect to that of the third line in the Horatian Alcaic) is seen in such lines as

> Brachia spectavi sacris admorsa colubris,
> Et trahere occultum membra soporis iter (iii. 11. 53);
> Est mala, sed cunctis ista terenda via est (iii. 18. 22);
> Nec nostra Actiacum verteret ossa mare (ii. 15. 44);
> Murmur ad extremae nuper humata viae (iv. 7. 4).

There is a grandeur as well as solemnity imparted to the thought of love triumphing over fate and death in

> Traicit et fati litora magnus amor (i. 19. 12);

while all the tender regrets associated with death are touched by the contrast between the spirit of youthful adventure and the pathetic memories suggested by the funeral urn—

> Sic redeunt, illis qui cecidere locis (iii. 12. 14).

Great historic and legendary associations are evoked in such weighty lines as

> Consule cum Mario, capte Iugurtha, sedes (iii. 5. 16);
> Cimbrorumque minas et benefacta Mari (ii. 1. 24);
> Curia, praetexto quae nunc nitet alta senatu,
> Pellitos habuit, rustica corda, patres (iv. 1. 11);

and more recent associations, solemn or serious, in these—

> Iura dare et statuas inter et arma Mari (iii. 11. 46),

and

> Maecenatis erunt vera tropaea fides (iii. 9. 34).

The awe inspired by the blind forces of nature and their cruelty finds a natural voice in such lines as

> Aspice, quam saevas increpat aura minas (i. 17. 6),

or

> Alternante vorans vasta Charybdis aqua (ii. 26. 54).

But his language and rhythm express not only the Roman sense of awe and solemnity in presence of the thoughts, memories, and aspects of nature which rouse these emotions. They are pervaded also by the Italian 'mollitia,' a susceptibility to the sweet and musical sound of language in harmony with a luxurious and voluptuous sentiment, often not unmixed with melancholy, awakened by the thought of the tender joys of love, the softer influences of nature, the musical charm of poetry and song. Here too the charm of sound and sense is in the pentameter—

> Omnia si dederis oscula, pauca dabis (ii. 15. 50);
> Ulla dedit collo dulcia vincla meo (iii. 15. 10);
> Non oculi, geminae, sidera nostra, faces (ii. 3. 14);
> Sit Galatea tuae non aliena viae (i. 8. 18).

So, too, in the descriptions of nature, how the sound is suggestive of the sparkling of a running brook in the line

> Et sciat indociles currere lympha vias (i. 2. 12);

of a rich and tender beauty and of its transitoriness in

> Vidi ego odoratum victura rosaria Paestum,
> Sub matutino cocta iacere Noto (iv. 5. 61);

of all the softer charm of nature in

> Mulcet ubi Elysias aura beata rosas (iv. 7. 60),

or

> Luna moraturis sedula luminibus (i. 3. 32),

and of its more picturesque aspects in—

> Nec vaga muscosis flumina fusa iugis (ii. 19. 30).

Again, how the slumberous charm of the occupation is suggested by these lines—

> Nam modo purpureo fallebam stamine somnum,
> Rursus et Orpheae carmine, fessa, lyrae (i. 3. 41).

How the musical sweetness of poetry is heard in

> Sed potui blandi carminis obsequio (i. 8. 39),

and in the reference to the poems of which that musical sweetness is the principal charm—

> Tu canis umbrosi subter pineta Galaesi
> Thyrsin et attritis Daphnin arundinibus (ii. 34. 67).

If the rank of a poet were to be assigned by the weight and power of single lines and phrases, no Roman poet would be more worthy than Propertius to be placed beside Lucretius and Virgil. No others show in their language so much energy and variety of imagination, so vivid a susceptibility to powerful emotions, so much capacity of receiving and interpreting certain aspects of beauty in art, in nature, and in human passions. Yet not only have his poems as a whole failed to gain the ear of the world, as the Odes of Horace and the short lyrics and iambics of Catullus have gained it, but there is no single poem of his which is stamped throughout with the classical perfection of many of the poems of these two great artists. It is not that Propertius was indifferent to art. He is ever straining after perfection of execution, but the full torrent of his emotion and conception constantly overflows or strays from the channel into which he wishes to direct it. There is, if not a narrower range of interests, a greater monotony of mood in Propertius. Yet it would be a wrong impression to form of him that he is solely the poet of his own love for Cynthia, or that he is not a powerful interpreter of other moods, and other aspects of life and nature, which are the material of poets of all ages. His first claim to distinction is that he is pre-eminently the poet of passionate love. From no other ancient poet do we realise so completely the daemonic spell which this passion could exercise on the whole life, its power for joy and grief, its power to exalt and to paralyse the energies of life, to inspire poetry and yet to subdue to its own service the gifts and aspirations which raise the poet into a higher and purer region of feeling and contemplation. He claims to be for the young lovers of both sexes the interpreter of their feelings. In some of his poems he tries to express his sympathy with the love affairs of his friends, but in the earlier stage of his passion he is too self-absorbed to rise to the disinterested joy in another's joy which Catullus makes us feel in the Acme and Septimius, and in the ringing Glyconics of the Epithalamium of Manlius and Vinia. But after the fervour of his own love has cooled, he

exhibits in the remonstrance with Postumus and in the epistle
of Arethusa to Lycotas a higher ideal of the love of woman
than anything else which we find in the other amatory poets.
It is to the credit of Propertius that neither his own experience
of infidelity nor the irregularity of his life destroyed his faith in
this ideal. He becomes neither cynical nor blasé. The sentiment expressed in the epistle of Arethusa,

> Omnis amor magnus, sed aperto in coniuge maior,

is in direct antagonism to the philosophy fashionable among
the votaries of pleasure, of whom Ovid was the high priest—

> dos est uxoria lites (A. A. ii. 155).

There is more strength and reality of feeling, and a truer insight
into the human heart in this epistle, vivid with all the actual
experiences of the present, than in the creations of fancy in
which Ovid reproduces the imaginary sorrows of his heroines.

The thought of death is vividly present to many of the
Roman poets, as a reminder, in the midst of all their luxury
or violent pleasure, of the transitoriness of their enjoyment.
But more than any, Propertius broods on the idea and on all
its accessories with a morbid intensity of feeling. He is
haunted by the foreboding that it is his doom and his glory to
die of love—

> Laus in amore mori (ii. 1. 47).

Perhaps the most powerful lines in which this foreboding is
expressed, mingling as they do a feeling of tragic awe with the
imaginative sense of a mysterious invisible agency, are these
from the fourth poem of Book ii—

> Quippe ubi nec causas nec apertos cernimus ictus,
>   Unde tamen veniant tot mala caeca via est.
> Non eget hic medicis, non lectis mollibus aeger,
>   Huic nullum caeli tempus et aura nocet:
> Ambulat, et subito mirantur funus amici:
>   Sic est incautum quidquid habetur amor.

This sense of the imminence of death sometimes suggests to
him, as to Catullus, the lesson of the more passionate enjoyment
of the present:

> Quare, dum licet, inter nos laetemur amantes:
> Non satis est ullo tempore longus amor (i. 19. 25).

But he can think also of the strength of love surviving the funeral pyre, and recalls the tale of Protesilaus as a testimony of this enduring love—

> Illic Phylacides iucundae coniugis heros
> Non potuit caecis immemor esse locis (ibid. 7).

The elegy on the death of Paetus (iii. 7), one of the truest elegies in the Latin language, realises with all the vividness of Lucretius the shock caused to surviving friends by the premature cutting short of a young and adventurous life, the horror, more natural in ancient than in modern times, of perishing at sea—

> Paete, quid aetatem numeras? quid cara natanti
> Mater in ore tibi est? non habet unda deos—

the contrast between the delicate frame and the pitiless cruelty of the waves which it had to encounter—

> Huic fluctus vivo radicitus abstulit ungues,
> Et miseri invisam traxit hiatus aquam—

the contrast between the familiar resting-place among his kinsmen and the 'vast and wandering grave' which received him—

> Nunc tibi pro tumulo Carpathium omne mare est.

This poem naturally suggests a comparison with another lament for the loss of a young friend by shipwreck. Both the lament for Paetus and the lament for Lycidas are powerful and musical elegies over the extinction of youthful promise. The actual details of the shipwreck are more vividly realised by the Latin poet, but perhaps it is a higher art to soften all these accessories by the delicate use of pastoral and mythological imagery, as is done by the English poet, than to present them in such grim realism as

> Et nova longinquis piscibus esca natat.

Even in the use of the ancient mythology the modern shows his superiority to the ancient poet, whose

> Infelix Aquilo, raptae timor Orithyiae

and

> Sunt Agamemnonias testantia litora curas,

simply check the feeling of pathos without mitigating the horror of the situation. The lines

> 'Ay me! whilst thee the shores and sounding seas,' &c.

reveal richer and more powerful imagination than the single line, weighty in its vague suggestiveness,

> Nunc tibi pro tumulo, &c.

Propertius expresses powerfully the common sorrow for the common lot. There is the true feeling of Italian piety in the complaint addressed to Neptune—

> Portabat sanctos alveus ille viros—

and in the longing of the dying Paetus to be borne to the shores of Italy, and to be restored even in death to his mother's care—

> At saltem Italiae regionibus advehat aestus:
> Hoc de me sat erit si modo matris erit.

The sorrow for Lycidas is for one cut off from a richer and nobler life than that which falls to the common lot. The spiritual piety of the English poet, if somewhat marred by the polemical passion of the time, affords a grander ideal than the piety of simple affection. But the truest note of difference between the modern and the ancient poet is struck in the last lines of their respective poems; in the sense of pastoral peacefulness and the thought of the consistent dignity of life, in the close of Lycidas—

> To-morrow to fresh woods and pastures new—

and the sense of almost heartless levity, and the thought of a marred and restless life which are left on us by Propertius :—

> At tu, saeve Aquilo, numquam mea vela videbis:
> Ante fores dominae condar oportet iners.

Milton's great saying, 'that he who would not be frustrate of his hope to write well hereafter in laudable things, ought himself to be a true poem,' never received more confirmation than in the art and life of Propertius. What prevented him from bringing his great powers of genius into perfect harmony so as to realise his great aspirations, was that he could not harmonise his life.

The lament for the young Marcellus (iii. 18) is a real elegy, but rather of imagination than of feeling. The thought is the commonplace one of the vanity of all earthly state, the unavailingness of worldly greatness and popular favour to avert the common doom; but it is expressed with great pomp and solemnity of language and rhythmical movement—

> I nunc, tolle animos et tecum finge triumphos,
>   Stantiaque in plausum tota theatra iuvent.
> Attalicas supera vestes, atque omnia magnis
>   Gemmea sint ludis: ignibus ista dabis.

The same thought of death as the universal leveller is expressed with the solemnity of Lucretius in an earlier elegy (iii. 5. 13–16)—

> Haut ullas portabis opes Acherontis ad undas,
>   Nudus at inferna, stulte, vehere rate.
> Victor cum victis pariter miscebitur umbris:
>   Consule cum Mario, capte Iugurtha, sedes.

In the poem in which Cynthia's ghost appears to him, she tells him that there is a separation in the world below between those who have kept faith and those who have violated it. This is the one human relation rewarded or punished. In the thought of a future life we recognise no definite belief, but the vague influence of old religious traditions and the ghostly terrors of the supernatural world, blending sometimes with the happier dreams of poets. We find a lingering survival of the primitive belief in the presence of the spirit in or near the grave, and still retaining the feelings of suffering or terror of which a living being would be conscious. It is this survival of belief which imparts such a grim horror to the curse invoked on the 'lena'—

> Terra tuum spinis obducat, lena, sepulcrum—

and to that which Cynthia invokes on herself, if she has been untrue (iv. 7. 53)—

> Si fallo, vipera nostris
> Sibilet in tumulis et super ossa cubet.

The feeling with which Propertius realises the thought of death and what comes after it has nothing of the austere fortitude with which Lucretius, or the quiet resignation with which Horace looks it in the face, nor anything of the gentle charm of poetical fancy with which Tibullus eludes it, but is rather the natural foreboding of a restless and melancholy nature, whose restlessness and melancholy are intensified by vivid imagination and uncontrolled by consistency of thought or character.

Though in common with all the other Italian poets he feels deeply the power of certain aspects of nature over the imagination, he does not seem to derive from them the sense of peace or consolation which Virgil and Lucretius, Horace and Tibullus, find in such refuges from melancholy thoughts, or from the cares and distractions of life. He seems to have keenly enjoyed the spectacle which Rome presented in her porticoes, temples, theatres, and triumphal processions. He has left a vivid account of the artistic glories revealed at the dedication of the temple of the Palatine Apollo (ii. 31), the columns of marble, the figures of the daughters of Danaus, the statue of the god himself, the four cattle of Myro—

> Quattuor artificis, vivida signa, boves—

the ivory gates of the temple on which the avenging power of the god was made visible in the representation of the Gauls driven from Delphi, and of the punishment of Niobe. In the poem (iii. 21) in which he expresses his intention of visiting Athens, he anticipates the delight to the eye from the art of the painter and sculptor—

> Aut certe tabulae capient mea lumina pictae,
> Sive ebore exactae, seu magis aere manus.

He has a great feeling of the beauty of gems, of robes of Coan silk, and other ornaments of luxury. When he describes a familiar scene from nature, it is that of the Tiber, with the boats passing up and down its waters, as seen from a wooded villa overhanging them. There are few traces in his poems of his having moved often from his home on the Esquiline. In one of his fits of despair, during the year of estrangement, he takes refuge among the solitudes around the sources of the Clitumnus, and pours out his sorrows to the woods and lonely rocks—

> Sed qualiscumque es, resonent mihi Cynthia silvae,
> Nec deserta tuo nomine saxa vacent (i. 18. 31).

In a happier mood and in one of the most charming of the poems of the second book, he writes from Rome to Cynthia, who had gone before him to spend some time among those lonely scenes—

> Sola eris et solos spectabis, Cynthia, montes
> Et pecus et fines pauperis agricolae (ii. 19. 7)—

and contrasts the primitive innocence and piety of the country with the temptations and luxury of the town—

> Illic te nulli poterunt corrumpere ludi
> Fanaque peccatis plurima causa tuis;
> Illic assidue tauros spectabis arantes
> Et vitem docta ponere falce comas;
> Atque ibi rara feres inculto tura sacello,
> Haedus ubi agrestes corruet ante focos[1].

He looks forward to joining her there in a few days and enjoying the tamer sports of the field—

> Qua formosa suo Clitumnus flumina luco
> Integit, et niveos abluit unda boves.

As it is among the wilder scenes of nature that he seeks refuge in his despair, so it is among them that he would fain return with the object of his love to a more natural and simple life.

---

[1] The loneliness of the place is not much changed in the present day. The words
   Sola eris et solos spectabis, Cynthia, montes
will recur to any one familiar with Propertius, as he looks on the amphitheatre of hills to the south.

He feels the charm of natural beauty as it reveals itself in wild and lonely places—

> Surgat et in solis formosius arbutus antris (i. 2. 11);

and it is in some quiet spot remote from men, beneath the shade of trees, that he desires to be buried—

> Me tegat arborea devia terra coma (iii. 16. 28).

It is from the same impressibility to the solemn sights and mysterious agencies of nature, and the sombre feelings produced by them, that he represents so powerfully the effect of the blind fury of the sea ('vesani murmura ponti') and the loneliness of night on the imagination, as in the seventeenth poem of the first book, in which the situation and feelings of one in danger of shipwreck in a stormy night, and descrying in the late evening or early dawn the woods of an unknown shore—

> ignotis circumdata litora silvis—

are vividly brought before the eye and mind. The terror of the sea is the principal motive of more than one of his most powerful pieces,—of the lament for Paetus, in which the darkness of the night adds to the terror of the conflict of the elements with the helplessness of man, and the dream (ii. 26) in which he sees the shipwrecked Cynthia—

> Ionio lassas ducere rore manus.

The loneliness of the natural scenes which surround them heightens the romance of the illustrations and tales from mythology introduced into his poems. The first are indeed often brought in irrelevantly or in greater abundance than is needed. In one or two instances the heroines are degraded (though not so often or with the same cynicism as in Ovid) by being identified with the realism of Roman passion. But in other cases the romance of ancient story enhances, without in any way suffering degradation, the passion of the actual situation. Thus the despair of Propertius, driving him into the solitudes of the bare Umbrian hillside, gains a certain glory from its association with the romantic tale of Milanion's sufferings among the wild Arcadian mountains. And no actual description of her personal beauties would affect the imagination of contemporaries familiar with the paintings and sculpture of the time so powerfully as the comparison (i. 3) of the sleeping Cynthia to Ariadne, just after the departure of Theseus,

> Languida desertis Gnosia litoribus;

to Andromeda,

> Libera iam duris cotibus Andromede;

and to the Bacchante, when, wearied with the wild revelry of the dance, she has sunk to sleep on the grassy bank of the Apidanus.

The most powerful union of a tale of adventure and terror in combination with the solitariness, the wild forces, and mysterious agencies of Nature, is seen in the treatment of a subject which had been famous in the Greek and Roman drama, and in many works of art, the escape of Antiope from the jealous tyranny of Dirce, and her recognition by her sons Zethus and Amphion (iii. 15)—

> Inde Cithaeronis timido pede currit in arces.
> Nox erat, et sparso triste cubile gelu.
> Saepe vaga Asopi sonitu permota fluentis
> Credebat dominae pone venire pedes,
> Et durum Zethum et lacrimis Amphiona mollem
> Experta est stabulis mater abacta suis.

The comparison that follows—

> Ac veluti, magnos cum ponunt aequora motus,
> Eurus ubi adverso desinit ire Noto,
> Litore sic tacito sonitus rarescit harenae,
> Sic cadit inflexo lapsa puella genu—

illustrates the power, not only of his meaning but of the movement of his verse, to stir the imagination with a vague sense of the analogy between the rise and subsidence of the stormy forces of nature and the forces of human passion, similar to the effect produced by the passionate lines of Shelley—

> Some respite to its turbulence unresting ocean knows . . .
> Thou in the grave shalt rest.

He is appreciative of the softer beauties as well as the sterner and more majestic aspects of nature. But these too appear in her solitudes, owing nothing to the care of man. The most elaborate description of a beautiful scene is presented in union with the adventures of the lonely wanderer Hylas (i. 20. 33)—

> Hic erat Arganthi Pege sub vertice montis
> Grata domus Nymphis umida Thyniasin,
> Quam supra nullae pendebant debita curae
> Roscida desertis poma sub arboribus,
> Et circum irriguo surgebant lilia prato—
> Candida purpureis mixta papaveribus.

His general treatment of mythology is merely allusive. Though it not infrequently seems frigid and pedantic to modern readers, yet it had a vital meaning in his own day for those who had not only the works of the Greek poets in their hands, but before their eyes the innumerable works of art inspired by them. In telling the tale of Hylas, or the flight of Antiope, or in recalling the kindly communing of Pan with the kindly and uncorrupted people of primitive times (iii. 13. 25–50), he shows a deeper insight into the romance and the tragic significance of the tales of the old mythology, a deeper love for nature, and a worthier sense of her influence on the heart and imagination, than the poet who by his power of narrative, and the facile working of a vividly pictorial imagination, has been the chief medium by which the romance of early Greece has passed into the imagination of the modern world.

The public events of his own time or within recent memory which made the most impression on his imagination, were the victories of Marius over the Cimbri, the death of Pompey, the horrors of the siege of Perusia, the career of Cleopatra, the danger with which she threatened Rome, and the sense of indignity which she left on the Roman mind[1]; the power of her fascination, and the tragedy of her death. And generally it is by the tragic issues of the time, more than its peaceful or warlike glories, that his imagination is moved. Yet he has

---

[1] Cf. p. 125, *supra*.

a just appreciation of the exceptional part played by Maecenas in history, of his prudence, his loyalty, his suppression of all personal ambition. He feels the magnitude of the issue involved in the battle of Actium—

> Huc mundi coiere manus—

and he avails himself happily of the resources of poetry, mythology and sculpture, to glorify the part which the patron God of Augustus is supposed to take in the struggle—

> Non ille attulerat crines in colla solutos
>   Aut testudineae carmen inerme lyrae,
> Sed quale aspexit Pelopeum Agamemnona vultu,
>   Egessitque avidis Dorica castra rogis,
> Aut qualis flexos solvit Pythona per orbes
>   Serpentem, imbelles quem timuere lyrae (iv. 6. 31).

We recognise a powerful stroke of the individualising power of his imagination in the suggestion of the whole spectacle of a Roman triumph by the vivid presentment of a single incident in it—

> Ad vulgi plausus saepe resistere equos (iii. 4. 14);

just as in a previous poem (ii. 1) he enables us to realise the regret which Maecenas may feel for his untimely death by the picture which he calls up before the mind, of Maecenas stopping his carriage as he drives past the tomb of the poet—

> Si te forte meo ducet via proxima busto,
>   Esseda caelatis siste Britanna iugis.

Had he not thought it his greatest glory to be the poet of passion, or had his mind developed more slowly to its full maturity, instead of working with precocious intensity on his own feelings, he might, in all probability, have been valued, not only as the most powerful and sincere of the subjective poets of Rome, but in the first rank of the higher artists who give objective expression both to the great interests and the trivial incidents of their age.

In another sphere of objective art his success is not so great. The subjects which he chose from Roman ritual were not favourable for poetical treatment. Roman myths and Roman worship arose out of the most prosaic and utilitarian superstition. No poetry could be elicited from such an abstraction of the understanding as the god Vertumnus, or it was so mixed with prose as to leave no consistent poetical impression on the mind. The idea of the site of Rome, of the bare Tarpeian rock, and of the river, familiar to his childhood in its upper reaches, passing by these lonely pastures as a stranger, does indeed elicit two lines of powerful poetry,

> Tarpeiusque pater nuda de rupe tonabat,
>   Et Tiberis nostris advena bubus erat (iv. 1. 7);

and he recalls the life of its rude inhabitants with the realistic fidelity of Lucretius. The site of Veii also, reduced to its primitive condition from a powerful and warlike town, naturally stirs the imagination:

> Nunc intra muros pastoris bucina lenti
>   Cantat, et in vestris ossibus arva metunt (iv. 10. 29).

The martial memories of earlier Roman history are sometimes evoked with a power which shews that his literary sympathy with the genius of Ennius, which he indicates more than once, was more genuine than that of any other Roman poet except Virgil and Lucretius. Yet the poems dealing with these subjects are in diction and metre tamer and more prosaic than any of the others. Nor is their composition more artistically perfect. Such lines as

> Acron Herculeus Caenina ductor ab arce
>   Roma tuis quondam finibus horror erat (iv. 10. 9),

and

> Incola Cacus erat, metuendo raptor ab antro
>   Per tria partitos qui dabat ora sonos (iv. 9. 9),

are more in the manner of Ennius than of the Augustan age, nor are they redeemed by anything of the greater spirit of Ennius. The attempt to give life and artistic form to the national rites and belief, notwithstanding the occasional gleams of genuine poetry resting on this 'inculto tramite,' must be pronounced a failure. It will be seen later how far Ovid succeeded where Propertius failed. Virgil alone solved the problem by assimilating these materials with the life of the great national epic. The Aeneid is full of rites and aetiological myths even of the most prosaic kind, as the symbol of the white sow, the practice of eating the cakes on which the sacrificial feast was placed, etc. It is one of the greatest triumphs of Virgil's art so to fuse these and other heterogeneous materials in the elaborate workmanship of the Aeneid, as to make it the representative poem of Rome at all times.

This consideration of the art and genius of Propertius leaves us with the feeling that he was one of the most genuine and most poetical forces in Roman literature; that his poetry everywhere betrays the glow of a most ardent temperament and the energy of a vivid imagination; that he is original and forcible in his diction, and elicits at once a deep and a soft music from his metre; that besides his acknowledged familiarity with all the conflicting elements of human passion and the deeper sources of melancholy in human life, he has more than almost any ancient poet a sympathy with nature in her lonely desolate scenes, with her tempestuous forces, and with some aspects of her softness and beauty; and that he was capable of dealing with the tragic issues of his time and some of the events of the national history, and with the deeper personal experience of private life, in a more serious and sympathetic spirit than any of the other elegiac poets. Neither did he want altogether the faculty of dealing with the lighter comedy of life. He was no careless artist, but took assiduous pains and felt great joy in the effort to produce the effect described by him in the lines

    Exactus tenui pumice versus eat.

Yet with greater powers of imagination and feeling and a higher ideal of art than any of the other elegiac poets, he fails to produce the same harmonious effects. How far this failure is due to the fact that the larger part of his work never received the form and finish which he was capable of giving to it, it is impossible to say. The power of his imagination, both active and receptive, revealed in the energy of his diction and the solemn or softer cadences of his verse, must always exercise a spell over the lovers of poetry who master the difficulties, and are not repelled by the signs, if not of affectation, yet of straining after effect, by his irrevelant mythology, and above all by the iteration with which he harps on a single theme. He has the seriousness of mood which Ovid lacks, yet there is a want of a really masculine tone in his seriousness. In his frequent alternations of mood when he rises out of the depression indicated in the line

> Me sine, quem voluit semper fortuna iacere,

it is rather levity than cheerfulness and buoyancy of spirit that he betrays. He remains a great poet—a poet potentially greater than Ovid and Tibullus, not inferior to, in some ways greater than Horace or Catullus—but more than any other classic poet marred by irregularity and incompleteness, occasional want of taste, the inability to conceal the struggles to produce a great effect, the failure in the last accomplishment of art, absolutely harmonious composition.

CHAPTER V.

Ovid.

I.

Amores.

THERE is an essential difference between Ovid and Propertius or Tibullus as poets of love. Not only is he much more the poet of pleasure and intrigue, they of serious sentiment or passion; but they treat the feeling of love, not as mere desire, but as the admiration of something above them. They willingly accept the position of *servitium*, while Ovid in the Amores and the Ars Amandi shows us only transient desire, and regards the whole subject in the spirit of persiflage. He never deals with it seriously, except when it is the love of the woman for the man. With Ovid, love poetry is a study of psychological observation: with the others an utterance of their own feeling. Even in the Amores, still more in the Ars, Ovid is much more disinterested and objective: he is absolutely so in the Heroides.

The Amores, in which he first came before the world, were originally published in five books, but afterwards judiciously restricted to three: in the interval between the first and second draught of this record of his personal experience and feelings, appeared at least ten of his Epistles. In these three books of Amores he carries on the rôle of Tibullus and Propertius, but in a very different spirit. The love poems of the two older poets are essentially elegies, plaintive in the former, passionate and melancholy in the latter. They have their source in actual experience and real feeling. The persons who inspired the feeling were not only actual women of the time, but one of them certainly lives before us in her lover's verse as a very distinct individuality. The spirit in which Ovid appears as the poet, not of passion but of pleasure, is entirely light and frivolous. His personification of the elegiac Muse—

> Forma decens, vestis tenuissima, vultus amantis,
> Et pedibus vitium causa decoris erat—

declares the scope of his art. While Propertius appropriately calls his elegies 'lacrimae,' and describes his art by the word 'flere,' there are no poems in Latin or indeed in any language to which the words used by Catullus, Virgil, and Horace, as well as by Ovid himself, for the expression of the gayer and lighter fancies and experiences of life, 'lusus' and 'ludere,' can be more properly applied. They share with the elegies of Tibullus and Propertius the tone which gained for this kind of verse the epithet 'imbellis'; but for the other epithet expressive of the spirit of the Roman elegy, as it was of the primitive Greek elegy, 'flebilis,' Ovid substitutes the words 'Musa genialis.' He is the poet of fashionable society in its laxest moods: no love-sick youths or maidens could appeal to him as 'ardoris nostri magne poeta.' Once indeed his verse does assume a sadder note, when in words of true feeling and graceful appreciation he mourns for the untimely death of Tibullus; then he utters under the influence of the genuine elegiac spirit —the spirit of the original θρῆνος and 'nenia'—not the self-regarding wail of unsatisfied or unrequited passion, but the lament for departed worth and genius and beauty of character:

> Flebilis indignos, Elegeïa, solve capillos:
> A nimis ex vero nunc tibi nomen erit.

It is indeed as the poet of love that Tibullus is there lamented; but it is not with its pleasures or its fanciful complaints, it is with its tenderness and truth, both in life and in the picture of life beyond death, that the thought of him and of the heroines of his song is associated; with all that can make love and death more beautiful. The thought of death brings much that is sad, but not the gloom, morbid and unrelieved, with which the thought presents itself to the mind of Propertius. In this, almost the only poem in which he is deeply pathetic, Ovid shows himself a truer master of pathos than Propertius with all his 'lacrimae.' The only other opportunity which he has for pathos is in the pretty and fanciful lament for the parrot of Corinna, a poem which enters into rivalry with the matchless dead sparrow of Catullus. Here there is a playful fancy rather than any real feeling, though the elegy has the plaintive note and movement as distinct from the rapid and lively movement, the tone of a gay, witty, and pleasure-loving society, which is the note of the purely love elegies:

> Quid referam timidae pro te pia vota puellae,
> Vota procelloso per mare rapta Noto?

Who was Corinna, the heroine of these poems, and what was Ovid's relation to her and his feeling towards her? Was she, like Lesbia, Delia, Cynthia, a real person whose fascination and waywardness really exercised a great influence on the life and art of her lover? Or is she a mere 'nominis umbra,' a figure round about whom a number of imaginary experiences—imaginary, though reflecting the ordinary life of pleasure and intrigue of the time—are gathered as they might be about the heroine of a modern novel? is she a study of character rather than a portrait? In a poem published twenty years later, he tells us that people in Rome are still asking who Corinna was. This suggestion of mystery led some of the older critics to take up the idea—a belief seen in a writer of the fifth century, Sidonius Apollinaris—that Ovid was the favoured lover of the most brilliant, most distinguished, and one of the most beautiful women of the time, the imperial Julia; and that he was capable of writing of her favours as Corinna's. That Ovid may have been a favourite poet of the lover of Iulus Antonius, and that he may have been admitted to her society, as unfortunately for himself he evidently was at a later time to that of her daughter, is extremely probable. But that, either in the time of her young widowhood or while the wife of Agrippa, she became for the time the mistress of Ovid, and allowed him to celebrate her charms with that absence of reticence which is more conspicuous in him than in Tibullus, is one of the most preposterous suppositions into which the license of learned conjecture has ever been betrayed. A much more probable solution of the secret is that Corinna was no person in particular, but only a name about which Ovid grouped many experiences and memories, and something of a continuous story. As she appears in the poems, she is little more than a κωφὸν πρόσωπον, with no individuality of temper or circumstances, nor are her personal traits and accomplishments distinct like those of Cynthia. There is more reality about the 'ancilla' Nape. Ovid represents his heroine as being 'ingenua,' and as accompanied by her 'vir' on one of the early occasions of their meeting. But as a mercenary 'lena' plays her part in the social drama, and as Ovid professes a scrupulous regard for the 'vitta' of the married woman, and in his Tristia declares that he gave rise to no domestic scandal, it follows that whether she was one special mistress to whom for a time his volatile nature was attached, or a generalised creation of fancy, she belonged to the class to which Cynthia and Nemesis belong. She simply serves as the theme of Ovid's poetry, in which he traces the progress of an ordinary intrigue, without any of the passionate alternations of feeling that meet us in Propertius, or the real pain and happiness of Tibullus. It is a tale, not like theirs of true love, but of a love that runs with a smooth enough, not to say a facile course, till it loses itself, one does not exactly see how, in the usual way, the lover professing to be tired of the infidelities of his mistress. The incidents out of which the story, or rather series of sketches, is made up are of the slightest kind, and many of them are suggested by previous poetic treatment. There is the introduction of himself as pierced by Cupid's arrow, the first conventional declaration of his susceptibility, then the statement of who and what he is, and the selection of an object both of his love and art. There is no resistance, there are no difficulties in the way of his conquest: Corinna, though 'ingenua,' is compared at the very beginning to Laïs. He begins with protestations of simplicity—

> Nudaque simplicitas, purpureusque pudor;

and with professions of his own fidelity and desire of hers. The fourth Elegy contains his anticipation of meeting his mistress, with directions in the style of the Ars Amandi how she is to behave. In the fifth a meeting is recorded with that unreserve and sensuous allurement characteristic not only of Ovid's temperament, but of the feebler restraint then exercised by the manners and the taste of society. Following this comes the familiar complaint against her door-keeper who refuses to admit him; his penitence for having struck her—

> Nam furor in dominam temeraria brachia movit—

the graphic and humorous denunciation of the 'lena'—'Dipsas anus'—whose nature answers to her name. Then come general reflexions; a comparison of the lover and the soldier; a pleading against mercenary love. The eleventh poem is imitated from the 'lost tablets' of Propertius (iii. 23); the twelfth continues the theme. The next Elegy is a lover's complaint of the importunate haste of Aurora. The fourteenth remonstrates with Corinna for dyeing her hair. The last poem of the first book is a defence of himself against the charge of 'ignavia,' and a fine vindication of the greatness of poetry, and of the immortality enjoyed by the great poets of the past.

The other books are made up of similar slight incidents and reflexions. They more than once treat lightly the things that caused real torture to Propertius. Ovid indicates (ii. 7) that his own tendency to admire other women (of which, in the spirit of the Ars Amandi, he makes no secret) excites his mistress's jealousy. He himself expresses the jealousy and antagonism of the cultivated classes at Rome towards the military adventurer: but there is no real rage or suffering either in his own jealousy or that which he supposes he inspires. The end of it all seems

to come simply because he has no more to say. It is still more
true of Ovid than of Propertius that

> maxima de nihilo nascitur historia.

but Ovid's 'historia' contains no real story, no alternations of
genuine feeling, no vivid presentment of a real personality. It
is a succession of lively, sometimes sensuous situations, the
movements of a gay, cheerful, and unrestrained fancy under
a transient allurement, expressed in witty, refined, easy language,
and smooth, rapid flow of metre, with the light of poetic imagination from time to time striking on the current, or lingering on
it where his narrative power asserts itself in longer reaches. It
is only of love in its shallowest vein that Ovid is the poet in the
Elegies. He has no belief in fidelity; as false himself as he
expects his mistress to be, he desires only the illusion of being
deceived for the moment into the belief of it. He re-echoes the
thought, extracted from Propertius as a miserable consolation
after much torture—

> Rusticus est nimium quem laedit adultera coniunx,
>   Et notos mores non satis urbis habet :
> Si sapis indulge dominae, vultusque severos
>   Exue nec rigidi iura tuere viri.

If this is irony, it is said without any bitterness. He has already
much of the experience and much of the good-natured cynicism
which twenty years later were declared with such maturity of
art and knowledge in the Ars Amandi. It would be to confuse
the cause with the effect, perhaps, to speak of the writings of
Ovid as an active agency in the demoralisation in which he
shared; but in so far as the charge is true, it is as true of his
earliest as of his latest work in this vein. The plea with which
he excuses the Ars Amandi, that it was not intended for those
who wore the matron's 'vitta,' is no more and no less true of
the Amores than of the more mature and notorious work. The
popularity of Ovid as a poet was due not merely to the favour
of the young and of the class of which Corinna was a specimen,
but to the universality of the love of pleasure, and the attraction

which the refined and yet free treatment of the subject had for that fashionable society of which Julia was the queen.

II.

Heroides.

OVID had two great claims on the attention of his contemporaries, and still has two sources of interest for his readers. He was one of the gayest and most cultivated members of a pleasure-loving and refined society, superficially cultivated and brilliant, which lived its life, careless of any more serious interests. He shared the feelings of that society and the same standard of conduct, enjoyed the same things, and spoke its language. His writings were the mirror in which it saw itself reflected. He was happy to be born in such a time, not on account of its greatness or splendour, but because it was then that 'rusticity'—including good faith and all the old restraints on inclination—was finally disappearing, and good taste, quickness of wit, readiness of resource, became the guides of life. These were the qualities which he had in a supreme degree. A less subtle and intellectual urbanity than that of Horace or Cicero, with no such ethical content as their urbanity had, and the command of facile, fluent, and witty verse shewn in the Amores and Ars Amandi, with their rapid alternations of mockery and voluptuousness, fitted him to be the poet and interpreter of this new phase of life.

But he had other and special gifts derived from nature, the accompaniment of the strong vitality and richness of sensuous temperament which he drew from his Pelignian home. More than any of the Roman poets he retained through life the child's faculty of living in a world of fancy; and the natural tendency to animate the beings of his imagination gathered strength with the maturing of his powers and the enlargement of his knowledge of life. It is as a creator, not indeed of a highly ideal or tragic life, of characters capable of playing a great or noble part

on the world's stage, but of the romance of love and adventure
at a time when the world was conceived as young—full of vital
force and impressibility and yet far removed from the actual
rudeness and hardships of uncivilised society—that Ovid has
a place among the creative poets. And this gift he exercised
coincidently with, or shortly after, his first essay as an interpreter of the actual life of his age. While his own mind
and the minds of all the youth were absorbed in the pursuit
of pleasure, enhanced and refined by sentiment, he found
another channel for expressing all the varieties of that sentiment, a theme admitting of a more ideal and passionate treatment than the light intrigues and infidelities of actual life, in the
far renowned brides and heroic maidens of ancient song. He
made them tell their story, express the constancy of their devotion, the vehemence of their passion or the anguish of their
desertion in the conversational manner of the refined literature
of the day. He selected, as the medium of their expression,
the form of the epistle, which about the same time Horace was
using for his comments on the conduct of life. But Ovid's use
of his instrument shows the influence of the rhetorical training
of the time, rather than the natural style of the ordinary epistle
which Horace so successfully adopts. In the pleas urged by
his heroines to recall or retain their lovers, we seem to trace
the practised hand of one who was trained to composition by
the 'suasoriae' of the schools. There is much of artificial
rhetoric both in the substance and the manner of the pleading.
The various heroines have too much the same rapid, animated,
antithetic manner of expressing themselves. 'Dolor ira mixtus'
is the tone of all. None of the impersonations can be called
great dramatic conceptions, as the Dido of Virgil can. In none
is there the vivid truth of the Attis of Catullus; nor is any
situation set before us with the combination of inward passion
and pictorial symbolism in harmony with that passion, which
we recognise in his Ariadne. There is much more nature in
a poem which admits of a close comparison with the Heroides,
the Epistle of Arethusa in Propertius (iv. 3). Yet we find in

Ovid's treatment of his subject great animation and rapidity of narrative—he has much more power of telling a story than Catullus—an imagination that seizes what is most poetical and most characteristic of the situation, and a sympathetic insight, which we should hardly have looked for in the author of the Amores and the Ars Amandi, into the purer and nobler and more abiding sources of woman's love.

Among the Epistles which profess to be written by Ovid, some are probably to be rejected as not genuine. These, though careful imitations of his manner, are both more diffuse, and are conceived on a more vulgar and conventional level of feeling than the others. This is especially the case with the letter professing to be written from Paris to Helen, and her reply. Paris is there a commonplace gallant carrying on a commonplace intrigue: he addresses her in something like the terms of gallantry which Sir Piercie Shafton uses towards the fair daughter of the mill. Whatever Ovid is when he deals with his own age, he has too true a conception of the ideal of a heroic time to allow it to be so vulgarised. It is not irregular passion which is inconsistent with that ideal, but the treatment of intrigue as a matter of ordinary course, with nothing either of romance or generous passion about it. Ovid cannot indeed conceive of woman as Homer did of Helen and Penelope, as Sophocles of Deianira, as Virgil of Dido; but in none of the impersonations in which he walks in the footsteps of the great masters of Greek epic and Greek tragedy does he vulgarise the ideal as in the Helen of these two Epistles.

He tells us in the Amores (ii. 18) that he is the author of the letters of Penelope, of Phyllis, of Oenone, of Canace, of Hypsipyle and Medea, of Ariadne and Phaedra, of Dido and of one written by Sappho, 'Aeoliae Lesbis amica lyrae.' He tells us further that answers to six of these letters were written by Sabinus on his return from the grand tour. A passage in the same Elegy seems at first to imply that Macer (to whom the Elegy is addressed) found time while singing of war to write the epistles of Paris and Helen, and of Laodamia.

But a different interpretation is given by Professor Maguire, in the Preface to Professor Palmer's Heroides, namely that 'Ovid is here speaking of episodes on these subjects introduced by Macer in his epic poem on the Trojan war[1].'

In some of these poems, probably in all, he has taken his facts from older epic and tragic sources. The Briseis and the Penelope tell over, rapidly though somewhat tamely, the story of the Iliad and the Odyssey. The letter of Laodamia (regarded by Professor Palmer as from the hand of the author of the letters of Paris and Helen) is no doubt based on the Cypria. For the two letters addressed to Jason, there were available the poem of Apollonius Rhodius and the tragedy of Euripides, and recent interest attached to the subject from the poem of Varro Atacinus. The Hippolytus has given both facts and fancies to the Phaedra, and the Trachiniae to the Deianira. A play of Euripides contained the story of Canace.

Ovid did not try to keep up the antique character of his personages. The Epistles are thoroughly modern: they express the feelings and speak the language of refined women in a refined age. Penelope is not the Penelope of the Odyssey, the worthy wife of the great Ulysses, but a Roman wife of the Augustan age longing for the return of her husband from the war. She writes with no sense of the greatness of the issue, but with the petty jealousy of the conventional wife,

> Forsitan et narras quam sit tibi rustica coniunx.

Yet the ideal of loyalty and affection first given to the world of early Greece in the Odyssey is not wholly obscured, and the poem rises into a higher strain near the end:

> Nec mihi sunt vires inimicos pellere tectis
> Tu citius venias, portus et ara tuis.

---

[1] There is no good reason to question (though in one case Lachmann has questioned) the genuineness of the nine poems mentioned first by Ovid, or the spuriousness of the letter attributed to Sappho; nor to attribute to any other writer the poems assigned to Briseis, Deianira, Hypermnestra, and Hermione, whether they were in the first draught of the work or not. Though here again the letters of Briseis, Hermione, and Deianira are suspected in addition to that of Medea, by Lachmann.

What Penelope wants in Ovid is the quality that Ovid himself was so deficient in—dignity. The story of Laodamia, another type of the virtuous and constant wife, had been told with more passionate power by Catullus. In Ovid's representation there is nothing heroic; Laodamia is tender and loving, but not the heroic wife of a brave soldier. Dido falls below the Dido of Virgil in queenliness and dignity.

Those of the Heroides seem most poetical which have some element of picturesqueness and romance in the situation, something of the wild feeling of the sea, mountains, and woods. Such is the story of Phyllis, the young Thracian princess, with her trusting eager heart, mounting the rocks and looking out for the return of the ship of Demophoon—

> Saepe notavi
> Alba procellosos vela referre Notos.

Ovid attains real pathos in her words:

> Fallere credentem non est operosa puellam
> Gloria.

In the Oenone, too, there is the romance of the nymph, the daughter of the river-god, and her association with the glories of Ida: there is pathos, as in the line

> Sed tua sum tecumque fui puerilibus annis.

The spirit of the chase and of the mountains is in it also, as the spirit of the woodlands is in the Phaedra, and some modern touches are added to the antique romance—

> Incisae servant a te mea nomina fagi.

Briseis is a barbaric captive raised by her love of Achilles into something greater, but not forgetful of country and kindred:

> Perque trium fortes animas, mea numina, fratrum
> Qui bene pro patria cum patriaque iacent.

There is an element of barbaric horror in the Canace, in the union of wild passion with girlish simplicity, and in the savagery of Aeolus. Perhaps the most elaborate is the Medea, the subject which he afterwards worked out into a drama.

The elegiac metre in the Heroides is proved excellent for rapid narrative, for recalling a familiar tale to the mind or presenting a rapid succession of impressions. It has not the gravity of the Latin hexameter nor the intensity of the Greek iambic: with Ovid it is apt to fall into the mannerisms of epigram and antithesis. There is more nobleness in the metre of Propertius; the hurry of Ovid's verse is inconsistent with dignity[1]. It may be maintained however that dignity is not the proper virtue for this style of poetry—

> imparibus vecta Thalia rotis—

and that Ovid has found or invented the most fitting instrument to express the livelier and the more pathetic, if not the deeper and more tragic feelings.

III.

Ars Amandi.

The Ars Amandi was not published till nearly twenty years after the first draught of the Amores was completed, though only a few years after the second, as in Amores ii. 18. 19 Ovid professes to be engaged on the composition of this work. He had passed by this time from youth to middle age. He had added to his reputation by the composition of a work of serious art, the tragedy of Medea. He was married—as it seems, happily—to the last of his three wives, and continued to take part in the life of pleasure and social enjoyment as before. The greater among the contemporary poets were now dead; with the younger poets, with those among the great families who encouraged literature, the houses of Messalla and Fabius, he enjoyed the highest favour. Those relations with members of the imperial family which appear later in his life were already established.

Roman society, of which Horace wrote in apparently sincere

---

[1] His sense of the slightness of his metre is expressed in Fast. vi. 22,
Ause per exiguos magna referre modos.

optimism in the fifth Ode of Book iv, had rushed headlong into the pursuit of pleasure under the leadership of Julia. Public affairs continued prosperous. The Empire was in its full external splendour; Rome now had become 'a city of marble.' Porticoes and temples charmed the sight and afforded meeting-places for all who were bent on amusement. The life of ease and enjoyment had at its command theatres and public games of all sorts, and 'convivia' in which both sexes met. Probably at no time was the position of the demi-monde so luxurious and refined. Rome was the capital of pleasure. A change had taken place in the life of the Emperor. Maecenas and Agrippa, the earliest partners of his youthful enterprise, the trusty counsellors who had done so much not only to consolidate but to elevate his rule, were both dead; and Augustus was now under the influence of Livia. Tiberius had retired in sullen disgust, owing partly, it is said, to the reckless gaiety of his wife and her associates, and partly to the opening career of the young Caesars, grandsons of Augustus. Literature was cultivated as ministering to the universal desire for pleasure. The object of education was no longer to fit men for the Forum or the Senate, but to make them socially agreeable. The poets were read to add to the attraction which men and women had for one another in their intrigues: music and singing, and the arts of conversation and correspondence, were cultivated for the same purpose; and among the many instructions given by Ovid in the Art of Love none are more sensible and applicable to all times than what he says on this subject (i. 463—8). The culmination of this reckless pursuit of pleasure was the exposure of the intrigue of Julia and Iulus Antonius. Almost coincident with this was the appearance of the Ars Amandi, the professed manual of refined life for the time, which held up the mirror to a society whose sole occupation was, in the words of Tacitus, 'corrumpere et corrumpi.' Religion and morality were both reduced to the smallest compass:

> Expedit esse deos, et ut expedit esse putemus:
> Dentur in antiquos tura merumque focos

is Ovid's theory of religion, while morality is summed up in

> Reddite depositum; pietas sua foedera servet;
> Fraus absit; vacuas caedis habete manus.

The Art of Love is carefully planned and composed. The form of literature, so peculiarly Roman, which had been employed by the most serious Roman poets, Lucretius, Virgil, and Horace, with a grave purpose, speculative, ethical, or literary, with the intention of making thought, life, and literature more elevated, serious, and severe, was chosen by Ovid to add all the allurement of art and genius to that aspect of life which for his readers required no adventitious attraction. There seems a kind of ironical pedantry—for Ovid had too keen a sense of humour to be really pedantic—in taking the medium of didactic poetry, which Virgil had adopted to elevate his homely theme, for the purpose of laying down minute precepts for seduction. It is in a spirit of playful mockery that he assumes the office of 'praeceptor amoris' and carries out his plan; a contrast to the spirit in which the great serious poets of Rome delivered their 'praecepta idonea vitae.' In the same tone of mockery he disclaims all higher inspiration, and professes to give only the results of his own experience;

> Non ego Phoebe datas a te mihi mentiar artes.

Yet, as with Byron in Don Juan, there is none of the works of Ovid in which a truer vein of poetry occasionally mingles with the cynical worldliness and warm sensuousness of his writings. He shows this even in the lines in which the higher inspiration is disclaimed: he knew and had drunk from the purer sources, and awakens the sacred associations of poetry;

> Nec mihi sunt visae Clio Cliusque sorores
> Servanti pecudes vallibus Ascra tuis:
> Usus opus movet hoc.

It is said sometimes that didactic poetry is altogether a mistake; and it is true that it is only among the least naturally poetical of those nations who have produced a great poetry, or in their least poetical epochs, that didactic poetry has succeeded. If justified at all, it can be justified only by the value of the ideal which it seeks to realise, and the power with which that ideal is presented. A great contemplative ideal inspired Lucretius in the conception and execution of his work; a great practical ideal, of a life of industry, simplicity, piety, affection, in closest union with all the charm of outward nature, and associated with the thought of patriotic memories and duties, inspired the Georgics. The purely didactic works of Horace are on a lower level of poetry: he probably would have denied to them the title of poetry altogether : yet whatever claim they have to be poetry, at least as much depends on the truth and value of the views of life and art inculcated, as on the mode of treatment. Something of an ideal on which the mind can rest as true is to be gathered from the Epistles of Horace. The ordinary didactic poem, conveying, in verse, prosaic precepts on a subject that associates itself with no ideal of the imagination, can be raised by no treatment to any rank in literature. If the didactic poem of Ovid were to be judged by the ethical value of its ideal, on the principle of laying down precepts 'idonea vitae,' no work of art could have less claim to rank as great. The attitude of a teacher assumed by him denies to him the plea that the artist has nothing to do with the moral, good or evil, of his representation. The aim of the didactic poet is 'idonea dicere vitae,' and it is that claim which Ovid puts forward. And if life is anything else than the eager pursuit of pleasure, to the sacrifice of all the more enduring sources of worthy happiness, no precepts could be more antagonistic to the rational conduct or rational estimate of it. The art he professes to teach is the art of lying as much as of loving. Deceit, in friendship as in love, is inculcated as the way of the world :

> Ei mihi, non tutum est quod ames laudare sodali;
> Cum tibi laudanti credidit, ipse subit—
>
> . . . . . .
>
> Nil nisi turpe iuvat; curae sua cuique voluptas:
> Haec quoque ab alterius grata dolore venit.
>
> (i. 741-2, 749-50.)

As superstition was the enemy against which Lucretius warred with all the force of his reasoning and imagination, so the enemy to be got rid of, against which all the force of Ovid's wit and knowledge of the world is directed, is what still remained of what he calls the rarest virtue of the age, 'simplicitas,' which the best Romans of every time, and some who were far from the best, such as Martial, and Ovid himself in his better mood, prized among the chief qualities in man. Sincerity seems another name for rusticity, the one thing intolerable to the society of the time. The peculiarity of Ovid's treatment of his subject is his total unconsciousness that it needs any apology. Why should the world, at least the world of fashionable society, safe and prosperous beyond all past experience under the government of Augustus, have any other care than how to enjoy itself? A similar feeling found expression in a ruder form in one of the prologues of Plautus (Truculentus 55–57), when the long strain of the war against Carthage had been removed; but even in the plays of Plautus, intended merely for the amusement of a short holiday, not for the whole conduct of life, there runs an undercurrent of restraining feeling or of good-humoured ridicule of the weakness and folly of youth. In Ovid almost alone of the poets who treat of the passion or pleasures of love, there is no trace of the old restraining instinct, so strong in the Italian races, and the source in ancient times of what was the secret of their greatness, their family life. Nor is there any feeling of satiety, any admixture of the

> amari aliquid, quod in ipsis floribus angat.

The attraction of the poem, to his own and to other times, was the presentation of the pleasure unmixed, not, as in Tibullus and Propertius, accompanied by the pain of the pursuit, and still less by any foreboding of the 'pede poena claudo' which follows it. No prophetic insight among the men of that time could have anticipated from the gaiety and brightness and rich colour with which the subject is treated by Ovid, the gloom and sense of satiety and disgust with which the same subject was presented to the Romans of a century later in another masterpiece, the sixth Satire of Juvenal. These two works, in which the fascination and the repulsion of a licentious life are presented in perhaps the most vivid colours ever used in literature, are simply different stages in one course of development. Yet this, if not the greatest, is probably the sincerest work of Ovid, the maturest expression of what he actually thought of life. If in the Georgics and the Aeneid we find a great ideal of human life and national greatness as it stamped itself on the pure and elevated imagination of Virgil in the opening years of the Empire; if in Horace we find the larger representation of many phases of the life of all classes before the glory of the new Empire had begun to fade and the republican memories to be forgotten, in the Ars Amandi we seem to have the picture of the age before the gloom of the last years of Augustus and the oppression of Tiberius settled down upon Rome, but after all the high ideals of the early Empire, its hopes of a great national, moral, and religious revival, had proved illusory. The interest in and anxieties about the Empire are no longer actively present: the only semblance of national feeling is in adulation of the imperial family, as in the anticipation of the return in triumph of the young Caesar from the East (i. 213); and men seem for a time to have lost the power and pleasures of thought and serious intellectual work.

The Ars Amandi is not only Ovid's sincerest poem, but it is one which called into play some of his most characteristic faculties and qualities. A great English critic, Macaulay, thought it undoubtedly his greatest work. The claims of the Metamorphoses, both on the ground of higher imaginative genius and a more potent influence on the world, may be urged to dispute this verdict. But on the same ground as Don Juan (or at least the earlier books of it) is regarded as the greatest of Byron's poems, it may be argued that the didactic poem on the Art of Love is the greatest work of Ovid. His power over his favourite instruments of metre and language is then at its height. His vivacity and energy of conception are unimpaired, and are tempered by stronger judgment than in the Amores. The abundance and at the same time the obviousness of his illustrations from natural objects and mythology are quickened and enlarged by experience and knowledge of the world. His wit is as unfailing, his insight has become juster and more penetrating. He has not the knowledge of men which Horace displays in all his works, because he wants Horace's sympathy with many and important phases of human life, but no poet ever understood society better—the society of an educated and luxurious circle, living for pleasure and mutual entertainment. His didactic poem is full of the common-sense which is often so strong in men who live only for pleasure; which is so weak in Propertius, a man who lived only for passion. It is shown in his denunciation of all magical arts and love charms. It is shown in the practical precepts

> ut ameris amabilis esto

and

> Ingenii dotes corporis adde bonis,

which are to put the poor lover on a level with the rich; in the inculcation of energy, unselfishness in small matters, good-nature in dealing with servants. The lover's presents are not to be costly, but judiciously chosen. All the *petits soins* of courtship, of which Propertius is by his own admission neglectful, are carefully observed. It is essential that the lover should not make himself a bore:

> Sed neque declament medio sermone diserti,
> Nec sua non sanus scripta poeta legat.

All these are admirable precepts for social life, apart from the special purpose with which they are given. There is similar sense in his advice to the other sex, especially as to the style of their correspondence:

> Munda sed e medio consuetaque verba puellae
> Scribite; sermonis publica forma placet.

But with all his realism he does not forget his special poetic faculty as a painter of bright figures and scenes from the world of fancy. It is in the Ars Amandi, next after the Metamorphoses, that we find those representations which have been or are best capable of being transferred to the canvas of painters. It is the deserted Ariadne of Ovid, rather than the Ariadne of Catullus, which seems to have been present to the imagination of Titian. There are many other tales, pictorially represented, both from Greek and Roman story; the tale of Pasiphae, of Daedalus and Icarus, of Atalanta (largely borrowed from Propertius), of Cephalus and Procris, of the rape of the Sabine women. All these are probably transferred from works of art, or influenced by them. Besides these historical pictures, there is a charm, not to be neglected, in some of the short descriptions of nature—

> Saepe sub autumno cum formosissimus annus
> Plenaque purpureo subrubet uva mero (ii. 315);

or

> Palluit ut serae lectis de vite racemis
> Pallescunt frondes quas nova laesit hiemps (iii. 703).

Here, as elsewhere, it is the beauty of colour, rather than of form, that Ovid recognises.

IV.

Metamorphoses.

In the first Elegy of the last book of the Amores, Ovid in his lightest and gayest spirit describes himself as walking in one of those scenes which had a peculiar charm for his fancy, a grove with its sacred spring and overhanging cave, and listening to the rival claims urged upon him by the light Muse of elegy, who added grace and refinement to the life of pleasure—

> Rustica fit sine me lascivi mater Amoris—

and the severer Muse whose function it was to represent the actions of men. He claims a short time to be given to the Muse that first awoke to life the seeds of his genius, 'felicia semina mentis,' and promises to devote himself afterwards to a greater work:

> Exiguum vati concede, Tragoedia, tempus;
>   Tu labor aeternus; quod petit illa breve est.
> Mota dedit veniam; teneri properentur amores
>   Dum vacat; a tergo grandius urget opus.

In this passage he expresses the struggle—if such a word can be applied to a process which seems to have been altogether unaccompanied by effort—between his keen interest in his own life, and the impulses of his creative imagination; between the impulse to celebrate the life which he lived and saw others living, and the life of an imaginary world which existed for himself alone, but which by his genius might be made one of the permanent possessions of mankind.

The earliest form in which he sought to realise that higher impulse was the Heroides, a work in which the ideal personages of an heroic past were animated with the feelings and fancies of the actual world. Even in the Ars Amandi we may note the constant tendency to tell some legend. But it was his ambition to find a more legitimate vehicle for his gift of dramatic impersonation, and to gain at last for Roman tragedy an artistic perfection such as had been given to Roman epic by Virgil and to Roman lyric poetry by Horace:

> Nunc habeam per te, Romana Tragoedia, nomen,
>   Implebit leges spiritus iste meas.

The work accomplished by him, the Medea, received the highest praises of Roman critics. The subject had so strong an attraction for Ovid's imagination that he treated it at considerable length, both in the Heroides and the Metamorphoses. But it cannot be inferred from either of these renderings what crisis of her fortunes and of her passionate or cruel moods he selected for dramatic treatment. The total failure of two such poets as Ovid and Varius, aided by the criticism and stimulus given in the Ars Poetica of Horace, to secure either immediate or permanent life for a Roman drama, shows that the time had passed when literature could assume that form in Rome. The audiences were too vast and too unsympathetic to appreciate this refined form of intellectual pleasure. A popular dramatic poet was under the Empire as much an impossibility as a popular political orator. Bathyllus and Paris enjoyed the favour which in the more intellectual time of the Republic had been enjoyed by Aesopus and Roscius. Tragedy, though in its highest development it becomes ultimately independent of them, depends for its immediate success on the art of the actor and the sympathy of the audience. It was not in the nature of Ovid to make any further attempt to work at so thankless a task. Ovid could only gain access to the select and limited class who cared for literature by works directly addressed to them. And from this necessity he found a medium more suited to his genius than the regular drama. His faculty was much more that of the story-teller than of the regular dramatist. In the exuberance of fancy which creates materials for narrative, in the power of presenting it with rapidity and brightness, and in the power of making natural scenes and the picturesque movement of life present to the eye [1], no Roman poet of any age equalled him. He gives little indication of the power of conceiving and embodying the nobler types of character, actuated by heroic impulses, nor of reaching the deeper sources of tragic passion. His vivid and energetic faculty of expression is more oratorical than purely dramatic, though it is an oratory often expressing itself in the tones of refined conversation. His imagination was discursive rather than concentrative. It ranged rapidly over the whole world of ancient fable and romance, over every region of the three continents known to story, every picturesque aspect of

---

[1] The vividness of Ovid's power of presenting images to his own mind is shown in the Tristia and Ex Ponto, where he so constantly speaks of the presence of friends and places to his imagination. Cf. Ex Ponto i. 8, 31—

>Nam modo vos animo dulces reminiscor amici,
>   Nunc mihi cum cara coniuge nata subit;
>Eque domo rursus pulchrae loca vertor ab urbis,
>   Cunctaque mens oculis pervidet illa suis:
>Nunc fora nunc aedes nunc marmore tecta theatra,
>   Nunc subit aequata porticus omnis humo, &c.;

ibid. i. 9, 7—

>Ante meos oculos tanquam praesentis imago,
>   Haeret et exstinctum vivere fingit amor.

the natural world, but did not take up its dwelling at 'Thebes or Athens' and regard them as the scene of some complete action of deep human significance. Though accompanied by accurate observation, and intuitive insight into the inner life and feelings of many varieties of men and women, yet in no poet of equal eminence is the imagination so little combined with rational reflexion on the laws of life. We cannot say that he had either belief or disbelief in any providential overruling of human affairs: the gods in whom he finds it expedient to believe are capricious agencies who by their jealous interference bring about the vicissitudes of human life, but afford no light or help in its perplexities. Neither religion nor human or divine will has any existence for his mind. Passion of every kind, desire, vanity and irritation, quickness of intelligence, the influence of custom,—these are the moving powers of his world of natural and supernatural beings. Nothing higher or more serious comes within the range of his art. He has little power over the springs of pathos. Deeds of horror and cruelty he can describe picturesquely, but they do not seem to move him deeply. A great sorrow, a great affection, a great cause or a great crisis, awakens in him little corresponding emotion.

The real importance of Ovid in literature, the inheritance which he left, and through which he powerfully influenced some of the greatest poets and painters of the modern world, was in the new and vivid life which he imparted to the fables of the Greek mythology. Those fables, many of which must have been old in the days of Homer, had already gone through various phases of their perennial existence. To the great Greek lyric poets they existed as the bright morning, the memory of which added a divine glory and ideality to their still bright midday. To the great Athenian poets, living in that age of the world when more than in any other the old forces of religious belief and reverence met with the awakening forces of art and philosophy, they supplied a large store of ideal situations, personages, actions and catastrophes by which they could express their interpretation of human life. Great artists in every kind of material had made the personages of this time present to the eye of later generations, and according to their own conceptions had made their power present to the spirit, or the interest of their story present to the curiosity of later times. To the imagination of the Alexandrian poets they supplied that element of a fuller and fresher life, a sense of movement and adventure and susceptibility to pleasure and pain, which was impossible in the routine of actual existence. But, living in an age of learning, science, and criticism, rather than of action, creation, and speculation, they brought nothing new from the spiritual life of their own time to enrich this heritage while it passed through their hands. They lost the sense of the heroic proportions in which the imagination of an earlier time had set it forth. It tended to pass into learned antiquarianism, the colours obscured, the outlines of the figures ill defined, the passions and feelings reproduced from older works, not created from living sympathy. The Greek imagination was too languid, too sophisticated, too much overgrown with learning, and, though not with thought, yet with the accumulated results of thought, to renew the life of this old mythology. The medium, too, the artificial epic diction, was incapable of imparting freshness to the treatment. Both conception and language, too far removed from the original sources, had become like a river flowing through level flats, dried up by the heat of an African sun. To impart to that mythology a new life, and thus to transmit it to a time which could enter into its enjoyment with all the sensuous vitality with which it first passed into poetry and art, required the fresh sensibility of a new race, and also the medium of a language which, while enriched and refined, had not lost its sensitiveness and its power of producing immediate impressions on the inner eye of fancy.

The first attempt to make this old world of romance and human passion live in Latin was made by the early tragic poets. What life they gave to the stories with which they dealt, and how they gave it, it is impossible to discover. We can only say that they dealt with them in a serious spirit, dealt with the manlier passions and made them a medium of moral teaching. But it was not through the masculine spirit and moral fervour of the Roman tragic poets that the Greek mythology was destined to live a second life in Roman literature, and thereafter to pass with renewed vitality into the art and poetry of the Renaissance. The Italian sensuous fancy, not the Roman serious spirit, was the power by which it was revived; and it was in Ovid above all other ancient Italian poets that this sensuous fancy was embodied. He had all the knowledge of the Alexandrians; and the knowledge of the fables of the past and the varied regions of the world, which in them was dead learning, was in him combined with vivid curiosity and active creative power.

The time in which he lived was analogous in many ways to the Alexandrian age, but much more quickening to the imagination. There was the same want of original speculation or real learning, but much curiosity and interest in books; the same tendency of a tame and blasé time to seek an outlet for itself in an imaginary world of adventure, and an idyllic restoration in the imaginary life of woods, streams and mountains, like the idyllic return to Nature that preceded the French Revolution. It was Ovid's great gift that, feeling these needs of the real world, it came naturally to his imagination to create the other. He had no vague sentimental longing, no regrets for an ideal past. But he had the power of directly making present to the minds of others what seemed to rise spontaneously in his own fancy. He had a keen enjoyment in the life of Nature, in the outward refreshment to the eye and ear, if not the inward contemplative enthusiasm of Lucretius or the deep meditative joy of Virgil. His visits to the Pelignian mountains, the charm of all the varied scenes in Sicily, Greece and Asia through which he had travelled, whatever he had received through books or observation or social intercourse, became a vital influence in his poetry. Though no one could be more thoroughly a child of his own age, yet from the sensuous richness of his nature, the buoyancy and youthfulness of his spirit, the activity of his fancy, even his deficiency in critical and reflective faculty, it came as naturally to him to recreate the stories of gods and nymphs, of heroes, or even peasants, of a primitive time, as it came to Scott to recreate, out of his keen interest and his abundant treasures of reading, the romance and human story of the Middle Ages. He had no belief in the supernatural, but it was as vividly present to his fancy as if his reason had accepted it for a reality. Curiosity, not faith, was the source of his inspiration. The interest appealed to is simply the love of the marvellous and the love of the picturesque in human action and in outward scenes. It was by a rapid and orderly succession of new and vivid surface impressions, not, like Lucretius and Virgil, and, though in a much inferior degree, Propertius, by making one deep concentrated impression, that he spoke to his own and to later times. He is more like Horace in the variety of the aspects of life which he presents. But he has none of Horace's ethical quality. He keeps entirely to observation and intuition. Horace tells a story not so much for its own sake as for the lesson it conveys. Ovid seems absolutely unconscious of having any lesson to impart. If any moral may be drawn from his tales, it is not to take the world too seriously. Punishment is meted out, not for offences against duty, good faith, affection, reverence, but for stupidity, austerity, vanity, and ungraciousness.

In his absence of reflexion and any kind of ethical feeling, he was true to his own nature; and he probably satisfied the taste of a shallower, if more light-hearted generation than that for which Lucretius, Virgil, and Horace had written. The gaiety of youth was the ideal for which society lived, and Ovid more than any other Latin poet kept alive in him—till his great misfortune—the spirit of youth and gaiety. It is their 'inconsumpta iuventas' that attracts him to the gods and nymphs and youthful heroes of the ages of romance. He gives us Homer's gods, but with a difference. It is not exactly in the spirit of Aristophanes or Lucian, but in a light artistic half-belief that he brings them back again, emptied of all majesty and grandeur. There is probably no intentional, or at least no systematic satire in this; no thought that the things attributed to them are unworthy of the gods in whom the world had believed. He does not ask whether these light lovers among woods and streams, these sharp avengers of slights to their vanity, are the ultimate powers who determine human destiny for good or evil. He rejoices in their youth and vigour and grace, and their free power of ranging over sea and air, and the beautiful places of the earth. Though in no ancient poem do the old gods play a larger part, no work is more irreligious. If the gods of Olympus first assumed their attributes and took their place in the belief of men through the poems of Homer, in the Metamorphoses of Ovid they seem to reappear again divested both of their original majesty and of all the other attributes which the reverence of the wisest of Greek artists and poets had added to their original endowment.

The Metamorphoses, while perpetuating the outward forms and many of the tales of the old mythology, must have been more fatal to any belief in a Divine Providence or a spiritual life than the iconoclasm of Lucretius. The feeling of Lucretius in regard to all the symbols and objects of old religious belief is really nearer to that of Virgil than to that of Ovid. The great gods of Ovid are in all the moral attributes of man much more below the average standard of humanity, than the gods and goddesses of Homer are below his human heroes and heroines. The exercise of power to avenge some slight to their dignity is the mode in which they chiefly make their presence felt in the world. The 'semidei,' the Fauns and Nymphs with their human sensibilities and their life fused in the life of Nature, with their favourite haunts, the spring and river-bank, the lonely mountains of Arcadia, the woods and groves, have a charm which does not belong to his representation of the greater gods. His imagination is more at home in their forests than in the celestial spheres. He cannot conceive what calls for reverence or inspires the spirit of awe. He has no sense of mystery, no feeling of anything sacred either in life or above life. Hence his great gods are merely the old elemental powers, animated with the most elementary of human instincts and passions, but vigorous with the fresh and perennial force of the elements, and superadding vigour and grace of movement to the force that comes from Nature.

It was the fashion of the times for ambitious poets to take up some of the great subjects of heroic action and adventure, and reproduce them in elaborate epic poems. Thus Ponticus, the friend of Propertius and of Ovid, aspired to tell over again in a Latin epic the story of the war of Thebes: Macer, the friend with whom Ovid travelled, to tell anew 'the tale of Troy divine.' The ambition of Roman writers, both great and small, inclined them to works 'de grande haleine.' Ovid, though professing in his earlier poems the spirit of a trifler, had abundance both of ambition and industry. He lets us know how he contemplated his completed work of the Metamorphoses. He makes for it as strong a claim to immortality as Horace does for his Odes:

> Quaque patet domitis Romana potentia terris
> Ore legar populi perque omnia secula fama,
> Si quid habent veri vatum praesagia, vivam.

He regarded this as the serious work of his life, and in his despair at not having been able to give the finishing touches to it he endeavoured to destroy it, as Virgil for the same reason had endeavoured to destroy the Aeneid. He never regards it, like his Elegies, as mere pastime. He discarded the form and metre of which he was so practised a master, and adopted that which from the time of Ennius had become the recognised metre for all long and ambitious undertakings. In adopting the metre he did not aim, as later epic poets for the most part did, at reproducing the intricate harmonies of Virgil, but gave an entirely new movement to the hexameter, making it a more fitting medium for the buoyancy of his own spirit, and the variety and rapidity with which his imagination worked. Concentration on any single action and group of figures, and the elaboration of a poem according to the rules of epic art, were repugnant to his versatile genius, with its abhorrence of monotony or satiety. His artistic instinct, as well as his natural liveliness, preserved him from the attempt in which so many of his countrymen failed, to make an epic out of some one of the great themes of epic poetry in the past,—a Thebaid, an Achilleid, or a new version of the adventures of the Argonauts.

Lucretius, who added a rich endowment of fancy to his great intellectual gifts and the Roman gravity of his temper, had shown his susceptibility to the charm of the old stories. The taste and instinct of Catullus had taught him to paint one or two idealised pictures from the large world of fancy, in the form of epic idylls. Propertius satisfied himself with recalling to the imagination some poetic aspects of some of the many ancient tales of love, by which he might enhance the glory or the misery of his own. Horace used mythology as an artistic embellishment for his graver or lighter admonitions. Ovid conceived a much more ambitious plan. It was to embrace in a long series of tales, bound together by a thread of connexion and yet each complete in itself, the great mass of tales of supernatural agency and heroic adventure, to tell the story of the world from its origin out of Chaos down to his own day, in so far as it was conceived of as the sphere of supernatural agency. The idea which gives unity and continuity to this great mass of traditional fancy at first sight seems too slight and trivial to give coherence to so vast a work. It is the idea of the transformation of human beings by superhuman power into constellations, stones, trees, plants, birds, beasts, serpents, or insects, and in some cases the reverse process, as in the re-creation of the human race from the stones thrown down by Pyrrha, or the creation of the Myrmidons from ants. Thus, much of what is most familiar in ancient legendary story, especially in the border-land between history and fable, does not come within the scope of his work; yet it is wonderful what a mass of incident and adventure, famous in older story and connected with the great heroic families, comes through some incident within the range of his plan, and also how many representations of homely incidents and personages otherwise unknown he is able to work into his poem. He moves from first to last in a region of fable and miracle, and yet through all the phases and vicissitudes of this region he makes us feel that we are in the closest contact with human nature, from heroes and heroines of the great princely houses, to peasants and fishermen.

He described his subject as 'mutatae formae.' Both the title and the actual subject were apparently suggested by the work of an Alexandrian poet, known as Ἀλλοιώσεις[1]. How far he borrowed his materials and methods from that or any other single work it is needless to inquire. But if the Metamorphoses are the result of large reading and a memory of wonderful retentiveness, no work of ancient or modern literature produces the impression of more prodigal invention, of greater ingenuity in varying the methods of telling a story, of keener observation or greater command over all the details of description. Ovid has the liveliest sympathy with the beings of his fancy, and the keenest curiosity about all they do and feel, and the transformations through which they pass; the keenest enjoyment in all that meets their eyes, and all the environment of wood, mountain, sea, and lake with which he surrounds them.

This world of romantic adventure and supernatural agency is not represented either as a mere dream of the imagination or as a thing of the past. The same power which had worked so many miracles in the morning of the world, is again, in these later times, made visible in connexion with the central fact and dominant sentiment of the age, the elevation of Augustus to supreme power and divine honours. This sense of a vital connexion between the world of fancy and the world of reality does not indeed pervade the Metamorphoses as it does the Aeneid. There are only the most incidental allusions to the actual life of the present, as where the dwelling of the Sun-god is called the 'alta Palatia caeli,' where the laurel into which Daphne is changed is said to be destined to adorn the brows of Roman generals, or where the amber into which the tears of the sisters of Phaethon are changed is spoken of as being ' nuribus gestanda

---

[1] Parthenius, Virgil's master and the friend of Gallus, had written a work called Μεταμορφώσεις.

Latinis.' Again, among the rivers whose waters are burned up by the conflagration of Phaethon, we read of the Tiber—

'Cuique fuit rerum promissa potentia Thybrin.

These slight threads of connexion with the actual life of the present gave something of an epic unity and a kind of credibility to a collection of tales, the motive of which was an agency irreconcilable with the rational convictions of the time. But the great difference between an epic poem such as the Aeneid and an epic or long narrative poem such as the Metamorphoses is that, in the one, this central idea of relation to the Rome of the Augustan age is what chiefly imparts interest to the details, in the other it seems to come in only as an afterthought. The Aeneid is essentially a Roman poem: the Metamorphoses are Greek, though coloured by Italian vivacity, sensuousness and love of Nature.

The chief attraction of the stories, as of the old stories of chivalry, is in love and adventure—adventure of the chase, of battle with fabled monsters of all kinds, of the sea, and of war. The tales of love are generally of the love of gods for mortals or nymphs of the woods and fountains. The great charm of them is derived from the picturesque scenes in which the adventure is laid, and the atmosphere of idyllic sentiment that surrounds it. It is the intermingling of the sensuous feeling of human relations with the sensuous feeling of natural beauty in its purest and freshest influence, which has made these tales of Ovid as favourite a subject for modern, as similar tales seem to have been for ancient painters. It is on the actual figures and the scenes in which they move that the attention is centred, much more than on the inward emotions, which Ovid, with only partial success, had attempted to reproduce in the Heroides. In such a scene as the rescue of Andromeda it is the outward spectacle, not the inward drama of emotion, that he sets before us. The elegiac poets speak sometimes as if love and war were the only themes for the art of the poet, and they speak of them in their elegies as if they were antagonistic to one another, and as if their own genius were only fit to deal with the former. Ovid, however, not only does not shrink from reproducing the details of single combats either with human antagonists or with the fabulous monsters, superhuman in force, who play so large a part in all mythologies, but goes into all the details of wounds and carnage in the long account of the battle of the Centaurs and Lapithae which he tells through the mouth of Nestor. Perhaps the manner in which this is done is characteristic both of the society for which it was written and of the temperament of the author: though at first sight nothing seems more irreconcilable with the soft, pleasure-loving, essentially kindly nature of Ovid than such ghastly details. The descriptions of wounds and violent death are sometimes objected to even in Homer, who spoke to a warlike people who probably had no rest from actual warfare, and for whom it was a necessity of life for each man to know how to defend himself, and even to take delight in slaying his adversary. In Ovid the details of wounds and slaughter are even more ghastly than in Homer. In the luxurious and effeminate society for which he wrote, there still survived so much of the old instinct of the she-wolf as to make them gloat upon the horrors of the gladiatorial spectacles. 'Sated lust' found a new stimulus from scenes of death. In the artistic temperament of Ovid there is that strange juxtaposition of what might be regarded as ὄξος τ' ἀλειφά τ', if similar sentiments, apparently mutually destructive, were not observed in the artistic temperament of a modern nation: the sensuous delight in beauty and a ghastly enjoyment of the outward manifestations of disease, decay and death. There is nothing in Homer like this—

> Prosiluit, terraque ferox sua viscera traxit
> Tractaque calcavit, calcataque rupit, et illis
> Crura quoque impediit, et inani concidit alvo.

After this incident in the battle of the Centaurs comes an account of the fall of a young warrior, which brings to the mind of Ovid some masterpiece of ancient statuary:

> Gratus in ore vigor, cervix humerique manusque
> Pectoraque artificum laudatis proxima signis.

This is immediately followed by the death, by her own hand, of his young wife Hylonome. The passage seems to challenge comparison with the deaths of Lausus and of Pallas in the Aeneid, and makes apparent the immense inferiority of Ovid to Virgil in pathos and all the elements of ethical grandeur. And though he deals, both in his battle-pieces and in his adventures of the chase and of what would in modern times be called knight-errantry, with the heroes and heroines to whom the poets and sculptors of the great time of Greek poetry and art had given the most heroic qualities—qualities which seem to have been at least appreciated by the Roman tragic poets who rudely reproduced the Greek originals—yet he seldom utters any heroic sentiment. One exception to this, striking from the rarity of similar passages, occurs in the account of Meleager feeling the first consequences of the fatal brand burned by his mother Althea—

> caecis torreri viscera sentit
> Ignibus, at magnos superat virtute dolores:
> Quod tamen ignavo cadat et sine sanguine leto
> Maeret et Ancaei felicia volnera dicit.

As in the Heroides Ovid falls far below the Penelope of Homer, so he fails to rise to the heroism of any of the great characters as presented fully in the Iliad or Odyssey and in Sophocles, or as hinted in a few pregnant words by Pindar. This is true even of his great rhetorical effort, the contest for the arms of Achilles between Ajax and Ulysses. We have here neither the Ajax of the great play, nor the Odysseus of either the Iliad or the Odyssey; we have two admirable specimens of rhetorical declamation calculated to bring down the applause of the recitation-rooms, which evidently retained their popularity as such till the time of Juvenal.

In the beginning of the poem, with its account of the gradual creation of things out of Chaos, Ovid enters into competition with the philosophical and didactic poets. The opening is frigid, a contrast to that of the Georgics, and makes the subject —'mutatas formas'—appear trivial. The prosaic definiteness of the conception of creation contrasts with the imaginative sense of wonder in Lucretius: the definite statement of fact destroys all mystery[1]. There is no sense, as there is in Lucretius, of the infinite and eternal, no thought of the 'ratio.' Ovid has nothing of the higher speculative curiosity as to the laws and processes of Nature; his curiosity is that of observation, not of speculation; the curiosity of one to whom the outward spectacle of things is sufficient. Everything with Ovid is too definite and sharp-cut: for it is before they have been made, as Ovid makes them, clear and definite to the understanding, that scientific or philosophic truths have power to act on the imagination. It is when he reaches the description of the real world that Ovid becomes poetical. At the end of the poem he returns again to philosophy in the discourse of Pythagoras, who is ingeniously made to illustrate the doctrine of Metamorphoses, and to supplement the mythological legends with the theory of the transformations of the elements into one another. Here again Lucretius is approached by Ovid, in the passage on the waxing and waning of nations:

> sic tempora verti
> Cernimus, atque illas assumere robora gentes
> Concidere has.

But the grandeur of the idea—

> Augescunt aliae gentes aliae minuuntur—

is much more remarkable in Lucretius than in Ovid.

It is not only in the science of the opening passages that Ovid's excess of definiteness detracts from his poetry. There is the same exuberance of fancy, and the same limitation of pure imaginative suggestion, in his account of the Golden Age. Whenever he has an opportunity of describing the sensuous beauty of the world, there is poetry:

---

[1] The opening of the fourth book of the Fasti, and its matter of fact and definite statement, may in like manner be contrasted with the invocation of Venus 'Aeneadum genitrix' by Lucretius.

> Ver erat aeternum, placidique tepentibus auris
> Mulcebant Zephyri natos sine semine flores.
> Mox etiam fruges tellus inarata ferebat,
> Nec renovatus ager gravidis canebat aristis.

But there is not the charm that belongs to Virgil's rendering of the same ideas[1]. Ovid keeps to the religious tradition, but it has for him no ethical significance. So too his clear description of the council and the dwellings of the gods is wanting in that sense of the moral government of the world so dominant in Virgil. Jove has not the majesty of Homer's Zeus: he is not the paternal and providential ruler, as in Virgil, nor the lord of the universe, as in Horace,

> Qui terram inertem qui mare temperat.

Heaven is compared to Rome—

> Haud timeam magni dixisse Palatia caeli.

The great gods are a class of nobles, under an emperor, distinct from the plebs—

> Plebs habitat diversa locis: a fronte potentes
> Caelicolae, clarique suos posuere penates.

There may be some irony in the degradation of Jupiter and Juno, and in the history of the Court intrigues of Heaven. The effect produced is as if the world had gone back to a pre-Homeric childishness, and yet retained the cynicism of an age that has survived all illusions.

Ovid is more in his element when he passes from the creation and the counsels of Heaven to the adventures of the young gods and the nymphs of the woods and streams; the love of Phoebus and Daphne, the wanderings and sorrows of Io, the slaying of Argus by Mercury, the tale of Pan and Syrinx, with the pastoral associations of the Arcadian mountains where the music of the flute was first discovered. The fresh feeling of

---

[1] Ovid's shallowness and superficiality of feeling are generally manifest when he treats the same subjects as other poets; compare his account (Fast. iv.) of the search for Proserpine in Sicily—a mere enumeration of names—with Virgil's power of evoking great associations in the voyage past Sicilian shores.

natural beauty in connexion with Arcadia returns again in the story of Callisto, the huntress-nymph of the mountain Nonacris:

> Miles erat Phoebes: nec Maenalon attigit ulla
> Gratior hac Triviae.

The mountains and streams of Arcadia have a peculiar attraction for the mind of Ovid, to whom Nature appealed in its picturesque and wilder aspects, rather than in its tranquil beauty or sublime grandeur.

The range of Ovid's imagination and his command of detail appear at their greatest in Book ii., in the description of the Palace of the Sun, and of Phaethon's attempt to guide the coursers of the Sun over the heavens. The whole passage, which contains the wonderful description of early morning that gave the idea of Guido's famous picture of Aurora, has the characteristics of the mythological pictures of the Renaissance, the spirit of youth, grace, and vivid life, with an absence of the spiritual meaning of the sacred subjects. The imaginative power of Ovid is nowhere greater than in his description of the career of Phaethon through the sky, when

> ita fertur ut acta
> Praecipiti pinus Borea, cui victa remisit
> Frena suus rector, quam dis votisque reliquit.

This power is manifested not only in the conduct of the narrative, but in the wakening of poetical associations connected with the great mountain ranges and the rivers and springs old in story:

> Athos, Taurusque Cilix, et Tmolus et Oete,
> Et nunc sicca, prius celeberrima fontibus Ide,
> Virgineusque Helicon.

Parnassus and Eryx and Cithaeron are named, and lastly

> Aeriaeque Alpes et nubifer Apenninus:

while after the great rivers of distant and half-known lands, Euphrates and Ganges and Tanaïs, those of the West close his catalogue—

> Rhenum Rhodanumque Padumque,
> Cuique fuit rerum promissa potentia, Thybrin.

Here again Ovid is 'nimium amator ingenii sui,' and forgets the greater effect of leaving his story half-told; but certainly the imaginative value of the whole legend is greatly enhanced by this rapid recalling to the imagination of the great natural features of the earth, or of those sacred places which had long ago awakened the minds of men to the sense of their secret poetry. There is a similar excess, combined with much poetical beauty, in the complaint of the Earth—

> Hosne mihi fructus, hunc fertilitatis honorem
> Officiique refers? quod adunci volnera aratri
> Rastrorumque fero, totoque exerceor anno—

the last words recalling, though with a slight difference, the thought of Sophocles (Ant. 338)—

> θεῶν δὲ τὰν ὑπερτάταν Γᾶν
> ἄφθιτον ἀκαμάταν ἀποτρύεται,
> ἰλλομένων ἀρότρων ἔτος εἰς ἔτος,
> ἱππείῳ γένει πολεύων.

Ovid's ingenuity, no less than his higher poetical qualities, are illustrated in the story of Phaethon. The legend, which so far has had no direct connexion with the theme of the 'mutatae formae,' is brought into the general scheme by the change of Cycnus, the half-brother of Phaethon, into a swan, and of the weeping sisters into amber-dropping trees—

> Inde fluunt lacrimae, stillataque sole rigescunt
> De ramis electra novis; quae lucidus amnis
> Excipit, et nuribus mittit gestanda Latinis.

Throughout the poem, indeed, Ovid shows extraordinary dexterity in the way in which different stories are introduced with perpetual variety. Thus the celebrated story of Pyramus and Thisbe (one of those mentioned by no other ancient author) is told by one of the Minyeïdes to her sisters as they sit at the loom, and so engrafted into the story of their transformation into bats on account of their perverse and unseasonable industry; and that of Baucis and Philemon is one of the tales told by the various guests at the table of Achelous, when he entertains Theseus on his return from the hunt of Calydon.

There is a want of seriousness and depth in the Metamorphoses: but this does not involve any failure in the description of different mental conditions, though the interest of these is subordinate to that of the story and the spectacle. There is genuine psychological insight, as well as imagination, in the account of the dwelling of Envy—

> Risus abest nisi quem visi movere dolores
> Nec fruitur somno vigilacibus excita curis;
> Sed videt ingratos intabescitque videndo
> Successus hominum, carpitque et carpitur una
> Suppliciumque suum est (ii. 778).
> Vixque tenet lacrimas quia nil lacrimabile cernit (ibid. 796).

The same qualities are to be found in the descriptions of the abode of Sleep and the temple of Rumour, which have suggested subjects to Chaucer, Spenser, and Pope.

One of the most human elements in the poems is the survival of the old feelings and features in the transformations, as when the feelings of Callisto the huntress pass into the hunted bear, or the savage character of Lycaon is repeated in the wolf—

> Fit lupus et veteris servat vestigia formae;
> Canities eadem est, eadem violentia vultus,
> Idem oculi lucent, eadem feritatis imago est.

Cadmus and Harmonia, broken-hearted by the misfortunes of their house, are changed into serpents among the Illyrian brakes—

> Nunc quoque nec fugiunt hominem nec volnere laedunt
> Quidque prius fuerint placidi meminere dracones.

The poetry of this treatment of mythology is best recognised in Arnold's modern version of the same story. The idea of metamorphosis seems to serve as an explanation of the moral affinities of animals to human beings, and to explain the analogies of grace and tenderness in trees, plants, and flowers.

As we have in many of the tales the romance of the mountain and forest, the stream and the lake, in some others, as might be expected of tales that have their origin in Greece, we find the romance and the terror of the sea. The adventures of Acoetes the Lydian mariner and follower of Bacchus make us feel the brightness and freshness of the sea about the 'nitentes Cycladas' (iii. 577). And one of the most charming and pathetic of all the stories, that of Ceyx and Alcyone, is a genuine sea-idyll. Though, as so often happens, overlaid with detail, it makes us feel with the life of those τοῖσίν τε θαλάσσια ἔργα μέμηλεν, more than any other ancient work except the Odyssey. The essential charm of the poem is the mutual devotion of Alcyone and Ceyx, and the triumph of love under new conditions, when Alcyone and the shipwrecked Ceyx are changed into the birds that presage calm. As with Cadmus and Harmonia, the old love remains—

> fatis obnoxius isdem
> Mansit amor, foedus nec coniugiale solutum.

This is one of the poems in which Ovid shows the power of sympathy with the purer affections. A like sympathy reveals itself in some of the homelier stories: among these none is finer than the account of Baucis and Philemon. In a very different vein is the grim humour and satirical power of the story of the gluttonous king Eresichthon, and of the avaricious king Midas of Phrygia. The same satirical purpose appears in the story of the countrymen changed into frogs for refusing water to Ceres in her thirst. The truth of Ovid's psychological insight and his unfailing power of graphic and vivid portraiture give human life to a poem which might seem to deal only with unusual conditions and impossible incidents.

THE END.

OXFORD
PRINTED AT THE CLARENDON PRESS
BY HORACE HART, M.A.
PRINTER TO THE UNIVERSITY

16/1/99

Clarendon Press, Oxford.

SELECT LIST OF STANDARD WORKS.

STANDARD LATIN WORKS	Page 1
STANDARD GREEK WORKS	,, 3
MISCELLANEOUS STANDARD WORKS	,, 7
STANDARD THEOLOGICAL WORKS	,, 8

1. STANDARD LATIN WORKS.

Avianus. *The Fables.* Edited, with Prolegomena, Critical Apparatus, Commentary, &c., by Robinson Ellis, M.A., LL.D. 8vo. 8s. 6d.

Caesar. *De Bello Gallico.* Books I-VII. According to the Text of Emanuel Hoffmann (Vienna, 1890). Edited, with Introduction and Notes, by St. George Stock. Post 8vo, 10s. 6d.

Catulli Veronensis *Liber.* Iterum recognovit, Apparatum Criticum Prolegomena Appendices addidit, R. Ellis, A.M. 8vo. 16s.

Catullus, *a Commentary on.* By Robinson Ellis, M.A. *Second Edition.* 8vo. 18s.

Cicero. *De Oratore Libri Tres.* With Introduction and Notes. By A. S. Wilkins, Litt.D. 8vo. 18s.
Also, separately,
Book I. 7s. 6d. Book II. 5s.
Book III. 6s.

—— *Pro Milone.* Edited by A. C. Clark, M.A. 8vo. 8s. 6d.

—— *Select Letters.* With English Introductions, Notes, and Appendices. By Albert Watson, M.A. *Fourth Edition.* 8vo. 18s.

Horace. With a Commentary. By E. C. Wickham, D.D. *Two Vols.*
Vol. I. The Odes, Carmen Seculare, and Epodes. *Third Edition.* 8vo. 12s.
Vol. II. The Satires, Epistles, and De Arte Poetica. 8vo. 12s.

Juvenal. *Thirteen Satires.* Edited, with Introduction and Notes, by C. H. Pearson, M.A., and Herbert A. Strong, M.A., LL.D. *Second Edition.* Crown 8vo. 9s.

Manilius. *Noctes Manilianae; sive Dissertationes in Astronomica Manilii. Accedunt Coniecturae in Germanici Aratea.* Scripsit R. Ellis. Crown 8vo. 6s.

Merry. *Selected Fragments of Roman Poetry.* Edited, with Introduction and Notes, by W. W. Merry, D.D. *Second Edition.* Crown 8vo. 6s. 6d.

Ovid. *P. Ovidii Nasonis Ibis.* Ex Novis Codicibus edidit, Scholia Vetera Commentarium cum Prolegomenis Appendice Indice addidit, R. Ellis, A.M. 8vo. 10s. 6d.

—— *P. Ovidi Nasonis Tristium Libri V.* Recensuit S. G. Owen, A.M. 8vo. 16s.

Oxford: Clarendon Press. London: HENRY FROWDE, Amen Corner, E.C.

STANDARD LATIN WORKS.

Persius. *The Satires.* With a Translation and Commentary. By John Conington, M.A. Edited by Henry Nettleship, M.A. *Third Edition.* 8vo. 8s. 6d.

Plautus. *Rudens.* Edited, with Critical and Explanatory Notes, by E. A. Sonnenschein, M.A. 8vo. 8s. 6d.

—— *The Codex Turnebi of Plautus.* By W. M. Lindsay, M.A. 8vo, 21s. net.

Quintilian. *Institutionis Oratoriae Liber Decimus.* A Revised Text, with Introductory Essays, Critical Notes, &c. By W. Peterson, M.A., LL.D. 8vo. 12s. 6d.

Rushforth. *Latin Historical Inscriptions, illustrating the History of the Early Empire.* By G. McN. Rushforth, M.A. 8vo. 10s. net.

Tacitus. *The Annals.* Edited, with Introduction and Notes, by H. Furneaux, M.A. 2 Vols. 8vo.
  Vol. I, Books I–VI. *Second Edition.* 18s.
  Vol. II, Books XI–XVI. 20s.

Tacitus. *De Germania.* By the same Editor. 8vo. 6s. 6d.

—— *Vita Agricolae.* By the same Editor. 8vo. 6s. 6d.

—— *Dialogus de Oratoribus.* A Revised Text, with Introductory Essays, and Critical and Explanatory Notes. By W. Peterson, M.A., LL.D. 8vo. 10s. 6d.

Velleivs Patercvlvs *ad M. Vinicivm Libri Dvo.* Ex Amerbachii Praecipve Apographo edidit et emendavit R. Ellis, Litterarvm Latinarvm Professor pvblicvs apvd Oxonienses. Crown 8vo, paper boards. 6s.

Virgil. *With an Introduction and Notes.* By T. L. Papillon, M.A., and A. E. Haigh, M.A. 2 vols. Crown 8vo. Cloth, 6s. each; *stiff covers* 3s. 6d. each.

Also sold in parts, as follows— Bucolics and Georgics, 2s. 6d. Aeneid, in 4 parts, 2s. each.

King and Cookson. *The Principles of Sound and Inflexion, as illustrated in the Greek and Latin Languages.* By J. E. King, M.A., and Christopher Cookson, M.A. 8vo. 18s.

—— *An Introduction to the Comparative Grammar of Greek and Latin.* Crown 8vo. 5s. 6d.

Lindsay. *The Latin Language. An Historical Account of Latin Sounds, Stems and Flexions.* By W. M. Lindsay, M.A. Demy 8vo. 21s.

Nettleship. *Lectures and Essays on Subjects connected with Latin Scholarship and Literature.* By Henry Nettleship, M.A. Crown 8vo. 7s. 6d.

—— *Second Series*, edited by F. J. Haverfield, with Memoir by Mrs. Nettleship. Crown 8vo. 7s. 6d.

Nettleship. *Contributions to Latin Lexicography.* 8vo. 21s.

Sellar. *Roman Poets of the Augustan Age.* By W. Y. Sellar, M.A.; viz.
  I. VIRGIL. *New Edition.* Crown 8vo. 9s.
  II. HORACE and the ELEGIAC POETS. With a Memoir of the Author by Andrew Lang, M.A., and a Portrait. 8vo. 14s.

—— *Roman Poets of the Republic.* *Third Edition.* Crown 8vo. 10s.

Wordsworth. *Fragments and Specimens of Early Latin.* With Introductions and Notes. By J. Wordsworth, D.D. 8vo. 18s.

Oxford: Clarendon Press.

2. STANDARD GREEK WORKS.

Chandler. *A Practical Introduction to Greek Accentuation*, by H. W. Chandler, M.A. Second Edition. 10s. 6d.

Farnell. *The Cults of the Greek States.* With Plates. By L. R. Farnell, M.A.
Vols. I and II. 8vo. 32s. net.
Volume III *in Preparation.*

Grenfell. *An Alexandrian Erotic Fragment and other Greek Papyri*, chiefly Ptolemaic. Edited by B. P. Grenfell, M.A. Small 4to. 8s. 6d. net.

Grenfell and Hunt. *New Classical Fragments and other Greek and Latin Papyri.* Edited by B. P. Grenfell, M.A., and A. S. Hunt, M.A. With Plates, 12s. 6d. net.

———— *Menander's* Γεωργόc. A Revised Text of the Geneva Fragment. With a Translation and Notes by the same Editors. 8vo, stiff covers, 1s. 6d.

Grenfell and Mahaffy. *Revenue Laws of Ptolemy Philadelphus.* 2 vols. Text and Plates. 1l. 11s. 6d. net.

Haigh. *The Attic Theatre.* A Description of the Stage and Theatre of the Athenians, and of the Dramatic Performances at Athens. By A. E. Haigh, M.A. Second Edition, Revised and Enlarged. 8vo. 12s. 6d.

Haigh. **The Tragic Drama of the Greeks.** With Illustrations. 8vo. 12s. 6d.

Head. *Historia Numorum:* A Manual of Greek Numismatics. By Barclay V. Head. Royal 8vo, half-bound, 2l. 2s.

Hicks. *A Manual of Greek Historical Inscriptions.* By E. L. Hicks, M.A. 8vo. 10s. 6d.

Hill. *Sources for Greek History between the Persian and Peloponnesian Wars.* Collected and arranged by G. F. Hill, M.A. 8vo. 10s. 6d.

Kenyon. *The Palaeography of Greek Papyri.* By Frederic G. Kenyon, M.A. 8vo, with Twenty Facsimiles, and a Table of Alphabets. 10s. 6d.

Liddell and Scott. *A Greek-English Lexicon*, by H. G. Liddell, D.D., and Robert Scott, D.D. Eighth Edition, Revised. 4to. 1l. 16s.

Monro. *Modes of Ancient Greek Music.* By D. B. Monro, M.A. 8vo. 8s. 6d. net.

Paton and Hicks. *The Inscriptions of Cos.* By W. R. Paton and E. L. Hicks. Royal 8vo, linen, with Map, 28s.

Smyth. *The Sounds and Inflections of the Greek Dialects* (Ionic). By H. Weir Smyth, Ph. D. 8vo. 24s.

Thompson. *A Glossary of Greek Birds.* By D'Arcy W. Thompson. 8vo, buckram, 10s. net.

Aeschinem et Isocratem, *Scholia Graeca in.* Edidit G. Dindorfius. 8vo. 4s.

Aeschylus. *In Single Plays.* With Introduction and Notes, by Arthur Sidgwick, M.A. New Edition. Extra fcap. 8vo. 3s. each.
 I. Agamemnon.
 II. Choephoroi.
 III. Eumenides.
 IV. Prometheus Bound. With Introduction and Notes, by A. O. Prickard, M.A. Third Edition. 2s.

Aeschyli *quae supersunt in Codice Laurentiano quoad effici potuit et ad cognitionem necesse est risum typis descripta edidit* R. Merkel. Small folio. 1l. 1s.

Aeschylus: *Tragoediae et Fragmenta*, ex recensione Guil. Dindorfii. Second Edition. 8vo. 5s. 6d.

———— *Annotationes* Guil. Dindorfii. Partes II. 8vo. 10s.

Apsinis et Longini *Rhetorica.* E Codicibus mss. recensuit Joh. Bakius. 8vo. 3s.

Aristophanes. *A Complete Concordance to the Comedies and Fragments.* By H. Dunbar, M.D. 4to. 1l. 1s.

—— *Comoediae et Fragmenta,* ex recensione Guil. Dindorfii. Tomi II. 8vo. 11s.

—— *Annotationes* Guil. Dindorfii. Partes II. 8vo. 11s.

—— *Scholia Graeca* ex Codicibus aucta et emendata a Guil. Dindorfio. Partes III. 8vo. 1l.

—— *In Single Plays.* Edited, with English Notes, Introductions, &c., by W. W. Merry, D.D. Extra fcap. 8vo.
   The Acharnians. *Fourth Edition,* 3s.
   The Birds. *Third Edition,* 3s. 6d.
   The Clouds. *Third Edition,* 3s.
   The Frogs. *Third Edition,* 3s.
   The Knights. *Second Edition,* 3s.
   The Wasps. 3s. 6d.

Aristotle. Ex recensione Im. Bekkeri. Accedunt Indices Sylburgiani. Tomi XI. 8vo. 2l. 10s. The volumes (except Vols. I and IX) may be had separately, price 5s. 6d. each.

—— *Ethica Nicomachea,* recognovit brevique Adnotatione critica instruxit I. Bywater. 8vo. 6s. *Also in crown 8vo, paper cover,* 3s. 6d.

—— Contributions to the Textual Criticism of the Nicomachean Ethics. By I. Bywater. 2s. 6d.

—— Notes on the Nicomachean Ethics. By J. A. Stewart, M.A. 2 vols. 8vo. 32s.

—— *Selecta ex Organo Aristoteleo Capitula.* In usum Scholarum Academicarum. Crown 8vo, stiff covers. 3s. 6d.

—— *De Arte Poetica Liber.* Recognovit Brevique Adnotatione Critica Instruxit I. Bywater, Litterarum Graecarum Professor Regius. Post 8vo, stiff covers, 1s. 6d.

Aristotle. *The Politics,* with Introductions, Notes, &c., by W. L. Newman, M.A. Vols. I and II. Medium 8vo. 28s.
Vols. III and IV. [*In the Press.*]

—— *The Politics,* translated into English, with Introduction, Marginal Analysis, Notes, and Indices, by B. Jowett, M.A. Medium 8vo. 2 vols. 21s.

—— *The English Manuscripts of the Nicomachean Ethics, described in relation to Bekker's Manuscripts and other Sources.* By J. A. Stewart, M.A. (Anecdota Oxon.) Small 4to. 3s. 6d.

—— *Physics.* Book VII. Collation of various mss.; with Introduction by R. Shute, M.A. (Anecdota Oxon.) Small 4to. 2s.

Choerobosci *Dictata in Theodosii Canones, necnon Epimerismi in Psalmos.* E Codicibus mss. edidit Thomas Gaisford, S.T.P. Tomi III. 8vo. 15s.

Demosthenes. Ex recensione G. Dindorfii. Tomi IX. 8vo. 2l. 6s.
Separately—
Text, 1l. 1s. Annotations, 15s.
Scholia, 10s.

Demosthenes and Aeschines. The Orations of Demosthenes and Aeschines on the Crown. With Introductory Essays and Notes. By G. A. Simcox, M.A., and W. H. Simcox, M.A. 8vo. 12s.

Demosthenes. *Orations against Philip.* With Introduction and Notes, by Evelyn Abbott, M.A., and P. E. Matheson, M.A.
   Vol. I. Philippic I. Olynthiacs I–III. Extra fcap. 8vo. 3s.
   Vol. II. De Pace, Philippic II. De Chersoneso, Philippic III. Extra fcap. 8vo. 4s. 6d.

Euripides. *Tragoediae et Fragmenta,* ex recensione Guil. Dindorfii. Tomi II. 8vo. 10s.

Euripides. *Annotationes* Guil. Dindorfii. Partes II. 8vo. 10s.

—— *Scholia Graeca*, ex Codicibus aucta et emendata a Guil. Dindorfio. Tomi IV. 8vo. 1l. 16s.

Hephaestionis *Enchiridion,* Terentianus Maurus, Proclus, &c. Edidit T. Gaisford, S.T.P. Tomi II. 10s.

Heracliti *Ephesii Reliquiae.* Recensuit I. Bywater, M.A. Appendicis loco additae sunt Diogenis Laertii Vita Heracliti, Particulae Hippocratei De Diaeta Lib. I., Epistolae Heracliteae. 8vo. 6s.

Herodotus. *Books V and VI,* Terpsichore and Erato. Edited, with Notes and Appendices, by Evelyn Abbott, M.A., LL.D. 8vo, with two Maps, 10s. 6d.

Homer. *A Complete Concordance to the Odyssey and Hymns of Homer;* to which is added a Concordance to the Parallel Passages in the Iliad, Odyssey, and Hymns. By Henry Dunbar, M.D. 4to. 1l. 1s.

—— *A Grammar of the Homeric Dialect.* By D. B. Monro, M.A. 8vo. *Second Edition.* 14s.

—— *Ilias,* ex rec. Guil. Dindorfii. 8vo. 5s. 6d.

—— *Scholia Graeca in Iliadem.* Edited by W. Dindorf, after a new collation of the Venetian MSS. by D. B. Monro, M.A. 4 vols. 8vo. 2l. 10s.

—— *Scholia Graeca in Iliadem Townleyana.* Recensuit Ernestus Maass. 2 vols. 8vo. 1l. 16s.

—— *Odyssea,* ex rec. G. Dindorfii. 8vo. 5s. 6d.

—— *Scholia Graeca in Odysseam.* Edidit Guil. Dindorfius. Tomi II. 8vo. 15s. 6d.

Homer. *Odyssey.* Books I–XII. Edited with English Notes, Appendices, &c. By W. W. Merry, D.D., and James Riddell, M.A. *Second Edition.* 8vo. 16s.

—— —— Books XIII–XXIV. By D. B. Monro, M.A. [*In the Press.*]

—— *Hymni Homerici.* Codicibus denuo collatis recensuit Alfredus Goodwin. Small folio. With four Plates. 21s. net.

Homeri Opera et Reliquiae. Monro. Crown 8vo. India Paper. *Cloth,* 10s. 6d. net.

Also in various leather bindings.

Oratores Attici, ex recensione Bekkeri:

Vol. I. Antiphon, Andocides, et Lysias. 8vo. 7s.

[*Vols. II and III are out of print.*]

—— *Index Andocideus, Lycurgeus, Dinarcheus,* confectus a Ludovico Leaming Forman, Ph.D. 8vo. 7s. 6d.

Paroemiographi Graeci, *quorum pars nunc primum ex Codd. mss. vulgatur.* Edidit T. Gaisford, S.T.P. 1836. 8vo. 5s. 6d.

Plato. *Apology,* with a revised Text and English Notes, and a Digest of Platonic Idioms, by James Riddell, M.A. 8vo. 8s. 6d.

—— *Philebus,* with a revised Text and English Notes, by Edward Poste, M.A. 8vo. 7s. 6d.

—— *Republic.* The Greek Text. Edited, with Notes and Essays, by B. Jowett, M.A. and Lewis Campbell, M.A. In three vols. Medium 8vo. 2l. 2s.

—— *Sophistes* and *Politicus,* with a revised Text and English Notes, by L. Campbell, M.A. 8vo. 10s. 6d.

Plato. *Theaetetus*, with a revised Text and English Notes, by L. Campbell, M.A. *Second Edition.* 8vo. 10s. 6d.

—— *The Dialogues*, translated into English, with Analyses and Introductions, by B. Jowett, M.A. *Third Edition.* 5 vols. medium 8vo. Cloth, 4l. 4s.; half-morocco, 5l.

—— *The Republic*, translated into English, with Analysis and Introduction, by B. Jowett, M.A. *Third Edition.* Medium 8vo. 12s. 6d.; half-roan, 14s.

—— *With Introduction and Notes.* By St. George Stock, M.A. Extra fcap. 8vo.
 I. The Apology, 2s. 6d.
 II. Crito, 2s. III. Meno, 2s. 6d.

—— *Selections. With Introductions and Notes.* By John Purves, M.A., and Preface by B. Jowett, M.A. *Second Edition.* Extra fcap. 8vo. 5s.

—— *A Selection of Passages from Plato for English Readers;* from the Translation by B. Jowett, M.A. Edited, with Introductions, by M. J. Knight. 2 vols. Crown 8vo, gilt top. 12s.

Plotinus. *Edidit F. Creuzer.* Tomi III. 4to. 1l. 8s.

Polybius. *Selections.* Edited by J. L. Strachan-Davidson, M.A. With Maps. Medium 8vo. 21s.

Plutarchi *Moralia, id est, Opera, exceptis Vitis, reliqua.* Edidit Daniel Wyttenbach. Accedit Index Graecitatis. Tomi VIII. Partes XV. 1795-1830. 8vo, cloth, 3l. 10s.

Sophocles. *The Plays and Fragments.* With English Notes and Introductions, by Lewis Campbell, M.A. 2 vols. 8vo, 16s. each.
 Vol. I. Oedipus Tyrannus. Oedipus Coloneus. Antigone.
 Vol. II. Ajax. Electra. Trachiniae. Philoctetes. Fragments.

Sophocles. *Tragoediae et Fragmenta*, ex recensione et cum commentariis Guil. Dindorfii. *Third Edition.* 2 vols. Fcap. 8vo. 1l. 1s. Each Play separately, limp, 2s. 6d.

—— *Tragoediae et Fragmenta* cum Annotationibus Guil. Dindorfii. Tomi II. 8vo. 10s.
 The Text, Vol. I. 5s. 6d.
 The Notes, Vol. II. 4s. 6d.

Stobaei *Florilegium.* Ad mss. fidem emendavit et supplevit T. Gaisford, S.T.P. Tomi IV. 8vo. 1l.

—— *Eclogarum Physicarum et Ethicarum libri duo.* Accedit Hieroclis Commentarius in aurea carmina Pythagoreorum. Ad mss. Codd. recensuit T. Gaisford, S.T.P. Tomi II. 8vo. 11s.

Strabo. *Selections*, with an Introduction on Strabo's Life and Works. By H. F. Tozer, M.A., F.R.G.S. 8vo. With Maps and Plans. 12s.

Theodoreti *Graecarum Affectionum Curatio.* Ad Codices mss. recensuit T. Gaisford, S.T.P. 8vo. 7s. 6d.

Thucydides. Translated into English, with Introduction, Marginal Analysis, Notes, and Indices. By B. Jowett, M.A. [*Reprinting.*]

Xenophon. *Ex recensione et cum annotationibus L. Dindorfii.*
 Historia Graeca. Second Edition. 8vo. 10s. 6d.
 Expeditio Cyri. Second Edition. 8vo. 10s. 6d.
 Institutio Cyri. 8vo. 10s. 6d.
 Memorabilia Socratis. 8vo. 7s. 6d.
 Opuscula Politica Equestria et Venatica cum Arriani Libello de Venatione. 8vo. 10s. 6d.

3. MISCELLANEOUS STANDARD WORKS.

Arbuthnot. *The Life and Works of John Arbuthnot.* By George A. Aitken. 8vo, cloth extra, with Portrait, 16s.

Bacon. *The Essays.* Edited with Introduction and Illustrative Notes, by S. H. Reynolds, M.A. 8vo, half-bound, 12s. 6d.

Casaubon (Isaac), 1559–1614. By Mark Pattison, late Rector of Lincoln College. *Second Edition.* 8vo. 16s.

Finlay. *A History of Greece from its Conquest by the Romans to the present time,* B.C. 146 to A.D. 1864. By George Finlay, LL.D. A new Edition, revised throughout, and in part re-written, with considerable additions, by the Author, and edited by H. F. Tozer, M.A. 7 vols. 8vo. 3l. 10s.

Gaii *Institutionum Juris Civilis Commentarii Quattuor;* or, Elements of Roman Law by Gaius. With a Translation and Commentary by Edward Poste, M.A. *Third Edition.* 8vo. 18s.

Hodgkin. *Italy and her Invaders.* With Plates and Maps. By Thomas Hodgkin, D.C.L. A.D. 376–744. 8vo. Vols. I and II, *Second Edition*, 2l. 2s. Vols. III and IV, *Second Edition*, 1l. 16s. Vols. V and VI, 1l. 16s. Vol. VII. *In the Press.*

Hooker, Sir J. D., and B. D. Jackson. *Index Kewensis.* 2 vols. 4to. 10l. 10s. *net.*

Ilbert. *The Government of India;* being a Digest of the Statute Law relating thereto. With Historical Introduction and Illustrative Documents. By Sir Courtenay Ilbert, K.C.S.I. 8vo, half-roan, 21s.

Justinian. *Imperatoris Iustiniani Institutionum Libri Quattuor;* with Introductions, Commentary, Excursus and Translation. By J. B. Moyle, D.C.L. *Third Edition.* 2 vols. 8vo. 22s.

Machiavelli. *Il Principe.* Edited by L. Arthur Burd. With an Introduction by Lord Acton. 8vo. 14s.

Pattison. *Essays by the late Mark Pattison,* sometime Rector of Lincoln College. Collected and Arranged by Henry Nettleship, M.A. 2 vols. 8vo. 24s.

Ralegh. *Sir Walter Ralegh.* A Biography. By W. Stebbing, M.A. 8vo. 10s. 6d.

Ramsay. *The Cities and Bishoprics of Phrygia;* being an Essay of the Local History of Phrygia, from the Earliest Times to the Turkish Conquest. By W. M. Ramsay, D.C.L., LL.D. Vol. I. Part I. *The Lycos Valley and South-Western Phrygia.* Royal 8vo, linen, 18s. *net.* Vol. I. Part II. *West and West-Central Phrygia.* Royal 8vo, linen, 21s. *net.*

Stokes. *The Anglo-Indian Codes.* By Whitley Stokes, LL.D. Vol. I. Substantive Law. 8vo. 30s. Vol. II. Adjective Law. 8vo. 35s.

Strachey. *Hastings and The Rohilla War.* By Sir John Strachey, G.C.S.I. 8vo, cloth, 10s. 6d.

Thomson. *Notes on Recent Researches in Electricity and Magnetism.* By J. J. Thomson, M.A., F.R.S. 8vo. 18s. 6d.

Woodhouse. *Aetolia; its Geography, Topography, and Antiquities.* By William J. Woodhouse, M.A., F.R.G.S. With Maps and Illustrations. Royal 8vo, linen, price 21s. *net.*

4. STANDARD THEOLOGICAL WORKS, &c.

St. Basil: *The Book of St. Basil on the Holy Spirit.* A Revised Text, with Notes and Introduction by C. F. H. Johnston, M.A. Crown 8vo. 7s. 6d.

The Coptic Version of the New Testament, *in the Northern Dialect, otherwise called Memphitic and Bohairic.* With Introduction, Critical Apparatus, and Literal English Translation. The Gospels. 2 vols. 8vo. 2l. 2s.

Bright. *Chapters of Early English Church History.* By W. Bright, D.D. Third Edition. 8vo. 12s.

Canons of the First Four General Councils *of Nicaea, Constantinople, Ephesus, and Chalcedon.* With Notes, by W. Bright, D.D. Second Edition. Crown 8vo. 7s. 6d.

The Book of Enoch. *Translated from Dillmann's Ethiopic Text* (emended and revised), and Edited by R. H. Charles, M.A. 8vo. 16s.

Conybeare. *The Key of Truth.* A Manual of the Paulician Church of Armenia. The Armenian Text, edited and translated with illustrative Documents and Introduction by F. C. Conybeare, M.A. 8vo. 15s. net.

Driver. *The Parallel Psalter,* being the Prayer-Book Version of the Psalms and a New Version, arranged in parallel columns. With an Introduction and Glossaries. By the Rev. S. R. Driver, D.D., Litt.D. Extra fcap. 8vo. 6s.

Ecclesiasticus (xxxix. 15— xlix. 11). The Original Hebrew, with Early Versions and English Translations, &c. Edited by A. Cowley, M.A., and Ad. Neubauer, M.A. 4to. 10s. 6d. net.

Hatch and Redpath. *A Concordance to the Greek Versions and Apocryphal Books of the Old Testament.* By the late Edwin Hatch, M.A., and H. A. Redpath, M.A. In Six Parts. Imperial 4to. 21s. each.

Ommanney. *A Critical Dissertation on the Athanasian Creed. Its Original Language, Date, Authorship, Titles, Text, Reception, and Use.* By G. D. W. Ommanney, M.A. 8vo. 16s.

Wordsworth and White. *Nouum Testamentum Domini Nostri Iesu Christi Latine,* secundum Editionem Sancti Hieronymi. Ad Codicum Manuscriptorum fidem recensuit Iohannes Wordsworth, S.T.P., Episcopus Sarisburiensis; in operis societatem adsumto Henrico Iuliano White, A.M. 4to. Pars I, buckram, 2l. 12s. 6d.

Also, separately—
Fasc. I. 12s 6d.; Fasc. II. 7s 6d.;
Fasc. III. 12s. 6d.; Fasc. IV. 10s. 6d.
Fasc. V. 10s. 6d.

Oxford
AT THE CLARENDON PRESS
LONDON: HENRY FROWDE
OXFORD UNIVERSITY PRESS WAREHOUSE, AMEN CORNER, E.C.

www.ingramcontent.com/pod-product-compliance
Lightning Source LLC
Chambersburg PA
CBHW030602300426
44111CB00009B/1075